In My Time

Thomas H. RADDALL

IN MY TIME
A Memoir

McClelland and Stewart

Reprinted 1977

The Canadian Publishers
McClelland and Stewart Limited
25 Hollinger Road, Toronto M4B 3G2

ISBN: 0-7710-7250-3

Photographs contained in this book are taken from
the Thomas H. Raddall Collection in the Special
Collections/Archives of the Killam Library of
Dalhousie University, except those of the Simeon
Perkins House and old King's College, which are
from the Public Archives of Nova Scotia, Halifax,
N.S.

Printed and bound in Canada by
T. H. Best Printing Company Limited, Don Mills, Ontario

Contents

About This Book

Shortly before my seventieth birthday, Dalhousie University made arrangements to obtain for its library the original scripts of my published and unpublished work, together with research notes, correspondence, diaries, public addresses and other papers.

I mention the diaries particularly because the book now in your hands does not hold the haphazard recollections of an old mind groping through a haze of time. I began to keep a diary when I went to sea as a boy and retained the habit all my life, and so this account of it is based firmly on a continuous record extending over more than half a century. Memory alone is not dependable. In old age it tends to blur times and events and to ignore or gloss over blunders, follies, quarrels, despairs, wrong judgements and other vagaries of human fault that old age would rather forget.

In the portion of this chronicle from youth to middle age there is frequent mention of money. I have done this to show something of the struggle for a living in my time, when I worked long and hard for paltry wages from the age of fifteen. I never cared a rap for money as money. I did value it as a prop, however slender it might be, for the independence of thought and action that has been precious to me all my life. Industry and thrift eventually made me financially secure, and money ceased to matter after that.

In my novels and short stories I never sought to teach or to preach. My aim was intelligent entertainment, and if the reader got some information along the way I made sure that it was true. When I wrote history as such I sought to make the truth as interesting to the reader as it was to me.

Whatever the merit of my published works now or in the future, I may be remembered as a Canadian author who chose to stay at home, writing entirely about his own country and its people, and offering his wares in the open market of the world.

I may be remembered also as one who never asked a penny of subsidy from any fund, institution or government, even when such money became easily available. From first to last I paddled my own canoe, and this is a condensed but frank account of my voyage.

January 3, 1976   T.H.R.

In My Time

1903
1913

The Cornish live like their fellow Celts on the west fringe of Europe, driven there by pressure from the east. There they are fighting all the time mainly against the elements. Therefore they are in no way soft; yet often they display a remarkable indolence, and again a startling capacity for intense effort. This contradiction is carried right through their character; harshness and gentleness; cruelty and tenderness; gaiety and melancholy.

J.W. Lambert

The Raddalls were Cornish folk, and most of my ancestors on that side were farmers or small tradesmen in the region of Launceston. My grandfather Thomas Raddall ventured elsewhere and set up a clothing shop in the busy naval town of Portsmouth. His wife, Eleanor, was a daughter of the sporting Head family, well known in their day in the horsy world of Tattersall's.

Thomas and Eleanor had several daughters and one son, Thomas Head Raddall, who became my father. The Portsmouth business was prosperous for years, but eventually Thomas senior became addicted to alcohol, and one day he collapsed, physically and financially. His wife became a nervous invalid, and suddenly their family had to seek a living any way they could. One daughter, afterwards my beloved aunt Jessie, became a schoolteacher in London. My father went there too and got a job as an office boy. He was fourteen. Long years later he told me how he hated this petty drudgery indoors after the free and sunny life at Portsmouth and how each noon he sat in one of the quiet pews of Saint Paul's, munching a sandwich and wondering what was to become of him.

When he was a few months past fifteen in 1892 he met a recruiting sergeant of the Royal Marines, splendid in scarlet coat and ribbons. He had seen and admired the Marines in Portsmouth and he asked the sergeant to enlist him as a drummer boy. He was sent to the depot of the Royal Marines at Deal, on the Kentish coast, where he plied his drumsticks in the band until he was eighteen. Then he became a rifleman in the Royal Marine Light Infantry, and he was a slim handsome lance-corporal in that famous corps when he met Ellen Gifford, a small brunette from a village near Canterbury.

For centuries the Giffords had been farmers in the fertile country between Canterbury and the Channel coast, and they were content there and never left the place except to fight in England's wars. (All of Ellen Gifford's six brothers fought in the 1914-18 war. Five survived and returned to Kent for the rest of their lives.) The Giffords were easy-going people with soft speech and tranquil ways. A greater contrast to the dark mercurial Celts of Cornwall could not be found in the length and breadth of England.

* * *

Soon after he met Ellen, Thomas Raddall was sent away on foreign service, and he spent the next four years with the Royal Navy in the Far East, cruising between Hong Kong, Wei-hai-wei, Kobe and Nagasaki. For a time he was one of the Royal Marine guard at the British consulate in Seoul. He and Ellen wrote to each other regularly, and when he returned to England towards the end of 1900 they were married in her parish church at Ash, near Canterbury. Their first child, my sister Nellie, was born in the married quarters of the Marines at Deal.

Thomas was an athletic and abstemious man. Remembering what had sent him to that dreary London office, he never took a drop of strong drink in his life. He had become a crack rifleshot and was eager for a military career. About fifteen miles westward from Deal along the Channel coast was the little town of Hythe, where the British Army's famous old School of Musketry now trained its men in the use of modern rifles and machine-guns. The instructors were all marksmen, and when a Marine sharpshooter named Raddall applied for a post there he got it, with a warrant-officer's rank.

As a minor result of this, I was born at Hythe in 1903. To be exact, I was born in the married quarters of the School of Musketry, and a neighbouring Army wife, coming in to see my mother and her new infant, blurted out, "Oh, Nellie, how unfortunate for the poor child to be born on a Friday the thirteenth!" Consequently my good mother always celebrated my birthday on the fourteenth of November. I never knew the awful truth until I had to prove my

British birth to Canada's Department of Naval Service. There it was, on the birth certificate. In physique I grew up to be like the stocky Gifford farmers, with my mother's brown eyes and fresh complexion. In mind and temperament I was all Cornish Celt.

In my childhood Hythe and its environs, Seabrook and Sandgate, formed a sleepy watering place that straggled along the Channel shore into the morning shadow of Shorncliffe. The fashionable seaside town of Folkestone lay just beyond. The School of Musketry was a cluster of brick and stone buildings on the western edge of Hythe, with an ancient defence canal winding through pastures before it and trailing away through the flat reaches of Romney Marsh. The canal and a row of crumbling martello towers along the Channel shore were relics of Mr. Pitt's measures against the threat of invasion by Napoleon a century or so before. Between the canal and the towers lay the fringe of the town, then pastures, and finally a great stretch of pebbles called The Shingle, once washed smooth by the sea but now a dry stony flat, very useful for the shooting ranges of the School.

I was christened in the old parish church on Hythe hill and later attended a school for boys, Saint Leonard's, in the town below. Otherwise I saw little of town life. As an infant I learned to walk in the barrack square. Our main existence was confined to a small world of khaki (red coats on Sunday parades) enclosed by stone walls and a tall iron fence. A day-long crackle of rifles and Maxim guns on the ranges echoed against the ridge behind it. Long columns of infantry marched down from Shorncliffe Camp to shoot on the Hythe ranges under the direction of the School staff. In summer there were tent camps in the fields that made a green stripe between the canal and The Shingle. After its recent bloody lessons in South Africa, Britain was training a small compact army of professional soldiers who could aim a rifle in the cool and deadly fashion of the Boers. Machine-guns, two to a battalion, were regarded merely as an accessory to the more exact fire of the riflemen.

My father was one of the thinking soldiers in those days who saw that the machine was much more deadly than the man and that in the event of a continental war an army with plenty of machine-guns would give one armed mostly with rifles a very rough time. Many of his off-duty hours were spent in studying the small arms of the chief European powers, of which samples were available at the School, and in forming theories about their use, especially the use of machine-guns. He put his ideas on paper. I have a clear memory of my father's lean tanned face under the evening lamp, and a brown hand writing crisply and neatly with an old-fashioned "stylus" fountain pen. What his superiors did with these earnest compositions I know not, but I can guess. The British Army of that time did not look for ideas in the ranks, and anyhow the War Office in its time-honoured way was determined to fight the next war with the weapons and tactics of the last.

* * *

The precincts of the School were forbidden to civilians, so that the staff and their families were a small military enclave, entertaining themselves with their own concerts, amateur theatricals and card parties, although the town was open to them, and staff people like my parents had friends there. Once a summer there was a day's picnic, when the military families rode in horse-drawn char-à-bancs ("charrabangs" to us) along the coast road to Dymchurch, where The Shingle gave way to long soft sands. At Christmas there was a concert or a full-dress pantomime in the Lecture Hall, followed by a children's party in the officers' mess, complete with Christmas tree and Father Christmas himself with gifts for us all.

Eventually, owing to congestion in the married quarters, some of the staff were permitted to live outside the School, and my father rented a house on the Dymchurch Road. There we entered more into the life of the town and countryside, notably the countryside. There were walks under tall old elms beside the military canal and wonderful explorations of the Roughs, the original chalk bluffs of the coast, left high and dry since Roman time by the shifting waters of the Channel and now green with turf and bushes of gorse. In spring there were strolls to pick bluebells and primroses in the woods and hedgerows of Ashford Hill.

On summer Sundays we had jaunts by horse-tram along the seaside promenade from Hythe to Sandgate. My father was an ardent cyclist, and when I was small he took me, perched on a cushioned seat attached to the handlebars, on tours of the country within a few miles of the town. Less than a mile behind the School, and soon within reach of my own young legs, was Saltwood Castle, a place of awe where King Henry's courtiers had tarried and plotted on their way to murder Thomas à Becket at Canterbury – all sitting in the dark, according to legend, so that none might see another's face.

When I was about six years old a tremendous thing happened. A

Frenchman named Louis Blériot flew an airplane over the Channel and landed beside Dover Castle, twelve miles or so from the School of Musketry. This feat in 1909 set all Europe agog, and in Britain there was a scramble to get into the air. Within a year or two my parents took me to see several airplanes rising from a racecourse, skimming over Hythe like canvas birds, and settling again.

There was a military side to all this. In 1911 or 1912 a mysterious encampment of Royal Engineers sprang up like canvas toadstools in the field beyond our house, and after a time we saw a round and bloated monstrosity rising in its heart. It was a captive balloon. Next day the balloon soared high over the rifle ranges, dangling far below it a wood-and-fabric replica of an airplane as a target for the troops. It was the first attempt at anti-aircraft fire – a term then unborn.

I remember my father laughing about it after his first experience of modern warfare at Ypres in 1915. In those pre-war days at Hythe the soldiers soon got bored with firing at a lifeless object hanging before them in mid-air, and high above was the balloon, a fat and tempting mark. Tommy Atkins was nothing if not a humorist. Inevitably a bullet found the balloon, which began to wilt visibly. The Sappers hastily reeled it down, patched the gasbag, pumped in more gas, admonished the troops, and sent up balloon and target again. This little comedy was repeated and repeated. Finally the experimenters abandoned what was certainly the worst possible training for troops against aircraft, as any hunter of wild fowl could have told them.

Again, I recall the headmaster of Saint Leonard's turning all of us out of doors one day to see a small airship of the kind known later as a blimp, soaring over Shorncliffe and Hythe. The British Army had two of them at this time called *Beta* and *Gamma*, but which this was I never knew. The Royal Navy was said to be putting together an airship called *Mayfly* because, my father quipped, it might not. The Germans were experimenting in those days with the huge Zeppelins, some of which were rumoured to be flying over southeastern England at night. Mysterious lights had been seen in the sky over Chatham and Dover.

There were evening discussions at our house, where serious men talked with Father about these and other manifestations of German military activity. It was all a mystery to me, of course, a curious boy standing by Father's chair, but it remains in my mind because one thing was repeated and accepted. The Germans were preparing for a great war of conquest, and sooner or later the British would have to fight them.

Years later when I found a few of Father's notes, I caught a glimpse of these prospects as British soldiers had seen them in the last years of peace before 1914. I realize, too, that the khaki columns I had seen marching down from Shorncliffe Camp or tenting in the fields by the rifle ranges were soon to become famous as The Old Contemptibles (from Kaiser Wilhelm's quip about "the contemptible little British army") who stood in the path of the German war machine through northern France and Belgium in the summer and autumn of 1914. All unwitting I had seen them preparing for the stop-gap role to which they rose so superbly, and in which they died.

* * *

Thus by the age of nine I knew quite a lot about the realm of the sword. There was another realm close about me, that of the pen, of which I knew nothing. It was not until my mature years on the other side of the Atlantic, when I looked back with curiosity at my first years on this earth, that I realized how complete a cyst the School of Musketry had been in its surroundings. Of all English soil that small part of Kent is perhaps the richest in its literary associations, for it was the chosen habitat of many famous writers. Some of them were living and writing close about Hythe in my childhood days, but excepting H.G. Wells they seem to have ignored the School of Musketry as the School ignored them. And no wonder. With its killing tools the School was as incongruous in that beautiful milieu as a loaded pistol in a poet's bower.

To go back a long way, this was the country of *The Ingoldsby Legends*. It was the favoured haunt of Dickens, who sang the praises of Folkestone as "Pavilionstone." He was a frequent guest at the old Pavilion Hotel, and he wrote a lot of *Little Dorrit* while staying there. William Wilberforce and G.A.H. Sala often stayed at Sandgate, and Ruskin lived there for a time, exulting in the Channel sunsets.

In my childhood other famous pens were close at hand. Kipling did not live there, but he spent much time roaming our region, especially Romney Marsh; and it was on the very scene of our summer picnics that he conceived the story called "Dymchurch

Flit," with which he was always so content. In scenes within an hour's bicycle ride of Hythe, Arnold Bennett laid *The Gates of Wrath*, John Masefield laid *Jim Davis*, and Jeffery Farnol laid *The Amateur Gentleman*. And there was H.G. Wells, who had been apprenticed to a Folkestone clothier in his youth. Long later he said, "If it was not for the fact that my health failed, probably I should now be the proprietor of a little business over the door of which would be inscribed 'Herbert G. Wells, Draper.'"

Wells lived several years at Sandgate after he became a writer, and it intrigues me to reflect that when I was being trundled along the Hythe streets in a go-cart, Wells must have been walking there with a sharp eye for the scenes he described in one of his best novels, *Kipps*. Kipps's boating holiday on the old military canal I might have seen myself. Kipps's excursions through Hythe ("where the machine guns of the Empire are forever whirling and tapping") were in my own little world, and possibly at times the guns he heard with Wells's ears were those of a squad under my father's direction.

You may remember how Kipps finally settled with Ann in Hythe and how Old Kipps recommended to Ann a house with a billiard room because "As you get on you'll be 'aving visitors. Friends of your 'usband's p'raps from the School of Musketry, what you want 'im to get on with. You can't never tell." And of course you can't. I am sure my father would have enjoyed meeting Wells-Kipps, billiards or no billiards.

In my toddling days at Hythe, too, Henry James was living in Rye, at the end of Pitt's old defence canal, and dictating the last of his convoluted novels about the little Anglo-American world in which he had lived for so many years.

But far above all to me stands the figure of Joseph Conrad, then living a few miles behind the School of Musketry at Pent Farm. This was Conrad's home base during his best period, from 1898 to 1907, in which he wrote *The Nigger of the "Narcissus"*, *Lord Jim*, *Youth*, *Heart of Darkness*, *Typhoon*, *Nostromo* and *The Secret Agent*. Sometimes when Father wheeled through the little hamlet of Postling with his small passenger we must have passed the man himself and certainly the house with its great barn, all overshadowed by a tall bluff called The Pent. The old house had been occupied for a time by Walter Crane, and it must have been Crane who painted on the lintel over the front door:

Want we not for board nor tent
Whilst overhead we have The Pent.

* * *

Like many sailors who have had enough of the sea, Conrad chose to live out of sight of it when he retired, but never far away. Of his various country houses after his marriage, nearly all were in Kent and only a few miles from salt water. This enabled him to take another look at the sea on which he had struggled so much and so far. The shore at Hythe was no more than an hour's leisurely amble by pony-cart from Pent Farm. On the beach at Sandgate, Conrad had dug his fists into the sand and exclaimed to H.G. Wells and Lewis Hind, "Ah, if only I could write zee English good, well! But you will see! You will see!"

At Pent Farm, too, Conrad was in easy reach of his sometime collaborator Ford Madox Hueffer at Aldington, of Stephen Crane and Henry James at Rye, and of Wells at Sandgate. John Galsworthy had met Conrad the sailor on a voyage from Australia to South Africa, and after Conrad retired to write in the quiet country behind Hythe he came down frequently to visit. Long afterwards he wrote: "Pent Farm, that little, very old, charming if inconvenient farmhouse with its great barn beyond the yard, under the lee of the almost overhanging Pent. It was a friendly dwelling where you had to mind your head in connection with beams. He liked those quiet fields and that sheltering hill. In Conrad's study at The Pent we burned many midnight candles, much tobacco."

* * *

I first encountered Conrad's books when I went to sea myself in small steamers out of Halifax and Sydney, Nova Scotia. In these I found an occasional veteran of the Bluenose windjammers reading much-thumbed pages of *Youth* or *The Nigger of the "Narcissus"*, and vowing that there, by God, was a man who knew sailors and the sea. After that I read everything of Conrad's that I could find, with an enjoyment that continued all my life, but it did not strike me right away that by one of the odd chances of life I had spent my childhood where and when he was writing so many of the pages that entranced me now.

With all this in mind you may see why I muse on the strangely contrasted worlds in which my first few years were spent. None of this had a thing to do with my future, of course. That I went off to sea out of Halifax at the age of fifteen was a blind chance. That I became a writer of sorts in my twenties was another. That I became a soldier of sorts at nearly forty was a comical anticlimax.

As a small boy in Hythe my mind was filled with soldiers and the sounds of war. In the library at Saint Leonard's I found another and much more interesting kind of war in the American forest with Fenimore Cooper and his Indians and Leatherstockings. If I thought of the pen at all it was only because my schoolmasters made what seemed to me an inordinate fuss about it.

In retrospect what impresses me most is that odd little fountain pen in my father's hand, whispering over the sheets beneath the lamp and setting forth the ideas of a soldier whose vision was years ahead of his time. On a hot day in 1918, leading a battalion of hard-fighting Canadians against the last German defences beyond Amiens, he proved with his life that the old sword-and-pen adage was wrong. In the final dash of what Ludendorff called "Germany's black day in this war" he was killed by a burst of machine-gun bullets.

1913
1918

Apart from his military studies and duties, Father was fond of music and often sang at staff concerts and other musical occasions in the School of Musketry. Despite his small pay he bought a piano and sent my elder sister and me to take lessons from a little old ape-faced man with white side-whiskers who lived in the town of Hythe. Our teacher beat the time with a silver-mounted ivory baton, yellow with age, and whacked my fingers with it when I made mistakes. My sister went unwhacked because she seldom made mistakes and soon played well. I never did, despite many lessons in Hythe and later on in Halifax.

Early in 1913 the Canadian government applied to the British Army for some experts on small arms. They would join the Canadian Army for the instruction of regulars and militia at various places across the country. Father then was about thirty-five. The Hythe post was an obvious dead end for a man of ideas and ambition, and he wanted better opportunities for his children; accordingly he applied for one of the Canadian posts and got it. When the word came through there was a great scurrying and packing. Even our piano was crated and shipped, a handsome old walnut thing with swinging brass candle-brackets each side of the music rack.

Father took us to London first, to see the heart of the Empire before we went abroad, with his sister Jessie as our guide. My clearest memories of it are Madame Tussaud's waxworks (especially the Chamber of Horrors) and, in dignified contrast, King George V, riding at the head of the Guards one afternoon near Buckingham Palace.

*　*　*

In May 1913 we sailed from Liverpool in a small steamer with one funnel, the *Carthaginian* of the Allan Line. My hapless mother was seasick most of the way, but Father soon recovered the sea legs of his younger years on the China station. We kids enjoyed the whole trip. The *Titanic* had sunk with an appalling number of her people just a year before, and our first sight of icebergs filled us with awe. *Carthaginian* had a small steel cabin bolted to her upper deck as if it were an afterthought of the builders. So it was, and from it came mysterious crackling noises. One day I peered in there and saw a wireless-telegraph operator at work. I was to see a lot more in time to come.

The ship carried cargo as well as passengers and stopped for a day or so at St. John's, Newfoundland. Two weeks out of England we came into the port of Halifax. Officially the British Army had left the Halifax fortress for ever in 1906, so the Raddalls chanced to be the last of a long procession of British soldiers and their families who had settled there all the way back to 1749.

Halifax was a small and depressing community when we saw it in 1913, a huddle of shabby buildings on the harbour slope, mostly wooden with little fresh paint. The streets were dusty in fine summer weather and muddy in the rains. The town was just beginning to revive from the financial depression that sank upon it soon after the confederation of Canada in 1867, and it had a look of stagnation during the past forty years. In contrast the setting was beautiful, for the sides of the long fiord were still largely wooded then.

Father rented a small wooden house on Chebucto Road, a few yards from Chebucto School. It had a bath and water closet but no electric light, so we lighted our darkness with kerosene lamps and candles. We were on the western outskirts of the city, and our next-door neighbour to the west had the sole sanitary facility in an old-fashioned privy in the back yard. Chebucto Road had a scatter of such dwellings on its way down to the rustic hamlet of Armdale, and between and behind these dwellings were small dairy farms and pastures.

Father began his duties at once, giving lectures and demonstrations to the regulars in Wellington Barracks and the militia in their armouries. He took an interest in the cadet corps of the Halifax schools and went with the older boys when they shot on the ranges at Bedford and McNab's Island. We kids attended Chebucto School, and I became one of its cadets. The uniform was a thin khaki blouse and breeches, puttees of the same material, brass buttons bearing an enamelled green maple leaf, and a hat of the Mounted Police type. We were armed with .22 calibre rifles on the Ross pattern and fired them on a miniature range in the school basement.

* * *

Father made a tour of militia camps and armouries across Canada that summer and came back enthusiastic about the country and its people. He was glad that his children would grow up as Canadians and, unlike my wistful mother, had no regret about leaving England.

In July 1914 he took me with him to a militia camp on McNab's Island, at the entrance of Halifax harbour, where I spent a week or two under canvas with a few other soldiers' sons, roaming the woods and shores through the lovely summer days. Fort McNab, which pointed its big guns seaward from the hilltop site of the old McNab mansion, was quite near the camp. A little cluster of McNab tombstones remained within the fort enclosure, the best-guarded graveyard in the world. From old inhabitants of the island we heard interesting tales of the McNab family and their Highland retainers and piper. We scrambled out to the tip of the long stony spit where in Nelson's day the Royal Navy used to gibbet the bodies of sailors hanged for mutiny or desertion.

On a misty evening, with the sea muttering on the stones and a foghorn groaning where the dead men used to keep watch on the harbour channel, that was an eerie place. So was the knoll called Thrum Cap, where in olden times the McNabs buried the bodies of shipwrecked sailors. These and other tales and impressions of the island stayed in a recess of my mind until, many years later and after careful research in archives, I poured them forth in a novel called *Hangman's Beach*.

In August 1914, when the Germans made their long-planned attack on France through Belgium, Father was in a militia camp near Calgary. He was ordered at once to Valcartier, Quebec, where the First Division was assembling for transport overseas. It was obvious that skilled instructors would be kept on training duty in Canada for the duration of the war unless they moved fast. Like a well-trained light infantryman, Father moved fast and soon found that Colonel Lipsett of the Winnipeg Rifles wanted a machine-gun officer. Lipsett pulled wires, and Father joined the Rifles as a lieutenant. He was thirty-seven.

The division went overseas in September, sailing from Quebec so that there was no chance for Father to see his family in Halifax. After a wet and chilly winter in tents on Salisbury Plain, the Canadians crossed over to France early in 1915 and in April fought their first battle at Ypres, where the Germans attacked them with great force and a terrible new weapon, poison gas. Wounded in the head and arm, Father recovered in hospital in England, and in June he came home on convalescent leave.

I was in my twelfth year. In the past six I had grown deeply resentful of my father's discipline, which he carried into family life and especially to me, the only boy. He had a natural affection and concern for his children, but he had come under the severe discipline of the Marines as a boy himself and accepted it as a way of life.

After his experience in the shambles of Flanders there was a change in him. He was a man of middle height, lean and muscular, with keen grey eyes in a face that seemed cast in a stern bronze mould. Now this mask dissolved and revealed to me a new and warm personality. He drew me into talks about my interests and studies and took me on walks about Halifax, pointing out the places of historical interest, all in a spirit of comradeship that delighted me.

Looking back, I know that close contact with Canadian troops had done much to change his outlook. They were nothing like the rigid automatons, exemplified by the Guards, that were regarded as ideal by the British soldiery. The camaraderie between Canadian officers and men at first amazed him, and he said so; but in the field he found them remarkably effective at war. They had no use for stiff and blind discipline. Efficiency was their ideal in war as it

24

was in peacetime at home, whether building a railway, or running a farm or a logging operation, or whatever. To achieve that they would accept cheerfully as much discipline as was necessary for the good of the job, but they would work or fight their best only for an officer who knew his own job thoroughly and, as they said, shaped up as a man.

In those summer days of '15 Father talked to me about my future. He also sought out and talked with my teachers. I was no student at all in the academic sense. I cared for nothing much but history and English composition. Not English grammar, though. The complicated rules of that subject were a bugbear, and I cannot recite a single one now in my seventy-second year. I enjoyed the actual writing of the English language, and the only prizes I won in school were for essays and other compositions. The explanation, as Father saw, was my delight in reading, which enabled me to write by instinct when I had occasion to push a pen. From this time until his death in battle three years later, he rummaged the London bookshops whenever he was there on leave and sent me all kinds of reading, from R.M. Ballantyne to Kipling, which he knew I would enjoy and which incidentally would show aspects of good English style. In talk with Mother he said, "I think the boy should go in for journalism. He seems to have a definite bent."

He was not permitted to enjoy all of his hard-earned leave at home. As the first wounded soldier to return to Nova Scotia from "the Front," he was beset by people wanting him to speak at various public affairs. On one occasion Mrs. F.B. McCurdy, wife of the federal cabinet minister from Nova Scotia, begged him to make an appearance and say a few words at a gala she was holding for the Red Cross at her home, Gorsebrook, a stately old Georgian house that stood among acres of trees and lawns in the swank south end of Halifax. She sent her limousine and chauffeur, and Father took Mother and me along. It was my first ride in a motorcar and the only time I saw the inside of Gorsebrook before its last days in decay.

The greatest demand came from the army, which asked Father to make a tour of the province, speaking at what were called "recruiting rallies" for volunteers. He hated it, but he complied; and according to the newspapers his talks about the war were good ones. When Army suggested a recruiting or training job in Canada, however, he said firmly, "My place is with my regiment in France."

He left us to return to the war on a sunny day in August 1915. At

25

that time there were some taxis in Halifax, but most travellers still preferred horse-drawn cabs of one sort or another. Like his mother's family, the Heads, he loved horses, and he had learned to ride well in France. On this day he engaged a smart pony-trap to take him to the railway station. He was smiling as he kissed us all good-bye, but his eyes were full of tears, like ours. The Cornish are a people with the gift or curse of second sight, like so many of their fellow Celts in Wales, Ireland and Scotland, and I have always felt that some such instinct told him that this was the last time he would see his family. I can still see the trap trotting away, the driver flicking his whip, and the man in khaki dabbing at his eyes with a handkerchief.

Three years later, almost to the day, he was lying dead on the battlefield of Amiens.

He rejoined the Winnipeg Rifles with the rank of captain and was adjutant in the battles of 1916, notable the long and bloody struggle on the Somme. In the spring of '17 he was wounded again at Vimy Ridge, but he recovered in time to fight that autumn in the mud and blood of Passchendaele, as major and second-in-command. He was given full command of the Rifles soon afterwards. Between spells in the line the Canadian Corps trained for open warfare all through the spring and early summer of 1918, and in August they made a secret march to link up with the Australians in the swift thrust out of Amiens that opened the way to the war's end three months later.

Years after the war several veterans of the Winnipeg Rifles wrote to me. Some visited me at my home on the south shore of Nova Scotia, and I met others in Toronto. All spoke of Father with affectionate admiration – "A strict disciplinarian but always just" – "A true British soldier under whom I was proud to serve" – "A man absolutely without fear." His vigilant care for the welfare of his men earned him the nickname Uncle Tom. One captain wrote to me, "I know he relished the name as a mark of the popularity which he indeed enjoyed."

Out of these soldiers' reminiscences came some lines I penned for their regimental association:

> Where the dead lay thickest, there they found
> My father with the sunset on his face
> Amid the wheat. There was a cheerful sound
> Of skylarks, nothing else, as if that place

Had never known a battle. The dead lay
As athletes fling themselves to earth at last.
The trampled wheat, the shattered roofs of Caix,
And these, marked where the regiment had passed.
He was their colonel, they had loved him well.
And so they buried him amid the grain
With three score men beside him where they fell.
And when their marching came that way again
They placed a signboard MANITOBA there
To show that prairie men were taking rest
In this half-acre, free from war and care
Amid the wheat, and dreaming of the West.

* * *

I have a small packet of my father's letters to me. The first was
written from Salisbury Plain in the autumn of 1914. The last was
headed simply "In the field, July 22, 1918." This was the date
when the Canadian staff were forewarned of a move by night to the
south to make the great all-out attack for which they had been
training.

He mentioned nothing of that, of course. It was the usual brief
father-to-son letter, urging me to persevere in my school studies,
my piano lessons, and so on. He closed with, "If I live through this
war I hope to see you graduate at Varsity. In any case take the ideal
for your goal and strive to make a name for yourself."

* * *

Halifax in wartime was an exciting place. The constant passage of
troops and warships and merchant convoys had many distractions
for a boy like me, brought up in a military air and no lover of the
schoolroom. As the war increased there was much emphasis on
training the cadet corps in the various city schools, and at times we
were turned out en masse for inspection by important-looking brass
hats. I remember an assembly of all the Halifax school corps on the
North Common, where we were inspected by Canada's Governor
General, the Duke of Connaught, a son of the late Queen Victoria.
I can still see this dour old gentleman with his white moustaches
and his general's uniform, tramping solemnly past our ranks and
stopping to speak briefly to a boy here and there. This must have
been in the spring or early summer of 1915, because soon after that

27

the Common was covered with long grey huts for troops awaiting embarkation.

In November '15 we were turned out for a very different occasion, the funeral of Sir Charles Tupper. The grave was in Fairview Cemetery, at that time a long march out of the city. Troops lined the route through the city streets, and the various cadet corps lined the narrow dirt road to Fairview. Our Chebucto company, clad in thin khaki drill, had the farthest post of all, on the slope down to the cemetery gate. It was a wintry day with a bitter wind off Bedford Basin, and we shivered there for about two hours before the procession came along. We had been drilled in the correct posture – at attention, head bowed, with the rifle muzzle on our right boot toe and our hands resting on the butt.

I think every motorcar in the city must have been pressed into service for the cortege. None of us had ever seen so many in one place at one time. Eventually I got bored with staring at my boots and counting the cars as they passed a couple of yards from my toes, so I looked up. At that short range my eyes met the hard stare of a face very familiar from newspaper and magazine photos and cartoons. It was Sir Sam Hughes, in the general's uniform he loved to wear. He was in hot water at Ottawa over the Ross rifle and other army supply scandals ("Sir Sham Shoes"), and probably he was thinking of them as he gazed out of the car. I knew nothing of that, of course, and to me his glare meant severe disapproval of the one boy in the line who dared to break the military pose. Hastily I stared back at my boots and didn't look up again until the last car had gone by. Of the important corpse in the hearse I knew very little. I daresay most of the boys thought of him for a long time as the cause of a dreary march and a cold vigil at the end of it, while a lot of well-clad gentlemen rode past comfortably on wheels.

* * *

In the spring of 1917, with manpower scarce and farmers clamouring for help, authorities thought up a way to use the energy of teen-aged boys in the summer holidays. We were urged to become "Soldiers of the Soil" and offered a small metal badge bearing these words to wear in our lapels. The pay, if any, was a matter for the farmer. The inducement to the boy was free entry into the next school grade whether he had passed the end-of-term exams or not. As it happened I had passed by a hair the exams which led to

Grade Nine, the top class at Chebucto School, but I became a Soldier of the Soil anyhow.

My employer was a Scotsman, sixtyish, who had been in this country a long time. He met me at the country railway station of Stewiacke and with horse and buggy took me about five miles, mostly through woods, to his farm. It was a region of poor soil and scrub forest with a small tributary of the Stewiacke River flowing through the woods and pastures. The man's wife was English, a little grey sparrow of a woman. They had no children and their only help was a poorly paid "hired girl" from another farm along the road.

They were kindly and hardworking, but frugal in the extreme. In Scotland the man had been a carpenter. He and his wife had crossed the sea about thirty years before and bought this poor little farm because they could not afford the rich soil of the Stewiacke Valley itself. They practised a rigid economy in everything, including the food they raised and could sell. I was in my fourteenth year, with a healthy appetite, and working outdoors from morning till night put a sharp edge on it. At table, however, the food was measured exactly to the needs of old folk, with no "seconds," and I went to bed hungry every night. I suppose they never knew.

There was plenty of work, though. I was taught to do the barn chores, to slay potato bugs (they couldn't afford to spray the plants with Paris green), to drive a horse and wagon or the horse-drawn mower, to hoe weeds, to repair old wire fencing and to put up new, and to take a hand with clearing and burning operations in the woods across the stream. The only breaks in this week-long routine came on Saturday afternoon, when the good woman took me in the buggy for a bit of shopping in Stewiacke village, and on Sunday, when she and I hitched up the buggy and drove to church at East Stewiacke. The farmer himself took no time off and grumbled at the Sunday expeditions, especially in haying time.

Mother had given me money to pay my rail fare to Stewiacke and back to Halifax, and at the end of two months, the stipulated time of service for Soldiers of the Soil, I announced that I was going home. I wanted a small holiday before starting the new school term. The farmer urged me to stay longer, but I shook my head. I expected some pay for two months' hard work, but I was too shy to ask for it, and neither he nor his lady mentioned it. She drove me to the railway station, kissed me good-bye, and that was that.

In September 1917 I entered Grade Nine, which was conducted by the headmaster himself as preparation for entry into the prestigious Halifax Academy next year. At the same time I acquired a paper route. My paper was the *Daily Echo*, published in the afternoon. The distributing point was a stationer's shop on Gottingen Street, more than half a mile from the school. I hoped to earn enough money to buy a bicycle.

Each afternoon after school I walked to Gottingen Street, picked up my bag of newspapers, and trudged around the route. I had a few deliveries to make on Gottingen, then along North Street to Chebucto Road, down Chebucto almost to Armdale, and thence up Quinpool Road to my final deliveries at Bloomingdale Terrace and Rosebank Avenue. My customers were widely scattered, and they covered the social scale from the poor folk of Gottingen to the well-to-do of Bloomingdale and Rosebank.

On Saturdays, while delivering the heavy weekend papers, I had to collect the week's money from my customers. We were paid a percentage of the cash we collected, and a bad debtor cheated the boy as well as the *Daily Echo*. I learned a lot about good and bad debtors in this business. Indeed, I learned a lot about people in general. Among other things I found that on Saturdays the poor people usually had the cash ready for me, whereas the well-to-do usually kept me standing (often in rain or snow) while they rummaged about for change. Also, my biggest and most careless debtors lived in plush homes at Bloomingdale and Rosebank. All together the route from the school and the roundabout course back to my home was over three miles, so that in the course of each week I did a lot of trudging in all weathers for small pay. As a bonus, which I did not appreciate at the time, I got lessons in human nature far more useful than anything taught at school.

*   *   *

When winter came there was a terrible new lesson, which also began for me at Chebucto School. On December 6, 1917, a French ship named *Mont Blanc*, crammed with powerful explosives, blew up while passing from the harbour into Bedford Basin. The resulting terrific blast destroyed the northern parts of Halifax and Dartmouth and smashed doors, windows, and much interior plaster in the rest. About two thousand people were killed at once or died later of their injuries. The exact number was never known. About nine thousand others were injured but survived, many of them hideously mutilated. A lot of them were blinded by slivers of window-pane driven with the force of rifle bullets.

Chebucto School was a brick structure of two storeys, with room for about seven hundred pupils, built in 1910 to cope with the expected growth of the city towards the west. The swarm of people into Halifax for war work soon crowded all the schools, and at Chebucto even the big auditorium was filled with makeshift desks, chairs and screens to provide extra classes for junior grades.

In this fourth winter of the war there was a heating problem. The fuel was coal from Nova Scotia mines, in short supply, and the school board ordered the janitors to bank their fires at night. At Chebucto School this brought a special problem in the morning, for the rooms remained chilly until about ten o'clock. Hence another decree. Only Grade Nine, the oldest pupils, would start the day at the customary nine o'clock in the morning. The rest would arrive one hour later, when the rooms were more comfortable. By chance this decree prevented a frightful loss of life and limb (and eyes) in our school on the morning of December 6. The only class in session at 9.05 was my own, whose room was on the south side. The great blast came from the north.

We had just finished singing the morning hymn, "Awake, my soul, and with the sun /Thy daily stage of duty run," and were in the act of sitting down when we felt two distinct shocks. The first came from the deep slate bedrock on which the city stood, a sort of earthquake in which the floor seemed to rise and drop in several rapid oscillations. A few seconds later the air blast smote us. In the same order there were two tremendous noises, first a deep grumble from the ground and then an ear-splitting bang. Some people afterwards said there were two explosions from the ship, but they were mistaken. Anyone who has heard the explosion of a depth charge at sea would recognize, on a minor scale, the same two sound effects.

It was like being shaken by a maniac giant with one fist and then slammed on your head with the other. I was able to move and talk rationally, but the concussion left me in a dazed state for many hours, during which I regarded strange and horrible sights as calmly as if they happened every day. My left hand was cut by flying glass, but that soon healed. The concussion was something else. For the rest of my life a sudden loud noise behind me, where I could not see or anticipate such things as a dropped tray or a slammed door, sent agony through my nerves. This was followed by furious anger at the person or persons who caused the noise. I had to learn to control this reaction but didn't always succeed.

The effects in the classroom were swift and destructive. The windows vanished. The thick opaque glass in the upper half of each door, with wire netting embedded to prevent ordinary breakage, flew out whole. Behind my row of desks a door-glass tipped forward, shot horizontally over our heads, and sliced deeply into the wall in front of us. Fortunately we were sitting by that time. Had it been twelve inches lower it would have decapitated most if not all of us in that row. The big clock on the wall just missed the headmaster and shattered on his desk. All the plaster sprang off the walls in large and small chunks, and filled the room with a fog of white dust. We jumped to our feet, staring at each other. One girl screamed (her cheek was cut from mouth to ear), but I don't recall much crying out. For a few seconds we stood like a lot of powdered clowns with badly applied daubs of red paint here and there; then with the instinct born of routine fire-practice the boys and girls dived through their separate cloakrooms, snatching coats and headgear off the hooks or off the floor and clattering away downstairs to run home.

By that time the cold air, rushing in through empty window frames, had blown the white fog away and I could see the whole room clearly. I found myself like Casabianca's boy upon the burning deck whence all but he had fled. I was the sole remaining pupil, and I stood by my desk gazing mutely at the headmaster. I had no conscious thought in staying. I suppose it was the instinct of any boy bred in a military life, looking to my commander for permission to leave, come hell or high water.

He was known affectionately and irreverently as Old Gander, a gaunt man with a long neck, bushy eyebrows and moustache, and a pate getting bald, with wisps of side hair brushed across it. He looked very wild now, with specks of plaster caught in all these hairs, and his eyes bulged. He said, "Thomas – is that you, Thomas?" I answered, "Yes sir!" Then he stammered something that seems madly ludicrous today. Actually it was quite sensible. At the first shock, like everyone else in the city, he thought the explosion was confined to the building in which he stood. Many people, including my mother, thought the house or shop or office had been hit by a shell fired by a raiding German warship off the harbour mouth.

With a long experience of school troubles, Old Gander put it down to something else. He said shakily, "Some . . . of the little boys . . . must have been . . . playing with dynamite . . . in the basement." Kids sometimes stole dynamite from construction works like the new railway cutting a mile to the west of us. It was possible that some of the juniors, not due until ten o'clock, had come early to play in the warmth of the basement, where the furnace was. Then Old Gander said more crisply, "We must search the building. I shall look downstairs. You go through the classrooms on this floor. If you find anybody injured, or see any sign of fire, come to me at once."

We parted on these errands at a run. I found the upper classrooms wrecked and littered but empty. Before I could peer into the auditorium I had to tear away some wreckage in a doorway. It was a spectacle. The architects had placed it on the north-facing side of the school and lighted it with a procession of large windows. The great blast had driven all of these windows inward, sashes and all, and they had swept the chairs and desks into a tangle of splintered wood against the farther wall. An hour later those chairs and desks would have been filled with tots of the lower grades.

I rejoined the headmaster in the first-floor hallway. He had just come up from the lower floor and basement, where he found no sign of life. Even the janitor had abandoned his furnace and fled. At the end of the hall was the ornate main entrance of the school, with tall and wide doors facing Saint Matthias's church, and above them an arched fanlight of coloured glass in various hues. The doors had gone out into the yard and so had the fanlight. A thin snow lay on the ground, and the fragments of coloured glass were scattered over it like a tumbled jigsaw puzzle. Old Gander and I walked out and saw at once that the origin of all this amazing destruction was not even near the school. The smoke of the explosion, a high pillar in the northern sky, was unfolding rapidly at the top in black and white convolutions to form a huge and hideous mushroom, growing incredibly in the sunshine of a winter's day.

Indoors, with our south-facing windows, we had not seen the direct flash of the explosion, which was far brighter than the sun to those who did see it. The evil fungus in the sky was sprouting from the direction of the Narrows, where Halifax harbour leads into the big inner anchorage called Bedford Basin. After the explosion there was an eerie silence, possibly because we were all deafened and in a state of shock, but now we heard a medley of shouts and cries and a great stir of people.

All of the houses across the street had shattered doors and windows like the school, and I realized suddenly that this calamity must have smitten my own home, less than two hundred yards away along Chebucto Road. I trotted into the road. Opposite the school an Imperial Oil wagon stood at a rickety angle on the edge of the sidewalk, with a pair of big horses lying on the road, harnessed to the shaft. The teamster was squatting with a hand on each head, as if in benediction, and saying to me in a bewildered voice, "Would you think a man could stand a thing that killed a horse?" I made no answer and trotted on my way. Actually the horses were stunned, and some time later the teamster got them on their feet and hauled the wagon away, leaving a small puddle of kerosene on the road.

When I reached our house it was like the school, with all the doors and windows gone and an avalanche of plaster covering the furniture and floors. Rags of window curtains waved in the cold breeze. I heard voices in the garden at the back and found Mother there, bleeding from breast and forehead, and my sisters Nellie, Winifred and the baby Hilda apparently unhurt. Mother said, "The Germans – those beasts – they're shelling the city. We must stay out here behind the house." She and the girls and the woman next door were all facing rigidly southward towards the invisible sea. It seemed incredible that they had not noticed the frightful mushroom still growing in the northern sky. I pointed to it saying, "Something has blown up in Bedford Basin."

An hour or so later the neighbour's husband came home. He worked in the north railway station and was one of the few who got out of it alive. His face was cut and smudged with soot, his clothes were torn, and he was gasping after his long run, but he was able to tell us that a cargo of munitions had exploded in the Narrows, the whole north end of Halifax was smashed, and much of it was burning.

We went into the house. Like most Halifax dwellings of the time it was heated in winter mainly by a tall iron stove (a type called Silver Moon was the favourite), which burned anthracite coal. From it a long stovepipe rose over the staircase and plunged into a chimney on the second floor. The explosion had blown down this stovepipe and buried it under a mass of plaster. Fortunately the stove remained upright, and without more fuel its fire went out.

Like every other family in the houses still standing, our job was grim and simple. It was to make one room habitable for the coming night, and that room had to be the kitchen, whose cooking stove and short stovepipe were still intact.

I fetched a shovel from the cellar and cleared out the mess of plaster and glass on the kitchen floor, heaving it through the gaping window frames. The door leading into the hall and another into a small scullery had been blown off their hinges, but Mother and I managed to nail them together in a rough fashion and prop them into place. Next we had to cover the window frames. I found an old storm window in the cellar. It did not fit our kitchen frame, but we got it up and nailed it into place on the side facing west. For the north window we dragged a carpet out of the living room, folded it to get several thicknesses, and nailed that in place. All of this, done in a hurry by an injured woman and a boy of fourteen, was a very inefficient job, but it had to do. We could not look for any help. Our neighbours had their own survival to worry about.

Mother had tied a piece of torn bedsheet about her forehead, but she was still bleeding badly there and from her breast. She had been looking out of a north window at the moment of the explosion, and by a miracle she was not blinded as so many were. She remembered that "all the house windows on North Street blazed as they do sometimes in a summer sunset," and then, minutes later, she was picking herself up from the floor. My sisters were unhurt, although Nellie had an amazing escape. She had not gone to school that morning because she had a cold, and she was lying in her bedroom on the north side of the house when the blast came. The window blew inward right over her bed and drove slivers of glass through the panels of her door. She ran downstairs barefoot over all the litter of rough and sharp debris without getting a scratch.

Much later in the winter, when a crew of carpenters and glaziers from the Halifax Relief Commission got around to our house, they found a piece of iron weighing several pounds stuck halfway through the roof. It was part of a ship's davit. Such relics of the *Mont Blanc* were scattered all over Halifax and Dartmouth. The cannon at the stern, with its muzzle broken off near the tip, was found on the shore of a lake outside Dartmouth. An anchor shank weighing half a ton fell into the woods across Northwest Arm, after an enormous toss into the sky. The rest of the ship became a rain of twisted scrap, ranging from the size of a walnut to that of a blanket.

Many people were killed or wounded by this murderous shrapnel from the sky after surviving the blast itself.

When we got the kitchen cleaned up, Mother opened her dress and found a glass sliver deep in her left breast. Without hesitation she pulled it out, and we were appalled by the rush of blood. At that moment I heard a motor truck coming along Chebucto Road, and I ran out and waved it to a stop. It was one of the garrison lorries. I said my mother was badly hurt and must be taken to a hospital. The soldiers took her to Camp Hill, a hospital newly built for the treatment of severely wounded soldiers coming back from France and not yet fully staffed or furnished. Camp Hill was now jammed with badly hurt civilians, like every other hospital in the city, with patients lying on the beds, under the beds, even in the halls. The hard-driven doctors and nurses could only patch up those who were able to walk and send them home, and about an hour later another lorry brought Mother back.

Towards noon, as we sat about the kitchen stove, we heard shouting in the street and ran out again. This time it was a pair of army lorries with soldiers of the Home Guard yelling, "Get out of your houses! Get out in the open! Another explosion coming! Dockyard magazine's on fire!" By the time they had passed our house we saw men, women and children hurrying along Chebucto Road towards Armdale. Soon the whole street became a rush of frightened humanity, many with bloody bandages and smears of soot. A lot hadn't stopped for hats or coats. There were women in housedresses and aprons, one of them still holding a broom.

We donned coats and hats. Mother picked up the baby, well wrapped, and we joined this dazed procession. Not far from our house we came to some small fields in which two or three wooden houses were under construction. There we turned aside with about a hundred others. Half an inch of snow lay on the fields, and from the builders' lumber piles we took boards to make warmer footing.

The rest of the human stream from the city hesitated, seeing us there, and then came cries of "Too near! Keep on! Take to the woods!" Most of these people hurried on to Armdale, and many did not stop until they were deep in the woods beyond the Dutch Village Road, which crossed the isthmus of the Halifax peninsula. One was a woman who lived near us, aged sixty or so, the wife of a sea captain. Without hat or coat she tramped all the way to those woods and stayed there in the snow for hours.

By this time the huge mushroom in the sky had dissolved in a cold breeze from the sea, but we now saw masses of brown and black smoke surging up from the burning suburb of Richmond to the north of us. It was very cold in the field, especially for my injured mother and the baby; and we were hungry, for we had eaten nothing since breakfast. I walked back to our house and got some bread, jam, a knife, a blanket, and an eiderdown quilt. While I was getting the quilt the bedroom door slammed shut in the breeze. It had been open at the moment of the explosion and was undamaged, except that the outer knob had broken off. When I tried to reopen it, the inner knob came away with the shaft, and for a time I thought I was trapped there with another blast coming at any moment. After some fiddling with the catch I got out and rejoined my family with those oddly assorted supplies.

I don't know how long we stood there. It seemed like most of the afternoon. Eventually army trucks appeared again, this time with shouts that the fire in the magazine had been put out and we could go back to our homes. Actually the whole thing had been a false alarm, started by some panicky fellows who saw flames in a demolished building near the magazine. The magazine itself was well guarded by soldiers and sailors and was never in danger. Our little group of Raddalls had only a few hundred yards to go back to the shelter and warmth of our kitchen. The refugees who fled to Armdale and the woods beyond were still straggling back at evening.

As the afternoon waned a scud of cloud began to cover the sky, with a rising wind from seaward, and by dark it brought specks of snow. In the course of the night this became a howling blizzard that covered the shattered city. In our kitchen we kept alive by sitting close about the stove. With all the plaster off the walls and ceiling, most of the stove's heat escaped between naked laths. Our makeshift window coverings were far from proof against this kind of weather, and the storm blew fine snow between the nails that held the carpet in place. The glass chimneys of our kerosene lamps were broken, and when darkness came we had only a few candles, which we used frugally, one at a time. At every blast of the storm the candle flame flickered blue. I fetched bacon and eggs from the shattered pantry, and we ate supper sitting about the stove.

Later there was a tapping at the front of the house and a man's voice calling "Anybody here?" Mother took the candle and I went with her into the hall. A soldier stood in the entrance where the front door had blown off. He wore the long khaki greatcoat, the brown fur cap, and the clumsy red rubber galoshes of the Home Guard. He said, "Does a boy named *Raddle* live here?"

Mother said, "If you mean Raddall, yes. What do you want with him?"

He explained that he and some other soldiers had been sent to Chebucto School "for a partic'lar job." His "awfcer" had been in touch with the headmaster, who said a boy named *Raddle* lived in the third house west of the school, and *Raddle* could show the soldiers where to find light switches, water taps, toilets, and so on.

I put on cap and coat and walked with the man the few yards to the school. A small group of soldiers stood outside a broken door, and in a few moments a sergeant came down from the first floor with the small flame of a match fluttering behind his hand. He said, "No use looking for switches; there's no juice, and all the light bulbs are smashed anyway."

My soldier said, "Here's the kid, sarge."

I led the way down concrete steps into the basement, which seemed to be the main place of their interest, and we made a tour of it with the sergeant striking matches as we went along. All the windows and doors had gone, of course, and the fire in the big furnace had died out long ago. The sergeant declared, "Hold a thousand, easy." He produced a bottle of rum, took a swig, and passed the bottle around.

Their conversation was mysterious and aloof, and I wondered how long I was supposed to stay. I walked up the basement steps and stood in the entry, peering out at the night. Not a light was to be seen anywhere, and now the snow was falling fast. Suddenly I was aware of a faint glow swimming towards me in the whirl of snow. It became a light of some kind. Behind it moved a white shape much too big for a man. I was scared, but I stood my ground as this apparition turned off the street and into the school yard. I called out "Hello!" in a shaky voice, and the thing swam up to the basement entry. It was one of the white horses that ordinarily pulled the Black Maria (the prisoners' van) about the streets. A plainclothes policeman, probably one of the city detectives, was riding it bareback, and from a rope loop about the horse's neck a lantern swung like a bell. The man called out, "Any soldiers here?" and when I answered Yes, he said, "Tell 'em the first wagon will be right along." He turned the horse and disappeared the way he had come. I passed the message down to the soldiers and remained where I was.

Soon another lantern appeared through the snow, with a faint rattle of wheels. This time it was a horse drawing a low flat wagon of the kind known in Halifax as a sloven, which normally clattered about the streets with freight from the waterfront and railway station. This one's freight was covered by a tarpaulin. In the light of the lantern the sergeant whipped off the tarpaulin and revealed the bodies of six black men and women, some clad in a few rags, the rest naked. They were frozen stiff and must have come all the way from Africville, on the Bedford Basin shore. The soldiers carried them down the steps one by one and dropped them with a distinct "flap" on the cement floor. The sergeant struck matches while they arranged the bodies in a row. Soon another sloven came with a load of white bodies, each gashed and bloody, and there was the same flap on the floor. Before long the wagons became a procession. The sergeant borrowed a spare lantern from one of the teamsters, and in the light of it the rows of bodies grew along the floor. After what seemed an eternity the sergeant noticed me still there and told me to go home.

Mother greeted me anxiously. What kept me so long? And what were soldiers doing at the school? I didn't care to say. I wanted to get those nightmare pictures out of my mind. I muttered, "They just want to fix up the school a bit." We sat huddled in blankets about the stove. From time to time I went to the fuel bin in the cellar and brought another scuttle of coal. When the candle burned down to a stub I replaced it with a fresh one. It was a long night and none of us could sleep. As the storm increased, the snow coming in through the gaps in our window coverings formed white fingers on the floor.

My father and mother were devout Anglicans, and it had been Mother's custom from the departure of Father overseas to hold family prayers before going to bed, each of us kneeling at a chair. Several times in this night, with Mother leading, we prayed again, but we had to sit with our feet perched on the chair rungs, for the floor was freezing. After a meagre breakfast Mother determined to send a message to Father, assuring him that we were safe. She gave me some money and I trudged to the cable telegraph office, far downtown. Its windows were boarded up, but there was light within; and I joined a queue of people with messages to send. On my way back I got a newspaper, a single sheet with a headline in huge letters, HALIFAX WRECKED. As I passed my school the wagons were still busy with their stiff and mutilated freight.

39

The grocery stores were all of the small neighbourhood kind and their stocks were soon gone, so the authorities set up food depots, doling out a daily ration. The depot for our district was an old church on Windsor Street. The process had to be simple, and it was. You went to the depot with a basket, gave your name and the number of people in your family, and received tins of baked beans, bully beef, condensed milk, tea, stale loaves of bread, and a small pat of butter. As new supplies came into the city by rail and ship the variety and quality improved. There was no attempt to collect money, and the inevitable swindlers made the most of the opportunity. Some would send two or three women, girls or boys to the depot, each with a basket, giving various names. Within a week or two our neighbourhood grocer was able to patch up his store and stock his shelves, and from that time we bought our own supplies.

By letting the taps run day and night we kept the water pipes from freezing in the wide-open bathroom and scullery. Fortunately the great snowstorm was followed by a thaw. Day after day I worked through the house with my shovel, scooping up a composite mess of plaster, glass and slushy snow, and flinging it through the gaping window frames. It was a slow job and hard work. You cannot realize the bulk and weight of the plaster on the walls and ceiling of even a small room unless you find it heaped on the floor and have to remove it.

On errands abroad I always stopped at the school and walked into the basement with the dreadful fascination of my visit to Madame Tussaud's Chamber of Horrors. Eventually the whole floor was covered with bodies, and a crew of professional morticians, most of them volunteers from other Canadian cities, took over the care of them. The soldiers had hated it. I remember one young soldier, serving his first turn at washing the gashed and awful faces, running outdoors to vomit.

My school was chosen as the emergency morgue for the city because it was close to the devastated area and because its draughty basement could indeed "hold a thousand, easy" as the sergeant said. Through this frigid place every day passed hundreds of survivors seeking to identify someone they had lost, and every day the wagons brought more human debris as other lots were taken away. The worst began to arrive when the troops, having searched through the splintered wrecks of houses and small shops and factories, turned to the grimmer job of shovelling and raking through the ashes of the burnt ones. Charred human remains came to the school in all sorts of receptacles found on the scene such as tin bathtubs, washtubs, pots and pans, and the morticians searched these grisly things for dentures, rings, watches and other clues to identification.

Most of the twelve-hundred-odd bodies actually found were identified at the school and taken away by relatives and friends, but many remained, mutilated or charred beyond recognition or with nobody living to claim them. These finally were placed in large and small coffins in front of the school for a mass funeral service, conducted by clergy of all denominations. Some of these nameless dead were buried in a single grave in Mount Olivet Cemetery, but most of them went to Fairview. Other bodies were found as late as the summer of 1918, when the last heaps of rubble were being carted away. These went to the paupers' burial ground on Bayers Road and were marked with a single stone monument. Forty years or so later the city bulldozed the paupers' graves flat and built a school (Saint Andrew's) over them. Only the stone monument over the last bodies of the 1917 disaster remained, concealed in a clump of shrubbery.

A few days after the explosion I walked through the ruins of the Richmond suburb. We had friends there, a family whose husband and father was in the army overseas like ours. They lived on a street at the north side of ancient Fort Needham, and their house had been smashed and burned like every other in that area. In the street itself, just in front of the cellar, I found some fragments of the *Mont Blanc* and a thick pool of congealed blood mingled with long strands of black hair. It looked as if our friend and her four children had perished. But on further search and inquiry I found that they were alive. The three older children had been at school in the centre of the city and were unhurt. Mrs. G. was thrown into the cellar with her youngest child and pinned down by the wreckage of the house, which soon began to burn. With one arm and one leg broken, this heroic woman dragged herself and the baby through all that tangle of wood to the street, and she was now in hospital.

Chebucto School remained in its wrecked state for many weeks. Eventually my class resumed study in the Halifax Academy downtown, alternating with one of the Academy classes, each for half a day. It was a long walk there and back in the capricious weather of a Nova Scotia spring, but of course to kids of that era walking was the natural way of getting anywhere in any weather.

On Father's insistence, after we came to Halifax I had resumed piano lessons. My teacher was an elderly spinster who taught in her home in the south end of the city, another long hike that I had to make twice a week. This had its own peculiar hazard. A boy carrying such a sissy thing as a music case was fair game for any gang of tough kids along the route. I learned to keep a wary eye and evade trouble when I could, but there were times when I had to conduct a running fight there and back.

I hated the whole music thing, not least because in addition to the lessons at Miss Hoyt's I had to spend an hour in practice at home every afternoon or evening, when my more fortunate chums were out having fun. And it was all so useless. All the lessons and all the glum practice of years could not alter the shape or size of my hands and fingers, which were much better suited to a sailor than a budding Paderewski. The worst of my musical ordeals, however, were Miss Hoyt's annual "recitals," which were staged in the auditorium of the Ladies' College on Barrington Street. She had about thirty girl pupils but only half a dozen boys, and she arranged the program so that every boy had to make two or three appearances on the stage, while the girls got away with one. To a boy in the shy and awkward teens, the lonely glare of the stage, the audience of parents and other adults, mostly female, the very attitude of the grand piano with its white teeth waiting to entrap one's stumbling fingers, all added up to torture. Many years after the Ladies' College removed to the west end of the city, the old building was taken over to provide a lounge and canteen for servicemen in War Two. One day I walked into the familiar auditorium and felt a reminiscent qualm. I sometimes remarked, not wholly in jest, that it was a piano that drove me away to sea.

The truth was that enforced lessons of any kind now gave me a spirit of revolt, and school had become an ordeal. The long daily tramp to the Academy, the difficulty of home study in our battered and poorly lit house, the lasting effect of the stunning explosion and the macabre scenes that followed all gave me a desperate longing to get away and do something new somewhere else.

In the spring of 1918 I was in my fifteenth year, and Mother bought me a new suit that included my first long trousers. The trousers made me feel so much a man that one afternoon, on my way down Cunard Street to pick up my bag of newspapers, I turned in to the Armouries and tried to enlist in the army. During this war, especially after several long and bloody struggles on the Western Front, the army readily accepted teen-aged lads if their health was good, if they were strong enough to carry a rifle, and if they were ready to fib about their age on the enlistment papers. Several boys from Chebucto School had done so and gone overseas. One of our neighbour's sons had enlisted at sixteen and was killed in France at seventeen. But I was recognized by a recruiting sergeant who knew my father, and he told me bluntly to go back to school.

The working schedule of our parish church, Saint Matthias's, had been upset by the explosion like everything else, and many weeks passed before it was repaired and in use. I was supposed to receive the rite of confirmation at Easter, but all that had been put off. I was secretary of the church boys' club, in which the choirmaster took an interest because he was testing voices for a boys' choir. He was a spry old gentleman who sometimes took a few of us on walking tours about Halifax and Dartmouth and gave us a dish of baked beans and a slice of pie at a restaurant at the end of the afternoon.

In May 1918 he invited three or four of us to accompany him to Encaenia at King's College, Windsor, Nova Scotia. In asking Mother's permission he mentioned that King's was the proper place for the higher education of Anglican boys, and he took some of them to see it every year. For generations the springtime Encaenia had been such an event that the railway ran a special excursion train from Halifax. So, for the first and last time, I saw the venerable wooden college in its setting of rich fields and orchards. It was destroyed by fire in 1920. I was enchanted with the college, the scene, and a dream of life as a student there; but the return to Halifax brought back the cold facts of my life, especially my deficiencies as a student. With my restless mind I couldn't hope to graduate from the Halifax Academy, let alone King's or Dalhousie, as my father wished.

All of this came to a head in August with a telegram from the Department of National Defence. Mother hesitated one or two minutes before opening it. She had gone through this experience twice before, when Father was wounded in 1915 and 1917. I watched her face as she drew the telegram from its envelope, and in a moment I knew. My sisters wept with her, but I had no tears, only a stony resignation.

I went out and sat on the front steps in the hot sunshine, wondering how anything could ever be right again. After a time I made my way to a telephone and asked the rector of Saint Matthias's to come and comfort my mother. He came at once, but he could only offer the doubtful balm of prayer and his face was sad. After four years of war this was a too familiar task, and he must have known how hopeless it was.

In myself I felt the first stirrings of a doubt that grew as the years went by. If there was an all-powerful and merciful God, why all the suffering I had witnessed in my home and in the city during the past eight months? And what about the suffering on the battlefields, where upright and devout men like Father had been cut down as ruthlessly as the sinners? In spite of all the prayers at home! It seemed to me that what we had been taught was nonsense. In the course of experience, like the ancients of Greece and Rome, I found the world a tough place where appeal to the gods met only silence or a mocking echo. Prayer with shut eyes and bended knees, addressed to some mythical Power, was like shouting down a drainpipe in the dark. It was better to face things on your feet and with eyes wide open, watchful for trouble and maybe a bit of luck here and there along the way.

Naturally at fifteen I did not think of these matters in the words I have just written, but they became my sentiments. As time went by I saw no reason to change them. From time to time I went to church, possibly from some unrecognized but wistful longing for the peace of mind my parents had found there, but mainly because in the small towns and villages where in the course of my life I came to work, and particularly in winter, the church was the only place where you could find most of the people you knew gathered at one time. Some were religious, but religious or not most of them went to church as I did, for the pleasure of seeing each other and chatting after the service. My unfailing interest and belief was in people. God remained invisible and aloof.

1918
1923

The pensions board at Ottawa notified Mother that as the widow of Major T.H. Raddall, DSO, she would receive a pension of eighty-five dollars a month, with an additional small allowance for each child under the age of fifteen. This meant no allowance for the support of my sister Nellie, who was nearly seventeen, and none for me after November when I would pass the age of fifteen.

Later on, through the insistence of one of my father's comrades, the pensions board checked over army records. Father had commanded the Winnipeg Rifles as acting lieutenant-colonel from the winter of 1917 to his death in the following August. Owing to some careless idiocy the rank had not been confirmed until a hasty entry in the records during his last few days of life, and this entry had been overlooked. Mother's pension was raised eventually to something like $110 monthly. How a private soldier's widow could have existed on a pension of about thirty-five dollars, as it was then, I cannot imagine. I know that Mother found herself in a frightening position in that last autumn of the war. Rent, food, clothing, fuel, everything necessary for existence had rocketed in cost since the war began, and now the cost was climbing faster than ever.

Her one hope was a return to England where her Canadian pension dollars would buy more, in spite of the war; but while the war lasted it was impossible to get steamship passage for mere civilian mouths, and meanwhile there was the difficult problem of paying for the passage. Father's cash savings had been pitifully small. Mother discussed all this with Nellie and me. Obviously we two must get jobs of some kind. In my case Mother remembered that during his home leave in 1915 Father had met William Dennis, owner of the Halifax *Herald*, and in conversation mentioned that his son seemed to have a flair for writing. He hoped to put him through college, but "if anything happened" the boy should go in for journalism. Dennis replied that "if anything happened" he would see that the boy got a chance with the *Herald*.

With this in mind I went to the *Herald* offices on Sackville Street and explained my errand to one of the young ladies on the ground floor. She went upstairs and returned saying Mr. Dennis was too busy to see anyone today. I went back another day, and another, with the same result. A lot of things had happened since the summer of '15, and the war had brought tragedy to Dennis himself. It was impossible for a hard-driven man in this battered city to remember a casual offer made all that time ago.

I tried the other paper, the *Morning Chronicle*. Gentlemen there gave a hearing to my shy little story of journalistic ambition and even read one of my carefully written essays. They offered a job as office boy. They were just being kind, I think. Obviously a lad of fifteen who was not even a graduate of Grade Nine in the public schools had nothing to recommend him for training as a reporter. I could see that in their faces. I thanked them politely and said that wasn't what I was looking for. I remembered Father's experience as an office boy.

Outside the *Chronicle* building and looking down Prince Street I saw an old stone structure known as the Queen Building. Its third-floor windows had stencilled gilt letters reading "Canadian School of Telegraphy." Among the newspaper advertisements of jobs available I had noticed one inserted by this school. It mentioned openings for all types of telegraphers and said there was a special demand for wireless operators in the merchant marine. The school had a complete radio apparatus of the type used in most British and Canadian ships, with every facility for practice, and there were lectures by a naval expert from the Halifax Dockyard. The school was privately owned, and the fee for the wireless course was eighty dollars.

I came home and begged Mother to let me take the course. The minimum age for a first-class seagoing certificate was eighteen, but I could fib my way to that, as so many boys had fibbed their way into the army. She was dubious. The war was still banging away, and the U-boats were still making the North Atlantic dangerous, despite the convoy system. Some had even bobbed up off the Nova Scotia coast this summer and shot up the fishing fleet. On the other hand there was the strong possibility that my fib would be detected and the training fee would go down the drain. I had to persuade her that I could get away with it. The more I talked, the more enthusiastic I became, and finally she gave in.

It was September 1918. After the breakthrough at Amiens in August, the British, French and American armies were following up with attacks along the whole front, and the Germans were pulling back from all of the old churned-up battlefields of the past four years. But it was a fighting retreat. Nobody believed the Germans would surrender until the Allied armies got across the Rhine, a very long way on the map. With bitter memories of the blood-and-mud campaign in the previous autumn, it seemed clear that the enemy could hold out for at least another winter. The general talk in the newspapers and in the streets was that the final campaign would come in the spring and summer of 1919.

I began my studies at the School of Telegraphy with happiness and zeal. First we had to memorize the alphabet in the international dot-and-dash code. Then, day after day and week after week, we practised at the heavy brass radio-telegraph keys and at the "phones," working towards a speed of twenty words (one hundred letters or figures) per minute, the minimum for a first-class certificate. We had to memorize a whole booklet of rules for wireless telegraph "traffic." We had to learn how to maintain and repair various kinds of wireless apparatus and how to install everything from a ground wire to the aerials aboard a ship. I soon discovered that the word "wireless" was a misnomer. Every radio outfit contained an enormous amount of wire, much of it as fine as a hair.

All my classmates were older than I, with the usual male distractions in booze and girls. My age absolved me from all that. I was so keen that in addition to the daily routine I spent every evening in practice at the instruments. I was joined in this by another teenaged lad named Edwin Turner, who also intended to fib his way to sea service.

He and I were still plugging away at the wireless course when the

Germans and their unhappy partners surrendered in November. However, the victorious allies had involved themselves in a whole new war by that time, backing the Russian white armies against the reds. They had landed troops, including Canadians, at Murmansk and Archangel and on the Pacific side at Vladivostok. On the face of it, this war might last even longer than the German one.

Shipyards on both coasts of Canada were still turning out steam freighters by the dozen, some for the British Ministry of Transport but mostly for the new Canadian Government Merchant Marine, known for short as the CGMM. (It was known abroad facetiously as the Rat Line because Canadian ships flew the British merchant jack with a beaver in the fly. Nobody outside of North America knew what a beaver was, and at a distance the rodent on our flag was hilariously familiar to every sailor in the world.)

All of these ships needed wireless operators so there was a continuing demand for "Sparks" or, in the telegraphers' own slang, "brasspounders." Early in the spring of 1919 Turner and I passed out of the School of Telegraphy and went to the RCN dockyard for official examinations. The examiners were naval officers who gave us stringent tests in sending and receiving messages at twenty words a minute, using the big brass key and the uncomfortable phones with their steel head-clamps. We had oral examinations on the regulations for wireless telegraphers in the Canadian sea service and on the care and maintenance of apparatus. In addition we had to write papers on these subjects that went to the Department of Naval Service at Ottawa for final review, along with the report of the examining officers at Halifax. These papers had to be accompanied by a birth certificate or some other good proof that you were of Canadian, or anyhow British, birth.

Mother had a copy of my birth certificate, so that was no problem. The problem was whether the examiners at Ottawa would notice that I was about two and a half years younger than the bold "18" I had written as my age on the exam papers. I turned the birth certificate in with the papers and hoped for the best.

At this time the manager of the Marconi Wireless Telegraph Company's office at Halifax, W.J. Gray, was beset with demands for qualified brasspounders, so he kept in close touch with the School of Telegraphy and with the dockyard. When he learned from the dockyard examiners that Turner and I had passed the tests there and that our papers were excellent and bound to pass the Ottawa board, he got in touch with us and offered jobs. I forget where Turner went, but I was sent to the wireless station on Partridge Island, at the entrance to the port of Saint John, New Brunswick, to get some watchkeeping experience until my certificate arrived.

When I caught the afternoon train for Saint John I was wearing the grey suit with long trousers that Mother had bought the year before. She had sewn a black mourning band around the upper left sleeve. My suitcase was one of my father's, and most of my shirts, socks, ties and handkerchiefs were his too, part of the mufti outfit he kept for off-duty hours at Halifax. I was even wearing a pair of his shoes. They were a bit too big but not enough to bother me.

The Marconi office gave me travelling money, and my good mother scraped up another fifty dollars for emergencies, the chief emergency in her mind being, as she put it, "if you find the sea life too hard. Then you're to tell them your real age and come home." She wept a little when we parted, but I was as blithe as could be. I would soon be off to sea as an officer, in a uniform splendid with gold braid on the cuffs, and with the whole wide world for adventure. What more could anyone ask?

* * *

The station on Partridge Island had been built in 1905, a small rectangular wooden shack, painted grey. It sat under a tall mast and aerials like a matchbox under a naked umbrella. The watch room was at one end and the engine room at the other, to keep the noise as far away as possible. Between them lay a kitchen-dining room, a bedroom for the chief operator and his wife, a storeroom, and next to the watch room a small coop with two-tier bunks for thc other two operators.

We had a lighthouse on one side of us, at a distance of perhaps a hundred yards, and a foghorn on the other. Spring is a foggy time in the Bay of Fundy; thus we had the intermittent roar of the horn ending with a dismal diaphone grunt much of the time day and night. This was disconcerting when you were trying to read a faint signal in the phones.

As the raw hand I got the graveyard watch from midnight to eight o'clock in the morning. Life was dull on Partridge Island with its cluster of deserted army huts, the dismantled battery, and few inhabitants. When the fog lifted at night, sometimes we could see the lights of Saint John not far across the water, inviting and tantalizing. Our only means of getting there was an absurd little tug named *Sissiboo*, which came with the mail each morning and made a trip for the quarantine doctor in the afternoon. This schedule and our own routine made it impossible to spend an evening in the town. At best I could go there on *Sissiboo*'s return trip in the morning, do a bit of sightseeing, lunch in a café, and come back on the afternoon trip.

After my careful training at Halifax I had no difficulty with the apparatus, and the ripple of dots and dashes was as natural as ordinary conversation. I was impatient to be off to sea, and in May the word came. I was to return to Halifax for a short leave and then join S.S. *War Karma* as junior wireless operator for a voyage to Europe. I left Partridge Island in good cheer and arrived home to find a cardboard tube and letter from the Department of Naval Service awaiting me. In a nautical phrase, they brought me up with a round turn. Someone at Ottawa *had* compared the date of my birth certificate with the age given on the examination papers, and my hopeful fib had been spotted. I have the letter still. It reads:

Sir:

The following table shows the marks you obtained in the various sections of the examination you attended for Certificate of Proficiency in Radio-telegraphy at Halifax on 8th April 1919: –

Section	Marks obtained	Minimum required
Technical	91	75
Diagram	94	50
Handling of traffic	93	50
Sending	100	100
Receiving	100	100
Practical	85	75

As you will not be 18 years of age until 3rd [*sic*] November 1921 you are not eligible for a First Class Certificate at the present time. A Second Class Certificate is however being issued in your favour and will be forwarded to you by registered mail. On receipt you will please sign your name on the line provided for that purpose on the back of the Certificate, in the presence of a Collector of Customs, a Justice of the Peace, or a British or Canadian Radio-telegraph Inspector. The witness will check your photograph and description, and sign his name.

I am, Sir
Your Obedient Servant
G.J. Desbarats
Deputy Minister

* * *

Obviously Mr. Desbarats was not my obedient servant, but I couldn't quarrel on that account. It was nice to know that I had passed for a first-class "ticket" with 563 out of a possible 600 marks and well over the 450 minimum required, but the second-class ticket in the cardboard tube meant that I could not take a senior post on any ship carrying more than one operator. Nor could I take a post as the lone operator aboard any ship that required a first-class man. In other words, I could serve only as the junior operator in ships having more than one, and I could take sole charge only in a slim choice of trawlers, colliers, and small tramps.

The photograph mentioned in the letter had been taken when I finished the wireless course at Halifax. It was now firmly glued to the back of the certificate and embossed with the seal of the Department of Naval Service. Also on the back was my physical description:

Height, 5 feet 8 ½ inches. Colour of eyes, Brown. Colour of hair, Dark brown. Complexion, Medium. Peculiarity, Birthmark on right ankle.

There was a place for my signature, and I signed it under the eye of a justice of the peace who had a little office on George Street and did much business in this line with officers of the merchant marine.

I smile when I look at the photograph now. A solemn boy with much dark hair, searching brown eyes, a straight mouth and, to offset the eyes and mouth, an almost girlish face with a dimpled chin. I was wearing my grey suit, a celluloid collar, and a badly knotted four-in-hand necktie. When I regard this obvious truant from Old Gander's classroom and then turn to the face of the certificate, with the signature of G.J. Desbarats, Deputy Minister of the Naval Service, I wonder how I got away with even a second-class ticket.

The dire shortage of ship wireless operators, and the fact that I had actually passed the first-class exams, decided W.J. Gray to

51

offer me a post. I know, too, that he was impressed by my passionate desire to go to sea. Many years afterwards at a book-autographing party in Montreal I met Gray again, and he told me this, and so did his wife, who in 1919 had been his secretary in the Halifax office.

*　*　*

Armed with this certificate and the letter to prove that I had passed the first-class exam, I signed the crew list of *War Karma* as "Jn. W. Opr." on May 17, 1919. She was an iron steamer of about two thousand tons, built at Three Rivers in 1918 for the British Ministry of Transport. Canadian yards had been turning out many like her, usually of bigger tonnage, and all named War-something. Some were built of iron or steel, some of wood. Most of the wooden ones were built in British Columbia yards and brought around to the Atlantic via the Panama Canal. They were not made to last long, and they didn't. A lot broke down after a few voyages. The iron *War Karma* was sold in France a year or two after my voyage in her, and eventually she went to the Greeks, who have a knack of buying supposedly worn-out ships for little money and keeping them staggering about the seas for years afterward. Incidentally, *Karma* is from the Sanscrit, meaning "fate-by-deeds" or something like that. If I needed a motto for my life, there it was.

Our captain was Charles Hunter of Tusket, Nova Scotia, a master of Bluenose square-riggers who had gone from sail to steam before the war. He had now shipped his son Walter as an ordinary seaman with a view to a career in the Canadian merchant marine, coming up the hard way as he had himself. Walter had been born at sea in his father's barque, returning from a voyage to India. He was a few years older than I, blond and stocky, cheerful and easygoing, and we became chums. Eventually he became a wireless operator himself and spend the rest of his lifetime in the Canadian sea service.

The senior wireless operator of *War Karma* was a tall gangling fellow of twenty-six, known as Skin because, as his shipmates said, he was as thin as a fathom of pump water. He knew his job well and spent his lifetime at it. Shortly after War Two, still pounding brass aboard a freighter, he died and was buried in the Caribbean Sea.

*　*　*

The Halifax tailors were booked up far ahead because men were pouring out of the armed services eager to get into "civvies" again. Consequently I had no uniform when *War Karma* sailed from Halifax twelve days after I signed the ship's articles. I was conspicuous in the officers' quarters for that reason and because my age and inexperience were obvious. I came in for a lot of good-natured ribbing. In those days, like a middy in the navy, a merchant service brasspounder was considered, and frequently told, that he was the lowest form of marine life. He sailed the sea in a chair, fiddling with knobs and switches and making noisy electrical sparks. So Sparks was his nautical nickname. In uniform he wore the wavy gold braid on his cuffs, but on Marconi pay he got less money than the navigating officers and engineers. Indeed, as the greenhorn junior operator at forty-five dollars a month I was paid less than a seaman or fireman.

Skin and I shared a little cabin across an alleyway from the radio room. At sea we kept continuous watch, each doing six hours on duty and six off, around the clock. The ship ran into stormy weather soon after leaving Halifax. Deeply laden, and carrying a large deck load of timber, she rolled and pitched unmercifully. For forty-eight hours or more I was miserably seasick and homesick, but I never missed a watch. Whenever Skin came to rouse me I got up at once, clenching my teeth and staggering to the radio room. For the next six hours I sat at the instruments, bracing myself against the violent movements of the ship and dutifully making a log entry every fifteen minutes, recording the names or call letters of ships engaged in wireless traffic.

In our passage across the sea we frequently "spoke" other ships by radio and exchanged information about the latest navigation warnings. The war had left a lot of floating wreckage in the North Atlantic, including dangerous wooden derelicts. Also, a multitude of mines had gone adrift from their moorings about the North Sea coasts during the war and now were floating far and wide. Each night we tuned in to broadcasts from Poldhu, Cornwall, and "F L" (the Eiffel Tower in Paris) and copied long lists of such sightings, with latitude and longitude given to the last fraction of a degree. From Cape Race, Newfoundland, we had similar warnings of icebergs in the northerly routes to Britain.

We wrote our log entries on long yellow sheets with a carbon copy. At the end of a voyage the log sheets, together with copies of all messages sent and received, had to be mailed promptly to Canadian Marconi headquarters in Montreal, whose code name was

ARCON. The logs were subject to scrutiny at ARCON, and any lax or faulty operation brought a sharp reproof.

In the whole Canadian Marconi service, ship and shore, Atlantic and Pacific, a message from ARCON was a word from God. AR-CON could pluck a man from a comfortable shore station like Montreal or Vancouver and send him to some desolate cape or island far up the map towards the Arctic. On the other hand, it could take him off a deadly dull post like the Lurcher lightship in the Bay of Fundy and place him aboard one of the smart new CGMM freighters bound to South Africa, India, Australia and other strange romantic places. It could take him from the barren sands of Sable Island and set him down at North Sydney, say, where the radio station was right in town and he could live like a blooming gentleman.

I made personal entries in a small pocket diary. This got soaked in a boarding sea, and anyhow it was inadequate. Eventually I copied the contents into a larger journal and went on from there. The diary habit stayed with me the rest of my life. When I became a writer the diaries gave story material here and there, and after I reached the age of fifty they became intensely interesting, bringing back clearly people, places, adventures and misadventures that had faded or slipped away from my memory altogether.

Part of my diary entry for June 3, 1919, says: "On watch . . . very homesick but no longer seasick." In fact I now had sea legs which seldom failed me afterwards. Like many other sailors, including Lord Nelson, when I put to sea in rough weather after a long stay in port I got a headache and didn't care to eat on the first day, but never again did I have to run for the lee rail.

Small and overloaded, *War Karma* took the weather badly. One midnight after taking over the watch, I slipped along the deck to fetch the usual "mug-up" from the galley. I was on my way back to the radio cabin with a sandwich and a mug of hot cocoa when the ship rolled deeply to starboard, and a huge sea came out of the darkness as if it had been waiting for that moment. In a moment I was neck-deep in the North Atlantic and would have been dragged over the rail if I hadn't been able to fling one arm about a stanchion and hang on. After what seemed a very long time the ship recovered and rolled the other way, and I made my way, chilled and soaked, to the cabin. The sandwich was gone and so was the cocoa, but I was still clutching a mug full of sea water.

Later that night another sea poured a lot of water down the open skylight of the engine room, filled the stokehold with steam, and injured one of the firemen. The engineer of the watch, feeling the violent jar to the ship and seeing the in-pour of water, thought we had struck a floating mine. With his wartime instinct he shut off steam to the engines to stop further headway, and the ship fell off broadside to the seas and took several in succession.

The blows and sounds were tremendous. Half the deck cargo and part of the bridge were carried away, portholes and doors were smashed, alleyways were awash to the full height of the door coamings. Roused thus from sleep, Skin stepped over the coaming into our alleyway, intending to take charge in the radio cabin. When his bare feet plunged into something like twelve inches of icy water he thought the ship had sunk that far, and he burst in on me with his mouth agape and his pale blue eyes popping. This surprised me, and I had a silly feeling of triumph over my superior officer. The truth was that he and others in the ship's company were still on edge with the long tension of the U-boat war, while I was just too green to be scared.

Our first destination was "Fastnet for orders," Fastnet being a lone rock, bearing a famous lighthouse and signal station, that stands out of the sea off the southwest tip of Ireland. From the remote days of the transatlantic trade this rock, or Brow Head on the coast beyond, was the chosen landfall of vessels bound to English ports or to continental ports along the Channel and North Sea. Our final destination had been given us by wireless, and when we sighted the Fastnet's flutter of signal flags they merely confirmed what we knew. We were to proceed to Manchester by the normal peacetime route.

In a mild June night we passed up Liverpool harbour and entered the first lock of the ship canal to Manchester. The next day we went up the canal, a strange sensation after our stormy ocean passage, steaming slowly inland for thirty-five miles and passing small villages, farms, and pastures with grazing cattle. We moored in Salford, the dock district of bustling Manchester, and lay there two weeks while the cargo was unloaded and the ship repaired. With the aerials lowered and coiled out of the way of the cargo derricks there was nothing for a wireless operator to do. Day after day, and evening after evening, I walked through the dock gate and explored Salford and Manchester.

My chosen chum was Walt Hunter. He didn't drink but he liked a pretty girl, and Manchester was full of them. Before long he was much attached to a demure little waitress in a cafe, and as her girl friend also worked there it followed that I made the fourth in a quartet. It tickled me to pose as a man like Walt, strolling along arm-in-arm with a pretty girl. She was Irish and her name was Bridget, but she preferred the diminutive Bridie. She had Titian hair, a soft milk-and-roses skin, violet eyes that sparkled with fun, and what was rare in working girls in England then, she had perfect teeth. When the girls had an afternoon off we went with them to various Manchester parks or to the perpetual carnival of the Bellevue Pleasure Gardens, and in the evening we treated them to meals and movies. None of this entertainment was extravagant, but it took most of the fifty dollars Mother had given me for "emergencies" as well as an advance on my pay.

Now the captain had further orders. As soon as the ship was ready, *War Karma* was to proceed to Cardiff and load a cargo of munitions for the white Russian army at Archangel. We were told that Archangel was jammed with shipping and some ships, including ours, would remain through the winter, acting as floating storehouses which "the white Ruskies" would unload over the ice. Meanwhile the red Russian armies were closing on Archangel, and if any of them penetrated to the shore of the bay any time between November and May, the ships frozen in the ice would be sitting ducks for their artillery.

Fortunately for us the Allied governments were now making up their minds to abandon the crazy adventure at both ends of the enormous Russian mass. Towards the end of June, Captain Hunter got orders to pay off the crew and proceed with the Canadian officers to London.

In the custom of wireless operators paid by the Marconi Company, Skin and I had signed the ship's articles (thus bringing us under the ship's discipline) at the nominal pay of one shilling a month. We signed off *War Karma* in the Salford shipping office, and under British Board of Trade regulations we now received the little blue-covered book so important to every British mariner, entitled "Continuous Certificate of Discharge." In this is written a description of every voyage you make or period of service you put in, the name of the ship and her captain, the date and place of engagement and discharge, your rank or rating, and the captain's opinion of your ability and general conduct. We also received the Identity and Service Certificate with a photograph.

As usual in Manchester rain was falling, but in spite of it the photographs were taken in the little courtyard of the shipping office. Mine was a quick head-and-shoulders. I have these documents before me now. In the picture I show my opinion of the fuss and the Manchester weather, and I look much older than the boy on the back of the Naval Department's second-class ticket. Not merely the frown and the set mouth but something else, the mark of a hard voyage and the conquest of homesickness and mal de mer all at one time.

On the first of July we Canadians left the ship and caught a midnight train jammed with people, including a lot of glum Tommies returning from leave to rejoin the army on the Rhine. Early in the morning we arrived in London at St. Pancras station and found quarters for ourselves. Walt and I shared a room at the Imperial Hotel in Russell Square.

While Captain Hunter and the others reported at the Furness Withy offices for orders, Skin and I reported at Marconi House in the Strand, which was international headquarters for all seagoing Marconi personnel. We found ourselves in a throng of other brass-pounders sitting in a long waiting room on plain wooden chairs. The routine was this: you registered your name and last ship and took a seat if you could find one empty, and you listened to an intermittent stream of dots and dashes from buzzers on the wall, each calling a man by name and summoning him to Office Number This or That. It was an efficient system in those days before the vocal intercom was invented but a bind on the men in the waiting room. They had to be there listening every morning and afternoon as if on watch at sea, until some office type was ready to deal with them. A chap sitting next to me had been there four days without a single buzz from "those fucking desk-blokes inside."

Skin and I were more fortunate. A buzzer snapped our names within two hours. In one of the offices a very brisk desk-bloke ordered us to join the transport *Prince George* at Southampton and gave each of us an advance of five pounds on our pay. When I rejoined Walt at the hotel I found that Captain Hunter and the others were posted to *Prince George* also. Before the war she and her twin ship *Prince Arthur* had been smart little freight-and-passenger liners on the run between Boston and Yarmouth, Nova Scotia. In 1916 the British Admiralty leased them for the Channel run between Southampton and Le Havre, carrying mails and soldiers on leave. Now the Admiralty was returning them to the owners in Boston, and in this way our *War Karma* party would work their passage home.

I took the tube from Euston to West Hampstead and called on my aunt Jessie Raddall, much to her surprise. The Raddalls have a chronic aversion to writing letters, so she didn't even know that I was out of school and off to sea. She and another teacher shared a flat near Hampstead Heath, and the two ladies bombarded me with questions. My aunt kept saying, "How you've changed!" As I told her truly, a lot of things had happened since she saw me last, more than six years ago.

Our party of *War Karma*s arrived in Southampton on an afternoon train and found the twin ships tied up at adjoining quays. Our captain and son Walter were familiar with them from pre-war days. Each had two funnels and a lean look in its naval grey paint, and they had a speed of twenty knots. Because they were designed for the Boston-Yarmouth run and could not carry enough coal for the transatlantic passage, carpenters were boarding up the rails on the lower decks to stow extra coal. Even with this the ships could only reach Horta in the Azores, where they would coal again for the run to Boston. The Hunters shook their heads over the condition of the ships after three years of troop carrying. Most of the crewmen were RNVR types at a loose end after the war, glad to work a one-way trip to the States and then get a paid passage home. We made bets with the officers of *Prince Arthur* that our twin would beat theirs to Horta and again from Horta to Boston.

Both ships left Southampton together, with a crowd of friends and relations waving on the quays and the crews singing the chorus of a wartime song, "Goodbye-ee, goodbye-ee, /Wipe the tear, lady dear, from your eye-ee. /Though it's hard to part I know, /We're just tickled to death to go." The weather was warm, the Channel calm, and the English coast lovely in the evening light. By the next evening we were rolling heavily in a beam sea out of the Bay of Biscay, which gave me a headache and twinges of nausea, like Lord Nelson long before me, but I kept my watch. On orders from London we listened carefully for radio signals from *R-34*, a British copy of the Zeppelin, which had crossed over the Atlantic to the United States and was now on its way back. We heard nothing. On July 13, Poldhu station advised all ships that *R-34* had returned safely.

Besides the shortage of bunker space there was a shortage of tank space for fresh water, so all hands were rationed to a quart a day. This had to provide for meals, washing, shaving and drinking.

At midsummer the latitude of the Azores was hot; with a cloudless sky and burning sun we minded the water shortage. Less than six days out of Southampton, however, we sighted the first of the Azores, a wide sprawl of volcanic peaks that stand out of the sea in tall green cones. In a few more hours we anchored off Horta, a pretty little town in pastel colours with the steep green vineyards of Fayal island for a backdrop. We had won the first half of our bet, for *Prince Arthur* was just passing Hera Cruso island, miles astern. It meant that we would have first turn at the coaling equipment and thus a head start for the second bet to Boston.

The coaling method was primitive. The Welsh coal came off to us in lighters from the storage heaps, and a gang of chattering Portuguese workmen rigged wooden stages up the ship's side. Two ragged fellows stood on each stage and swung the coal up in two-handled baskets to the deck, where it was dumped into the bunkers. Horta was a sleepy out-of-this-world place in those days. Men returning from a brief run ashore, or chaffering with bumboats alongside, brought aboard a lot of cane furniture, lace, wine, plaited grass basketwork, and caged canaries. By nine that evening we had finished coaling and topped up our water supply. We left the anchorage at once, and *Prince Arthur* took our place.

A precocious romanticist wrote in my diary, "The lights of Horta twinkling farewell. A perfect night, warm and voluptuous, a big moon peeping over the black bulk of São Miguel, and the faint music of the military band drifting over the water. Walt waxing sentimental again. A senhorita this time."

Captain Hunter, a sportsman, notified *Prince Arthur* that he would wait off the west end of the Fayal Channel so that the second half of our race to Boston would start fair and square. The captain of *Prince Arthur*, a very different kind of sportsman, played his second bet strictly to win. He drove the stevedores hard in the night and then slipped away by the east entrance of the Fayal Channel, which lies between the islands of Fayal and São Miguel. He ordered his wireless operators to keep silent and headed for Boston at full speed. When he failed to appear at the west entrance, and when our wireless calls got no reply, Captain Hunter guessed the game, and we were off. By the next afternoon we had dropped the peak of Corvo astern, our last view of the Azores.

It was a pleasant voyage. There was some excitement, a fire in one of the bunkers, and the stokers and trimmers toiled for hours to get at it. Early one morning I picked up dot-and-dash signals from

Sable Island, like a voice from home. After many clear hot days and nights we were now in fog, and the fog became thicker as we drew toward Cape Cod.

Here I must mention RDF (Radio Direction Finding), then fairly new and in the minds of many merchant skippers a very doubtful contraption. During the war, U-boats surfaced at night to charge their batteries and communicate by radio with each other and with Germany. Consequently in 1917 the British Admiralty set up RDF stations. When U-boats began to raid the east coast of Canada in 1918 the Canadian Navy built RDF stations at Chebucto Head (Halifax), Canso, Nova Scotia, and Cape Race, Newfoundland. Any two of these stations could take bearings on a radio transmitter within their range and thus get a "fix" on it. The system was imperfect. It was bothered with night variations which often made a fix impossible; but in daylight it could locate a trans-mitter with ease, and usually the fix was sharply accurate.

At the war's end it was obvious that RDF would be of great help to ships in fog or snow and for any reason doubtful of their position, so the RDF stations remained in operation. The difficulty now was to convince old-fashioned captains that anything contrived by "those wireless blokes" could be worth a damn in the field of navi-gation. Skin and I had told Captain Hunter about this new aid to navigation. I happened to have the watch as we approached Cape Cod in a wet blanket of fog, and the captain asked me with a scepti-cal grin to get him a position by RDF.

If any U.S. naval RDF stations were manned for general use at this time we were not advised of it, but I had picked up good signals from the Canadian stations at Chebucto Head and Canso. In our position far to the south this meant an acute angle for the bearings, not the broad angle that gave best results. Anyhow, I called them for a fix by cross-bearings. The method was for the ship to transmit the figure two (two dots and three dashes) for a full minute. This gave a good signal for RDF purposes. Then the two shore stations compared notes, and the nearer one (in this case Chebucto Head) gave the cross-bearings.

I carried the message up to the bridge and watched eagerly as the captain and chief officer drew the bearings on the chart. A smile spread over the Old Man's face. He thumped a big fist down on the chart table and declared, "They cross between my funnels!" The RDF fix was near enough to his own reckoning at any rate, and from that moment he was sold on the newfangled and indeed fantastic idea of getting a ship's position actually through the skull of Sparks.

Naturally this position of ours was picked up by *Prince Arthur*, and next morning she broke her long silence and called the Canadian RDF stations for a fix. We copied it and sent it to the bridge. The Old Man worked it out on his chart and said cheerfully, "Well, the bastards are ahead of us. Not far, mind you. But we can't catch 'em now." When we slipped out of the fog and into the sunshine of Boston harbour on July 25, we found *Prince Arthur* neatly tied up at an East Boston dock and her officers calling out to us, "Where've you been?"

Walt and I explored Boston and its environs in the next three or four days. The most interesting place to me was the Harvard campus, whose open spaces had been covered with wooden barracks during the war as the chief training school for U.S. Navy radio operators. We inspected and admired the equipment, which was about to be dismantled along with the barracks. At the end of the month our two crews signed off, and the British personnel went home by passenger liner. Captain Hunter and Walt remained a day or two longer to visit friends and relatives around Boston. Skin and I took train for home.

So ended my brief service with the British Ministry of Transport. My first experience of the sea in *War Karma* had been a rough one, and then came the warm and pleasant voyage in *Prince George*. I had enjoyed working at my job. I had enjoyed the illusion of being a man full grown (in spite of Mr. Desbarats) and seeing strange towns and people. But what I enjoyed most was that brief glimpse of lush green islands in a sea of marvellous blue and their easy-going olive-skinned people, all placed beyond an enormous reach of ocean as if for the reward of way-worn sailors, like the Isles of the Blest in Masefield's ballad. I knew there were many such places in the world. Bermuda, for instance, or Tahiti, magic name, or Hawaii, or Conrad's enticing East as he sniffed it first from a small boat in *Youth*. I longed to set my feet on such places, to feel myself part of them for a time and then go on to the next. Why else do young men go to sea? And it was no mere fantasy. Born of a war-time emergency, the Canadian Government Merchant Marine was now determined to stay in peacetime business, sending its numerous ships about the world as in the good old days when Canada's "wooden ships and iron men" went everywhere and carried anything. Most of the CGMM ships required a single operator, and he had to have a first-class radio ticket, a passport to dreamland for which I must wait another two years and some months. Meanwhile I must take any job I could get.

I spent two weeks with my family in Halifax, the last I was to see of them for almost three years, except for a few days in the summer of 1920. Mother was preparing to sell her furniture and depart for England. I felt guilty about the money I had spent. I was broke and unable to repay the cash she had put up for the wireless course and for "emergencies." I resolved to take any job at all, as soon as possible, and to set aside all pleasure until that money was back in her hands.

In mid-August of 1919 I was called to the Marconi office, where Mr. Gray talked to me like a father. His discourse went something like this. "Raddall, there's a job in the offing for a second-class operator, but I think I should tell you a few things about it first. The ship is a small freighter called *Watuka*, about one thousand tons, launched at New Glasgow last year. She soon showed a tendency to roll her rails under in anything more than a moderate sea, and right now she's hauled up on the marine slip at Pictou getting a stabilizing fin riveted along her port and starboard bilges.

"When she comes off the slip she's to take a cargo of timber to Britain from a sawmill on the Miramichi. After that she'll spend the autumn and early winter months on cold and dirty trips between Cape Breton and Newfoundland, taking coal and supplies to the iron mines at Wabana and coming back to the Sydney steel mills with iron ore. In short, she's anything but a pleasure boat.

"However, that's not the main point. I must warn you that her skipper is a tough old relic of windjammer days. I believe he had quite a reputation as a bucko mate and captain of the fist-boot-and-belaying-pin type. Nowadays of course he does his hazing with his tongue, but that's bad enough. He can't keep a crew. The only mates he can get are men down on their luck, and he makes them get their meals in the engineers' mess. Regulations oblige the ship to carry a wireless outfit and an operator rated as an officer, with an officer's full accommodation; consequently he eats in the cabin with the captain."

Gray paused and looked at me shrewdly. He was a former brass-pounder himself, a Scot from the Shetlands who had been in charge at Cape Race when the *Titanic* sent out her dramatic SOS. "So

62

you'd find yourself eating three meals a day in his company, not merely because regulations demand it, but because he wants someone to haze at the table. In his rambunctious way he enjoys that. You see, the mates won't talk back to him. They're afraid of losing their jobs. Radio operators are paid by the Marconi Company, and they're mostly spirited young chaps. When the skipper goes into his tirades about the worthlessness of wireless apparatus, the incompetence of the operators, and all the rest of it, they're inclined to hold up their end of the argument. Finally it always comes to a thundering row, and he orders them off the ship. The ship's only been afloat about a year, and in that time he's fired five wireless operators. The owners have to pay for the operators' journey home, so the skipper always fires them in Sydney or Halifax where it doesn't cost much."

The superintendent paused again. "Think you could take it on?"

I said, "Mr. Gray, if you'll give me the job, I promise you I'll try to stick it out." I didn't feel as brave as that, of course, but I had to have that job.

So Gray gave me journey money and a letter of identification for the captain when I reported aboard. He shook my hand and said, "You know, I'd like to convince the owners that our operators are competent and steady-going, in spite of what the captain says. Your best policy is silence. When he raves, let him rave and keep your own tongue in your cheek. And if you do hold the job longer than the others – five months, say – I promise you a transfer to something better."

With that promise I departed for Pictou. I found *Watuka* high and dry on the marine slip outside the town and climbed aboard by ladders and stagings. I got a sailor to hoist my sea chest aboard with a rope, and while that was going on I reported to the man whom I shall call Captain McAhab, which of course was not his name. I don't want to imply that he was at all like the hero-villain of *Moby Dick*, except that he had an obsession. Melville's skipper was intelligent, despite the obsession. My skipper's intelligence was not much higher than his boiling point, which was just a few degrees above zero.

He was thickset, with a grey Edwardian beard, and he brushed wisps of thin grey hair across a balding skull. His eyes were those of a codfish, with large drooping sacs below. During the next few months I attributed these sacs to heavy drinking, which according to his steward he did mostly at night in the solitude of his cabin. I suspect now that they were symptoms of liver disorder, which accounted for some of his bad temper. His upper teeth were false and cheap and ill-fitting, and their phony whiteness made a sharp contrast with the yellow snags remaining in the lower jaw.

I presented the letter from the Marconi office, and he looked me up and down. "Where's your certificate from the Navy Department?" I passed him my second-class ticket and watched his face. He ran a fishy gaze over the front of it and then turned to the back, reading the physical description and glancing from the photograph to me. The photo taken nearly a year ago caught his suspicion at once.

"How old are you?"

"Sixteen, sir." This was stretching the truth a bit.

A bellow. "So they've sent a sixteen-year-old kid to run my wireless! Those Marconi people have a hell of a nerve!"

I produced the Board of Trade discharge book, showing my voyages in *War Karma* and *Prince George*, with the reports on ability and general conduct both marked "Very Good" and signed by the captain. He gave these a long stare and growled at last, "Well, I'll have to take what I can get, I suppose." He produced the ship's articles, and I signed them for the usual nominal sum per month.

The radio cabin was amidships, a small uncomfortable coop on the port side. It contained a half-kilowatt transmitter, whose noisy spark was muted in a wooden cabinet with thick walls like an old-fashioned icebox. There was a tiny desk just big enough to hold the receiving tuner and transmitting key. The bunk had three wooden drawers underneath. The cabin floor space was so small and narrow that I had a whimsy of being pushed out through the porthole if anyone suddenly opened the door.

I made a routine check over the apparatus and spare parts. On deck I noticed that the ship's masts were being cut down close to the height of her funnel. The mate informed me that this was being done so they could pass under the bridges over the Liverpool-Manchester canal. In my former ship *War Karma*, the designers had taken care of such a contingency with a mast in two sections. The full height of these at sea gave the wireless outfit a good range, and on entering the canal the upper mast and aerials were easily lowered out of the way.

I pointed out to Captain McAhab that cutting the masts short, as the Pictou ship-riggers were doing, would bring my aerial wires perilously close to the funnel top. The loss of height would seriously shorten the hearing range of the apparatus, and in sending messages the high voltage in the aerials would probably make a spark-jump to the metal of the funnel, with another loss of signal strength. The skipper could not understand this, of course. He snarled that I didn't know what the hell I was talking about, and anyhow the masts were his business, not mine.

I was pleased to find that I was going to Manchester again, remembering those happy-go-lucky jaunts ashore with Walt Hunter and the girls, but I was to find little happiness or luck aboard *Watuka*. With such a misanthropic tyrant for a captain the officers and crew were bound to be a poor lot, and they were. The first mate was an elderly Englishman with a master's ticket, reduced by booze to jobs like this and visibly frightened whenever McAhab barked in his direction. The second mate was a taciturn Newfoundlander, stoically putting in time until he could fill a vacancy among the harbour pilots at St. John's. The chief engineer chose to eat his meals in the junior engineers' mess instead of taking his place at the captain's table, where the chief engineer rightfully sits in a well-conducted tramp. He found his own men better company. Apparently so did the two deck officers, who also ate there.

I struck up a friendship with one of the sailors, a young Nova Scotian named Shaw of better education and moral fibre than the rest. Like me he had been drawn to the sea by a romantic will-o'-the-wisp that promised the far, the strange and the beautiful, and like me he soon found that *Watuka* would never take him there.

When the ship came off the slip she moved across the harbour to Pictou Landing to take on pig-iron ballast and bunker coal. This was a pleasant place in August, with summer cottages inhabited by families from New Glasgow, Trenton and Pictou, and a camp of teen-aged girls. Some of the girls came aboard the ship and I made their acquaintance, or they made mine, "because we want to see the wireless." A happy memory is a trip by motorboat to a sand beach near the harbour lighthouse on a warm moonlit night. We bathed and then talked beside a driftwood fire for hours.

At last *Watuka* sailed for Newcastle, New Brunswick, and the captain began his customary war with the wireless operator at once, ordering me to make contact with the radio station at Pictou and one on Cape Bear, Prince Edward Island. These were small stations, manned only in winter for communication with the Magdalen Islands when the mail service was shut off by ice. I told McAhab this, but he insisted; and I made persistent calls throughout the day and of course got no reply. At evening the skipper snapped that either I was no good or the Marconi outfit was no good. As soon as we got to Newcastle I must wire to the Marconi office at Halifax to "send a wireless engineer to overhaul the gear."

We entered the mouth of the Miramichi River and about two hours later tied up at a sawmill wharf across the bridge from Newcastle town. I sent a telegram to Gray with the captain's demand. That afternoon I walked over the bridge and through the town to see a big wireless station built just before the war by the Poulsen Company of Denmark for transatlantic messages. The Canadian Navy had taken it over during the war and kept a bored staff monitoring the main German naval radio station at Nauen. Now it had been offered to the Marconi Company, and a Marconi engineer was there looking it over, together with an engineer representing the Poulsen Company. They showed me the whole thing, and Murphy, the Marconi man, mentioned that he kept in touch with Gray in Halifax.

Two days later I had a wire from Gray. "Pictou and Cape Bear stations shut, so impossible communicate them, but get Murphy to overhaul set to satisfy captain." It was an old story to Gray, but he did not always have an indisputable expert just across the river from the ship. Murphy came to inspect my apparatus, and out of curiosity the Poulsen man came with him. I think my snarling grey-whiskered skipper interested them as much as anything else. They went over my apparatus carefully, found nothing wrong, and told Captain McAhab that with my aerial wires slung so low he could not expect much of a range. His answer was a grunt.

In those days Newcastle was a little town supplying sawmills and their outlying logging camps. Now that the last of the soldiers were home from the war, the town had a celebration. The ex-soldiers marched in their wartime uniforms behind the town band, and there were speeches in the town square. In the evening there was a fair, with fireworks. The popular tune of the year was "I'm Forever Blowing Bubbles," and the band played it over and over again.

Early in September the *Watuka* went down the river and crossed over the Gulf of St. Lawrence to North Sydney, where she topped up her bunkers and food stores. Two days later we sailed for England. Just as we were leaving the coast I heard North Sydney wireless station telling Cape Race that "V C T" (the station on Sable Island) had been destroyed by fire last night.

                         *   *   *

On Sable Island long afterward I picked up the story behind that
bald announcement. It is an odd bit of Canadian radio history, and
I might as well record it here.

The radio station on Sable Island, like many others on the east
and west coasts of Canada, was built in 1905, and it was the usual
rectangular one-storey shack. A big horizontal one-cylinder gasoline engine whirled the dynamo. For safety in case of fire the drums
of gasoline were placed on a sand dune whence they could be rolled
easily down to the fuel tank.

The chief operator in 1919 was a veteran Marconi hand whom I
shall call Brand. At the outbreak of war in 1914 the Canadian
Navy took charge of all the coastal wireless stations, and in the long
course of the war the stations became staffed by a mixture of veteran Marconi hands and Navy hands. When the war ended in 1918
the naval operators, who had enlisted for the duration of hostilities,
demanded and got their discharge. Thus at a time when the Marconi Company was trying to find brasspounders for Canada's rapidly growing fleet of merchant ships, there was a sudden shortage
of hands for the shore stations.

At Sable Island in the late summer of 1919 Brand had a crew
long overdue for relief. Owing to the wreck of a government supply
ship, several remote lighthouses and radio stations, including Sable
Island, had passed the winter and spring of 1918-19 on short supplies. The operators on Sable Island now saw the approach of another winter, and they were apprehensive and angry. Their feelings
were aggravated by their wages, which were still on a miserable
pre-war scale at a time when any experienced Canadian brasspounder could get a well-paid job in the States. Brand and his three
men sent a message to ARCON demanding immediate relief.
ARCON said it was impossible at the present time. So they mu-
tinied. In a message to ARCON, signed by all hands, they said they
would maintain regular watches and they would handle S O S calls,
but they would not accept a single paid message. This was shrewdly
aimed at ARCON's tender spot, the matter of money. At that time
Cape Race and Sable Island were the busiest and most profitable
stations on the Canadian east coast. Emigrants were pouring out of
Europe towards the United States, and all began sending radio
messages to relatives and friends there, via Cape Race and Sable
Island, in good time before they reached New York. In the other

direction the liners were filled with Americans eager to see Europe again after being shut off for the past five years, and these too sent a stream of messages. The Marconi stations had a fat rate for such traffic, and by the summer of 1919 money was pouring out of the North Atlantic air into ARCON's bank account in Montreal.

Soon after Brand's men sent their ultimatum they put it into effect. The veteran OIC (operator in charge) at Halifax called Sable Island and tried to reason with the mutineers. He got a reply too rude to set down here, even in dots and dashes. When this situation had existed for some time, the mutineers put their heads together again. They also put something else together.

Earlier that year a Greek steamer named *Plataea* had grounded on the island with a cargo of mixed freight that included some small drums of alcohol. To lighten the ship everything was dumped overboard, even the bunker coal, and she was towed off, one of the few ships ever to escape the clutch of the Sable Island sands. When I was posted to the station there two years later, some drums of alcohol were still stashed away in the dunes.

On the night of September 4, 1919, a brief ripple of dots and dashes came from the spark of the station:

> QST de VCT
> stn on fire
>   SK

In plain English:

> Sable Island calling all ships and shore stations.
> Station on fire.
>   End.

* * *

Halifax called VCT repeatedly for several days with no answer, and at last the authorities sent a ship to the island. The landing party found the wireless station burned to the ground, or rather the sand. Brand and his wife and crew were living a mile away in the lifesaving station. The ship took them off to Halifax, where there was a formal inquiry. The fire was blamed on an accident in the engine room, and there was no proof of any other cause. The only possible charge against the operators was their strange little mutiny, but like the war itself a lot of things were being written off the books just then. The Marconi Company simply released them from its service. They disappeared towards the States and no doubt lived happily ever after.

Later that summer a government ship went to Sable Island and put ashore the materials for a prefabricated wooden building, very much like the old one, together with new apparatus, furniture, stores, fuel, and brasspounders. This was the station to which I was posted later on, and I shall come to it in due course. I must return now to the little *Watuka*, laden with timber and bound across the sea to England.

*   *   *

Looking at my diary entries on that voyage, I find them written in a debonair and even cocky spirit as if I actually enjoyed the hatred of the captain, but it was the equivalent of a boy whistling past the graveyard after dark. I remember keenly the hours of loneliness and the private desolation of heart that came out of it. In the ship's company there was none of the cheerful camaraderie I had enjoyed in *War Karma* and *Prince George*. The mates and engineers kept aloof as if I were a pariah. They reckoned it safer, I suppose, knowing that the wireless operator was always the main object of the captain's wrath. They all feared the rough side of his tongue.

Captain McAhab thought nothing of bawling out an officer in front of his men. His normal voice was a shout, and his reaction to anything that displeased him was a stream of abuse that included just about everything blasphemous in the English tongue. His vocabulary impressed the steward especially, a furtive little Maltese man who once whispered to me, "That man is Satan! Satan! One day God will strike him dead!"

A psychiatrist would have found the captain's mind an interesting study and not least his monomania about wireless operators and their "gear." As I look back now myself, recalling some of the tales that were told about McAhab in Sydney and elsewhere, I can understand much more than was apparent to me at the time. According to the tales (as Gray had warned me), McAhab had been a bucko mate and master of sailing ships. He must have been something of a sadist even as a young man in the 1870s and '80s. That was probably why his wife ran away with another man – in fact a steamer man, and this in a time when steam was cutting out wind in every way.

At some time after the turn of the century McAhab had been obliged to go into steamships, like many other sailing masters, for lack of a sailing berth. He retained his bucko character, but he was then in his forties, no longer the invincible bruiser of his younger days. One day he attempted to haze a seaman and was knocked down an open hatch himself, in full view of his crew and an interested crowd of longshoremen. The hold was partly filled with cargo so he did not fall far enough to break his neck, but he was painfully hurt and had to spend weeks in hospital.

Tales like that spring up about a man of McAhab's sort, but these anecdotes of his past have the ring of truth when I test them, as one tests a coin, with a careful tapping on the counter of my own experience. They bear out what I saw of the man myself and give a source and meaning to his mania, which was so incomprehensible to me at the time.

What he had come to hate with all the sourness of his nature was *change*. He never concealed his contempt for engineers, oilers and stokers, regarding them as a lot of landlubbers going to sea in a floating machine shop. And now, by government regulations, even a small tramp like *Watuka* had to carry a wireless telegraph with an operator, another lubber who had never fisted a sail on a yard. What was worse, both outfit and operator had to be rented from the Marconi Company at what he considered an outrageous annual fee. Worst of all, by the same regulations the operator had to be ranked as an officer, with appropriate accommodation and meals. He signed the ship's articles for a nominal sum per month to bring him under the captain's authority like any other member of the crew, but he got his real pay from the Marconi Company. So the captain had no monetary hold over him as he had over every other man in the ship. Hence his furious and undying war with the Marconi Company and its personnel.

McAhab's war with me followed his pattern with all the former operators, a constant persecution to make my life as miserable as possible. By regulation the lone brasspounder in a steamer of this kind kept watch during certain daylight hours, with an evening watch that ended at midnight. Then he could turn into his bunk until morning. In actual practice, I kept watch throughout the day and the evening, ceasing only for brief meals and a walk on deck in the afternoon. I put in a long twelve-hour day at the phones. Even with the shrunken listening range, due to those low masts, I could hear the talk of other ships from time to time, far more interesting than anything to be heard aboard *Watuka*.

70

The regulations also provided for extra duty whenever the captain deemed it necessary, and McAhab made the most of it. In spite of his whisky, or perhaps because of it, he was a bad sleeper, and he had the old windjammer habit of popping on deck at odd hours of the night to check on the mate and helmsman of the watch. Whenever this happened he did not forget the wireless operator. Night after night I was roused out of sleep by a sailor or the mate of the watch with orders from Captain McAhab to make radio contact with Cape Race or some other shore station over an obviously impossible stretch of sea, or with some passing ship whose lights could be seen in the distance. The ships that passed in the night were small freighters, like *Watuka*, whose lone operator was asleep in his bunk, or sailing ships that carried no radio at all. The late war's demands had brought forth a lot of old and new windjammers, which were still to be seen about the seas in the early 1920s. McAhab knew this as well as I did, but he demanded the impossible; and I had to spend hours calling C Q (the hail to an unknown ship, like calling "Hey, Mac!" to a stranger in the street) and getting no reply.

The skipper never came to the radio cabin. He sent those messengers with his demands. Our meetings were limited to mealtimes, when with the repetition of a noisy parrot he informed me of my incompetence and that of the bloody worthless contraption with which the Marconi Company swindled his owner. He sat in the captain's place at the head of the table, and I sat in the usual place of the wireless operator, in one of the side chairs near the foot of it. The other seats were empty, where in any normally conducted ship the mates and the chief engineer would have sat. The little Maltese in his white jacket went back and forth, serving the food first to the captain and then to me. It was poor stuff, badly cooked, for no good cook would take a job in such a ship, and it added dyspepsia to the skipper's spleen and my discomfort.

There was one interlude on the voyage in which McAhab turned his entire hatred on his mates and crew for three days, and he had none left over for me. We ate together in a silence so absolute that the Maltese went about on tiptoes, as if afraid to break the spell. Finally the captain broke it with a loud demand. A passenger liner had passed us that afternoon. What had I heard from that ship? I answered, "Nothing, sir." He went into the familiar tirade, the utter uselessness of myself and my "gear," unable to hear a ship in plain sight, let alone stations on the "shore."

When he paused for breath I broke Gray's rule of silence and said quietly that passenger ships don't send messages all the time, and they have nothing to say to passing tramps. I went on to say that if he wanted to keep in touch with the land at distances of hundreds of miles, he would have to shove his masts up to a useful height and get his owners to rent more powerful apparatus. For a moment he looked as if he intended to rise and thump me with his fists – I am sure the notion was in his mind – but my father's blood refused any fear of this potbellied old windbag. I daresay he could see in my face the contempt I had for him. He contented himself with words in his customary strain, but they ended with something more.

"Ye can pack yer baggage when we git in."

I had been expecting that right along, and as I noted in my diary, "I thanked him politely."

In the following days I had dot-and-dash talk with various ships, one of which gave me several drifting-mine warnings for the Irish Sea. When we passed into that area I got cross-bearings from RDF stations so that the skipper could check his position exactly with reference to the warnings. At the same time I sent two messages. One was from Captain McAhab to the ship's agents, giving his expected date and time of arrival. The other was from myself to W.J. Gray at Halifax. It must have been glumly familiar.

"Trouble with captain. Discharging me Liverpool."

Gray told me afterward what happened when he got this message. On the phone to the owners he pointed out that I was the sixth operator McAhab had fired in a little more than a year, all of them qualified people with naval certificates, and that something obviously was wrong with the captain. He added that the owners would have to pay my way back to Canada at a first-class passenger's rate, plus all the expense of getting another operator in Britain, and on that score he was advising the British Marconi Company to send an inspector to get my story before they put a man aboard.

All of this produced interesting results when the ship reached Manchester and I was still on board. The Marconi inspector turned up promptly, made a thorough check on my apparatus and me, and took down my account in writing. He insisted that McAhab could not discharge me on a baseless whim and that I must await permission from ARCON before leaving the ship. This was a sharp disappointment. I had hoped to return to Canada at once. For a week or more nothing happened simply because the skipper had disappeared into the city, leaving the first mate in charge of the ship.

I visited my Irish girl. I got a uniform from a Salford tailor who specialized in quick work for merchant marine officers. The jacket cuffs bore the two stripes of wavy gold braid that marked a first-class wireless officer. (After all, I'd passed the first-class exams, hadn't I?) My girl was enormously impressed. Actually this was the only good clothing I had. The cheap grey reach-me-downs, bought in Halifax in the spring of 1918, were now very shabby and worn.

The mates and engineers of *Watuka* viewed me in this smart garb with utter disfavour. None of them wore anything like a uniform. Nor did Captain McAhab, who stumped about the bridge in a wrinkled suit of tweeds and a common cloth cap, which he exchanged for a bowler when he went ashore. Who the hell did I think I was?

Well, I thought I was soon to be free of *Watuka* and all these third-rate characters and on my way back to Halifax in a liner. Then I hoped for a post as a junior operator in one of the CGMM ships, where all the officers wore uniforms as their natural clothing. These rosy hopes perished in a sudden frost. The captain returned from a stay of several days and nights ashore. He greeted me in the dining saloon with one of his old vituperative blasts oddly mingled with a new indignation and amazement. Following Gray's ultimatum, the ship's owners had sent him one of their own. He was to retain his present wireless operator and stop his endless quarrel with the Marconi people, which had involved the ship in so much coming-and-going and expense. Apparently the owners were near the end of their patience with a man now obviously past a useful age and temperament, and they must have said so, for the skipper was visibly frightened behind his bluster. Where else, at his age and with his propensities, could he find another job?

So I remained in *Watuka* with disgust, and after this outburst McAhab did not speak to me for weeks. Indeed, he vanished into the city again and stayed there most of the time we were in port. There was much ribald speculation in the crew. The ship lay in Number Nine, the timber dock at Salford, where several other ships were unloading. The dockers were a leisurely lot, and the work of discharging our cargo went slowly. We were delayed further by a strike of English railwaymen, which of course stopped all movement of freight cars in or out of the dock. Sometimes I went to

a public reading room to glance over the newspapers and magazines. For study on board the ship at night I bought one or two
textbooks on the latest theory and practice of radio. The technique
was changing and improving rapidly, and I had to keep up with it
for my naval re-examination in 1921.

My young friend Shaw the sailor left the ship as soon as she
reached Manchester, so I had no companion aboard. In the captain's absence the chief mate was usually in a drunken stupor and
the crew amused themselves as they pleased. Salford was the
Sailortown of Manchester with plenty of pubs and prostitutes. Every night bevies of whores slipped through the dock gates, and
every ship became a floating brothel. My observation of this rude
side of life went side by side with my radio studies, a quaint
combination.

I made acquaintance with the radio operator of a big American
freighter, and sometimes we rambled ashore together. I was astonished to find that his pay was $200 a month, while mine was merely
$45. His training was no better than mine if as good. He had no
more experience than I, and far less interest in his work. In fact, he
hated the sea and his sole desire was to get a job on firm ground in
the States.

*   *   *

After discharging the cargo *Watuka* filled her bunkers for the voyage home. The coal was poor-looking stuff, like coarse black dust,
obviously "slack" from a screening process at the mine. We had a
new English second engineer who observed aloud that this coal
wasn't fit to take the ship down the canal, let alone across the sea.
The chief engineer merely shrugged. There was something mysterious about this bland acceptance of bad fuel. If it was bought at a
bargain it soon proved a very bad one.

We left Manchester in mid-October and went down the canal in
miserable weather, rain and hail, and lay at anchor in Liverpool
harbour all the next day. There was no cargo. *Watuka* was bound
across the North Atlantic "in ballast." When we went out from
Liverpool the firemen and engineers soon complained about the
wretched quality of the coal. It was impossible to work up a good
pressure of steam. The ship crawled at four or five knots all day in
the Irish Sea. At the afternoon's end Captain McAhab ordered the
helm put about, and we crawled all the way back to Manchester to
get rid of the bad coal and fill the bunkers with something better.

Even McAhab, with his penny-pinching ways, could not face a North Atlantic passage in late autumn, in an empty ship, with such stuff clogging the fires.

It is one thing to tip coal into a ship's bunkers and quite another to shovel it out again. We lay at a Salford dock five days and nights while this was being done. Several of the new hands deserted and were replaced by other riffraff from the Salford shipping office. Word of a ship like *Watuka*, with a captain like McAhab, soon gets about Sailortown, wherever it happens to be. When the bunkers were emptied we moved down the canal to a place called Partington, where we got better coal. During this extra stay in Manchester I had a note from my aunt Jessie saying that Mother and the girls had just sailed for England in the Furness Withy liner *Digby*. So we would pass at sea.

It was a rough passage. With her empty holds and water ballast, *Watuka* rolled, wallowed, climbed, shuddered and dived through one gale after another. The *Digby*'s radio call was M N G, and I listened for it eagerly. Late one night I heard M N G talking to another ship. The signals were far and faint. I called her repeatedly, but if *Digby* replied, her signals were drowned in the many noises of an empty tramp floundering along in a storm.

On a cold November day *Watuka* sighted Newfoundland and entered Conception Bay, with flat-topped Bell Island looming up like a tall coffin ahead. We moored at the ore-loading wharf under a cliff. The mine and village of Wabana lay two or three miles away across the coffin top, and pebble-sized chunks of red ore came along a narrow tramway in small trucks, pulled by an endless wire cable from the mine, an entirely automatic process. At the top of the cliff they decanted the ore into a vertical chain of buckets, which took it down to the ship. A continual procession of loaded iron cars crawled and groaned across the wintry flat to the ship, and then crawled and groaned empty back to the mine.

Most of our crew stayed aboard, for it took only a few hours to load a cargo of this heavy stuff down to our WNA (Winter North Atlantic) plimsoll mark, and Wabana was not worth a long hike in the cold. With my usual curiosity I went up the cliff in the "skip," a funicular thing with one platform going up and the other down, for conveying passengers and odds and ends of freight. I followed the ore tramway on foot, for the trucks went slowly in the freezing air and they left rusty stains on anything they touched. I noted in my diary,

The Island is a bleak table of barrens and swamps, with scattered trees and weatherbeaten houses. Wabana, where I spent the evening, is a long street with several shops and some fair houses. The movie is like an enlarged barn, with planks laid across chairs for seating. Most of the male customers are miners in their working clothes, and the women are poorly dressed. Three great coal stoves are kept red hot by patrons nearby and the rest of the crowd freezes. The pictures are as old as the hills and "the kid that handles the music box" has a lot to learn.

The ore was soon loaded but we did not leave the dock for two or three days, waiting out a long and violent gale. When we did leave Conception Bay a big sea was still smashing on the coast. As soon as I switched on my receiving apparatus I learned that an American freighter named *Polarland* had sent out an S O S a few minutes before. She had a cargo of wheat bound from Montreal to Europe, and in that gale her cargo had shifted, the dread of all grain carriers. She must have capsized soon after the distress call, for three ships searched about the position she had given and found nothing at all.

We discharged our cargo at Sydney for the steel mills there and went across the harbour to North Sydney, where we loaded coal, baled hay, dynamite and other supplies for the Wabana mine. The North Sydney wireless station was on Goat Hill, some distance outside the town. The operators were Marconi employees like myself, and I walked up there for a chat. North Sydney, known to brasspounders by its call letters V C O, was rated a soft post. The crew lived in the town, and since the station got its power from the town's own dynamo, there was no engine room nor kitchen nor sleeping quarters. It was just a small wooden shack containing the watch room, warmed by a small iron stove, and a spark disc and its electric motor sang *staccato* behind a thick partition, like a baritone shut up in a cupboard. The OIC, a serious man, informed me that Canadian Marconi operators, ship and shore, were in the process of forming a union to press for better pay and (on shore stations) better subsistence allowances. For backing they had sought and got affiliation with the prosperous and powerful Commercial Telegraphers' Union of America. At the OIC's suggestion I signed a form, and some weeks later I had a membership card. I have it still, a souvenir of my lone enlistment in the ranks of organized labour.

November 13, 1919, was my sixteenth birthday, and I celebrated it by taking the ferry to Sydney and buying Christmas presents for my mother and sisters in England. Two days later *Watuka* sailed for Newfoundland again. On the way I had a dot-and-dash chat with *War Witch*, a sister ship of my old *War Karma*. She now had my former captain Charles Hunter and his son Walt, and we exchanged happy greetings. I was to see Walt again years afterward, but not my good old captain.

Sometimes that winter we took coal to Halifax or to St. John's, apart from the Wabana trips. On one Halifax trip I reminded Mr. Gray at the Marconi office that my promised five months would soon be up. He answered that he couldn't relieve me at present, but he would see what he could do.

In December our obstreperous captain got his long overdue comeuppance. He fired a seaman and wrote him off the ship's articles in the little shipping office of North Sydney, a short way above the coal dock where we lay. After his habit, McAhab uttered some choice words in farewell when the sailor pocketed the small pay that was coming to him. The sailor's reply was a smashing volley of well-aimed fists. The shipping-master and *Watuka*'s second mate managed to rescue the skipper, but it took them some time to get him on his feet. Meanwhile the sailor ran down to the ship to get his dunnage, and we quickly passed a cap to provide extra money for travel in foreign parts. Away he went, a few minutes before the police arrived at the dock. McAhab was helped aboard much later. His false teeth were smashed, his face was cut and swollen, and he had a huge black eye. He was glum and wordless, and he remained an invisible presence when we sailed for Newfoundland that afternoon. When we got back again he departed in a taxi to a Sydney hospital. He made a brief return to the sea later on, but I had seen the last of him.

Another captain came, and the cold rough voyages went on through December. There was one interesting break. A few days before Christmas, on a passage to Newfoundland, we sighted what appeared to be an iceberg south of Saint Pierre. It was small and low, of the sort that Newfoundlanders call a growler, a fragment broken from a bigger berg. It proved to be the hull of a dismasted schooner bound from Sydney to Fortune Bay, completely shrouded by ice, with four men and a boy huddling in the cabin. We had another chief mate by that time, a veteran seaman who had started as a boy in the Bank fishery. He steered a boat to the wreck and took her people off, in squalls of snow and a heavy swell, with night coming down fast. Years later I wrote that into a story for *Blackwood's Magazine* and called it "The Road to Fortune."

In January 1920 the ship returned from another of those bleak voyages and I found a welcome telegram from Gray. He was sending a relief operator, and I was to report for duty at North Sydney wireless station, pending appointment to another ship. It was almost exactly five months since I joined *Watuka*, and I had outlasted McAhab after all. Our latest skipper was a good man in all ways, a Cape Bretoner known as Big Dan Macdonald. I liked him, but I was glad to get away from the ship with its gloomy associations and its bleak and dirty trade.

I moved my sea chest to a little old wooden hotel in North Sydney, where I shared a room with one of the wireless operators. It was really a big boarding house catering chiefly to the numerous Western Union cable operators, who got a lot more money than we did even with our improved wage scale. (Canadian radio-telegraph operators now started at sixty dollars a month instead of forty-five, with an annual increase of ten dollars to a maximum of one hundred and twenty. Those on shore stations like North Sydney also got a subsistence allowance of forty dollars a month.)

The inmates of the Albert Hotel were a merry crew and we got along like a band of brothers. Severe winter weather continued, and as I was given the graveyard watch every night I had frosty and stormy hikes up and down Goat Hill in the dark. Coming off watch one morning in a temperature of twenty below zero, my right ear became frozen. After thawing, it swelled to double the normal size and was very painful whenever I clamped the phones on my head.

Within a couple of weeks I was sent to another and much larger ship named *Hochelaga*, which was lying in the port of Louisburg, loaded with steel rails for Rumania. The Allied forces had withdrawn from the Black Sea, and the red Russians hadn't much of a fleet left there; but they could be a nuisance with what they had. The Black Sea was therefore designated a danger zone, and *Hochelaga* was ordered to carry an extra wireless operator. I was delighted at the prospect of seeing the Mediterranean, the Dardanelles, Constantinople and the port of destination, Constanza.

I stayed overnight at a Sydney hotel and caught the early morning train of the Sydney and Louisburg Railway. It was a coal company line, and the train was a string of coal gondolas with an ancient passenger car tottering along at the rear. Something went

78

wrong with the steam heat in this car, which contained only half a dozen people. At a place called Mira we were sidetracked for an hour with a sub-zero wind sweeping over the ice in the bay. The snow was deep everywhere, and when the train got to Louisburg I had to hire a horse and sleigh to carry me and my sea chest a mile or so to the dock. By that time I was starving and stiff with cold. The other two brasspounders poured cognac into me, and after a hearty meal I was ready and eager for Rumania and all those other romantic places along the way.

What a hope! The owners were getting bad news from the Black Sea, including doubt about the Rumanian ability or intention to pay for the rails. Because drift ice had appeared off Louisburg and might close it in, *Hochelaga* was sent down the coast to Halifax to await final orders. We went by night, and ours was the first ship to enter Halifax harbour the next morning. We cut our way through a thin sheet of ice after passing inside McNab's Island, a very unusual thing. That winter of 1919-20 was a bitter one. After several more days' delay at Halifax the owners of the cargo decided to sell it somewhere else, and as the ship would not need an extra brasspounder I was signed off.

I stayed a couple of days at a small hotel near the docks and visited old friends and neighbours on Chebucto Road. One day outside Chebucto School I met Old Gander, who shot up his eyebrows and exclaimed, "Thomas! Thomas Raddall! In a military uniform!" I thought the old chap had gone colour-blind. We exchanged a few pleasantries and passed on.

Early in February I was ordered to the wireless station at Pictou, another small affair. The operators boarded in homes nearby, and the town supplied the electric power. The Pictou station was a political device of the federal government, set up years before to please the French-speaking population of the Magdalen Islands, which voted as part of the province of Quebec. There was an all-year-round station on the Magdalens, a small relay station at Cape Bear, Prince Edward Island, and the terminal station at Pictou. During the winter months the folk of the Magdalens enjoyed a very cheap message rate. We passed back and forth long screeds in patois that cost the senders almost nothing.

Our station was in a low field near the Pictou Academy, and as we had a fine sheet of ice under our mast we enjoyed the company of young lady teachers, who came to skate and then to chat in the warmth of the radio shack. The OIC was easy going, and as long as we kept one ear alert for radio calls we could talk to the girls as much as we liked.

The Marconi Company used this subsidized station at Pictou as a winter parking-place for operators out of a berth, convenient to the ports of Halifax and Saint John when ships wanted a man and to various other land stations if one of their operators fell sick or left the service. Thus at Pictou there were many hands to make light work, and we enjoyed ourselves at hockey and other winter amusements. It was too good to last long, of course. There was a constant coming and going. In mid-February I was ordered to Halifax. Mr. Gray met the night train there and told me to board a cable-repair ship called *Mackay-Bennett* right away.

She sailed in the morning to repair the Direct United States ("DUS") cable between Halifax and New York, a cable so old and fragile that it would hardly stand being hauled to the surface, and this in a time of cold gales and heavy seas. The ship was heading for a long and nasty job. Built in Scotland in 1884, the *Mackay-Bennett* was small (984 tons) with big winches fore and aft for picking up and paying out deep-sea cables. Miles of new cable were coiled in round tanks below her decks, where other ships had holds. She had a graceful clipper bow, and when she was built she had yards and square sails on both masts, to save coal in fair winds. The yards and sails were gone now but she retained the tall masts.

Her owners were the Commercial Cable Company, originally formed in New York by American mining magnate John W. Mackay and newspaperman James Gordon Bennett. The ship had British registry, however, and she was based at Halifax with a crew of about seventy officers and men, some English and the rest Canadian. The captain was an Englishman. The two cable technicians, graduates of English electrical-engineering schools, were the most versatile officers in the ship, for they acted as wireless operators too. The senior technician was preparing to leave for another post in a few months' time. A new man, fresh out from England, was to learn telegraphy well enough to pass the Canadian naval examination for a second-class certificate. Hence I was borrowed from the Marconi Company to teach him and to take a watch myself until he could take over. I expected this to take about six months, but the new man was very slow to qualify for a ticket. I was in the ship more than a year.

It was a very happy ship after *Watuka*. The officers were cheerful and intelligent, and the food was first rate. I was still studying diligently the technical side of my profession, especially the new-fangled vacuum tubes, and the cable technicians taught me a lot about the budding science of electronics.

The ship's radio apparatus was new to me, a two-kilowatt transmitter using a "quenched" spark like those of the Americans, Germans and Japanese. The receiving apparatus had the familiar crystal detector, and for weak signals there was a vacuum tube amplifier. This was my first acquaintance with the tube that had already led the way to radio telephony and was going on to radio broadcasting and eventually to television and many another electronic miracle. With my training in the now defunct School of Telegraphy at Halifax I was like a whiz-kid with the bow and arrow suddenly finding a rifle in his hands and seeing in the shadows ahead the vague shapes of machine-guns, rockets, and other fabulous weaponry.

* * *

In chat with the officers I learned some interesting history. A few of them had been in *Mackay-Bennett* in 1912 when she went out from Halifax and picked up hundreds of dead from the *Titanic*, all afloat in their cumbersome cork lifebelts but killed in a few minutes by the icy water. They gave me one or two photographs of this grim cargo. The boatswain had been in the ship long before that, when she attended the international yacht races off New York in 1899. This was when Sir Thomas Lipton's first *Shamrock* tried to win the America's Cup and was beaten by the defending *Columbia*.

Guglielmo Marconi, eager to get publicity for his new invention, had persuaded James Gordon Bennett to use wireless telegraphy and provide a scoop for the New York *Herald*. Bennett was not only proprietor of the *Herald* but a partner with John W. Mackay in the Commercial Cable Company. The ship named after them was ordered to New York from Halifax. She acted as the "shore" station by anchoring off Sandy Hook and picking up a submarine cable to New York. Marconi installed one set of his apparatus on the ship's bridge and another on the American steamship *Ponce*. The *Ponce* followed the yachts around the course and reported their progress, tack by tack, through *Mackay-Bennett* to the *Herald* office. The winds were light, and there were a lot of tacks before *Columbia* defeated *Shamrock* in three races out of five.

According to our boatswain Bennett was delighted with his newspaper scoop, and he and Mackay bought the Marconi set aboard their ship. It remained in *Mackay-Bennett* until in time it was discarded and replaced with something up-to-date. The boatswain added that the original set was "still up in the forepeak somewhere." I persuaded him to help me find it and eventually we did, under a lot of odds and ends. I removed and still have the "coherer" signal-detecting device, consisting of two silver plugs wired inside a slim glass vacuum tube. Under a narrow gap between the plugs lay a tiny heap of fine metal dust. When a radio signal came down the aerial wire it magnetized the metal dust, which arose and formed a bridge between the plugs. This switched on an amplifier with a more powerful current.

Many years later I met a former purser of *Mackay-Bennett* who gave me some photographs he had taken in 1899 showing the radio outfit and operator in the chart room, the business of picking up the telegraph cable near Sandy Hook lightship, and the two yachts sailing past *Mackay-Bennett* at the start of the races. *Time* magazine once borrowed them from me but found them too faded for good reproduction.

* * *

Our cold and rough job on the DUS cable began somewhere off Cape Sable, Nova Scotia, in February 1920. The process was one of dragging a grapnel over the ocean floor until the cable was hooked and then hauling it slowly to the surface. This could be done only when the sea was not too rough, otherwise the heaving of the ship would break the cable. We rode out a series of gales and worked in the intervals. In my radio watches I picked up various distress calls, the usual casualties of winter in the North Atlantic; but other ships were nearer, and we were able to stick to our knitting.

One case was interesting because of its outcome. A large British freighter ran onto the Blind Sister ledge while heading towards Halifax harbour in thick weather. Her wireless operator had obtained RDF bearings that showed the ship to be in a dangerous position, but the captain ignored them. The ship broke in half, and seven men died before the rest could be rescued. The wireless operator was among the survivors, and he had clung to his radio log.

When the authorities finished their usual strict investigation of the wreck, they ruled that henceforth in thick weather every shipmaster must take heed of radio bearings if they show his ship to be in danger, notwithstanding his own reckoning. This official rule converted a lot of old diehards by the scruff of the neck. I could almost hear the roar of anguish from my old captain McAhab, wherever he was by then.

In mid-March our ship was diverted from the DUS job to repair a cable outside New York harbour. We got it up and found it badly "faulted" (skinned of its insulation) by a ship dragging its anchor. A violent gale forced us to lie to for three days, slowly steaming with our bow to wind and sea. Then we put in a new section of cable, spliced the ends, and lowered them to the bottom.

The owners sent us into New York for provisions and fuel, not to mention a few days of rest and recreation. We tied up at Staten Island, a short ferry trip from the Battery. With one or two other young officers I spent every possible moment in the city, enjoying restaurants and theatres. For the ship's radio set we got some of the new "honeycomb" coils and three-element tubes to rig up a much better signal amplifier. With this on March 20, 1920, we heard words and music from the Western Electric broadcasting station, my first touch with this marvel of the post-war years.

We finished our dreary struggle with the DUS cable towards the end of March and returned to Halifax to refit for a long job in mid-Atlantic. The refit included dry-docking and gave us a pleasant month in Halifax. In those times of Prohibition one notable amenity of the cable ship was a stock of wines and spirits, which the officers could buy cheaply free of customs duty. Hitherto I had sipped various kinds but disliked the taste of all. In *Mackay-Bennett* I found that after the sun got over the yardarm, talk and a dram of whisky and water went together when you were off duty, and I learned to linger over a dram for the sake of the talk. Only once was I drunk, and the cause of it was ignorance. A popular officer left the ship at Halifax, and the farewell party on board decided that nothing less than champagne would be appropriate. It seemed to me as pleasant as cider and no more dangerous, and my glass was refilled many times. Eventually I had to be carried to my berth, where I lay wretchedly dizzy and sick for hours. It was many years before I could enjoy champagne again.

At the end of April 1920 we sailed for St. John's, Newfoundland. Following a hard winter, icebergs were flocking out of the north, and one had drifted into Cuckold's Cove, just outside St. John's harbour, where it sat heavily on the armoured shore-end of a trans-atlantic cable and nipped it through like a bit of spaghetti. When we got there the berg was still aground, so we had to lay a loop of new cable around it. Since the berg would drift off again eventually and probably take our loop with it, we lay at a wharf in the port awaiting the event. It took two weeks.

During that time I explored the old city and met a young woman and fell in love. She was a pert creature of about eighteen, and one evening after some kissing I asked her to marry me. It was my first experience of love and the blindness it creates. I was still adding three years to my age when anyone asked me, and the lady could see me as a genuine matrimonial prospect. Usually I wore my uniform ashore, and at that time gold braid and brass buttons were impressive in St. John's, where eligible young officers were not abundant.

The lady treated my honourable proposal with a mysterious reserve, probably measuring the advantage and disadvantage of a husband at sea most of the time. I was so bemused that I didn't see anything suggestive in the name of Cuckold's Cove, the reason for my presence in my charmer's field of operations.

One day the berg slid ponderously out of the cove without damaging our new loop. The ship sailed at once for Sydney to top up her bunkers for the mid-Atlantic job. I was to see St. John's again that summer, but only for a few days, and I did not seek out the lady. In a casual conversation at sea, not knowing my interest, a shipmate mentioned her name with relish. He had slept with her, as the saying goes, but he used a shorter phrase and added details. My recovery from love's blindness was instant and complete.

At Sydney my ship coaled at Whitney Pier, on the other side of which lay an odd-looking ship named *Turret Court*, bunkering for a voyage to Europe. She was a whaleback, built like a floating cigar, with her topsides concentrated on a narrow deck. Her wireless operator was my old classmate at the School of Telegraphy, Eddie Turner, and we had a good yarn together and took snapshots of each other for souvenirs.

If *Turret Court* was odd looking, something odder still was squatting on the launching ways across the harbour at North Sydney. It was a small ship built of reinforced concrete, a wartime idea in late bloom named *Permanencia*. I went over there to see the launching, but she stuck on the ways. Afterwards I heard that she was wrecked at Saint Pierre on her maiden voyage. With a name like that she was doomed from the start.

We sailed a few days later and began a long summer's work. One of the main cables had developed an electric leak, and tests from both ends showed that the fault was almost exactly in mid-ocean between Ireland and Newfoundland. In that depth of water it took many hours merely to pay out the grapnel and a great length of wire rope. Then came the business of dragging the grapnel back and forth across the ocean floor until it hooked the cable. When this happened a dynamometer on deck showed an immediate jump of several tons in the grapnel strain, and then began the long and careful process of hauling the cable to the surface. There were frequent gales, and in the lift and fall of great seas we could do nothing.

Our captain was a tall Englishman with a walrus moustache under a Duke of Wellington nose. Despite his nautical uniform he looked like a cartoon of the retired English colonel Mark '14, and he had the same amiable eccentricities. One of his foibles was a seagoing conservatory, consisting of dozens of potted geraniums on shelves under the long skylight in the poop deck, which lighted and aired the officers' dining saloon. There were wooden slats to keep them in place, and twice a week old Jerry, the captain's personal steward, went about the business of watering them, using a portable ladder tipped with hooks to fit the slats. One night in a very wild storm the ship made a tremendous roll, the slats proved insufficient at last, and there was a cascade of pots falling and smashing on the saloon table. Then the whole mess surged back and forth for hours with the bucking of the sea. In after years, whenever I read some reference to "*Bounty*" Bligh and his breadfruit plants, I thought of Captain Stewart's geraniums.

After a month at sea we returned to St. John's to refuel and take on fresh water and stores. Four days later we sailed again. I had not seen my Circe. In the mid-Atlantic position our nightly reports on the day's work or inability to work went to New York by whatever shore station we could reach. Sometimes they went via Clifden, Ireland, sometimes by Cape Race, Newfoundland. One night after many fruitless calls to both of them, I got through to a station in Portugal on a freak "surge." With the apparatus of those days it was a miracle.

The cable was old, and the work was frustrating in that depth because it took so long to lower our grapnel to the bottom and many hours more to haul it up again. Then we found that the cable had parted on the way up, and what we had on the grapnel was a fragment. At last we had a good end at the surface and tested it through to the cable station at Waterville, Ireland. We spliced it to new cable in our tanks and began to steam towards our western

85

mark buoy, using the big winch aft, which was called the paying-out machine. But we were jinxed. The drum of the paying-out machine chose that time to collapse, so that the new cable had to be paid out over the bow sheave, using the forward winch, which was properly used as the picking-up machine. It worked all right, although the cable, with its growing weight as it slid overboard, rubbed against the bow.

The weather changed suddenly; wind and sea rose together, and after a time a seaman at the bow lost his footing and fell overboard. What was far more terrible, he fell astride of the new cable, and the tremendous pressure between cable and hull nipped off one of his legs at the thigh. The second mate and I were chatting on the well-deck aft when we heard the yell, "Man overboard!" We sprang onto the poop just as the man floated past and threw him a life-buoy, but he called up to us "My leg is gone," and drifted away astern, borne up by the air trapped in his oilskins.

We always had a boat ready for work with our mark buoys, and the boat's crew lowered it in three minutes and launched it while the ship was still moving, a dangerous feat in that kind of sea. They reached the sailor and hauled him into the boat, but he was beyond help. The ship's doctor said he had bled to death from the big femoral artery severed in the thigh.

Next morning, with the storm abating under a gloomy sky, our captain held the sea burial service in the presence of all hands. Sewn up in canvas with several iron fire-bars from the stokehold, the body slid down a tipped plank and vanished. The man had shipped from Dartmouth, Nova Scotia, an old fellow who had spent most of his life at sea, where he would stay now for ever. My experiences at Halifax in 1917 had given me a close acquaintance with sudden and ugly death, but then I was in a sort of trance from the shock of the explosion. This time I was keenly aware, and it hurt to see a shipmate die in such a way in what should have been a common day's work at sea.

Eventually we exhausted our supply of new cable and the owners ordered us to England, where we would take a full cargo direct from a factory on the Thames. When we reached Land's End our bunkers were so nearly empty that we had to coal at Plymouth before going on up the Channel.

We anchored in Plymouth Sound, and the coal came out to us in barges, a slow business. It had to be hoisted aboard in small wooden tubs, using windlasses turned by hand, a method held sacred by the local dockers' union. It was almost as primitive as the one I had seen at Fayal in the Azores. We were astonished. We had thought of Plymouth as a British naval base, bristling with efficiency. So it was, but the navy didn't have to deal with British labour unions.

I went ashore with the second mate, and we explored the town from the famous Hoe, where Drake played his game of bowls, to the Palace Music Hall. Late at night we got back to an ancient stone quay called the Barbican, from which the Pilgrims had made their final departure for America, and found that the last leave boat had returned to the ship. Other shipmates were stranded there, most of them drunk and hilarious. After some trouble we managed to hire a motorboat to take our own pilgrims out to the ship in the Sound. Several more were in a Plymouth clink, and the captain had to pay their fines and get them out before we could sail next day.

On later reflection it occurred to me that my father's birthplace was not much more than twenty miles from Plymouth. I might have spent my day ashore much better if I had gone by bus into the countryside and hunted up some of my relatives. The chance passed and never came again.

In fine summer weather the Channel was like a busy street with ship traffic of every kind. As we approached Beachy Head our bridge steering-gear broke down suddenly, and we nearly rammed another ship. Using the manual steering-gear aft we went on our way, and in the afternoon we passed an odd little procession going the other way, presumably to Portsmouth. It consisted of a German heavy cruiser and two destroyers, very battered and rusty, under tow by German tugs, and all under the escort of a British destroyer, H.M.S. *Vancouver*. Presumably these were ships so badly damaged in the battle off Jutland in 1916 that the Germans had never put them in repair, and so they were not in the fleet that surrendered and then scuttled itself at Scapa Flow in 1919.

We picked up a Thames pilot off Dungeness and about five o'clock in the afternoon passed my birthplace, Hythe. Towards evening we anchored in the Downs to repair the steering gear. We were actually lying off Kingsdown, where my mother and sisters had been living since they returned to England, but of course there was no chance of going ashore. Next morning we were in the Thames at Tilbury, waiting for the tide, and that afternoon we moored in the river at Woolwich. As the ship would be there about a week, I got leave to visit my family, took train to London, and from there went by the South Eastern and Coastal Railway (known as "the slow, easy and careful") to Walmer, the nearest station to Kingsdown.

My family were surprised and delighted to see me, as I was to see them after a year's separation. The next day we went by car to Ware, near Canterbury, and visited my grandparents at their farm. It was a big one with a fine old brick farmhouse, and my grandfather had a motor tractor and other equipment not usual on English farms in those days. On a tour of his fields the sturdy old man showed me a line of craters made one night during the war. A raiding Zeppelin, turned away by the London defences, had dumped its bombs there before recrossing the Channel.

Mother suggested a trip to London to visit Aunt Jessie and ramble about the city. We spent three happy days touring such old standbys as the Tower of London and the British Museum, and a new one, the first London airport at Cricklewood. The theatres were best, though, and I enjoyed especially the musical *Chu Chin Chow* at His Majesty's Theatre, with author-actor Oscar Asche still playing the leading role. My father had seen it during the war, and so had many other soldiers on leave from France. Indeed, it had been running so long that Asche's wife, Lily Brayton, who played a slave girl, became too fat and had to leave the cast.

Towards the end of July *Mackay-Bennett* sailed down the Thames for another bout with the old cable called Main Two. With her storage tanks chock full of new cable our little ship sat lower in the water than ever, and in any rough sea the fore and aft well-decks were awash. To get dry-footed from the poop deck to the bridge, and from there to the bow, one had to travel on "flying" gangways fixed there for the purpose. The wireless cabin sat in the aft well, so we had to step over a high protective coaming in getting through the doorway. When seas were coming aboard we had to watch our chance to make it, coming or going. At night this was often a very wet adventure.

We endured the usual storms and delays by mechanical and electrical failures of various kinds, but we managed to lay about eighty miles of new cable and lower the final splice to the bottom on Friday the thirteenth of August, 1920, which we considered a lucky day. Now we had our last job of the summer – or so we thought. Main Four was broken near the Irish coast. When we got there the weather was too rough for cable work and we tossed about for many hours. At last I was able to write in my diary,

"August 20. 7.55 P.M. Dropped final splice. Hurrah! We have completed the work we sailed to accomplish on April 30th and it has been a long and arduous summer with a persistent jinx seated on the masthead right straight through. Taylor put 'The End of a Perfect Day' on the gramophone tonight and there was a celebration."

* * *

The officers in charge of electrical matters, especially cable telegraph technique, were a pair of humorous and whimsical Englishmen, and their whims helped to pass the long monotony at sea. The senior was a bachelor of about thirty-five whose mother was an artist of some distinction. Harold had inherited some of her talent, which he put to madly inartistic use. There was a fad in those days for bawdy limericks, which men recited in clubs and pubs and other male chuckling-places. Harold got a large loose-leaf book in which he typed the pick of the limerick crop wherever we went. On an opposite page he made a pen-and-wash drawing to illustrate the point. In his adventures about the world on cable ships and stations, including such lively places as Havana and Manila, he had made intimate study of naughty ladies, and in his limerick pictures he portrayed them with humour and lusty skill. The book became famous in its way. In ports on both sides of the Atlantic, among them London and New York, more than one of our visitors was sure to be a well-dressed business type who made the usual inquiries about cable repairing and then said, "Isn't this the ship that has the illustrated limerick book?"

Many years after Harold retired, he picked up one of my novels and wrote to me in care of the publisher. In reply I asked, among other things, what had become of the limerick book. He answered, "Not long after you left the ship I was posted to England. I didn't want a thing like that in my baggage for customs inspection, and anyhow I thought it was time to make an end of it. So we went through the book for the last time, drank a toast in farewell, and consigned it page by page to the waters of Halifax harbour."

With a much more respectable turn Harold used to illustrate a small typewritten pamphlet that the purser and others put out from time to time for circulation aboard the ship. It contained little tales and sketches of our life at sea and in the ports. I was interested in these descriptions of places and matters I had seen myself and had a vague hunch that I could do that sort of thing if I really tried, but it went no further than that. My interest was concentrated on radio telegraphy.

The officers had another whimsy that came into play during long spells of bad weather at sea. In a toyshop somewhere they had bought a comical wooden duck, and they had got a girl friend to fit the duck neatly with a seagoing jacket and cap. Then they made a miniature cat-o'-nine-tails. The duck was fastened on the top of the radio receiving apparatus as the ship's mascot, with the whip in a socket nearby. In the worst of weather, with the ship bouncing and wallowing like a tin can in a millrace, the purser, one of the navigating officers, a cable technician and I held a solemn court martial on the duck for neglect of duty. The sentence of so many lashes with the cat-o'-nine-tails was duly inflicted, with all the vigour and punctilio of Nelson's day. By the end of that stormy year 1920 the duck was badly worn and so were we.

Before returning to our base at Halifax we went back to the Thames for another load of new cable, and on the way I heard radio-telephony for the second time. It came from the powerful station at Poldhu, Cornwall, talking to Marconi's yacht *Electra* in the upper waters of the Adriatic. They were proving that a large mass of land was no barrier to telephonic air transmission.

Among the various navigation warnings we were still getting notices and exact positions of explosive mines seen adrift about the British coast. Near the Owers Lightship we sighted and passed one, shaggy with seaweed and speckled with barnacles, a hoary relic of the war in the North Sea, as dangerous as ever.

In London the ship tied up temporarily in the West India Dock, in fabled Limehouse. I visited Aunt Jessie and went on to my grandfather's farm, where Mother and the girls were staying for a holiday. In the next few days I ranged about the countryside on a bike and then caught a train back to London. I found the ship at the Woolwich mooring, slowly taking in cable over the water from the Siemens factory. In London I hunted up an old chum of my school days in Hythe, like myself the son of an army man. He was now a clerk in a London bank and hated it. Eventually he went to Australia, became a hand on a Queensland cattle ranch, advanced to foreman, and at last was able to buy a pub, the Aussies' paradise.

On my last evening in London we went to a theatre and parted in Trafalgar Square soon after midnight. By that time the direct trains, trams and buses to Woolwich had departed on their final runs. My ship was sailing in the morning, so I set off in the direction of Woolwich on foot, trusting to a sailor's luck to get there. And I had it. I fell in with a young artilleryman bound for the Woolwich barracks, and he knew the ropes. By catching last buses to other places on a circuitous route we made it.

Next evening *Mackay-Bennett* anchored in Plymouth Sound and remained there two days awaiting orders. Shore leave was restricted, and again I got no farther than the town. Finally the orders came. Instead of sailing home to Halifax as we hoped, we were to do another repair job off the southwest coast of Ireland. A succession of gales kept us cruising off the mouth of Ballinskelligs Bay in County Kerry. The captain would have put into an Irish port for shelter, but the Sinn Fein "throubles" were in full fury, and anyone in a British uniform, even the uniform of a peaceable merchant mariner, was a likely target for skulking IRA gunmen. As the captain said, "Better a rough berth at sea than a bullet in the back." At last we got the job done and went in to the cable station at Waterville to pick up our mail. We found the cable operators living almost in a state of siege, most of them being English. In the surrounding countryside, so green and inviting to salt-parched mariners like us, every kind of outrage from cattle-maiming to human murder was being inflicted on anyone suspected of the slightest British sympathy. Elsewhere, especially around Cork and Tipperary, the auxiliary police, the Black and Tans, recruited among young British veterans of the late war, tough and trigger-itchy, were getting out of hand and committing reprisals on suspected Sinn-Feiners.

We left the Emerald Isle with no regrets. Rough weather clung to us all the way back to Halifax, which we reached just over five months after setting forth in the spring. Halifax was still in the throes of prohibition and bootleg brews, and as our ship had its own supply of good drink we had a lot of visitors. One of my girl friends ashore had a thirsty father, and when I left the ship for an evening at their home I carried in my overcoat pockets a quart or two of the best Scotch. At slop-chest prices they cost me only two dollars a bottle. I got dark looks from the chief steward, frowning at the large increase in my consumption, and some sarcasm from the purser, who assumed that I was engaging in wild parties ashore.

Within eleven days the ship was off again, this time for a job about four hundred miles east of Halifax. Two days after sailing we were hove-to in the lee of Sable Island, riding out a northwest gale.

The low sandy island was just a blur to windward, my first glimpse of the place. I was to see much more of it later on. When we got to the site of the cable break we had to play our wearily familiar game of fighting gales and beating the duck and working in the calms. We had to lay forty miles of new cable. When we got back to Halifax there was frost in the air and snow on the ground. We had spent most of the spring, summer and autumn on the barren face of the sea, and now here was the barren face of winter on the land.

After six months in so much racking weather our ship needed a long refit and she got it. During this time in port the mail brought a surprising letter from my mother. Life back in England had proved a disappointment. The friends of her happy young married life in Deal and Hythe were all military families. Most of the men had been killed or disabled in the late war, and their families had gone away. Excepting her own brothers and sisters she knew nobody, whereas in Halifax there were the good friends and neighbours of the more recent six years. Also, she was concerned about her daughters in the little backwater of Kingsdown, where there was no prospect of employment or of marriage in the future. In short, she had determined to return to Halifax, and she asked me to find a decent house, at a reasonable rent, somewhere near our former home on Chebucto Road.

I began this quest about the time of my seventeenth birthday in November 1920. Halifax was overpopulated. Many people had come to work for fat wages there during the war and stayed on hopefully. Many Halifax soldiers had returned from the war with English wives and children. An aura of prosperity had carried over from the war, and nobody suspected that it would vanish in another year. I found it impossible to get a decent house at a reasonable rent anywhere in the city. Real estate agents told me the only way to get a house at all was to buy one and turn the tenant out of it.

I went to a man I knew who owned two houses on Duncan Street, quite near our old house on Chebucto Road. He was willing to sell one for five thousand dollars, and he would take five hundred in cash and the rest in monthly payments on the hire-purchase system. During this year, so much of it spent at sea, I had saved out of my pay nearly six hundred dollars. I wrote to Mother that I would make the down payment of five hundred dollars if she agreed to the purchase. I got her reply just before Christmas. She was happy about the whole thing, and so I paid the money, arranged with a lawyer for the documents, and agreed that the present tenant could remain in the house until my family arrived next year.

Week after week the ship lay at her Water Street dock while the ship-fitters tore things apart and put them together again. Like all young sailors I enjoyed a good walk ashore, and as there was little snow in December I tramped often to Point Pleasant Park or around the Northwest Arm to the Tower park, or merely about the city streets. Some evenings I remained on board at my studies. Others I spent with friends at theatres and restaurants or chatting in their homes. Our former neighbours on Chebucto Road were hospitable folk, and often I lunched or dined with them. All were delighted to hear that my family was coming back next year. It was all very pleasant, but after a few weeks I was chafing to be off again. I wanted to work at my profession and I could do that only at sea.

I have mentioned how I got drunk for the first time in my life. On New Year's Eve there was another spree in the officers' quarters, but I stayed out of it. I noted in my diary, "They wanted to see the Old Year out but when midnight arrived they were sprawled around unable to see the New Year or anything else." These shipmates of mine enjoyed a few drams together but rarely got drunk. The sprees were a clear symptom of too long a time in port. The captain and some others had homes and families in Halifax and naturally were content with a long tie-up at the wharf. The bachelors got bored.

At that time Halifax was still shabby with the effects of the explosion in '17, and despite the prosperity of wartime its amenities were meagre and few. The restaurants were small, with nothing to wash down their dull food but tea or coffee. Movie theatres showed the silent black-and-white flickers of the time. The only "legitimate" theatre was the misnamed Majestic, where a third-rate American repertory company staged dreary third-rate plays. Two other theatres, Acker's and the Strand, offered vaudeville acts from the States touring what the performers openly called the sticks. For strong drink there were numerous "blind pigs" selling bad brews at worse prices. An organized rum-running trade with real booze from Saint Pierre was just beginning to operate.

For casual sex, the streetwalkers had basic competition from a lot of small brothels, staffed by one or two but never more than six "sporting girls," who charged two dollars a trick – I supposed in the sense of a seaman's trick at the helm, for most of them were on Water Street. For the public eye these places posed as tobacco shops and kept a small stock for sale, but the shop windows were empty and entirely obscured by large cardboard cigarette advertisements. The ladies revealed their more intimate wares in small bedrooms behind the shops.

One of these, run by a cheerful pair of trollops in their late twenties, was close to the shore-end of our dock and occasionally I stepped in to buy cigarettes. The first time, the girls glanced at my uniform and told me quickly what else they had for sale. When I said I just wanted smokes they looked at me more closely, guessed my age, made saucy remarks about my greenhorn state, and sold me the smokes. It was early afternoon, a time of slack business, and they engaged me in chat to pass the time. After that first encounter I learned a lot more about the life of Water Street from the viewpoint of the cigarette girls, a distinctly different view from that of Jack Tar, who thought he knew so much.

The ship sailed at last in the frigid weather of January 1921 for a cable-repair job roughly halfway between Nova Scotia and Cape Cod. Roughly is the right word. Our small ship plunged and rolled in icy seas and then abruptly set her stern down in a trough, as if she had slipped on invisible ice. With frequent squalls of snow the decks were covered with frozen slush, and every step was a hazard. I heard a radio message from a Yankee ship saying with an unusual flair, "Galley flooded. Fires out. Men on board who never think of God prayed."

Then came a miraculous spell of fine weather and light winds, and we made the most of it. Towards the end of January we returned to Halifax to load more cable from the dock warehouse. Then we were off again, and the winter gales were on again. One very wild night I picked up an S O S and phoned it to the bridge. The captain's voice answered curtly, "We can't do a thing. We'll be lucky to stay afloat ourselves."

I had got so used to our ship's antics and flooded decks in rough weather that his remark surprised me. It never occurred to me that she might roll under one of these big seas and never come up again. On the North Atlantic in winter the S O S becomes a familiar sound, and you think of danger and death as the misfortune of others, never of yourself. Later on I knew what was on my captain's mind that night. Shortly after I left *Mackay-Bennett* she was condemned as unfit for further sea service, and spent the rest of her long life as a cable-storage hulk in Plymouth Sound across the sea.

My own abode in the ship was not a real cabin at all but a

makeshift cubbyhole right aft, with a single porthole so close to the waterline that it had to be screwed shut and covered with a steel deadlight whenever the ship left harbour. For ventilation there was an electric fan drawing air through a metal grille from the saloon. It was an old-fashioned fan with eight-inch blades and no protective guard, fastened high on the bulkhead. The cubbyhole was over the shaft tunnel leading to one of the ship's twin screws. Whenever she dived in a trough of the sea, bringing the screws out of water, they raced like mad and set my little coop rattling and shuddering. One stormy night I wedged myself into the bunk in the usual way, by stuffing my lifebelt under the outer edge of the bedding so I couldn't be flung out of it, and went to sleep.

Months of vibration had loosened the four-bladed fan on its shaft, and suddenly it flew off and came whirling down on my face in the dark. I was startled more than hurt – a thump and a cut on my forehead – but I was always leery of that fan afterwards, and of the cubbyhole itself. As an extra and very minor officer, not contemplated in the original cabin accommodation, I had to put up with this claustrophobic kennel.

My dual job of watchkeeping and coaching the new electrician in the art of pounding brass lasted much longer than I had expected. Now he was getting to the point where he could pass for a second-class ticket, and I could get back to normal duty. I still cherished my dream of sea roaming in warm latitudes amid the world's more romantic scenes.

We got back to Halifax after another rough job off Nantucket in April 1921. The next day I got my discharge and returned to the regular Marconi service. I had no notion of what was to come. It turned out that I had left my last ship. In the past two years I had travelled something like thirty-five thousand miles on the cold and stormy North Atlantic. No Bermuda, no Tahiti, no Hawaii. Just one brief enchanting glimpse of Fayal in high summer.

I bade farewell to my shipmates in *Mackay-Bennett* with a blend of happiness and regret. I had found them good comrades afloat and ashore, mostly afloat and often in bad weather, a sure test of men in a small ship. And I had learned much about the new electronics, far beyond the needs of a mere brasspounder.

Apart from that I had learned a lot about the waterfront of Halifax, where the ship had been my home. I had talked and (much more important) listened to the folk who lived there – stevedores, wharfingers, junkshop keepers, bootleggers, whores, thieves, old seamen down on their luck, boardinghouse keepers – in fact, all of the human medley to be found only on Water Street, of which the office and shop workers and churchgoers of the port knew nothing whatever. There was much more to learn about life, of course. Sexually I was still virgin and seven months short of the magic age of eighteen, when I could gain my first-class ticket and set forth to taste the world's delights as a fully qualified young man.

*　*　*

The Halifax office of the Canadian Marconi Wireless Telegraph Company was a small one on Granville Street, a short walk from the docks. When I knew it first the office was run entirely by W.J. Gray and his wife, who was the stenographer. Since then Gray had been promoted to Montreal, and now I found a man in charge whom I shall call Cutler, with a male assistant, and a new girl at the typewriter. Both men were former brasspounders. Cutler had spent several years on east coast stations before getting an office post at Montreal. Now he had been placed in charge of all Marconi shore stations in the Maritime Provinces and was boss of all the seagoing Marconi operators whose ships were based there.

I reported to him after my release from *Mackay-Bennett*, and he said casually that I would relieve an operator on Sable Island as soon as the supply ship made her next call there. I was startled and then indignant. Sable Island was notorious as "the Graveyard of the Atlantic," full of wrecked ships and dead men's bones, a desert in the sea about 175 miles out from Halifax, visited four times a year by storeships of the Department of Marine and Fisheries. A posting there meant a year at least. After that, by an unwritten rule at the Halifax office made after the mutiny and fire in 1919, each operator was entitled to a furlough and then a more congenial station on the mainland. But a whole year! At my age, with my dreams of sea travel, it sounded like a sentence to Siberia, and I said so. What had I done to deserve a year on Sable Island?

Cutler's reply was a mixture of blarney and steel. I got the blarney first. Surely I realized that, second only to Cape Race, Sable Island was the busiest and most useful station on the Canadian coast, handling traffic with the big liners of all nations on the route between Europe and the States. A post there required a crack operator who could work at speeds as high as thirty words a minute, and because repair and maintenance on such isolated stations was a do-it-yourself business he had to be a competent technician as well.

He'd had good reports of me on both counts. I was a bright young fellow and what I didn't know I'd soon learn. A year at Sable Island would make me one of the brasspounders famous up and down the coast, and my future could go on from there. Look at himself. A few years at places like Cape Race, a spell at ARCON, and now here he was running the whole Maritime show! Ships? There was no future in pounding brass aboard a ship.

When I went on pleading for a sea job, Cutler gave me the steel. I had only a second-class ticket and couldn't get a first-class till I passed the age of eighteen – he knew all about that. The only sea job offering for a second-class operator right now was aboard a trawler fishing on the Banks. Did I want to bash my brains out in a trawler? Without waiting for a reply, he said coldly that he was giving me an order. I must go to Sable Island.

I knew it was that or quit the Marconi service, which meant practically the whole Canadian radio service. After making the five-hundred-dollar payment on my mother's house and buying necessary clothing and shoes I hadn't much money, so there was no chance of hunting for a sea job in the States. I had to hang on in Canada until my eighteenth birthday and the first-class ticket. So I resigned myself to what seemed an eternity on a desert island that hadn't even got a tree for a spot of shade. Even Robinson Crusoe had lots of that.

I took a room in a convenient but shabby little hotel near the docks. It was really a rooming house, and for meals you went along the street to Mader's Cafe. The house was a resort of sea officers awaiting a berth and of other port wanderers, including at this time some guys and dolls of a small burlesque show from the States ("Jimmy Evans' Varieties") then playing at Acker's Theatre.

One night a few of the burlesque performers had a party in a bedroom on my floor, and they invited me to join them in drinks and song. The drinks were bootleg stuff and the party got noisy and hilarious, especially when one of the girls doffed her clothes to the tune of "Mademoiselle from Armentières." Having been in trouble before, they had been warned by the formidable ogress who owned and managed the hotel, and she made them pay for their rooms well in advance. When things got literally out of hand I retired to my room at the end of the hall, leaving my door open and switching off the light. The ogress soon came upstairs with a policeman and ordered the party to pack up and get out of the house. After some interesting argument they all went shouting down the stairs. One of the girls was the estranged wife of Kid Burns, an American boxer. She marched past the ogress yelling, "I've been chucked out of better hotels than this dump!" I remembered that scene long afterwards when I wrote a novel called *The Nymph and the Lamp.*

All of this came to an end on April 21, 1921, when I packed my sea chest, hired a taxi, and crossed over the harbour to Dartmouth by the old steam ferryboat. A small steamship named *Dollard* was lying at the wharf of the Department of Marine and Fisheries, loaded with coal, gasoline, and general supplies for Sable Island. I was given a cabin furnished for occasional trips by officials of the department, so I travelled de luxe. *Dollard* left the harbour on the following morning. About twenty-four hours later she was anchored a mile off the beach at Sable Island, and I was heading for it in a surfboat laden with supplies and mail.

* * *

Including the crews of the lifesaving stations, the two lighthouses, and the wireless station, there were twenty men on Sable. Several were married, and their wives and children brought the population to about forty, scattered in posts along the length of it, which was then about twenty miles. From each end of it there were bars extending and gradually submerging for another fifteen miles or so. Thus the whole thing was a ship-trap roughly fifty miles long and shaped like a slice of the moon lying east-and-west on its back. The greatest width was about a mile in the middle, from which the island tapered towards the ends.

Except for an occasional small stone the island was all sand, heaped up in dunes or stretched out along the beaches. In some of the deeper gullies between the dunes there were ponds of fresh (rain) water. Most of the dunes were tufted with coarse marram grass, and some had the creeping vines of beach pea. Others lacked the anchorage of these roots and moved with the winds like drifts of snow. Cranberries flourished in a thin peat formed over centuries about the ponds, and in places wild strawberries, blueberries and various wild flowers were plentiful. Nothing grew higher than my knees. About three hundred ponies, whose origin nobody knew, fed on the dune grass and beach pea. They were wiry creatures with long manes and tails, roaming in gangs gathered by the more powerful stallions. The lifesavers had caught and tamed some for pulling their carts or riding on patrols along the beach.

In the days of sail Sable Island had earned its grim nickname. Since the installation of the first lifesaving establishment in 1801, successive "Governors" of the island had kept a list and eventually compiled a map showing the names and sites of about two hundred wrecks. Europeans had been sailing in these dangerous waters for at least three centuries before 1801, and there must have been many others. In the early 1500s the French even made one or two attempts to establish a colony there, God knows why; and in my day a part of the sheltered hollow occupied by the main lifesaving station was still known as Frenchmen's Gardens. Among the legends passed from one generation of lifesavers to another was one about the Singing Frenchman, whose ghost had been seen and heard. He was riding a big white horse unlike the wild ponies of the island and dressed in a costume of some ancient time.

Most of the people lived near the west end, where the west light, the main lifesaving station and the wireless station stood about a mile apart. The superintendent (always known as the Governor) had a two-storey house at Main Station, and there were also a small barrack for the lifeboat crew, another for shipwrecked crews (known as the Sailors' Home), a stable for a few tame ponies and two or three cows, a shed for the lifeboat and the wheeled carriage on which it was drawn by ponies, a shed for the Lyle gun and breeches buoy apparatus, and on the crest of a tall dune a wooden watchtower.

For beach patrols in thick weather, and quick shelter for castaways in winter, there were three houses spaced several miles apart along the island. In each of these lived a man with wife and family and a male assistant. In fog, sleet or snow the Governor ordered a daily patrol of the beaches in search of castaways. A rider left Main Station with a patrol ticket and travelled along the north beach to Station No. 2, where another rider took the ticket to No. 3, and so on. When the ticket came back to Main Station it bore the signatures of all the patrolmen from west to east and back again by the south beach, proof that every yard of the shore had been covered.

These arrangements had been in effect for at least seventy years, and some for a century or more, when I set foot on Sable. They had saved many lives in the time past, but for years now nothing much had happened. The waning of the windjammers and the invention of Radio Direction Finding had removed the Graveyard's chief menace. During my year on the island there was only one wreck, a fishing schooner, whose crew were rescued by another.

*   *   *

As I arrived at the wireless station, the operator in charge departed on leave to marry his fiancée in Newfoundland and would not be back until the supply ship came again in August. In his absence the temporary OIC was an Irishman named Cope, the son of a Dublin music teacher and a good pianist and violinist himself. The other operators were Newfoundlanders, who told me tales of the sealing ships and of life on little radio stations "up along the Labrador."

The Sable station building was fairly new, having replaced the one burned in 1919. It was a rectangular one-storey wooden affair with an apartment for the chief operator at one end. The rest of it included watch room, engine room, three small bedrooms and a bathroom. The architect obviously thought Sable was in the latitude of Bermuda, for there was no heating in the operators' quarters. A coal stove warmed the watch room; the busy gasoline engine naturally heated the engine room; but from October to May our bedrooms were like iceboxes, and again and again we had to thaw the bathroom pipes with a blowtorch.

In the early summer days I learned to swim in the salt lake or lagoon, eight miles long, that lay between the main island and the south bar. We bathed there every day, and after two or three weeks I felt bold enough to swim off the beach in the ocean itself, something never done by the lifesavers, who were full of dire warnings about the undertow. Also, I learned to ride the ponies – those broken to the saddle, I mean. They were far from broken, really, with sudden moods of bucking or wild galloping over the dunes, and any ride could end in a toss and a long walk back.

In the saddle or afoot, I came to know every part of the island, at all seasons, in all weathers. Because only two operators were off duty at any time, and one of the two might wish to sleep, I was usually alone on my visits to the various posts and lighthouses. All of the island families had come originally from villages on the coast, and in several cases the posts had passed in succession from father to son to grandson, all born on the island, with interludes on the mainland or in ships out of Halifax. They regarded Sable as their natural home and had tales and legends passed down from the remote past.

I learned for myself the strange fascination of this boneyard in the sea, where a long gale from an unusual quarter would expose old wreckage buried in the dunes, or the remains of a rude hut made from ship timber by castaways, or human skulls and bones that had been covered perhaps for centuries. Just off the north beach near the wireless station was the wreck of a steamer washed up there by a huge sea in 1906. Nothing remained visible but her Scotch boilers, still firmly fastened to the bedplates. When the wind got into the east and blew a gale, it set up a moaning in those old boiler tubes fit to stand your hair on end, especially if you heard it first (as I did) in the middle of a graveyard watch.

I learned how to shoot wild duck, which were plentiful in those days. Seals also were numerous, and I learned how to kill them too. At the first talk with my Newfoundland chum Williams about sealing, I refused to believe that such a large animal could be killed with two or three quick blows on the head, whereas bullets shot into the body were not so sure. I had a .32 Smith and Wesson revolver, bought for fifteen dollars in a Water Street hockshop (probably stolen and "hot"), which I kept in my sea chest. One day we put it to the test. Williams, an experienced sealer, had a club made from the loom of an old dory oar. We rowed across the lagoon and crept on our bellies towards a group of seals sunning themselves on the seaward side of the bar. When we jumped to our feet they flopped away towards the water, but our legs made better time. At a distance of only a few feet I fired all six of my bullets into the body of a large seal, which snarled at every impact but kept on going into the sea and swam away. The dense fat closed over each bullet so that there was no hole, merely a small round pink mark on the hide. How deeply the bullets penetrated I couldn't even guess. The seal was still swimming strongly when I saw it last, and I was astounded. Williams had been so interested in my shooting that he lost any chance to use his club.

Some days later we happened on a herd of seals on this bar, snatched up heavy oak staves from a broken cask nearby, and killed a big one with two blows on the forehead. It was really dead, too. I know, because I skinned it and made the hairy hide into a mat for my bedroom floor. Many years afterward (in the 1960s) a German newsman started a furore about the brutality of Canadian seal hunters, who clubbed the animals to death instead of shooting

101

them. Newspapers and humane societies in Europe and North America took up the cry, which was nonsense. I add that I never killed one of the seal pups ("whitecoats"), although my comrades did.

*   *   *

Nova Scotian and Yankee schooners came to fish on the Sable Bank in May. Their hulls, masts, sails and fishing methods were unchanged since Kipling described them in *Captains Courageous*. One of the Yankees was the famous *Esperanto*, which had beaten the Nova Scotia champion in the international fishermen's races off Halifax in 1920. Her skipper was a daring fellow named "Marty" Welsh who fished close to the island and often took a short cut across the west bar by a gully he had found. One fine evening *Esperanto* and another Yankee schooner named *Elsie* were fishing in company so close to the south shore that we could see their dorymen catching cod with handlines. Towards night they took up their dories and made sail, obviously intending to cross the bar and anchor off the north side of the island for the night. As darkness closed down we saw no more of them. Later we knew that "Marty" had taken too close a chance that night.

His schooner struck the sunken wreck of an iron steamer named *State of Virginia*, which had foundered off the west point in 1879. The impact tore a long gash in *Esperanto*'s starboard bilge, and she filled and sank. Luckily *Elsie* was able to come alongside and remove the crew. In the morning we saw a pair of topmasts sticking out of the sea. The lifeboat crew put off to investigate and found a schooner sunk with all sail set and all her dories nested on the deck. With a boathook lashed to a pole they managed to fish up the topmost dory and found the name *Esperanto* on it, so we sent a message to Halifax reporting that apparently she had gone down with all hands. We learned the truth when *Elsie* reached port.

This affair brought us an interesting visitation. At Gloucester, Massachusetts, the home port of *Esperanto*, a man named Abbott bought the sunken schooner from the insurance underwriters for a nominal sum. He then approached the Boston *Post* with the bold idea of resurrecting the American champion from the Graveyard of the Atlantic and sending her to the races next fall, like a ghost, to defend the cup she had won. They raised a fund, chartered a trawler named *Fabia*, engaged a crack hard-hat diver named Jack

Gardner, and sent them off to Sable Island with salvage gear, including ten collapsible air pontoons that worked like huge accordions. *Fabia* arrived at the wreck in June with several American newsmen aboard. They lost no time in getting ashore and sending long press messages from our station.

During the next three or four weeks we had light winds and the salvagers were able to work away. They managed to raise the hull several times, but whenever it broke the surface there was a tremendous surge that snapped the chains and cables of the pontoons, and down it went again. At last they gave up and vanished. In another week a heavy surf smashed *Esperanto* to pieces, and parts of her were strewn for miles along the beaches. We got a good dory and some of her sail canvas, which we painted and used to cover part of our bare floors. For small souvenirs I made a pair of miniature lifebuoys, carved out of a bit of deck planking, with beckets made from a codline and bound with threads from her sails. One of them hangs on the wall of my study today, beside the wreck map of the island.

*   *   *

On the first of June 1921 a friendly wireless operator on the Cunard liner *Saxonia* informed me that my mother and sisters were on board and would arrive at Halifax tomorrow. I promptly sent franked messages to friends there asking them to meet the ship and take my family to their new home.

To amuse myself in off-watch hours in the hot summer days, after the daily swim, I made a crude model of a brig, which I sailed on one of the ponds a mile or two east of the wireless station. After experimenting with the setting of rudder and sails for various winds, I began to learn something of the art of sailing a real square-rigger, an interest that remained with me many years, talking to old seamen, studying logbooks, models, sail plans, and so on.

In August the supply ship *Lady Laurier* brought our stores and fuel for the next three months and our chief operator, Walsh, and his bride, returning from their honeymoon. Among their new belongings was a piano, an awkward thing to get ashore in a boat and then over the dunes to the wireless shack, but we got it there without a scratch. As Mrs. Walsh would do the cooking for us all, our male cook departed gladly enough and so did one of the operators who had served his time.

Late in the summer I had a close brush with a messy death when

Walsh, Williams and I were duck hunting among the ponds. We were returning at dusk, walking in file with Walsh in the lead, Williams close at his heels, and I two or three paces behind Williams. A lone duck, hiding in the reeds, broke cover almost at my feet. Walsh swerved sharply, throwing up his gun with an instinctive finger on the trigger, and it went off. At that short distance the pellets had no chance to spread, and the tight bunch of lead shot whistled past my head. Walsh cried, "My God!"

Williams said, "You all right, Brud [Newfie for brother]?"

I chuckled and said "Sure!" At that age a miss of an inch is just as good as a mile.

On a graveyard watch that October, I amused myself by writing a little tale about one of the island ghosts, "The Singing Frenchman," which went by autumn mail to a short-lived Halifax newspaper called the *Sunday Leader*. It appeared in a December issue.

* * *

That autumn the department decided to remove fifty of the wild ponies and sell them at auction at Halifax. The order came, and toward the end of October the lifesaving crew made a roundup, western cowboy style, riding tame ponies from their various stations and driving several wild gangs into a corral concealed in a hollow near Main Station. They caught about sixty.

The ship arrived off the west end on November first, but the surf was rising to a dangerous point, and after putting the mail and some urgent small stores into one of the island surfboats she retired to shelter in Whitehaven, the nearest port on the mainland, eighty miles away. Ten days later she was able to land the rest of our stores and take off forty-one of the ponies. By that time the captives had been milling about the corral, without food, for two weeks. The lifesavers reckoned this to the good, because the ponies would be weak and easier to handle. I described the harsh method of getting them to the boats and then to the ship a mile offshore in my novel *The Nymph and the Lamp*. I was told long afterwards that somebody formerly connected with the department deplored my description in the book and said it was highly exaggerated. It was not. I have a set of photographs showing the whole wretched business. I didn't blame the lifesavers, who were given a job to do and did it.

I remain scornful of comfortable souls on the mainland who from time to time demand removal of the Sable Island ponies, professing the most tender motives, when they ought to know (or should be able to guess) what is involved in getting these wild creatures off the dunes and into a ship. Nowadays, with the invention of a device that shoots darts with a powerful anaesthetic and with the expensive use of helicopters, removal of the ponies might be made with much less pain and difficulty. Even so, I object strongly to the recurring idea that the Sable Island ponies would be happier on the mainland. Always lurking in the obscurity behind this sweet thought there is somebody hoping to make an easy profit by selling them, if only to the canners of dogmeat.

On this occasion in 1921 the hapless ponies were sold at auction in Dartmouth, but nobody bought one for a pet. They were too wild and too scrawny by that time. I saw some of them later on, pulling carts for poor whites and blacks who sold poultry and vegetables in the open-air market at Halifax. The ponies had been tamed to this drudgery by beating half the life out of them, and the sores were hideous.

*   *   *

The ship took away not only the wretched ponies but two very happy men, operators Cope and Williams, who had served their time on the island and were due for leave. As the OIC was now taking a regular watch himself, a lone relief operator came to us. He was about thirty, a sharp-featured man with the quick mean eyes of a weasel and the disposition of a rattlesnake. I shall call him Sharp. He had served during the late war in a Canadian Army signals company and was full of tales about his amours in France and about his other prowess, which was with his fists. According to himself, he was just about the toughest guy in an army of tough guys, and all his fighting had been done against other Canadians, not the Germans. His yarns usually ended with "So I flattened the son of a bitch."

In the new routine of watches Sharp's followed mine, and when I had the evening watch he was supposed to relieve me at midnight. But he did not. He liked his bed too much. Whenever I wakened him at a quarter to twelve he uttered an irritable Okay! Okay! and went to sleep again as soon as I left the room. Consequently in addition to my own watch I was serving twenty minutes to nearly an hour of his, depending on the number of times I had to waken him before he was ready to come forth. This went on all through November and December.

The simple pleasures that had passed the off-duty hours of the summer and autumn, the walks, the pony rides, swimming, spearing flatfish from a dory in the lagoon, sailing my little brig, and hunting ducks, all came to an end with the bleak winds of November. In that month I passed my eighteenth birthday and became a man, according to the Department of Naval Service. And Sharp arrived.

The OIC and his bride kept to their own apartment except when he took his turn in the watch room in the daylight hours from 8 A.M. to 4 P.M., leaving the evening and the night to Sharp and me. Thus in the monotony of winter Sharp and I were thrown upon each other's company, congenial to neither of us.

My patience ran out on a stormy midnight of wind and snow in January. I wakened Sharp with a long and forceful shaking, and he sat up in bed and favoured me with some choice army obscenities. I said quietly, "I want you at the phones in fifteen minutes. No more." Actually I waited twenty minutes and then found him asleep, or pretending to sleep just to see what I would do. He soon saw. I yanked him out of his blankets to the icy floor, gave his arse a hearty kick for emphasis, and returned to the phones and listened to some ship-talk for my regular log entry, which had to be made every quarter hour.

Sharp darted into the room in shirt and trousers, grabbed me about the throat as I sat busy at the phones, and yelled that he would teach me a lesson. After a wild struggle, stamping about the watch room floor, I managed to force his hands from my throat. The phones fell off my head. We bumped into the stove and nearly upset it. At the moment it held about half a bushel of red-hot coals, which would have set the station afire, so I said, "We can't fight here. We'll settle this on the beach in the morning." He nodded rapidly several times, a picture of fury and malevolent promise, and then picked up the phones and went on with the watch.

Tossing and turning in my frigid little bedroom all night, I could not sleep. After a silent breakfast we left the shack together as if for a walk. Walsh had taken over the watch and stood at the window with the phones on his head, guessing full well what was really afoot. It was a tradition on the station that quarrels of the fighting sort must be settled on the north beach, where the dunes shut off the OIC's view.

Last night's snowstorm had blown itself out. The tide had swept the beach and left it brown and frozen. As soon as we arrived there

Sharp flew at me in a style I had never seen before, whirling his arms and fists like windmills, and in a crouch, with his head down for a butt at my jaw. His first butt hit my cheekbone, and I had a big bruise there for days; but that was the only blow he landed on my face. My chest and shoulders took a lot of thumps. I soon saw that I should make a quick side step to avoid these wild rushes, at the same time swinging an uppercut at his face. This went on furiously for perhaps twenty minutes. By that time his right eye was swollen shut and he was bleeding from mouth and nose.

He made another of those strange headlong lunges and again I made the side step, but this time I set my feet on the frozen sand and, in sea slang, swung one right off the deck. I was simply aiming at that downturned face again, but by chance this blow struck his left eye socket just above the eye, where the bone is close to the surface. It cut right through the eyelid, which then drooped over the eye in a stream of blood. With both eyes sealed he was now helpless, and I was aghast. This self-styled tough guy was just a noisy swaggerer after all. Anybody who had learned to take care of himself when returning to the docks at night could have done exactly what I did.

I helped him to stumble back to the station, and Walsh got out the first-aid box and bandaged the cut. Properly it should have been sewn, but neither Walsh nor I had skill enough for that. When the cut healed the lid had a permanent droop. It did not impair Sharp's vision at all, but it added a more sinister touch to his visage, quite in keeping with the attitude he cultivated. After that he stood his watch on time and we got along.

As I have remarked before, my diary in these sea years is often precocious and smart-alecky, sometimes quite sensible, mostly just boyish and naïve. In the long months on Sable Island it makes frequent mention of tiffs and squabbles that arose in the wireless station. Much ado about nothing just to break the monotony, the common behaviour of human males in isolated posts the world over. In this case, however, the fight would have happened anywhere, and inevitably, with a man like Sharp. I never saw him again after leaving the island. Brasspounding friends of mine wrote me that he remained the lone weasel, disliked wherever he went, but he never pushed anyone into a fight again. Our strange brawl, starting in the watch room and ending on that wintry beach, became a part of Sable Island legend, repeated and embroidered wherever brasspounders chatted together, so I am setting forth the simple stupid facts with my old diary before me.

*   *   *

To get back to our work. In coastal traffic we communicated with Cape Sable, Halifax, North Sydney and Cape Race. In turn, Cape Race communicated with the chain of stations up the Gulf of St. Lawrence to Montreal and with a lesser chain along the northern coast of Newfoundland and "up the Labrador."

Much more profitable to the Marconi Company was our busy traffic with ships of all kinds, from trawlers to big British, French, German, Scandinavian, Italian and American liners, which sent and received a torrent of messages. For us at Sable Island each message meant a double job because it had to be relayed to or from the Halifax station. To avoid overlapping and interference ("jamming"), the rules required every ship to communicate with its nearest shore station. This was because we all worked on the 600-metre wavelength, like a lot of people talking or shouting to each other in one big room.

Thus the liners on their westerly passage to America poured messages to and from Cape Race until they steamed into the radio orbit of Sable Island. Then we got the whole stream until they passed into the orbit of Cape Sable, then Cape Cod, and finally New York. On the return passage to Europe the same thing happened in reverse.

With the faint signals that came through our old-fashioned crystals we could not use a typewriter, which would have drowned them out. Thus we had to write all messages with pencil, making a carbon copy. The busy liners often worked at a rate of thirty words a minute, as fast as the human hand could use the heavy brass keys of those days. In good signal conditions a liner might send groups of five or ten messages before pausing to hear the "Received" signal from us, a curt *R*. As prelude to each of these messages you had to write the ship's name, the date, and the exact time of reception, while the ship's operator whipped along at full speed with the message. Writing with one hand, changing carbon paper with the other, and taking regular glances at the clock on the wall all added up to something like a conjuring trick.

My opposite number on the same watch at Cape Race was a man named Jim Myrick, famous as the best brasspounder on the Canadian east coast. His "hand" was fast, accurate, and as graceful to the ear as fine handwriting is to the eye. "To send like Jim Myrick" was the ambition of every young brasspounder on the coast, and after some months as his opposite number I like to think I achieved it. When he first called me with a few messages to be passed to a ship far away to the southwest, "J M" detected a strange hand at Sable Island and cracked out "W O [Who are you]?" I couldn't use my initials as most operators did because *TR* was the prefix for a ship's position report, so I cracked back "R A D." The air was noisy with static electricity from a thunderstorm somewhere, and apparently it obliterated the dash in *A* and left only the dot before it. A lone dot meant *E*. Thereafter in our daily greetings and bits of personal chat Myrick invariably called me R E D – and I didn't correct him. Correcting the famous J M would have been something like blasphemy to our peculiar trade, so the Canadian brasspounders, ship and shore, who came to recognize my hand as well as Myrick's, assumed that I probably had red hair.

In the dull prison of winter, with Sharp as my sole companion in the operator's quarters, it was a marvellous release to take over the watch and become part of the busy world, cracking away at top speed with the liners and absorbing from their messages the interesting news and gossip of politicians, big businessmen, stars of the stage and screen, and other remarkable folk who travelled on the sea in those days.

For example, we got a lot of insight into the workings of Canadian federal politics when Prime Minister Arthur Meighen was returning from a visit to England to face the election campaign of 1921. Aboard the ship he was bombarded with messages through our station containing advice, questions, pleas, threats, and a lot of other interesting matter that never got into the newspapers; and we read his replies, always clear and incisive. He was defeated in the election and never had political success in that unlucky time after the war. I met him in Toronto many years later. Regardless of party politics I still rate his mind one of the best that Canada ever produced.

As a sample of the more amusing entertainment we got on our desert island there was the case of Harold McCormick, wealthy head of an American manufacturing firm, whose wife was Edith Rockefeller, wealthy herself. For years they were the chief patrons of the Chicago Opera Company. Then they separated but apparently at this time were not divorced. In 1921 McCormick made Mary Garden the director of the opera company, in which she had been prima donna for years. Apparently she had been McCormick's inamorata also during much of that time; but now she was well on in her forties, and he had found a new love in Europe, the luscious and much younger Polish opera singer Ganna Walska. His affair with Ganna was quite open and American newsmen were reporting it with glee. To add to the fun, McCormick had gone to Paris for the so-called monkey gland operation by the famous Doctor Voronoff, although it was said that he actually had purchased the sexual glands of a young blacksmith. One American news report included a wicked little rhyme:

Under the spreading chestnut tree the village smithy stands.
He isn't what he used to be, McCormick's got his glands.

*　*　*

All of this outraged the wary Mary in Chicago, foreseeing a successor on the stage as well as the couch. Wireless messages flew back and forth as the ship bearing McCormick to New York drew into our range. At the time, of course, I didn't know the full background of this affair, one of the juiciest scandals of the post-war years, but the messages were revealing. Rich and famous friends poured entreaties to McCormick aboard the ship, urging him to reconsider. One long message was from Mary Garden, begging him "not to wound the hearts of your friends," and so on. For her part, Ganna Walska in Paris sent long messages designed to keep his emotions and intentions warm. And there were sharp exchanges between McCormick and his wife.

Apparently they had two houses in or about Chicago, and he sent a message asking which she intended to keep, so that he could use the other. I can recall the exact words of her reply because it came in my watch, and the words were few and to the point. "I intend to keep both houses. You have much choice among your many friends in Chicago to find a place to stay." This was an obvious jab at Mary Garden and possibly other Chicago lady friends of his.

After the passage of juicy messages like this you could hear the listening brasspounders on other ships tapping out "H I!", the signal for a laugh. It was all such fun that we were sorry when the ship passed out of our range and turned this stream of entertainment to the operators at Cape Cod and finally New York. I don't know what happened afterwards to that notorious liaison. I do remember

110

a hilarious American news report that the blacksmith's glands weren't working so well in their new environment.

* * *

None of us realized that all this open chatter in the air, like the old-fashioned country telephone line, was coming to an end in a few more years. Danger or distress at sea continued to require a general watch on the 600-metre wave, but soon passenger liners would be equipped with additional wavelengths, enabling them to communicate swiftly and privately with New York and other far places regardless of the old nearest-station rule. Also, in liners the old-fashioned spark transmitters gave way to electronic tubes that gave clearer signals at longer range. With these tubes, too, the radio-telephone soon came into use. Thus the prosperous flood of messages through the Canadian stations at Cape Race and Sable Island ebbed away in the 1920s.

Their great days had begun in 1912 when the *Titanic* sank within their twin orbits. This disaster drew the seafaring nations into conference and produced new and strict international rules for ship and shore radio traffic. Among other things they ruled that all ships carrying a certain number of seamen (in the case of cargo ships) and all ships carrying passengers must have radio-telegraph apparatus with certified operators and regular hours of watch. This brought about the great volume of radio-telegraphy on the 600-metre wave which I had known after the forced sea silence of the 1914-18 war. At Sable Island I was hearing the last of it in full cry.

* * *

In December 1921 and the first weeks of 1922 the supply ship *Lady Laurier* made several sorties from the mainland, only to find that a sudden gale and a thundering surf made landing on our island impossible. Between these ventures she lay at Halifax or Whitehaven. We decided not to celebrate Christmas until we got our Christmas mail and supplies, whenever that happened. At last we were able to tell her that a calm at zero temperature was stilling the sea, and now was the time. She said she could not get to us much before night, but we assured her we could unload boats in the dark.

To speed things up the ship's motor launch towed our laden surfboats as far as the outlying shoals, and from there the oarsmen rowed them in to the beach, where the lifesavers handled their own supplies and we "wireless fellers" looked after ours. Sharp had the watch in the wireless station, so Walsh and I did the chores on the beach. It was hard and heavy work, especially with the coal sewn up in hundred-pound sacks and with the drums of gasoline. When each boat came in to the beach we had to wade into the water to steady it and unload it, and as we wireless fellers were not equipped with hip rubber boots, we got wet to the thighs. These labours went on far into the night.

When everything was ashore I picked up a big wooden box holding Christmas gifts, fruit, nuts, candy, magazines and books from my family and friends in Halifax. It must have weighed close to fifty pounds. I heaved it on my shoulder and trudged a mile along the beach and over the dunes to the wireless shack, with my frozen trouser-legs clashing like boards at every step. It was the toughest night I had spent in my life, but I revelled in it, as if I were fighting a battle in the dark against our bitter enemy, the sea, and winning it all by myself. It is wonderful to be in good health and just eighteen. Long afterwards I described that night in a piece called "Christmas at Sable Island," my contribution to a book for Canadian schools entitled *All Sails Set*.

In February I sent a message to the Marconi superintendent at Halifax making formal request for relief when the next supply ship came. So did Walsh, whose wife was pregnant. March crawled by. We heard that nor'west winds were shoving the winter's icefields out of the Gulf of St. Lawrence, and proof came in the first week of April, when a vast pack reached our island and covered the sea northward to the horizon. The sheer weight and pressure of this mass under a light breeze pushed thick floes far up on our sands. On the west bar the first floes grounded and the rest slid over them, one upon another like a spilled pack of cards, until the uproar was tremendous and, as the west lightkeeper said, the ice was "mountains high."

A gale cleared the pack away before the end of the month, when faithful little *Lady Laurier* came to us again. On the night of April 29, 1922, I had the graveyard watch, my last on the island. I passed some of this dull vigil in scribbling some doggerel, often quoted afterwards by old Sable Island hands.

FAREWELL TO SABLE ISLAND
Twelve months in any place, my friends, is quite a weary while,
And seems more like a century when spent on Sable Isle.

But now my exile's over and I've packed my little trunk,
I'm going to the mainland where a fella can get drunk.
There's girls and trees and taxicabs and movie shows and booze,
And I can walk for miles and feel hard earth beneath my shoes.
The only seals I'll see will be fur coats on ladies' backs.
And not a speck of sand within a mile of Halifax!

And when I have grown old and have grey hair beneath my cap,
Before I kick the bucket with a loud and fatal rap,
I'll drag my feeble limbs aboard the boat when sailing's nigh,
And have another look at Sable Isle before I die.
For when I've seen the breakers pound along that sandy length,
The thought of what a hell-on-earth it is will give me strength,
And when the Devil lets me into Tophet with a curse,
I'll tell him, "Nick, it ain't so bad, I've seen a place that's worse!"

*   *   *

Aboard ship on the way to Halifax I wrote a shorter comment in my diary: "I wish I could put into this ink one half of the joy with which I watched that strip of sand disappear below the horizon." Beneath this youthful exuberance my mind had stored deeper and more powerful impressions of the island and its life. These and other experiences and observations of the past three years lay dormant or maturing slowly, like wines in an underground vat, until they emerged years later in a blend called *The Nymph and the Lamp*.

On the first of May 1922 I landed at Dartmouth and took taxi and ferry across the harbour to Halifax. The unwritten agreement about service on Sable Island entitled me to two weeks' leave, but when I reported to Cutler he said he was short of men and I must go forthwith to Camperdown, the Marconi station at the mouth of Halifax harbour. His only concession was a couple of days in which I could see my family, shop for new clothes, bank my accumulated pay, take the examination for a first-class certificate at the naval dockyard, and get a new photograph for the ticket.

At the dockyard I showed my letter from the department in 1919, stating that I had passed the exams for a first-class ticket but could only have a second-class until I became eighteen in November, 1921. The chief wireless officer at the dockyard studied this for a minute. Then he said there was no need to repeat the written and oral examinations. He obviously assumed, however, that as a second-class operator my experience must have been in small tramps or trawlers where messages were few and slow, for he said he must test my skill with dots and dashes.

A first-class ticket called for absolute accuracy in sending and receiving at the rate of twenty words (one hundred letters or figures) a minute. Out of sheer swank I plied the testing key at thirty, as if I were talking to Jim Myrick, say, or *Mauretania* in a busy watch. The officer said with some surprise, "If they all sent like you we'd have no trouble." Then a suspicion hit his mind. "Where the hell have you been?" When I told him he chuckled, "Why didn't you say so in the first place?" So I passed for the long-wanted first-class ticket, and in due course it came from the Department of Naval Service at Ottawa. Glued to the back of it and embossed with the department's seal was a new photograph of me, looking nothing like the schoolboy on the other ticket.

I stayed this brief time with my family in the home I had got for them on Duncan Street. Then I hired a man with horse and buggy to take me out to Camperdown, fourteen miles away by a narrow dirt road around the head of the Northwest Arm. We passed through a small rustic hamlet called Spryfield (nowadays a sprawling and bustling suburb of the city) and bumped and lurched through woods to the village of Portuguese Cove. There I rented a bedroom in a fisherman's cottage and arranged to get my meals in the postmaster's house, the only substantial one in the place. My island chum Williams was here at Camperdown, and now came Walsh and his wife. The chief operator was an old hand named Inder.

Camperdown was the name of a small hill overlooking Portuguese Cove and the mouth of Halifax harbour, with an ancient but still operational army watch-post on its crest. Down the slope a bit stood the Marconi station, built in 1905, a grey shack containing a huge old-fashioned single-cylinder gasoline engine, a dynamo, and the usual instruments of a radio watch room. The OIC and his family lived in a house nearby. Other operators made their own arrangements for board and lodging in the village at the foot of the hill.

From the watch room we had a fine view across the harbour mouth to Devil's Island and the eastern shore. In the foreground, on the reef that sheltered Portuguese Cove, stood the rusty bow and forecastle of a large steamship. The rest had broken off and slid away into the depths long ago. It was all that remained of the Anchor-Donaldson liner *Letitia*, which was used as a hospital ship during the First World War. She ran aground here in a snowstorm in 1918. By great exertions the army and navy people at Halifax rescued everyone on board and took them away to the city in naval craft.

For several days *Letitia* lay abandoned, and fishermen from miles around came to loot everything that could be carried off – huge quantities of food, cots, bedding, tableware, carpeting and what not. When I sat down to meals in the postmaster's house, the tablecloth, plates, cups, saucers, knives, forks and spoons all bore the insignia of the Anchor-Donaldson Line. The wooden walkways around the house, and from house to barn, were composed of oak gratings from the ship placed end to end. The room I had in a poor fisherman's cottage was furnished entirely from the wreck: the bed, bedding, carpet, chair, mirror, wash bowl and jug.

On the gratings outside the postmaster's house, for lack of room in the cluttered little parlour, a daughter taught me the basic steps of modern dancing, humming waltz and fox-trot tunes in my ear as we pranced and twirled. She had learned these in visits to a married sister in Halifax. Most people in the fishing villages preferred old-fashioned but lively square dances, usually held in Sambro, about eight miles from Portuguese Cove by a rough road through the woods. Sometimes I walked to Sambro to attend one of these festivities, returning in the dark to take my watch. A closer pleasure on warm days was bathing in a small lake behind Camperdown hill, where the army signallers, Williams and I splashed and clowned like small boys.

Williams had bought a fisherman's motorboat, which enabled us to run up to the city much more easily than by road. For one of these trips I borrowed a tall kitbag from the soldiers, filled it with live lobsters, and took it home by tramcar from the Market Wharf. My family had seen lobsters only when they were cooked to a bright red. For fun I emptied the bag on the kitchen floor, and at sight of these crawling dark green monsters they screamed and fled to the bedroom stairs.

Since their arrival in Halifax last summer my two adult sisters had taken courses in typing and stenography and now had salaried jobs in the city. My mother's financial problem had been eased, although now she had to make the monthly payments on the house. She managed to keep up the payments, but from time to time in the years to come she fell short of paying the stiff city taxes, and I paid them out of my small salary as a bookkeeper in the backwoods.

* * *

Williams's ambition was an operator's job in the transatlantic wireless station at Glace Bay, Nova Scotia. The apparatus there was powerful and since the messages were taken down on typewriters, he had bought an old portable machine for practice and made formal application for a post. Towards the end of May he got it, and away he went in good cheer. I bought the typewriter for ten dollars to oblige him. I had no use for it except to peck out an occasional letter. One such letter I sent to the curator of the Nova Scotia Museum in Halifax. A fisherman had dug up in his garden a large military badge, and I made a drawing of it and sent it in for identification. The curator, a noted antiquarian and writer named Harry Piers, replied that it was a crossbelt plate of the 17th Regiment of Foot, which was posted at Halifax from 1783 to 1786. The fisherman donated it to the museum, and I took it there on one of my trips to the city, together with an ancient bayonet I had found on Sable Island.

In this way I made the acquaintance of a talented and dedicated man and formed a friendship that would last until his death. At Piers's request, I walked four miles from Camperdown to Herring Cove and inquired among the fishermen for traditions of H.M.S. *La Tribune*, wrecked there in a gale in 1797, and especially for the name of an orphan boy who rowed out alone in a small boat to rescue some of her crew. Subsequently the Canadian Historic Sites and Monuments Board erected a cairn there, with a plaque.

When Piers mentioned an ancient visual-telegraph system at Halifax, of which Camperdown was probably the outer post, I examined the old army building on our hill, took a photograph, and questioned the villagers. Such matters, and tours of the museum with Piers as my mentor, put a new keen edge on my schoolboy interest in history and the evidence of it still to be found, not only in documents but on the ground. Quite unconsciously I was mounting a hobbyhorse that I would ride for the rest of my life.

Up to this time my absorbing interest was in my profession as a brasspounder, and my plan for the next part of my life was still several years of sea roving about the world. A conversation with Inder at Camperdown finally shattered this romantic dream. I cannot recall his exact words, except some of the more pungent

116

phrases, but the gist was this: "Do you think for one minute that Cutler would let you go back to sea, especially in a ship on a foreign run where you'd be out of his bailiwick and all over hell's kitchen? Look, son, anybody can pound brass aboard a ship, but expert shore station operators are scarce, and nobody knows that better than Cutler. From my station alone three ops have drifted away to the States in the past year. More will be going from all over pretty soon because there's a rumour that ARCON's going to cut the pay."

Including the shore subsistence allowance of forty dollars a month, my pay was now $130. I was still incensed at Cutler's refusal of my well-earned leave, and the prospect of a future spent in barren spots like Sable Island did not enchant me. With rare exceptions all the Marconi stations along the Canadian Atlantic coast were on remote capes and islands. I could leave the Canadian service and go to the States, where the U.S. merchant marine readily hired Canadian operators with first-class tickets and experience and paid them much more money. The sticker was that they must make a formal transfer to American citizenship. My father had fought and died as a Canadian soldier, and I had served three years under the Canadian flag myself. I could not cut myself away from all that, for money or for dreams.

My studies of electrical textbooks had given me a sharp awareness of my lack of general education and a growing desire to make it up somehow. I couldn't go back to school because I had to earn my living, but if I could get work of some kind in Halifax I could live there with my mother, enjoying access to libraries and to the minds of men like Piers. I cannot say I thought it all out in this logical sequence. It was simply the instinct of common sense, working in the back of my mind as I gazed over the sea from Camperdown. I was no longer the penniless young fellow who spent a year of precious life on a desert island because he damned well had to. I now had more than a thousand dollars, a lot of money in 1922, which I never could have saved in the happy-go-lucky life of a seafaring brasspounder. In the seaman's term, I had a good anchor to windward if I wanted to shift my berth.

I wrote my resignation from the Marconi service in mid-June, giving the requisite two weeks' notice. Cutler phoned from the Halifax office, demanding my reason for leaving, and I told him. First he gave me the old blarney. The Canadian coastal service needed crack operators like me, and so on. When that didn't work,

117

he asked me to stay at least until the end of July, to give him a chance to find a suitable man. If I left at the end of June, Harry Inder would have to forgo a long-delayed leave, and surely I couldn't do that to Inder. It was a good point, and I agreed to stay through July.

The time passed quickly enough at my duty and, in off-watch hours, a pleasant and innocent flirtation with my charming little dancing teacher, who was a devout Catholic like most people at the Cove. On short trips to Halifax I inquired about the prospects of a job and was told I would have to "get into business." And how could I do that? The answer was in a commercial school that called itself the Maritime Business College. There young ladies learned the arts of typing and stenography, and young men the more complicated art of keeping accounts for trading and manufacturing concerns.

On the evening of August 1, 1922, at home at last in my nineteenth year, I wrote the closing entry in my diary as a brasspounder. "Left Camperdown this morning in Purcell's team. A farewell party at the military signal station last night, where I drank too much and made an idiotic speech. I'm going to have a good vacation and then study at the Maritime Business College."

The vacation I spent with former Halifax friends who now lived on a farm near Bridgetown, Nova Scotia. I bought a bicycle and took it there on the train for explorations of the Annapolis Valley, which I had never seen. The weather was marvellous, and after a year in an atmosphere of salt and sand the rich green fields and orchards were paradise. Heavenly too was the food: the corn, tomatoes, cucumbers, cabbages and potatoes, the fresh meat and poultry, and the delicious fruit. The contrast of all this with Sable Island was so striking that I never forgot, and I kept it in mind when, years later, I wrote *The Nymph and the Lamp*.

My new education began in mid-September. When I finished the course in the spring of 1923 I was ready and eager for the world of business, but I found the business world sadly unready for me. The post-war slump was sinking to its depths in Halifax, where experienced bookkeepers were trudging the streets, out of work, or taking a train for the States. A new certificate from a business "college" didn't mean a thing.

Somebody told me that the manager of the Canadian Press at Halifax was looking for a suitable young man to train for news writing. I hastened there to offer myself. His name was Andrew

Merkel, a man with an aquiline nose and a pleasant mouth and manner. He shook his head regretfully. He wanted someone of much better education, preferably a university graduate. He said gently that news writing required a special kind of talent and training, and I'd better try something else. It was a sharp disappointment, not only because I needed a job but because I remembered my father's notion that I should go in for journalism. I was to meet Andrew Merkel again many years later. He had forgotten this brief interview, and I did not remind him of it. I shall relate that meeting in its place in my life.

* * *

As a last resort I returned to the proprietor of the business college, a shrewd old gentleman named Kaulbach. He had been operating his school so many years that some of his graduates had worked up to executive positions. I had heard that when they wanted a book-keeper or a typist to start at a very low wage, they usually applied to him, knowing that his young men and women were ready in these times to take any job, anywhere, for any wage at all.

When I walked into Kaulbach's office on a day in May he said at once, "You're a lucky fellow!" He had two inquiries for a book-keeper. One came from the company that supplied electricity to the city of Sydney in Cape Breton, at a wage much lower than my Camperdown salary as a wireless operator. The other, at an even smaller wage, was from a little wood-pulp factory in the forest of western Nova Scotia. Quickly I said I would take the Sydney job. I knew people there from my seafaring days, and I wanted to live in a town, not the bush.

He paused and regarded me over his spectacles, which sat on a nose red and pitted like an enormous strawberry. He advised me to take the job in the woods, even though the wage to start would be only eighty-five dollars a month. He explained that on the Sydney job I would be stuck at a desk, entering monthly bills for house-holders or some such thing, year in, year out. At the wood-pulp mill I would have sole charge of the cashbook, the ledgers, the payrolls, the bank accounts – in fact, all of the clerical details, from the scalers' sheets in the logging camps to bills of lading for the ships at the river mouth. I would gain wider and better experience of business in a year there than in ten years at Sydney.

I was reluctant, saying I'd spent enough of my life in lonely places, but the old man persisted. "My boy, go and stay one year.

Just one year. With that experience I may be able to get you something better, perhaps right here in Halifax."

* * *

On May 15, 1923, I caught the early morning train for Liverpool, about a hundred miles west of Halifax, a little seaport at the mouth of the Mersey River, where my new boss would meet me with a company car and take me to the mill in the woods upstream. I was determined to stay just one year. Not a day more.

1923 1939

I got off the train at Liverpool in bright sunshine, and my boss was there, a short brisk man of about thirty-five, with shrewd grey eyes behind steel-rimmed glasses. His name was Gordon. He took me five miles or so to the north end of a riverside village called Milton. It was a part known by the Indian name of Potanoc, in the edge of the woods, where I obtained board and lodging. My employers, the Macleod Pulp and Paper Company, made wood pulp and sawed some lumber. The "Paper" in the firm's name was just an old lost hope. They had a small sawmill at Potanoc, a wood-pulp mill half a mile upstream at Cowies Falls, and another at Rapid Falls, a mile above Cowies.

Actually the Mersey had no real falls but rather a succession of rapids spaced at intervals from a place called Indian Gardens, where the river flowed out of its chain of lakes, to tidewater at Milton, three miles above the town of Liverpool. All together the mills employed about 150 men, working in twelve-hour shifts, six days and nights a week. The basic pay was $2.00 a shift – less than seventeen cents an hour – rising through the various jobs to that of foreman, which was paid $3.50 a shift. The manager got $150 a month, with a bonus at the year's end if the company made a profit.

I took the place of a tall young man named Austin Parker who was going to a much better job in the States. The Macleod Company had paid him $125 a month. As the greenhorn replacement I was given eighty-five dollars, with a vague promise of increase with experience. Out of this paltry wage I paid thirty-five dollars monthly for my food and bed.

I had sold my new bicycle in Halifax, thinking I could not use it in the backwoods, so now I bought Parker's old one for occasional trips down the river road to Liverpool. Each morning I left my lodging at Potanoc, called at the Cowies Falls mill for the previous day's payroll and production sheets, walked a mile or so along a railway track through the woods to Rapid Falls mill, got the pay and production sheets there, and then settled down in the office for the day's work, which lasted till five o'clock.

The office was a small wooden building in a charming spot where the tailrace of the Rapid Falls mill foamed away through the woods towards the mill at Cowies Falls. It was staffed by the boss, a typist, the mill superintendent and myself. Frequently it had another occupant, a timber cruiser working at his maps and estimates.

The Macleod mills were ramshackle wooden structures full of obsolete machinery, but the company owned large and valuable timberlands, a water-storage dam at Indian Gardens, and the best sites for future hydro-electric power dams on the river below. In 1919 the Macleod owners had sold all this to an American syndicate represented by a man named Barnjum. That was how he spelled it. I always felt it should have been Barnum, like that of the man who said a sucker was born every minute.

Barnjum was a slick speculator with a pompous front who made his official residence in Annapolis, Nova Scotia, and had a small office in Montreal. He claimed to be a native of Montreal, but he first came to public notice as a bold and successful timber speculator in the state of Maine, and when he died he was buried there. He had lived in Canada for years and was recognized as a Canadian citizen, busy with a newspaper campaign for conservation of the Canadian forests. Needless to say, he was not moved by patriotic Canadian motives. He had been picking up cheaply much woodland in Nova Scotia. When he and his Boston backers acquired the Macleod properties on the Mersey River their scheme was to promote a large paper mill at the port of Liverpool, within cheap sea-reach of New York's newspaper market. The timberlands and the undeveloped hydro-electric sites on the river would be sold as one package to the new paper industry at a profit of several million dollars. In the meantime the decrepit pulp mills, with their long working hours, miserable working conditions and poor wages, would continue to grind wood under the old Macleod name merely to pay the taxes on the lands until the big coup was made.

After fitting his own cheaply bought woodlands into the Mersey River package, Barnjum's next move was to campaign strenuously for a Canadian embargo on all exports of raw wood. His propaganda was issued from his Montreal office, run by a clever woman secretary, and as it was avowedly for the sole benefit of Canadian industry he had no trouble getting it into Canadian newspapers. Naturally the American mills importing wood from Canada raised a fund to combat the proposed embargo, and they placed it in the hands of a sharp entrepreneur who lived in Nova Scotia. He had various interests in the moneymaking line one of which was a company shipping raw wood to the States.

Actually, these shenanigans were going on at a time when really farsighted American industrialists were beginning to see the advantage of building paper mills in Canada, where there was cheap waterpower in the midst of uncut forest. With the old Macleod mills grinding pulp to pay their taxes, Barnjum and the syndicate could wait comfortably for the golden egg to drop into their Boston basket.

As the new bookkeeper I walked into this situation in the spring of 1923. It took me some time to see through the hide to the bones of it, and like Alice I found this wonderland curiouser and curiouser as time went on.

* * *

Many homes in the village had a small foot-pumped organ in the parlour and some had a piano, as prestige furniture, seldom played except in a two-fingered tune-pecking way. There was not a single radio. (There was no regular broadcasting station in Nova Scotia until 1926.) For entertainment the villagers had nothing but a few worn records for an old-fashioned gramophone here and there and, on Saturday nights, a journey of several miles down the river road to the silent black-and-white movie show in Liverpool. In these dull circumstances naturally there was much diversion of the kind that Eve discovered with Adam far away and long ago.

In the parlour of my lodging stood a silent piano. For something to do in the evenings I got an old book of ditties (*Heart Songs* was the title) and began to practise my long-abandoned music, even singing to my own accompaniment. It would have tortured poor old Miss Hoyt in Halifax, and I was surprised when my hosts and some of their neighbours began to slip into the parlour chairs, listening with apparent pleasure. Those painful lessons of my boyhood had been of some use after all. I heard myself described in the terse village way as "Nice fella. Plays pianna. Sings too."

My boss, a practical man, advised me to get a gun and fishing rod. He was an ardent hunter and angler himself, and in those days the forest on the Mersey watershed was a sportsman's paradise, threaded here and there by a rough logging road but mostly to be reached only by canoe or afoot. Trout splashed in every stream. Salmon swarmed up the river from May to August, and one of the best salmon pools was only a few steps from our office door. Moose and deer were plentiful, and there were multitudes of partridge, ducks and rabbits. Gordon kept a rifle and salmon rod in the office, and one day the typist casually picked up the rifle and shot a partridge from the doorstep.

I bought an old .22 rifle for rabbit hunting and a cheap metal rod for the trout. On my scanty pay I couldn't get a big-game rifle or a salmon rod unless I bought them with some of my hard-earned Sable Island money. I was going back to the city in twelve months, so there was no point in that. Except for ducks on the island I had never shot game. Indeed, I had never been in the woods in my life except on the fringe of the farm at Stewiacke. So I began to explore. Sometimes I joined our timber cruiser on a short local job. Then, for some of the finest trout fishing in the world my boss took me sixteen miles up the river to Indian Gardens, the site of a long-abandoned Indian village where the company had a storage dam and a small hunting lodge.

That autumn I went on a hunt for moose at the invitation of two brothers who had a shack up the river. They were good-natured lazy drawling men who worked in the pulp mills in winter and spent the rest of the year fishing, hunting, and just plain loafing. I had yet to learn that you cannot walk far in the Nova Scotia woods without coming to a swamp. I was dressed in ankle boots, puttees, thin drill breeches, cotton underwear, a flannel shirt and a cheap mackinaw jacket.

The brothers let me use their rifle, an old 38-55 Marlin, if I brought my own ammunition. We ranged a few miles about their camp but saw no game. They had shot over that area thoroughly.

Finally they took me some miles farther up the river by canoe and then struck off through the forest towards an open stretch of swampy wild meadows, a natural calling-place for moose. After a lot of wandering and arguing between the brothers about the right direction we reached it at nightfall. Without tent or blanket we cut brushwood for a bed, lit a fire, and lay down for the night. With feet to the fire, the brothers slept as cosily as hibernating bears while I lay awake, listening to their snores and the rattle of my teeth and getting up frequently to put more wood on the fire. There was ice on the swamp pools in the morning when one of the brothers began calling, using a birchbark horn like a speaking trumpet to utter the long imploring *moo* of a lady moose in want of love. The sound echoed for miles in the frosty silence.

After a time a bull moose answered far away, making sounds like a basso profundo with a very bad cough. Gradually the sounds came nearer. He burst into the open at a distance of perhaps five hundred yards and halted there. Quite rightly the brothers would not let me shoot at that range and went on calling to coax the bull further towards us. He was wary of crossing the open and did not move. After a time the air began to stir after the night's frost, and soon there was a breeze in which the bull caught our human scent and vanished. The breeze made further calling hopeless, so we tramped back to the canoe, again with much wandering and argument.

This expedition taught me two good lessons. The first was to dress suitably for a journey in the bush. The other and more important lesson was that the so-called born woodsman, without a compass and depending on instinct and "an eye for country," does a lot of wandering on his way from one place in the woods to another. With a good map and a compass even a greenhorn like me could walk a straight course and save time and sweat. After that I used my father's army compass, and when I wanted to explore I got the timber cruiser to draw a little map for my guidance. Eventually I was able to go anywhere I wished. Thus I discovered the marvellous freedom of the forest, where anyone with a good pair of legs and a compass could leave the highway's stink and noise and walk away into a green and quiet world. I did not realize the pleasure of this all at once. It came to me gradually in the course of time and increasing ventures into the woods and streams that covered the Mersey watershed.

*   *   *

The people of the village were friendly to the young stranger in their midst, and I enjoyed their talk about the river and the forest as well as the free and easy gossip about their lives. Most of those employed at the pulp mills had no education beyond the first few grades of the village school. After the first long winter at Potanoc, with occasional four-mile hikes or (if I was lucky) sleigh rides to town for the Saturday-night movie show, I began walking to the Anglican church at Liverpool on fine Sunday mornings. This was from no religious urge but to seek acquaintance with people who had books to lend. Once or twice I was invited to lunch there before tramping back to Potanoc; but most of the church folk I met were reserved in manner, as I was myself behind my inquiring face, and while I made a few acquaintances I cannot recall a single friendship arising from these pilgrimages.

*   *   *

I began to hear the story of this region during the past fifty years, in which Liverpool and Milton had declined from prosperity and a bustling population to their present state of doldrums and poverty. It had been the habit of most Nova Scotians to blame all their economic ills on the entry of their province into the Canadian federation in 1867. I learned gradually from local family history that the trouble had really begun in 1873, when a financial panic in the United States spread like a tidal wave from an earthquake. In this part of Nova Scotia it swept away the decayed structure of a wooden economy that had outlived its time.

During the prime of "wooden ships and iron men," Liverpool was busy launching windjammers and sending them in the carrying trade about the world. A few miles above Liverpool at the head of tidewater, Milton's sawmills prospered on the export trade to the West Indies and South America.

The panic of 1873-74 ruined the Liverpool banks and with them the whole business of Queens County. There was no chance of recovery. At that point in time the wooden windjammer was doomed by iron and steam. During the previous half century the lumbermen had cut most of the tall white pine that once covered a large part of the Mersey watershed. There was plenty of other wood in the forest, but the overseas markets wanted white pine and little else. By 1876 nearly all of the old established shipping and lumbering firms in the county were bankrupt, and their employees were

126

penniless. Their descendants in my day talked of "the time of the failures" as if it were the end of a civilization. In a way I suppose it was.

During the nearly half a century since the collapse many people had drifted away to the States or to western Canada. In Milton the three churches built in the bygone days were now far too big for the worshippers who came to the sound of the bells on Sunday morning. In winter, or when rain forbade the long tramp to Liverpool, I attended these churches in rotation. It was the best way to meet the people and compare their religious practices. Except for the rite of baptism (which someone described to me as "a choice of sprinkle or dunk") I could not find much difference, and I was astonished to see these people, with their small incomes, maintaining three preachers and three big echoing arks when all of the congregations together could hardly fill one.

There were puritans among them in a direct line of descent from colonial Massachusetts, whence most of their ancestors migrated to Nova Scotia in the eighteenth century, and I heard much denunciation of sin from the pulpits. Yet many of the men drank smuggled rum in this holy time of Prohibition, which the pulpits revered as an act of God, and the cheerful village tattle spoke of more than a few persons (even one or two ladies in church choirs) who did not seem to know about the sexual commandment in the laws of Moses. Gossip being what it is, no doubt there were breaches in the law about false witness, too.

* * *

One evening in the late summer of 1924 I went with a party of young men and women to a "corn boil" beside the Medway River. It was the first entertainment of this kind I had ever seen. The place was a grove of trees on a high bank, looking down on the river gleaming in moonlight, and someone had made a large stone fireplace in a clearing there for the benefit of parties like this. The lights and shadows thrown by the fire, the delicious taste of corn plucked fresh from the stalk and cooked and coated with butter, the young people laughing and singing, all made it a delightful affair.

After a time I noticed couples leaving the firelight and sauntering away into the darkness of the wood. I turned to a girl sitting beside me and suggested that we do that, too. She arose without hesitation. Her face was plain, but she had a friendly smile and the good figure and legs of a healthy country girl in her twenties. In the dark of the trees I put my arm about her waist and kissed her, and she responded warmly. We sank down in a mossy hollow. Without a word spoken she granted me release from the tension that had troubled me increasingly in the past three years.

I had seen and heard a lot about sex in my green years at sea, and I was revolted by its results in some of my shipmates; but now in this abode of clean femininity that bogey vanished. Suddenly now, in simple human nature, I had to prove my manhood to myself and to the girl. For all my supposed knowledge I was awkward about it, but happily for me the young woman had some experience and an amiable patience, for which I was silently and humbly grateful. On further occasions we enjoyed each other much better. Eventually, like so many Nova Scotian girls in those hard times, she went away to the States to train as a hospital nurse, and she married there. I never saw her again but I never forgot her.

It is droll to reflect that the Department of Naval Service had recognized my manhood with a first-class certificate, signed and sealed, when I passed the age of eighteen. My real certificate, unwritten and unsealed, was granted me at the age of twenty-one by a good-natured girl in the Medway forest.

Later on there were other light love affairs in the village and on Halifax holidays. None of the ladies were virgin, and the single ones knew that on eighty-five dollars a month I could hardly support myself, let alone a wife. I was no Don Juan, just a healthy young man subject to the male need, which is strong and often urgent to the point of torture. Thenceforth if I was fortunate at urgent times I met somewhere a woman of charm and warmth who sensed my need and was generous.

I am an old fogy now, of course, and there are some attitudes of youth in the present day that I dislike, notably an arrogant assumption that my war-bedevilled and hard-driven generation made a mess of the world for them to solve, but I cannot condemn with equal arrogance their own sexual emancipation. A determined and pitiless scheme of Nature (or Creation or whatever else it may be called) implants in every normal young man a sexual hunger that gives him no respite day or night, for even his dreams are part of the scheme, no matter how hard he works or studies or tires himself in athletic pursuits.

In my time, if he refused to submit his clean flesh to the foul pit of a Doll Tearsheet he usually had to suffer the hunger for years before he could afford to marry. Young and poor, I knew that ache until I found that in my world there were wholesome and pleasant women willing to give me the solace that only they could provide. Nowadays, with the Pill and other safeguards, a young woman can be as natural as Eve if she wishes, without any shadow of old taboos and punishments; and when she wants marriage and children she can select a mate with the wisdom of some experience rather than the blind chance forced on other generations of women by the hag-ridden age in which they lived. If there is true amity and not just stupid lechery, I see nothing wicked or harmful in tentative sexual relationships between young men and women who have discovered a liking for each other. Excess is the bad thing, and that is true of other natural needs and gratifications like eating and drinking.

The true enjoyment of life is not for gluttons.

* * *

I spent the Christmas holidays of that year with my family in Halifax, looked up old acquaintances, found some new ones, and made inquiries about a job. I found that the post-war slump in Halifax was getting worse instead of better, and I was advised to hang onto my job in the backwoods. So I stayed there after the one year I had set for myself, making the best of a very bad bargain at eighty-five dollars a month.

To extend my knowledge I started a correspondence course with the Nova Scotia Technical College, which gave me something to do on dull evenings. Not that all my evenings were dull. Apart from occasional lovemaking, which was always delightful, my social life found new interests. Down the river in Liverpool some young musicians had got together and organized dances in the assembly room of Town Hall, and there I made new acquaintances.

One was an American "millionaire" who turned up at the local hotel in midwinter, calling himself Lou Keytes. He was fortyish, bald, with a bushy black beard very uncommon at that time and invariably dressed in the style of a city slicker, from bowler hat to pearl grey spats. He spoke of the States with contempt and said he wanted to get away from it all. Our roads were not ploughed in winter then, and in late fall every motorist laid up his car until spring. Keytes therefore whiled away the winter cultivating the young dancing set in Liverpool. Because he had an ingratiating manner and was lavish in sending out for refreshments, we naturally considered him a jolly good fellow.

When spring came he bought an expensive car, and soon after that he acquired a large hunting lodge by the shore of a lake thirty miles away through the woods along the motor road to Annapolis. He spent about fifty thousand dollars making it over and furnishing it for the entertainment of his guests. I was one of the young people who enjoyed his parties there, travelling with fortunate friends who had cars. We were all astonished some months later when he was arrested in Halifax and revealed as a notorious Chicago swindler name Leo Koretz, wanted by police in the United States for using the mails to defraud. Away went our jolly millionaire to trial and an Illinois jail.

That summer I met other visitors who were not only charming and hospitable but also genuine, an American family that spent every summer in a rambling old house at Mill Village, twelve miles from where I lived. I was introduced to them by a Harvard student summering in Milton who knew their daughter and the daughter's guest, a girl about my age. They had what to me was a tremendous car, a Winton Six. In this on Saturdays the girls would pick me up after work at the pulp mill office, call for the student in Milton, and then whisk us away for a weekend with the family, playing tennis, swimming, and making short canoe trips on the Medway River. On other fine days at five o'clock the car appeared at the office with the girls and a hamper packed with food and drink, and away we went to the seashore for a bathe and a picnic. There were beautiful sand beaches within a few miles of Liverpool, not much frequented in that remote time when few people had a car, and usually on these occasions they were ours alone. The house at Mill Village was filled with lively and intelligent visitors, and the summer flew by. When the family returned to the States in the fall I had made friendships that continued for nearly forty-five years.

*   *   *

A very different but equally long and interesting friendship began when I found a band of Micmac Indians living a short distance through the woods from Cowies Falls. One or two of their men laboured in the mill there, but the rest would work only as guides to hunters and fishermen. Their women made baskets for sale in Milton and Liverpool. All spoke English well but they used their own language in the home, and the older ones knew much lore of their

130

people. At first I was interested in the meaning of Indian place-names on our timber cruiser's maps. As time went by I found their whole knowledge fascinating, and for better understanding I learned a smattering of their language.

*   *   *

In the autumn of 1924 I went moose hunting with my boss and the timber cruiser in the forest west of Indian Gardens. By this time I had waterproof boots and other suitable raiment for the woods. I borrowed an old Mauser rifle for the moose. We travelled by car on the Annapolis road to a place called Sixteen Mile, and from there walked eight miles behind a wagon over a rough tote road of the loggers to Indian Gardens. The simple hunting lodge of the Macleod Company stood on the west bank of the river, looking across foaming rapids to a level shelf at the foot of the east bank which the Indians had cultivated in a time going back into legend, before the coming of white men to the Mersey River. It was a lovely glen, surrounded by oak and other hardwood trees. The sole inhabitant was a man called Pete, who tended the water gates in the dam.

We stayed there overnight and the next morning tramped again behind Pete's wagon, laden with our canoe and supplies and gear. After two or three miles we came to a stretch of water called Kempton Lake, after the bygone logger who cut the virgin pine about it. The Indians had an older and much more significant name meaning Place-where-people-were-burned. It was where the ancient inhabitants of Indian Gardens had taken their dead for secret cremation and burial.

Pete dumped our stuff on the lake shore. My two companions paddled away to the western tip of the lake with the tent and some of the supplies, and one remained there pitching the tent while the other brought the canoe back for me and the rest of the gear. I had an hour or more of solitude in which to contemplate the lake, which was perfectly calm, like a mirror, reflecting the red maples along the shores. I had seen autumn colour on my travels with the two arguing brothers last year, but nothing to touch this. The rifle lay forgotten at my side. My friends had gone out of sight. The whole thing seemed a splendid secret hidden in the forest by Glooscap, the magician of the Micmacs, just for me. I was to learn in time that the hinterland of Nova Scotia had hundreds of such miracles, all linked by streams and portages for travellers like me.

This spell of contemplation was broken by the canoe returning for me, and I took up a paddle and worked my passage to the other end of the lake. In the evening firelight my companions told me that this lake and two others, Long Lake and Eagle Lake, lay very close together, screened from each other by narrow ridges of timber. Long ago the Indians had warned white loggers to keep out of the region about these lakes because it was haunted by frightful spirits. The loggers went in and cut the big timber anyway, and without harm, although some said they heard strange sounds at night. Old lumbermen in Milton still called it the "Injun Devil country." None of them had ever bothered to learn the Indians' name for Kempton Lake, and what it meant, and why. I did not realize myself, until I learned more of the language, that the Indians just wanted to keep white intruders from tramping over the ashes of their forefathers.

* * *

A sluggish stream flowed into the tip of the lake, draining miles of swamp and meadows covered with long wild grass, bushes of Labrador tea, and spindling hackmatack trees. Water lilies and their roots, a favourite food of the moose, flourished in its black pools. A short walk from our tent brought us to a wooded knoll like a small island in the eastern end of the swamp. It offered concealment for hunters with a long view up the meadows, and it was Gordon's chosen "calling place" for years. Wandering moose had worn a path across the knoll. Gordon and the cruiser posted themselves under an old pine at the west end where they had the long view. In case a moose came across the short space of swamp at the east end, they posted me in the path there. They suspected the greenhorn of "buck fever," and to make sure I didn't ruin everything with a wild shot at the wrong time they insisted that I must not have a cartridge in the old Mauser's breech. They would signal me, they said, when to "rack in a shell."

There had been a sharp frost in the night. With daylight a cold mist arose from the swamp and hung low over it. In the still air the conditions for "calling" were perfect. Gordon's imitation of an amorous cow moose went echoing far along the wooded borders of the swamp. Soon we heard a bull coming along the north edge, uttering a deep *whoof* from time to time, and banging his horns against trees to warn off any other bulls and to show the invisible lady what a hell of a fellow he was. He was wary enough to choose the short open crossing at my end of the knoll, and to stop whoofing when he left the cover of the trees, although he was still well hidden in the mist. There was a tremendous splash when he plunged into the stream but after that only a silence that prickled my ears. I was sure that the bull was coming up the old game path in which I crouched. Thirty yards away, Gordon and the cruiser were sure that the bull would come direct to the calling place, where they had killed others in the past. The top of the knoll was above the mist, and we could see each other clearly.

When I made a motion to "rack in a shell" they gave violent hand signals for me to keep still. There was a bend in the path just below me, and suddenly the bull appeared there with just his head and horns showing above the mist. The tip of the horns must have been eight feet above the ground, and as I was sitting on the ground he looked enormous. Again I turned to the others, pointing to the moose, which of course they could not see, and to the empty breech of my rifle. Again I got those urgent signals to keep still. I wondered why they wanted a better target. In a few more steps this monster would tread on me. A moose has a marvellous sense of direction and distance. The bull was staring over my head straight towards the pine tree whence the invisible cow had uttered her last call. Then he looked down and saw me.

Later experiences taught me that a bull moose may take an irate view of the swindle when he finds a mere human where he expected an inviting lady moose. The swindler may have to scramble up a tree if for any reason he can't kill the animal quickly. This bull, however, wheeled around and sprang away into the mist, and we heard the plunge as he recrossed the stream. My boss resumed seductive sounds with his birchbark horn but the game was up. A breeze began to sweep the mist away and to betray our scent. Gordon and the timber cruiser refused to believe that the bull had come so close to me until they saw his tracks in the frost.

For some days the wind persisted and made calling useless. We turned to "still-hunting" (moving stealthily to windward through the woods) with no luck at all. Then I had to return to my desk in Milton, and another man took my place as the greenhorn of the party, although he'd had some experience. On the next morning of frosty calm the party returned to the calling place and resumed the same posts. The newcomer, a middle-aged dentist from Liverpool, was placed in my spot at the bend in the path. Wiser than I, he concealed himself in a spruce thicket by the path and silently racked a cartridge into the breech of his rifle. Again a moose came to the call in the same way, and the same thing happened, up to a point – a point where the dentist poked his rifle out of the thicket and pulled the trigger. The moose fell dead almost at his feet.

Years afterward I wrote a novel called *His Majesty's Yankees*, and I opened it with a party of colonial hunters in that place, only a mile or two from the old beaver meadow where the people from Indian Gardens used to burn their dead. They believed that hostile strangers could work frightful mischief on the living tribe by some hocus-pocus over the dead, so they performed the death rites and buried the ashes in deep silt at the foot of the lake.

*   *   *

In time I learned from Gordon the art of moose-calling well enough to entice bulls close to me. I did it with interest in this old Indian skill and, I must admit, a pleasant sense of danger. I carried a gun in case of need but I never had to use it. I saw no sport in killing these huge animals after luring them within easy rifle shot, as most hunters did in the rutting season. I was not alone in realizing how rapidly the slaughter was increasing with the spread of motor roads and the swarm of hunters every year. As the caribou had vanished from Nova Scotia, so the moose would go because eventually the kill passes the point where survivors of the species can reproduce effectively, and then disease does the rest. The government of Nova Scotia banned moose hunting in 1938, in time to save them in the eastern half of the peninsula, but in our western half this splendid animal was never numerous again in my lifetime.

*   *   *

In the winter of '24 I heard much talk of politics. The Liberal Party had been in power at Halifax for more than forty years, and like any party in power too long it was lazy, arrogant and corrupt. All government supplies and works were delivered at a fat profit by Liberal merchants and contractors. All government jobs went to Liberals. Even to get a few weeks of summer work with pick and shovel on the roads, the poor labourers of the villages had to swear to illiteracy and make an open vote for the Liberals at every poll, or lapse into semi-starvation on the food dole from the local Poor Rates Committee.

As I have said, I was an instinctive rebel against oppressive power or the threat of it from anybody, beginning with my father's well-meant family discipline and continuing in my encounters with such people as Captain McAhab and the truculent weasel at Sable Island. Now I saw oppression in another and much larger form, and so did thousands of other young Nova Scotians of my time.

In the county of Queens where I lived the matter was somewhat complicated. The only visible owner of the Macleod pulp mills, Mr. Barnjum, had been an ardent supporter of the Liberal Party from away back when he wangled the infamous "Big Lease" of government timberland in Cape Breton. Barnjum got the lease for an American paper company which exported the wood raw. They got it for fifty cents an acre.

Since then Barnjum had used his Liberal influence to get cheap timberland for himself in western Nova Scotia. When he and his Boston backers put together their neat package of timber and waterpower on the Mersey River in 1919 they were confident in the benign indifference of the Liberal government at Halifax. But then for the first time something went wrong.

In 1919 that government created the Nova Scotia Power Commission to expropriate a partly built hydro-electric development at Saint Margaret's Bay. It was the enterprise of a private company (with too many Tories on its board of directors) that supplied electricity to the city of Halifax. On the face of it this takeover was made to please the numerous voters in Halifax, but there was a paragraph in the covering legislation saying that the new commission could expropriate any partly developed or undeveloped waterpower in the province. Barnjum and the Boston syndicate caught the whiff of danger to their cozy package on the Mersey. By 1924 Barnjum's acute political nose caught the unmistakable scent of something else. The post-war hard times in Nova Scotia, and the smug "I'm-all-right" attitude of well-paid Liberal officials in the midst of poverty, created a hot boiling in the old political pot for the first time in more than forty years. The Conservatives, so long a small and despised minority ("those Tories") in every town and village, now found themselves with a host of young veterans of the war and other sympathizers eager to "chuck out those fellows in Halifax." And a general election was due in 1925.

So Mr. Barnjum turned his coat and became an ardent Tory. First he ordered my boss to stand as a Conservative candidate in Queens County. Then, seeing the swift rise of the Tory tide, he ordered Gordon to step down and ran himself. In his nomination speech he promised to build a paper-manufacturing industry employing several thousand men in the woods, at the paper machines and in ships. He fetched a prominent American engineer (at four hundred dollars a day) to survey a site for the mill near Liverpool and draw an exact plan, showing all the buildings, railway sidings and wharves to be created there. Barnjum displayed this plan at all his political meetings in the spring of 1925.

Then a rival Santa Claus popped up on our rustic scene, a sharp and energetic man named Ralph Bell, whose various enterprises included a company shipping raw pulpwood to the States. Bell came to support the Liberal candidates in Queens County with a promise of his own. He would build a big paper industry at Liverpool, and like Barnjum he displayed an elaborate plan of it. Unlike Barnjum he was not running for office, as he carefully pointed out, so that on the face of it he had nothing to gain by fooling the electorate. That left Barnjum only one thing to do. He made a solemn declaration that he would resign the seat if *his* paper mill was not under construction within twelve months of his election.

*   *   *

I knew nothing of politics. As a soldier my father had a low opinion of what he called "politicos," and I felt the same; but like every other staff employee of the Macleod Company I was ordered to join the Conservative organization in the Milton district and get busy. In other circumstances I would have told Mr. Barnjum to take a long running jump into the river. My salary after two years' experience had been raised to one hundred dollars a month, but it was still poor pay. I knew, however, that salaries and wages in modern newsprint paper mills were among the highest in Canada. An industry of the size that both these promising gentlemen were talking about would not only restore the old-time prosperity of the county but boost it to a height never known before. I would have worked cheerfully for the Devil himself if I thought he would bring such a boon, and so I joined the band of Tory workers in Milton and began to learn the ins and outs of rural politics.

Again I felt like Alice in Wonderland. The old hands went over a list of voters in the Milton polling district and marked all dyed-in-the-wool "Grits" and "Tories" with a pencilled "L" or "C" as the case might be. This left a surprising number of others whose votes were for sale. Not all of these were downright poor. The payment of "boodle money" in the rural parts and small towns of Nova Scotia was an old and hoary practice, and many voters considered it their due at every provincial or federal election. When our old hands had figured out the exact number of boodle votes in our district it was enough to swing the majority to the party that had more money and rum than the other. It was as simple as that.

The ways and means committee of the Conservative Party at Halifax, allotting their funds among the provincial constituencies, decided that wealthy candidate Barnjum could take care of Queens County and so gave us nothing. When this was put to the gentleman himself, he struck an attitude of pious rectitude. He would pay legitimate expenses, yes, but not a dollar for boodle or for rum. The truth was that he was sure his promised paper mill would elect him and he need not spend much cash.

This created dismay among our Tory crew. Finally somebody or bodies scraped up enough cash to bid two dollars for every floating vote in the county and to provide enough smuggled rum. Then came another thunderbolt. Some mysterious person had given the Liberal Party in our small county thirty thousand dollars in ten-dollar banknotes, to be used as they saw fit. The result was hilarious. I found myself running about the western half of Milton in a Model T Ford, steered by the timber cruiser, and striving to corrupt the voters there with my pockets full of two-dollar bills.

My Liberal opponent in this half of the polling district, an amiable chap named Ralph Freeman, had a Ford of his own and his pockets full of ten-dollar bills. At the end of the day the Liberals had hauled to the polls not only the faithful of their own party but most of the boodles as well, but a transfiguration took place inside the booths. Nearly all of them voted Tory. What they really voted for, of course, was Barnjum's paper mill. They had no faith in Bell's. The same Tory tide flowed all over the province, paper mills or no paper mills, and the Conservatives had a smashing victory after forty-three years in the wilderness.

Barnjum tried to sell the Mersey River package within his specified twelve months, calling on paper interests in Canada, the United States and Britain. The trouble was that he and his American backers were too greedy. The price they demanded for their power-and-timber package was extortionate. More than that, people who investigated the Mersey proposition in depth soon found that the professed ownership of the waterpower through the dummy Mersey Hydraulic Company had a very shaky basis.

Among those who hired competent people to look into the Mersey package was a man with the quaintly appropriate name of Izaak Walton Killam, a Nova Scotian who had gone to Montreal as a young man and learned the art of angling for big money under the expert guidance of Max Aitken. When Aitken went off to fish the more promising streams of England (and to become famous as Lord Beaverbrook), he sold his Royal Securities Company to Killam. Working quietly through this company, Killam now devised real plans for a paper industry at the Mersey mouth, ignoring the Boston syndicate's woodlands and arranging for other timber supplies. For the huge power needs of such an industry, economically run entirely by electricity, he found the Nova Scotia Power Commission ready and willing to expropriate all the hydro-power sites on our river and to install the necessary dams and dynamos. Barnjum's wily switch of politics had done him no good at all.

At the end of the avowed year he resigned his seat in the Nova Scotia Assembly, which he had found a bore anyway. He went on seeking a buyer for the syndicate's timberlands and ramshackle pulp mills, and from 1926 to 1928 we heard rumours of his activities. I hoped that something would come out of all this, for I had changed my mind about going back to Halifax. I liked this region of forest and lakes and streams, and if I could make a decent living here, I wanted to stay.

* * *

There was another reason. I have mentioned Ralph Freeman and our merry boodling contest in the election of 1925. He was a jovial fellow in his twenties, a grandson of one of the well-to-do shipbuilders who were ruined in the 1870s, and much farther back his ancestors were Pilgrims at Cape Cod. His father had died shortly after Ralph's return from army service in 1919, leaving him the immediate task of supporting his mother and young brother in the small family home at Milton. A sister named Edith also lived at home, earning a slender income as a music teacher. She was about my age, not at all pretty, but a petite and amusing chatterbox who played a good game of tennis and loved parties. She did not take her music seriously and preferred to play waltzes and fox-trots.

Although her home church was Congregational, she had studied music at a Baptist ladies' seminary in the Annapolis Valley, and after graduation she spend an unsuccessful year trying to work up a piano-teaching practice in the town of Annapolis. She came home to Milton in 1924, the year after I arrived there. Soon I was invited to dine at the Freeman house. It seems a bit fantastic to me now, but before long I was spending whole evenings there and playing duets with the music teacher. Long afterwards she declared she had marked me down for a husband the moment she saw me, but married ladies sometimes amuse themselves with quips like that.

Anyhow, by the spring of 1926 we were engaged to be married the next year, and I gave her a ring with a small diamond, the best I could afford. Years afterward I could afford a much better one, but she refused and wore the small diamond to her death in 1975. As I now had three years' experience, I asked my boss to raise my salary to $125 (the pay given Parker before me) and he consented, although the value of wood pulp had gone down so far that the old Macleod mills were losing money. Indeed, soon after this he left his own job to look for a better one in the States.

I was lucky in finding a house for sale a few yards from my fiancée's home. She was delighted of course and so was I. It was an interesting old farmhouse in the Cape Cod style, built about 1815 at a guess, with several acres of land, an orchard, a huge barn, and a small clay tennis court. The house and barn were badly in need of repair, and I was able to buy the whole property for $500 cash and a mortgage for $1,400.

When my boss resigned his job the syndicate in Boston had to find another manager. The mechanical superintendent of the mills was a good old man named Freeman, a distant relation of my fiancée. He knew nothing of office business. I knew the office business but nothing of mill machinery. The manager had to be an all-round man who could deal with business affairs, find new ideas for nursing obsolete machinery, and take care of all that valuable timberland. My predecessor as bookkeeper, Austin Parker, had now spent three years with an American paper company, partly in New York and partly as assistant manager of their wood-pulp mill in Quebec. He was a capable and experienced man in every way. The syndicate got in touch with him. At first he could see no future in Milton, but he was offered a much larger salary and there was the prospect of an executive post in any new paper industry at Liverpool, no matter who built it. So he and his wife returned to Milton, and from that day to this they have been the closest and best of my friends.

For almost a year, from July '26 to June '27 when I was married, I kept bachelor's hall in my rambling old house, sleeping on a camp cot in the kitchen for the warmth of the stove, eating sketchy meals, spending my spare time, often till midnight, scraping and painting, installing carpets and linoleum, uncrating and setting up new furniture, and so on. Electricians came and rewired the house. Carpenters removed the moss-covered shingles on the leaky roof and replaced them with modern synthetic ones.

In the absence of her Congregational pastor my fiancée decided to marry me in the Baptist church across the bridge, whose pastor had served in the Royal Flying Corps during the late war. He had been shot down, spent a long time in German prison camps, and still suffered from nervous shock. Ours was his first church wedding. The poor man's hands trembled as he held his prayer book before us. When he came to the question, "Do you take this woman to be your lawful wedded wife?" he asked if I took "this man." Dutifully I said, "I do."

As we made our way towards the church door, the bride's long veil caught and tore badly on a pew corner. All in all it was an awkward affair, even when we got outside, for there a group of villagers were throwing rice and salt in our faces. Possibly in some ancient custom salt was supposed to bring good luck. Possibly it was just a whim of some joker in the pack. My mouth was open, laughing, when we passed through the doorway, and I could still taste the salt when I signed the register in the rectory across the street.

Years later, looking back on a marriage that was like the sea, sparkling and beautiful at times, dark and stormy at others, with long intervals in which I plunged myself into study and writing, I knew that taste of salt was an omen. Our differences of background, outlook and temperament were so wide that only the haze of young romance could have concealed them. Love really is blind. Like many other blind marriages in those days, when divorce was too difficult and expensive for any but the rich, ours had a lot of ups and downs before we learned how to live with each other on an even plane.

While the first delicious haze lasted it was wonderful, and we spent a happy honeymoon in the little hunting lodge at Indian Gardens. The Parkers took us in their car as far as Sixteen Mile, where I had a horse and buggy awaiting us, and I drove with my bride and baggage over eight rough miles of tote road through the woods and then crossed over the river on a precariously narrow dam. I have mentioned the beauty of the glen at Indian Gardens. We enjoyed it in the sunshine and moonshine of early summer, and the trout fishing was like all the rest of it, out of this world.

140

It was a paradise soon to be lost. Within a year a construction army bulldozed a motor road up the east side of the river from Milton, and at Indian Gardens they erected barracks, cookhouse and dining hall and began to build a high dam some distance below the Gardens at what our river-drivers used to call The Ledges. As the water slowly rose behind this dam it washed out of the slope on the east side of the river a vast scatter of stone tools, arrowheads, bits of pottery and other primitive artifacts. These exposures continued for many months until the water reached the crest of the old glen, revealing the full size of an ancient Indian town extending half a mile along the slope, which in our ignorance we had confined to the small flat once cultivated down by the river. Today the Indian Gardens lie under about seventy feet of water, and the site of our honeymoon lies drowned and buried with them.

*　*　*

When we returned to Milton I found bad news. The wood-pulp market had slumped so far that the Boston owners ordered Parker to close the mills, keeping only a few key men on reduced wages. My pay was cut back to $100 a month. Indeed, it looked as if I would be out of a job altogether before long. Some of our mill hands departed in search of a job in the States; others existed on their small savings or cast themselves on the meagre food chits of the village Poor Rates Committee. The days of unemployment insurance and a humane standard of assistance to the poor were far away in the future.

Most of my Sable Island savings had been spent on the house and furniture. I had to make regular payments on the mortgage or lose the property. For the benefit of my wife I had taken out a life insurance policy with an annual payment of $240. Within a few weeks of the honeymoon she found herself pregnant.

If the outlook needed a gloomier note, I found one in the hayloft of the barn, which had a small compartment at one end. Peering curiously into this remote coop one day I noticed an old organ stool lying on its side. Overhead was a loop of rope knotted around a beam, and the rope had been cut off, apparently with a knife, just below the beam. I mentioned this to old Jimmy the village cobbler, who had lived all his days across the road. He said, "Ah yes, I mind that well. Your house was Will Ford's long ago. Had a sawmill up to Potanoc. Got in debt. Lost everything. Hung himself up there in the barn one day in 1906."

141

My own troubles were not that bad but they made it urgent for me to earn more money somehow. I was a subscriber to *Maclean's Magazine* in Toronto, which claimed to be Canada's national magazine, and it occurred to me that I might try my hand at short stories or articles about Nova Scotia. I still had the battered old typewriter I bought from Bill Williams in my last days as a brass-pounder, and on this I began to experiment in the evenings after supper, with the machine on our dining table where the light was best.

Early in the winter of 1927 the managing editor of *Maclean's*, Napier Moore, wrote an editorial complaint about the quality of the fiction he received from Canadian authors and would-be authors. He wanted material with a fresh note and would prefer humour or at any rate something whimsical. So I sat down to write something fresh and whimsical. I chose a scene like Sable Island and worked out a fable that we brasspounders would have loved to happen.

It was about the descent of three pompous officials on a visit of inspection, landing from the supply steamer and intending to stay only a few hours. The weather turned bad suddenly. It was impossible to get a boat off the beach for many days, during which the visitors had to subsist on the depleted rations of the operators, eked out with gulls' eggs. In calculating supplies for the station every three months, the officials never made allowances for gales, surf, or other unkind acts of God, and the food was apt to run short before God relented. We actually did eat gulls' eggs at one time on Sable Island. I entitled the story "The Three Wise Men," and after many revisions it had about six thousand words. Shortly before Christmas I sent it to *Maclean's*.

As the year 1928 opened we had word from Boston that some of the baled pulp left on hand when the mills closed last year had been sold at a sacrifice price to a paper mill in Maryland. A steamer had been chartered to load the bales at Liverpool, and Parker was ordered to cut out every possible cent of cost in getting the pulp to the ship. Consequently he and the rest of us still on the payroll laboured along with the villagers hired for this job. It was hard and heavy work. Each bale had weighed 228 pounds when it came off the mill press, but since then in the open sheds it had absorbed

142

moisture and weighed up to three hundred pounds. These moist bales had now frozen together in their tiers to the shed roofs. Every bale had to be pried loose with peavies, manhandled down to the floor, placed on a big wheelbarrow, trundled up a gangway into a railway boxcar, and again stacked to the roof of the car.

Parker was a muscular six-footer of thirty-three. I was in my twenty-fifth year, not as tall or as strong but in the good condition that came from much travel in the woods. Even so, at the end of a day at this work I had barely enough strength to trudge two miles back to my home in the village. The poor labourers who worked alongside us for two dollars a day had been existing for the past six months on vegetables from their small gardens, then bread and molasses, wild rabbits, and moose meat when they could get it. Some were exhausted before the end of one day and had to drop out. The rest toughed it out with the desperation of men with hungry families. It was pitiful to see them, and in my heart I raged at the comfortable owners whose schemes and practices had brought about these conditions. Long afterwards, in a novel called *The Wings of Night*, I depicted those practices and conditions in a village I called Oak Falls.

*   *   *

In January 1928 there was deep snow about our silent mills and thick ice on the millponds. The mill canal, penstock and tailrace made a straight line across a large bend in the river in the place called Rapid Falls. With the canal gates closed, the whole torrent was pouring over the dam and down the rapids in its old bed. Merely for something to pass the time, our mill superintendent and a watchman, both old men, took axes one day and began to chop away some of the ice above the dam.

I was alone in the office when the watchman staggered in after a long run in the snow, gasping, "Tommy! Mister Freeman! Over the dam!" I ran like mad down to the railway bridge. Above it the rapids were too turbulent to freeze, but below lay the thick ice of Cowies Pond, a mile long. I knew that Freeman had been a good swimmer in his younger days, but every protruding rock in the rapids was now coated with ice, and he would be swept down very fast. My hope was that I might reach the bridge before he did and perhaps be able to stretch a hand to him. I waited there some time without sight of him and then hurried through the snow around the bend of the rapids to the mill dam. There was no sign of him anywhere. By this time Parker had returned from town. He quickly organized a search party with boats and makeshift grapplings. They had a dangerous job in the rapids, and nothing came of it. The poor old chap had been swept down the rapids and under the ice of Cowies Pond before I reached the bridge.

For the next ten days we worked from dawn to dark trying to find his body. Parker went to Indian Gardens and helped Pete to lower the wooden gates in the storage dam, holding back the whole flow of the river as long as they dared, to give us a better chance to search below. After that we obtained long ice-cutting saws and removed much of the winter cover of Cowies Pond, sluicing the stuff over the lower mill dam so that we could drag the bottom. Finally we had to give up. In winter temperatures the corpse would not float to the surface. We could only wait till spring. Parker told the Indians and others who lived near Cowies Falls that the company would pay a reward for anyone finding it. One day in April an Indian noticed something bloated and hideous caught in the log sluice at Cowies Falls. Parker and I, with most of the pulp mill people, attended the funeral service next day.

* * *

My diary gave a brief account of poor Freeman's death on January 23, 1928, written under the strain of the day. Then a curt note of something else. "Today I received cheque for sixty dollars from Maclean's Magazine, payment for my first short story Three Wise Men." Napier Moore had paid one cent per word. I wish now that I had framed the cheque for a souvenir, but I needed the money and cashed it. When the story appeared in the magazine I found that Moore or his sub-editors had changed my text in many places. For example, I had one of my characters saying in his natural idiom that the barometer was dropping like a gull's dung. According to *Maclean's*, the barometer was just dropping. Their readers must never suspect that gulls dropped anything, especially in unexpected moments like, say, a barometer on Sable Island.

* * *

The fuel of the village was hardwood, felled, sawn, split and dried through a summer in woodshed or barn, as it had been since colonial times. As a prudent householder I had to provide for my next year's supply while enough snow remained for sledding it out of the woods, so I hired a couple of out-of-work mill hands to cut birch and maple in tree lengths on a ridge of second-growth timber a few miles behind my house. In the last week of February I went with a teamster and horse and sled to get the logs out to the village. We had a rough job because the swampy places were not frozen under the snow, and the horse plunged and floundered in them, but in a couple of days we managed it.

This gave me another occupation for the evenings, by the light of a lantern, cutting the logs into stove lengths with a bucksaw, splitting them with an axe, and stacking the firewood in the barn to dry. I think it was *Poor Richard's Almanack* that said, "Cut your own firewood and it will warm you twice." Very true, and there is something warming to the spirit, too. Birch and maple wood cut in sunny days near the end of winter, when sap has begun to flow, gives off a rich sweet smell in drying, very noticeable in the confines of a barn or woodshed. Whenever I did my nightly chore of filling the firewood boxes in the house I paused in the barn just to sniff that fragrance. In memory I can smell it still, especially nowadays when we burn oil and there is nothing but a stink.

*   *   *

My wife had been getting huge and uncomfortable during the winter. In March the birth came. Her mother and a village midwife came to attend her, and I summoned a doctor from Liverpool as well. A fat impersonal type, he went into the bedroom with his stethoscope, returned to the living room, announced, "This is going to be a slow one," dropped into a chair, threw a newspaper over his face, and went to sleep. As screams arose in the bedroom I felt like kicking him as I had kicked the weasel at Sable Island, and for the same reason. He ought to be on watch. From time to time the midwife came and wakened him, whispering something. He merely grunted and went back to sleep. At long intervals he did go into the bedroom and returned, shaking his head. After an eternity of agony for my wife, the child was born dead, as the doctor had known from the start.

The next day, in a snowstorm (I am not making this up), I got the trustees of the village cemetery to mark off a burial plot. They informed me that a stillborn child was buried without religious ceremony, never having lived. A man who ran a little shingle mill at the riverside was also the village coffin maker and undertaker. His hearse was a plain black box on wheels, drawn by his truck horse, and he brought a small white coffin the next afternoon. I sat with him on the journey across the river to the cemetery and saw the child conceived in the beauty of Indian Gardens disappear into a hole among the tottering tombstones of the village. It marked the apparent end of a phase in my life. My wife shrank from going through all that again, and for her sake so did I.

* * *

A few days later I had something else to think about. Premier Rhodes of Nova Scotia announced that financier I.W. Killam had been granted cutting rights on government-owned timberlands on the condition that he built a paper mill to manufacture the wood in this province. He added, "Mr. Killam guarantees to build a fifteen-million-dollar newsprint industry within two years."

The work began within a month of the announcement. Engineers came to inspect the hydro-electric power sites on the river. Others came to choose and lay out a site for the new mill at Brooklyn, a mile below the inner harbour bar, where there was deep water for cargo ships. In May a construction company began to cut a road-way through the woods on the east side of the river from Potanoc to Indian Gardens. Other gangs cleared ground for a base camp near our Rapid Falls mill and extended the existing CNR siding to it. Barracks, cookhouse, dining hall, warehouses and offices sprang up on the spot like magic.

Up the railway line from Liverpool came tractors, power shovels, and other machines and tools, and as the new motor road stretched mile after mile up the river a fleet of big trucks carried stores and material to a growing chain of construction camps. By the midsummer of 1928 nearly a thousand men were at work on the river road, on the dam sites, and on the mill site at Brooklyn.

With all this in view I felt sure of a much better job next year, and I managed to defer payments on my mortgage until then. For the present I had worries enough on a hundred dollars a month. The pulp mills remained closed and my job could end without warning at a further pinch from Boston. I discussed this with my friend Parker, who agreed that there seemed to be no future in the old mills or in Barnjum's fantasies. He said, "Tom, you must do what you think best for yourself."

I walked over to the base camp of the construction company, asked for a job, and got one. Their office manager, a shrewd man from Ontario, said he would start me at the same pay I'd been getting from the pulp company, but he promised a substantial raise when I had proved I could do the job. I found the new work tedious and time consuming, although it did not require much intelligence or the training I'd had as an accountant. It was simply to keep stock records in the depot warehouses, which swallowed everything from shovels to cabbages as they came in carload lots up the railway line and then disgorged the stuff into a constant procession of motor trucks for various camps up the river.

My office was a coop of boards in a corner of the main warehouse with a window looking out on the camp yard. A gang of "muckers" was still busy there, levelling the yard with pick, shovel, and dynamite. They were lighthearted about the dynamite, merely covering each blast with a thin layer of brushwood weighted by a few railway ties. One day a tie sailed through my window like a wooden torpedo. Luckily, I had gone to consult the boss in the main office. My working hours were from 8A.M. to 6P.M., with an hour for lunch in the cookhouse. Otherwise I was busy every minute. Having sold my bike for needed money, I walked to and from the job, two miles each way.

Occasionally I got a motor ride up the new river road, and by September I was able to go all the way to Indian Gardens. The old beautiful glen was a sorry sight. The oaks and birches on both slopes above the river had been sheared and burned to clear the flowage of the new dam below. On the east crest a camp of wooden shacks held several hundred men, with their trucks, derricks, narrow-gauge railway, gasoline locomotives, and the rest.

The summer of 1928 had been hot and the river was low, for the water stored in the old wooden dam at Indian Gardens had run out by July. This made a problem for my friend Austin Parker. At his urging the Boston syndicate had decided to run the pulp mills long enough to use up the wood piled in the yard, before it began to rot. That could be done only with a strong flow of water in the river, which now depended on the autumn rains.

*   *   *

The Conservative government had been a little over three years in office at Halifax. They could stay another year before another election, but they were contemplating a dismal fact. After the enthusiastic tide that swept them into power in 1925 there had been a great ebbtide of disillusionment, because they had merely replaced

147

the notorious graft and corruption of the old Liberal regime with an equally blatant kind of their own.

One simple example. From my warehouse window I could see a string of railway boxcars on one of the sidings, filled with sacks of cement bought direct from the manufacturers at a price of sixty-six cents a sack. There was no room for it in the warehouses, so the construction company was paying demurrage to the CNR at a stiff daily rate for keeping the cars idle and in fact using them for storage. At the same time I could see trucks going up the road laden with cement from a Tory merchant in Liverpool, priced at ninety-five cents a sack. The construction boss had protested but he was told to shut up.

In the same way there was graft on the fleet of big construction trucks, all bought from a factory in Ontario that specialized in these vehicles and had no agency in Nova Scotia. A car dealer in Liverpool pulled the political wire to Halifax and got a fat commission on every one of them. Gloating as one Tory worker to another, he showed me a cheque for several thousand dollars and crowed, "This is the kind of thing you can get for nothing if you go after it."

The Conservative government decided to call an election in the early autumn of 1928, before the ebb got any lower. By that time I was utterly disgusted with it. So was my former boss Gordon, who had returned from the States in the hope of a job in the new industry. We made no secret of our disillusionment, but the Tory leader in Queens County continued to regard us as the key Tory devotees in the Milton polling district. In organizing the county districts for the coming election he did not neglect us. He called me on the phone and went into a long discussion of my prospects. Did I like the work I was doing now? The pay? The hours? He added that the construction work on which I was now engaged would be finished in a year or so.

I should have been suspicious but I was not. I knew he was no grafter himself. He was a well-to-do and clever man who played the game of politics as he played the game of poker, for the sheer pleasure of dealing, drawing, bluffing and playing absolutely to win. I liked him and would have taken his word for anything. At last he came to his point. He said he had been talking to the president of the new paper company, whose mill was now rising as big as a city block across the harbour from the little town of Liverpool. The president, an Ontario man, had asked him to recommend a young

Nova Scotian with business experience, preferably in the wood-pulp or paper business, and with the ability to compose and write good letters and reports. He wanted this young man for his personal secretary, and the salary would start at two hundred dollars a month. The Tory gentleman said he had told the president about me, my experience in the pulp business, and my sideline of "writing for *Maclean's Magazine*," and the job was mine if I wanted it.

Like a salmon fresh from the sea in spring, I leaped at this pretty fly and swallowed it without even thinking of a hook. I asked when I could have an interview with the president. Well, he was away on business in Montreal and New York. I would be notified later on. Just a week later on the provincial election was announced, and in all the polling districts the Tory workers were called together. Among other things we were told that the president of the new paper company was a red-hot supporter of the Conservative government, eager to bear a hand in the local campaign in every possible way.

When Gordon told me he had been promised a lucrative post as woods manager with the new company by the same Liverpool gentleman, in the same way, I had a qualm about what we had swallowed, but I put aside my suspicion. With the prospect of a new and interesting job at twice my present pay I worked hard in the campaign, going from door to door with persuasive talks and on election day visiting the voters with money in hand and a car to take them to the poll and back.

Barnjum and his embargo were now a dead issue, so we saw no more of him or Ralph Bell. When the polls closed our county had another Conservative majority but it was nothing like the triumph of 1925. All over Nova Scotia there was a big swing away from the Tories, and the government hung on with twenty-three members against twenty Liberals. The Liberals now were led by a supremely honest man, a young professor of law from Dalhousie University named Angus L. Macdonald. In later years I was to know him as a friend and admire him as a man.

Less than a month after the election I awoke from my giddy dream of affluence with the new company. The Tory gentleman in town evaded all my inquiries about the promised job, and I discovered that the president of the new paper company had brought with him from Ontario a very competent male secretary (who became a good friend of mine), just as Gordon discovered that the new mill had a woods manager, another man from Ontario. When I turned back to my boss at the construction depot on the river road, he blandly evaded *his* promise of a raise in pay when I had shown that I could do the job. As I had found with Barnjum and the Boston syndicate, the rule with distant owners and far-fetched bosses seemed to be that the natives of these parts weren't worth much, and the less you paid them the better.

Austin Parker now needed a bookkeeper for the active operation of the pulp mills, and I went back to my old job at the old pay. It was November, and although the river was rising with the fall rains there was not yet enough water to run the mills. But we had other work shipping the remainder of the stored pulp to the dock at Liverpool. Our penny-pinching owners in Boston had chartered an ancient American three-masted schooner named *Dorothy* to carry baled pulp to New York. Somehow, too, they had managed to place insurance on our cargo in this decrepit craft.

The owner-skipper of *Dorothy* was a lean Yankee, about fifty, with cold pewter eyes and a drawl. When his ship was loaded, he inquired the various depths of water on the inner harbour bar, cast off his lines, and adroitly ran *Dorothy* aground. When a tug pulled her off, the skipper invited an inspection by the local agents for Lloyds, a pair of retired mariners, who condemned the schooner as unseaworthy and notified the underwriters. The skipper produced his charter and insisted that *Dorothy* was ready and able to make the voyage to New York "after a few rudder repairs." Of course, the alarmed insurers of the cargo now insisted on transfer to a better vessel. As his next move the skipper got a lawyer to make a legal claim on our company for payment of his freight. He settled for two thousand dollars, and the bales of pulp were laboriously transferred at our expense to a stout Nova Scotia schooner for New York.

We found later on that *Dorothy*'s skipper had worked this game before and got away with it. He remained in Liverpool for a time. Then he saw a chance for some fruitful chicanery elsewhere and sailed away, leaving a lot of unpaid bills in his wake. Meanwhile I had interesting talks with him. He yarned freely of tricky adventures with old windjammers in the trade between New England and the West Indies. When in time I wrote a novel called *Tidefall* I set him forth as a secondary character named Captain Halkett.

* * *

Since my first tale appeared in *Maclean's Magazine* I had been working carefully on another, more to my liking because it was founded on fact, an incident some years before when an old Indian used to steal slabwood from a Potanoc sawmill for his stove on Two-Mile Hill. His face had been pitted by smallpox in his youth and he was known all his life as Scabby Lou. The mill owner sold his log slabs in the village for kindling wood. He did not mind Lou taking some, and told him so, but insisted that he must ask first. Lou heard this with disdain and went on stealing. Finally the owner took brace and bit, bored holes in some of the topmost slabs on the pile, and inserted a bit of dynamite. Old Lou's stove blew up one evening, and there was an amusing encounter at the sawmill next day.

I thought of some subtle but quite natural way for the Indian to return trick for trick, with no violence except to the owner's purse. I worked long and hard to put the story together in a style that suited my hand, and after many rewritings I gave it the title "Tit for Tat" and sent it to *Maclean's*. The manuscript came back with a letter from chief editor Napier Moore. According to him the story was worthless, and he listed all the things wrong with it. This was a sad blow. To me the story was a good one, and if I couldn't sell a genuine Canadian story to Canada's leading magazine there seemed no hope of selling it anywhere. I tore up Moore's letter and shoved the manuscript away in a drawer.

Something else had come to my notice. The New York firm of Street and Smith published a wide variety of fiction in unglazed paper ("pulp") magazines, one of which was called *Sea Stories*. Recalling my old yarn about the spook in the Graveyard of the Atlantic, I wrote another more elaborate version and sent it to New York. *Sea Stories* bought it for fifty-five dollars, one cent a word, the same rate as *Maclean's*. They published my story in January of 1929 and asked for more.

Owing to my daily work and my various chores, I had to squeeze time for writing late in the nights and on Sundays. During 1929 *Sea Stories* published five of my tales and paid as much as ninety dollars for one or two of them. They were written to the New York editors' taste, not mine. I considered them trash, and so they were; but I needed the money, and each effort taught me a little more about the art of telling a story. Another writer trying his maiden pen in *Sea Stories* at this time was Guy Gilpatric, afterwards famous for his tales of Mr. Glencannon, the Scottish marine engineer, and his hilarious adventures around the world.

One of my yarns in *Sea Stories* had to do with privateering in the

Caribbean Sea. A retired schoolma'am in Liverpool had told me a lot about that dangerous game as it was played by her own ancestor and other Nova Scotia seamen during the Napoleonic wars. The editor liked my story and so did his readers, who asked for more. Unfortunately the time was now the late autumn of 1929, when the collapse of the New York stock market started the business avalanche of the 1930s. Street and Smith decided to kill *Sea Stories* and several other magazines on their list that no longer made a profit, and they turned the editor of *Sea Stories* to another task. He was to organize a new monthly aimed at the lowbrow masses, to be called *Excitement*. He wrote to me, asking if I would undertake a blood-and-thunder serial story about pirates in the West Indies to launch the new magazine and carry it through the first year. Would I not!

I pecked away at my typewriter every minute I could scrape out of the next four months or so. The name of the chief character I took from an Australian bushranger who called himself Captain Moonlight (I had read about him in a book on the Australian mounted police), and that made the title of my story. An old seaport like Liverpool had charts in many an attic. I borrowed some of the West Indies. The result of all this was eighty thousand words of fanciful rubbish, for which Street and Smith paid me one cent a word in February 1930.

By that time I had become a mere bookkeeper in the office of the new paper company, at $125 monthly. Of my old job with the Macleod Company there is little more to say. By the end of 1928 it was clear to Parker and me that as soon as the wood on hand had been ground to pulp and sold, the Boston owners would shut down the old mills for ever. They could not compete for labour or for wood against the hustling new enterprise at the river mouth. The syndicate's policy now was to hang onto their timberlands in Nova Scotia, paying the taxes out of their Boston coffers, and figuring that the Mersey paper mill, devouring wood at a tremendous rate, would have to buy them sooner or later. They hung on grimly year after year in the Great Depression, paying the taxes with an almost audible gritting of teeth. By a natural phenomenon in the municipalities and school sections of rural Nova Scotia, taxes on the idle timberlands of absentee owners rose steeply all the time. At last the syndicate sold out to Izaak Walton Killam at the compleat angler's own price.

Nobody in Nova Scotia shed a tear for them.

The offices of the Mersey paper mill were still under construction when I joined the staff, and we were crowded together in a board-and-tarpaper shack until they were finished. Each morning I walked three miles to the coastal highway, where if I was lucky I could thumb a ride to the mill site at Brooklyn, two miles further on.

With two or three others I got my dinner at a private home in Brooklyn, where we had entertainment with the food, for the husband of the good woman who provided our meals at $1.50 was the village Munchausen. His repertory covered imaginary jobs all over Canada, ranging from an inspector of lighthouses on the Atlantic coast to the top hand on a paper machine in British Columbia. He was a genius in his way, known all over Queens County. People would ask, "Have you heard Homer's latest?" and go into a word-for-word recital, with all the Homerian gestures and grimaces. The portable tape recorder was a device of the future, unfortunately. Tapes of Homer reciting his fables would be priceless today. For each he prepared himself like any good author, carefully studying the detail and background from every possible source before putting the tale together, and while you hid your laughter you gave him full marks for research.

Later on I got my dinners in Liverpool, at the Chinese restaurant or a smaller one on the waterfront run by a pair of amiable Negroes. There I heard much talk about the rumrunners who were now using Liverpool as a refitting and fueling base for their triangular trade. From here they went to the French island of Saint Pierre, off Newfoundland, where booze was cheap and plentiful, and carried cargoes of it to various places off the United States coast, notably New York's "Rum Row," where the stuff was sold over the side for cash at fantastic prices.

The trade had begun just after the First World War, when the imposition of Prohibition created a vast North American thirst. At first the so-called rumrunners (which carried various kinds of wines and spirits actually) were a motley fleet of steam, diesel, and sailing craft, including a lot of fishing schooners from Nova Scotia. By 1927 the increasing size and efficiency of the U.S. Coastguard fleet required much better qualities in the smuggling craft.

Mysterious men with New York accents appeared in small Nova Scotia ports like Liverpool with exact plans and specifications for sleek fast wooden craft, drawn up obviously by experts. In Liverpool they persuaded the last surviving shipyard to turn from fishing schooners to these remarkable vessels. When they were launched, a local marine workshop installed powerful diesel engines and the latest radio and navigation aids. The cost of it all was paid in currency by other mysterious men, with American $1,000 and $100 notes. No bank accounts. No signatures. All perfectly legal in Canada.

Every time I passed over the river bridge at Liverpool I could see rum-running craft of all kinds refitting, fueling and victualling for the next voyage. After each trip between Saint Pierre and Rum Row they returned empty to Liverpool, showing a clearance from Saint Pierre "in ballast" so that there was no conflict with Canadian Customs regulations. On one occasion in the Liverpool post office I was accosted as "Cap'n Randall?" by a character right out of a gangster movie. I said I didn't spell my name that way and passed on. Obviously in his side-mouthed utterance he had asked someone to point out Captain John Randall, whose schooner *I'm Alone* was then based in our small port. Not long after this she became internationally famous, or notorious, when the U.S. Coastguard sank her by gunfire in the Gulf of Mexico.

Visiting these craft at the docks and chatting with their radio operators as one brasspounder to another, I learned a lot about the rumrunners. Later on I came to know a former rum-running skipper very well, a bold rascal whose adventures in sea knavery of various kinds would have filled a shelf of books. I did write one book years later which I called *Tidefall*. The leading character, Sax Nolan, like the lesser one, Captain Halkett, was drawn from life.

* * *

I continued to live in Milton, thumbing a ride when I could but often walking the five miles to and from the paper mill, in every kind of weather. We were driven hard in the temporary office, with its cramped space and poor facilities. I seldom got home until long after six o'clock. After a hasty supper I did my firewood chores and then settled down to writing.

In my seafaring, and later in Milton, I was seeing things and people and a way of life that were passing rapidly, for the 1914-18 war and its tremendous effects were changing everything. At sea I had seen the last of the square-rigged sailing ships. I saw the last real log drives come down the Mersey River and the closing of the last water-driven sawmills. Although I was only in my teens and twenties when these things were passing I felt a pang, for they seemed to me full of the romance of another time. I wanted to capture some of all this on paper.

I had discarded my old typewriter and bought a rebuilt office machine that made better copy. To please my wife, I put it aside now and then for small social affairs in the village, and for a time we performed in an amateur theatrical troupe, touring the county and playing in small halls and schoolhouses.

*   *   *

During the late war, the president of the Mersey paper company had commanded part of the Canadian Forestry Corps in France, supplying timber to the army, and after his return to peacetime affairs he was known popularly as the Colonel. He was a short brisk pot-bellied bon vivant, and a very capable businessman with ideas and interests as wide as the world.

Among other abilities he had a flair for publicity, very useful to financier Killam at this time when he was preparing a large sale of Mersey bonds to the public. The main selling point was that Liverpool harbour, free of ice all the year round, was only forty hours' steam from New York, the richest newspaper market in the world. No other Canadian mill had these advantages. Moreover the advantages extended to much wider markets. The mill could ship to Europe or South America at easier freight rates than any other in Canada. For that matter it could (and eventually did) ship paper via the Panama canal to New Zealand and Australia, and even to California, in direct competition with West Coast mills.

Killam and the Colonel were calling attention to all this in every way they could. The Colonel himself got right into the seafaring spirit, bought a Nova Scotia fishing schooner, and converted her into a yacht for entertaining prospective American customers. He renamed her *Awenishe*, after a sloop he had owned on the Great Lakes. It was the Ojibwa word for "Little Beaver," and he had a beaver carved in wood for the figurehead. For his crew on weekend cruises he commandeered the services of sea-wise Nova Scotians in the paper mill's employ, and when he discovered that I had been a seagoing brasspounder, I was bidden to join a cruise in August 1929. The Colonel thought that important American paper executives would want to be in touch with their home offices at all times;

accordingly I was to draw plans for a wireless outfit and then to act as operator on summer weekends and holidays. As a guest, of course.

I was quite happy about this. I made myself useful in handling sail and taking the wheel whenever I could, and for several summers I enjoyed cruises in the schooner. Eventually, however, the Colonel found that the cost of a radio outfit was much more than he expected. Also, the guests from American cities usually became seasick and prayed to get ashore. After that the Little Beaver was his own toy and he enjoyed it, blissfully regardless of hazards on a coast strewn with reefs and often obscured by fog or the thick storms that our fishermen call "smoky sou'westers."

He had an easy notion that in such weather, even in the blackest night, he could put a finger on the chart, tell the skipper to go in there for shelter, and expect it to be done at once, just as in his office he got things done by pushing buttons. The skippers of Little Beaver had adventures that prickled their scalps, and mine when I was helmsman, but nothing ever bothered the Colonel.

* * *

In my own way I had interests as varied as the Colonel's. I was one of a group that formed a historical society in Liverpool. The leading spirit was an old gentleman named Long, a native of the town who had spent much of his life as a newspaperman in the States, coming back to Liverpool every summer and rummaging about for documents and other items of its history. I spent hours with him, listening to discourse on the first Yankee settlers, the coming of the Loyalists, the development of shipbuilding and the West Indies trade, and the local effects of the American Revolution, the wars of Napoleon, and the War of 1812. He told me about a remarkable diary kept by a settler named Simeon Perkins from 1766 to 1812, a huge bundle of foolscap sheets lying in a cupboard in Town Hall. Perkins was a merchant, shipbuilder, sawmiller, owner of shares in merchant ships and privateers, colonel of militia, magistrate, and member of the provincial legislature. In these various capacities he knew all that happened in the town, and each night he wrote the gist of it. The diary proved to be one of the most informative and valuable colonial documents in Canada, and subsequently I made good use of it.

*   *   *

In the summer of 1929 fire destroyed the Baptist parsonage in Milton. I was one of the amateur firefighters who scrambled to the scene, and to save a fine old colonial house next door I perched myself on its roof, pouring water from buckets passed up a rickety ladder by a chain of men. I was scorched and half baked when the parsonage collapsed and the worry was over. The trustees of the church began a debate on whether to build a new parsonage or buy one of the existing houses in the village.

With another winter before me, I saw that I must move to the mill site at Brooklyn or at least as far as Liverpool. Those five-mile walks were getting to be a drag. I preferred to live in Liverpool, if I could, because apart from the convenience of shops and a movie theatre there was a small circulating library as well as books I might borrow in private homes like the Colonel's, and the Perkins diary and other colonial documents I was eager to study. I could not afford even a second-hand car, but many well-paid papermakers lived in the town and drove to the mill, and I could hitchhike readily in bad weather.

I offered the Baptist trustees my Milton property for what it had cost me in purchase and repairs. Owing to the influx of new people, housing in Liverpool was hard to find, so I stipulated that I should retain the use of the house until the next spring. The trustees agreed and in the old-fashioned way paid me $100 cash to bind the bargain.

By this time my friend Austin Parker had wound up the affairs of the defunct pulp mills and sent his resignation to the Boston syndicate. He applied for a staff post in the Mersey paper company, where his experience and capability soon made him assistant to the treasurer. Eventually he became treasurer, and when at last he retired he was vice-president.

During the first years of the paper mill's operation the bookkeepers were given various new tasks as they arose. At first I had charge of the cashbook, and among other things I had to sign (there was no machine for stamping a signature) all of the payroll cheques twice a month. This meant something like five hundred cheques in the mill and as many more in the logging camps. For the first time I knew what writer's cramp was. My title was cashier, but as my tasks increased cash became the least of my concerns.

Early in December, 1929, like a ghost from the past, my old ship *Watuka* came to the paper-mill dock with a cargo of coal. (She remained in the coal trade until the Second World War, when she was torpedoed off Cape Breton and went down in five minutes.)

I went aboard and chatted with the operator in the familiar little radio cabin. That night I wrote in my diary, "The sight of the dirty old ship brought a lump to my throat, though I can't understand why. Perhaps it was because she reminded me of my careless dreamy youth, lost and gone for ever. I thought I'd settled into the grind of business life but the lure of roving life comes back as strong as ever."

This sentiment, written at the age of twenty-six, was a symptom of my mixed feelings at this time. Marriage was not going happily for my wife or me. She loved parties and chatter any time and anywhere, but when I got home from the office I wanted to spend the evening in study or writing. Also, my salary was small. I had to be frugal with what I got, and there was not much money for fun. Much deeper than anything else however was a physical problem. After one painful and tragic experience my wife dreaded another pregnancy and so did I. We dared not risk another horror that might end with a dead mother as well as a dead child.

The drugstores of those days had no devices or materials for female contraception. With great secrecy they sold a crude rubber sheath for the male (each stamped "For prevention of disease only") that sealed off contact with the flesh and so abolished the ecstasy of natural intercourse for a kind of masturbation. Even this device was notoriously defective. English historian A.J.P. Taylor has said of this basic problem in married life, "The historian should bear in mind that between about 1880 when [family] limitation started, and 1940 or so, he has on his hands a frustrated people."

I cannot put it better than that.

Outside of my marriage I felt the pull-and-haul of opposite interests: on one side the old dream of roaming the world, and the sometimes desperate urge to get away to sea again and never come back; on the other side my growing interest in the forest and its lakes and streams, which required a firm base on the land. It was the same with my work. The accountant's need of a mind absolutely given to arithmetic was offset by my interest in people and the urge to put them on paper. To do my office work and pursue my hobby I had to split my mind into watertight compartments like an artificial schizoid.

* * *

Five hundred visitors came to the official opening of the paper mill. A special train from Halifax was laden with booze and VIPs. Premier Rhodes pushed a golden button and the mill's main doors opened to reveal the machinery in motion. Small souvenir news-papers (which I helped to write) were printed on paper coming off the machines.

None of the eloquent speakers on this occasion breathed a word about the recent collapse of the stock markets, but to those in the know it was plain that Izaak Walton Killam had a very big fish on a very thin line at the mouth of the Mersey River. A Canadian bank had lent him several million dollars on the security of a first mort-gage. He had planned to sell to the public a second-mortgage bond issue and some of the common stock for several millions more. That had gone with the wind from Wall Street, not to mention Saint James Street and Bay Street.

So there was a resort to expedients, which as cashier I was in a good position to observe. During the first two or three years of operation we were paying construction bills with money received from paper sales and letting huge debts accrue in other directions, notably the bills for electric power. As the Nova Scotia Power Com-mission was government owned, and the government was Conserv-ative, this ultimately caused a scandal in the legislature.

When the building contractors and machinery suppliers came to the end of their own financial ropes and threatened writ and sei-zure, the bank had to put up more and more money or see its main loan go down the drain. These additional loans were made through the local branch in Liverpool, whose manager simply acted as agent and watchdog for the head office in Montreal. The loans ranged from fifty thousand dollars upwards, and each required an official form headed "Loans under Section 88 of the Bank Act," in which the company pledged the mill, the timberlands, and every-thing else it had, from food and other supplies in the logging camps to finished paper in the holds of ships. I presented these to the bank manager, who always greeted me with a dour, "Well, what's the damage this time?" One day I said casually, "Oh, not much. Just three hundred thousand." Even his tight jaw dropped for that one.

Killam of course had cleared each of these loans with the head office, but to a small-town banker it looked like progressive ruin to the whole institution.

Long afterwards I was told that Killam pledged the bank everything he owned, including his house in Montreal, during these early struggles of the paper industry at Liverpool. He had faith in it, and willy-nilly so did the bank. The Mersey mill had the advantages I have mentioned, which kept its head out of the morass that sucked down so many industries in the depression of the 1930s. Even so, as Wellington said after Waterloo, "It has been a damned serious business – the nearest run thing you ever saw in your life." In its first ten years the Mersey company did not pay a cent of dividends. The outbreak of the Second World War and the subsequent demand for newsprint paper, at prices that rose higher and higher in the long boom after the war, put the mill on Easy Street and Killam on fat profits. He remained to his death the chief holder of the common stock, and when his widow sold Mersey and other profitable investments of his in the 1950s she got well over one hundred million dollars.

* * *

My diary entry for February 25, 1930, was, "My salary is increased to $175 per month. Also I received cheque from Street & Smith for $800, for my serial story Captain Moonlight." I bought my wife a fur coat, her first, as a peace offering for the many evenings when I rejected the social amusements of the village and to show her that these long hours of homework could pay off.

I wrote everything with pencil first and typed it later on. Thus I could work far into the night, scribbling and changing the scribbles, without keeping her awake with the racket of the machine. It was several years before I accustomed myself to writing directly on the machine in a distant room, pencilling corrections and changes on the typed sheets at the end of each night's work and finally transcribing this mixture of type and pencil into clean-typed copy for the printers. I must add here that the apparent success of "Captain Moonlight" was a delusion. The new magazine *Excitement* perished at the end of 1930 and with it my sole market, for by that time pulp magazines as well as slick-paper magazines were going down like ninepins everywhere.

Meanwhile my employers were piling the burdens on all their

people who did not come under protection of the powerful Paper-makers' Union and paying them as little as possible. The office workers, the loggers in the woods, and the seamen in the ships had to bear the combined pressures of long hours and hard labour for small pay. Throughout the 1930s the management continued to skimp in these departments. When I left their employ after nine hardworking years, my pay was exactly what it had been for the past eight, $175 a month.

In addition to the cash accounts, I kept the records of paper sales and wood purchases. The last of these became my greatest burden. In addition to wood from its own logging camps on the Mersey watershed, the company bought wood in four-foot lengths from farmers and fishermen all over Nova Scotia. Within a thirty-mile radius of the mill this wood came by motor truck. The rest came by rail or by ship. The company's agents bought any quantity down to five cords piled beside a truck road or a railway siding. Before long my wood ledgers resembled a rough census of woodlot owners in Nova Scotia, for ours was the only paper mill in the province.

Large or small, the wood suppliers wanted money as their work progressed. Loggers within trucking distance came to the mill office themselves, talked to officials in the woods department, and then arrived at my desk with paper slips in hand. So did the men from our own camps up the river, who were paid a meagre $1.50 for a cord of wood cut and piled, less a daily charge for their food. Busy as I was, I usually took time for a brief chat because I was genuinely interested in them and the forest in which they worked. Indeed I was one with them, for I knew how hard they worked for poor pay, and they had my warm sympathy. It was the same with the seamen in the company's employ, whom I paid in cash twice a month aboard their ships. I was one with them, too. After his retirement one of the chief logging foremen told me, "You know, Tom, we used to say you were the only really human guy in that whole dam' place." A bit of woods humour. There were a lot of really human guys in that place, but only one or two in executive chairs.

All of this piled my desk with work, and to keep abreast of it I often had to stay through the evening, getting home at ten or eleven o'clock. Even on Sundays and holidays I was subject to phone calls from important persons, demanding that I hurry to the mill at once for some financial information or to furnish them with travel money from my office safe.

I was not alone in working long hours. Two of my friends on the office staff were laden with work in their own lines. As it chanced, all three of us enjoyed getting into the woods whenever we could, in all seasons of the year, and in effect the woods became our refuge. On every possible weekend or holiday we made sure that we were far away from telephones and beyond the reach of messengers. As a result of all this I did no creative writing during the years 1931, 1932 and 1933. I had little home time for it, and there seemed to be no market anyway.

In the spring of 1930 I moved my small household to Liverpool, where I rented a second-storey flat on Main Street. It was in a quaint Victorian mansion, flanked by huge chestnut trees and so named Chestnut Hall, the last house in the old seaport to retain a watch cabin and a captain's walk on the roof. As we occupied the upper storey, I made use of the captain's walk, especially on hot summer nights when sleep was impossible. It gave a view over the inner harbour, where a few crumbling rock-and-cribwork docks and wharves remained from the windjammer days. The builder of the house, a retired naval officer, must have spent a lot of time up there. The ruined wharves, used so long in the West Indies trade, had seen a vast amount of rum, sugar and molasses in their day. Especially rum, which for many years was part of every workman's wage. When the old house and its chestnuts were demolished in 1962 to make way for a government liquor store and warehouse, it rang a chime somehow. A short walk from Chestnut Hall to the post office corner enabled me to thumb a car ride to the mill in wet or snowy weather, but when weather and footing were good I left home early enough to walk two miles along the shore by the railway track.

An unusually dry month of May gave us a break in the office routine. A series of forest fires broke out within a few miles of the mill, which shut down and turned out all hands to fight them. I became a hoarse and grimy member of a crew with a portable motor-pump. A gale pushed the worst fire down to the highway between Liverpool and Brooklyn and burned about forty homes and other buildings on the way. Our pump crew had many hot adventures, and I learned a lot about forest fires in a hurry. One thing was that they don't "roar" as newspapers say. A wave of intense heat sweeping far ahead of the fire turns everything green to a brown crisp, and as it comes towards you the noise is that of a million high-pressure steam pipes all broken at the same time. It is, believe me, a very nasty sound when you stand blinded by hot smoke, with a ridiculously small hose in your hands and a damp handkerchief over your mouth and nose as your only protection.

* * *

In May 1930 Ottawa announced a federal election. I soon received a cordial invitation to attend a caucus of Tory workers in our constituency. I ignored it. I had seen too much of politics as practised by both of the major parties and the greedy men who lurk behind their façades, and I refused to be a tool for them again. At various times in years to come I was asked by Liberal or alternatively Conservative spokesmen to run as a candidate or to speak for them, but in this as in every other aspect of my life I remained stubbornly independent.

During the summer of 1930 I spent a weekend in Halifax, and on a whim I went to a photographer and got a souvenir of what then seemed a bygone chapter in my life, a portrait of myself, pen in hand, as an author. The pose was so naïve that the picture struck me as ridiculous, and I thrust it out of sight. I did not see it again until I was rummaging my attic for these memoirs.

Late in 1930 I moved my household again, this time to a tiny bungalow near the railway station, with a coal furnace and a well-equipped bathroom, the first in my married life.

* * *

In 1931 the local war veterans formed a branch of the Canadian Legion. I had not fought in the war, but my subsequent service in the merchant marine was one of the Legion qualifications; and my friend Brenton Smith urged me to join. In this time of depression all over the country many war veterans were unemployed and destitute, with meagre pensions for wounds, inadequate medical treatment, and a general neglect by the people they had fought for. There was a big task for the Legion everywhere and I could take part in it, as my father would have done in his vigorous and outspoken way had he survived the war.

So I joined and for many years worked for the veterans in any way I could. Our branch of the Legion had no money for a social hall. We met in Town Hall on hard wooden chairs. Whenever the current president put the question, "Is any comrade in need of aid?" there were always comrades in need, for whom we strove to get pensions, medical treatment, jobs, shelter, food, and what-have-you.

163

That winter a young Liverpool lawyer took me to Halifax in his car. We stopped in the town of Bridgewater to look into the courthouse, where the preliminary hearing of a murder charge against a simple backwoods farmer was being held.

The German settlers of Lunenburg County in the eighteenth century had brought with them a superstitious belief in witchcraft, which they called *hex*. As late as the 1930s it still governed the lives of many people outside the towns, and one backwoods region particularly was known as "the witchcraft belt." The man charged with murder lived there. His village had been dominated many a year by an expert known openly as "de vitch doctor." Like all such doctors this man claimed to be in close touch with Jesus Christ on one hand and the Devil on the other, so he had all the answers. Every ailment of human beings, cattle, horses, sheep, pigs and what not was caused by a *hex* put on them by a human creature of evil disposition in the neighbourhood, who transformed himself or herself into a witch by night. By his magic powers "de vitch doctor" was able to detect such persons and put a counter *hex* on them, by weird rites and incantations. For this he demanded a stiff cash fee.

The prisoner in the court had been paying hard-earned money for a long time to cure an ailing child, with the "doctor" putting the *hex* on various suspects without result. At last it occurred to him that the evildoer was "de vitch doctor" himself, and he killed the sorcerer. When he was arrested he gave a full and frank confession to the police.

The lawyer appointed for his defence soon disposed of the confession. All the witnesses summoned by the police refused to testify. Called to the stand, they rolled their eyes to the ceiling and gabbled long quotations from the Scriptures. (They went to bed every night with a Bible under their pillows to ward off evil in the dark.) They weren't taking any chances with *hex* in or out of the courtroom. My friend and I left for Halifax while this was going on. I made careful notes of the case and subsequently learned much more about *hex* in Lunenburg. Eventually I wrote a short story called "The Powers of Darkness" and published it in one of my books. It has been performed as a play several times on radio and television. Some people think it a wild stretch of imagination. Witchcraft in Canada? In the twentieth century? Ha!

I have mentioned that I wrote no fiction from 1931 through 1933. (I sold "Tit for Tat" to *Blackwood's Magazine* in 1933, but it was written in '28.) However, in 1931 I wrote a bit of history about the Liverpool brig *Rover* and her adventures as a privateer in the Caribbean Sea during the years 1800-1804.

This was done for the Colonel, who had a new idea in his constant effort to advertise the paper industry at Liverpool. At intervals of a year or two I was to write a series of small books drawn from historic facts about Nova Scotia. The subjects must be interesting in themselves, and in addition they must show something of the wide sea-reach of Nova Scotia. For example, a map at the front and back of *Saga of the Rover* (my first subject) showed the whole east coast of the United States as well as the West Indies, and Panama was clearly marked.

I made research in the valuable Perkins diary, in the archives at Halifax, in the British *Naval Chronicle* and in *The Naval History of Great Britain* by William James, which gave an account of the *Rover*'s battle with Spanish warships off Puerto Cabello. I also consulted local tradition handed down by descendants of her crew such as my wife's family, who were descendants on the distaff side from Henry Godfrey, one of *Rover*'s powder monkeys.

To head each chapter I wrote a doggerel verse of the come-all-ye sort. Illustrations for the little book came from the hand of my friend Tom Hayhurst, an officer of the paper company's steamship *Markland*, whose hobby was painting windjammers in oils. He had never attemped the human figure and his pen-and-wash drawings for the *Rover* book confessed it. I assumed that the Colonel would engage a cartographer to prepare the important map, and for that expert's guidance I drew a crude sketch showing the main cruises of the privateer and their relation to Nova Scotia, the American coast and the Caribbean Sea. For fun I added a dolphin, a square-rigged ship, and a puff-cheeked character representing the trade wind. Whatever God meant me for, obviously it was not an artist, and I was dismayed when the Colonel used this awkward concoction for the book just as it was.

Saga of the Rover was printed and bound in hard covers by a firm in Halifax. One lot of 250 copies, containing a front sheet of advertising by the paper company, was distributed to editors or owners of large newspapers along the east coast of the United States and in New Zealand and Australia. (That was where Panama came in.) The other lot of 250 copies had no advertising. The Colonel turned them over to Hayhurst and me for our reward.

We put them on sale in a Halifax bookshop and another in Ottawa at a retail price of two dollars. Few were sold in those hard times. The rest we autographed and gave to our friends. The books came from a Halifax bindery in December 1931 and were gone by the end of 1932. Today they are collectors' items, with offers up to sixty-five dollars a copy and only rarely a taker.

In the spring of 1932 the Colonel called me into his office on another matter of publicity. The rapidly growing and already powerful medium of radio broadcasting was not to be missed. He had arranged to make a radio address on the paper industry in Nova Scotia and asked me to write it for him. From that time on he asked me to write scripts for other public addresses, and when newspapers asked for an occasional article on the paper industry, the conservation of the forest, or anything else, he gave me some of his ideas and I wrote the rest. These had to be written in my own time at home because my office work kept me busy all day. Apparently the Colonel thought I dashed them off in the office, for I got no pay for them.

* * *

In June 1932 the Colonel told me to start research for another little book, this one more difficult, an account of the old Norse voyages to America and their relation to Nova Scotia. The purpose was to show, by a back-track in nautical history, our ease of access to Europe, where the Colonel hoped to gain entry into British and continental paper markets despite stiff competition from the Scandinavian paper mills.

At that time scholars agreed that Nova Scotia was the Markland ("Wood Land") of the Icelandic sagas, hence the name of our company's first steamship. I made research in Halifax libraries. Strolling along Water Street one Sunday morning for the sake of old memories, I was astounded to see a Norse long-ship tied up at the wharf of an old Halifax firm, T.A.S. DeWolfe and Son, complete with striped sail, shields along the bulwarks, dragon's head at the bow and the tail sticking up astern. For a moment I thought I'd been studying too hard. I hurried down the wharf to board her while the illusion held and found that she was real, a full-sized replica built in Norway from the ancient model. Her owner-skipper was aboard, a fine old salt named Gerhard Folgero.

With a crew of young Norwegian adventurers he had sailed first to Gibraltar and around the Mediterranean, to get the feel of her in various winds with handy shelter in case of trouble. Then he had sailed from Spain to Cuba by the old Columbian route, taking ninety-three days on the passage. She was towed up the Mississippi for exhibition to the numerous people of Scandinavian origin in the Middle West, and thence by canals to the Atlantic seaboard. Now Folgero was sailing homeward by the old Viking route via Nova Scotia, Newfoundland, Greenland, Iceland and the Faroes.

He was delighted to find someone here who knew about the ancient Norse voyagers, including Thorfinn Karlsefni, who actually made a brief settlement in Markland. After long and eager talk about these matters Folgero invited me to join his crew for the passage back to Norway. I almost leaped at it. How often does a man get the chance to adventure more than nine hundred years back in time? But on reflection I had to say No, with regret. Including the various stops the northern passage would take many weeks, and to make it I would have to throw up my job. Jobs in Nova Scotia then were almost as scarce as long-ships in the North Atlantic, and I had a wife to support.

The next year I had to say Sorry again, when Folgero wrote inviting me to join in a leisurely cruise about the shores of the Baltic. Those golden chances never came again. In the course of our talk at Halifax I did learn essential points about sailing and handling this sort of craft, which proved useful when I wrote my little book.

On my return home I wrote to Halldor Hermansson, author of the article on Vinland in the *Britannica*, and got a list of books on the ancient Norse voyages that were not available in Halifax libraries. Some were out of print, but the Colonel pursued them through Brentano's in New York and eventually got enough to occupy my spare time in study for a year. I finished the manuscript in April 1934. As it was a much longer and more arduous task than *Saga of the Rover* the Colonel had the paper company pay me $250. Hayhurst had just completed his drawings for *The Markland Sagas* when he was killed in a motor accident at Philadelphia, where his ship was unloading.

This time there was a single printing of three hundred copies, and they came off the press in October. The Colonel sent most of them to newspaper executives in Britain and elsewhere. The plates for the illustrations of *Saga of the Rover* and *The Markland Sagas* eventually came into my possession, together with Tom Hayhurst's original drawings. I have one other memento of my friendship with poor Tom, a small oil of the famous fishing and racing schooner *Bluenose*, which he painted for me in 1932.

There were no more Sagas. By 1935 I had determined to try my luck as a professional author and to leave the company's employ as soon as I could work up enough magazine sales to make the venture possible.

*　*　*

Excepting my work on *The Markland Sagas* I wrote nothing in 1933, but in that year the writings of some other people changed the whole course of my life. A Liverpool bank manager, retiring on pension to his home in New Brunswick, gave me a bundle of back numbers of *Blackwood's Magazine*. I had read the famous old British monthly a few times in my seafaring days with passing interest. Now I thoroughly enjoyed this bounty of good reading. For its writers *Blackwood's* had a high standard in material, style and workmanship. Conrad had written *Lord Jim* originally as a serial for it. The stories and articles had to do with people in many parts of the world but rarely in Canada, and I wondered why. Was it possible that Canadian writers never thought of sending their work across the sea, as if there were no market beyond Toronto? Or had they found *Blackwood's* standards too high?

I thought of my story about the Indian, the lumberman and the dynamite. I had not looked at "Tit for Tat" since *Maclean's Magazine* rejected it as worthless in 1928. Now I dragged it out of the drawer in which it had lain for five years and sent it off to *Blackwood's*, expecting it to bounce right back. Instead I had a letter from old George William Blackwood himself, accepting the story with pleasure. "Maga" paid at the rate of one guinea a magazine page, and Mr. Blackwood enclosed a cheque for the sterling equivalent of ninety dollars. This was about 50 per cent more than *Maclean's* would have paid me for a story of the same length.

Blackwood asked to see more of my work, and in a silly flush of optimism I gathered up some flimsy things I had scribbled during 1930, when "Captain Moonlight" was running as a serial in *Excitement*. I had hoped to sell them to *Excitement* after the serial ended, but by that time the new magazine was foundering like *Sea*

Stories before it. As I should have expected with any common sense, Blackwood politely rejected this hasty rubbish and asked to see something more in the material and style of "Tit for Tat."

This was in the fall of 1933, and what with my office work and my studies for *The Markland Sagas* I had no time for the careful construction of magazine stories. When "Tit for Tat" appeared in *Blackwood's* I was gratified to see it printed as I wrote it, without the change of a word. Again the contrast with *Maclean's* was remarkable, for Canada's chief magazine was notorious for editorial chopping and changing. I resolved that whatever I might write in the future I would send nothing there.

* * *

During my busy summer of 1932, my friends Austin Parker and Brenton Smith built a roomy log cabin at Eagle Lake for hunting, fishing, and just plain getting-away-from-it-all. The lake poured its water down a steep mile of woodland into the west side of the Mersey River, where there was no road of any kind and consequently no travellers except one or two Indian trappers. The forest had been logged for its virgin pine about a century before and again for the lesser pine in 1905. The loggers' camps had crumbled to dust, and their tote roads had grown over or dwindled to mere game paths when we explored this region in the fall of '31.

I have mentioned the region before as the "Injun Devil country" of the old loggers. At the south end of Eagle Lake was a swampy wild meadow they called "the haunted bog," a natural place for moose calling like all such openings in the forest. Many years before us, a party of young hunters had bivouacked on a small wooded island in this swamp, intending to call moose in the morning. During the night, and again in the dim light of a misty dawn, they heard weird and frightful screams from something invisible rushing through the air about them. They cleared out in a hurry when full daylight came.

I knew these men in their old age, sensible and sober woodsmen all, and they still swore to their strange experience. One of them even came to Eagle Lake with Parker and me and led us to the approximate spot where they had spent that memorable night. When we scraped aside the dead leaves and other forest debris of nearly half a century, we found the ring of stones that had contained their camp fire.

They knew nothing whatever of *Windigo*, the evil spirit of the

169

Ojibwas, which rushed through the air, making dreadful cries but was never seen, or *Ska-de-ga-mut-k'* of Micmac legend, which does the same thing and is always a presage of death or disaster. For my part I can say only that my friends and I have used the cabin at Eagle Lake for more than forty years and explored every bit of the neighbouring woods and waters, including Long Lake and Kempton Lake, which make up the rest of the Injun Devil country, without hearing or seeing anything frightful. I have even called for bull moose by moonlight on "the haunted bog," and heard nothing worse than my own voice bellowing through a birchbark horn.

*   *   *

The building of the cabin was a unique affair which I described much later in my novel *The Wings of Night*. The idea was Parker's. When the old-time loggers felled a pine they "junked" it into twenty-foot lengths for hauling and stream-driving. Some of the upper lengths, averaging fourteen inches in diameter, were full of sap and sank when rolled into the water. The loggers did not care a hoot about the loss of these and left them on the bottom of the lake or stream. Lying submerged, every one of these logs was sealed against insects and airborne fungus spores and consequently remained as sound as the day it was cut.

Paddling a canoe around the shores of Eagle Lake, Parker and Smith noted traces of "landings" where logs had been hauled and piled in winter, ready for rolling into the lake when the ice went out. The water was comparatively shallow there in the heat of summer, and on calm days they could see the shapes of sunken logs under the thin silt of the years. Stabbed at one end with a pike-pole, these "sinkers" could be raised slowly to the surface, one on each side of the canoe, and held there by rope lashings. Then came a slow job of paddling canoe and logs to the camp site at the north tip of the lake. Sometimes it took all day to tow one pair to the spot. Others lay quite near the camp site. This work was done on weekends and holidays all through the spring, summer and autumn of 1932. The door, windows, furniture, boards for the floor and roof, the stove and other manufactured stuff had to be boated up the Mersey River from the hydro-electric dam at Big Falls and then manhandled a mile or more up an old trail to the lake.

Smith's father had been a shipwright in the last days of wooden ships, and in his seventies he was still a tall strong man. He brought his old broad axe, sharpened to a razor edge, and hewed the logs three-square, leaving one side round to face outdoors. Thus they fitted neatly upon each other. His hewing was so neat that some visitors inside the cabin thought they were looking at walls lined with boards.

We called it Kitpoo Lodge from the Indian name of the lake, *Kitpoo-ak-a-de* – "the eagle's place." Parker and Smith kept two canoes and a skiff there and invited me and two or three other cronies to share their enjoyment. Year after year, by canoe and afoot (on snowshoes in winter), we ranged the forest of the Injun Devil country. Moose were getting scarce and we made no attempt to shoot them, although moose hunting was not banned in Nova Scotia until 1938.

There were plenty of white-tailed deer, which offered a much greater challenge to the hunter. Unlike bull moose they could not be lured into the open, even with those silly "deer calls" that are sold in sporting-goods stores. Also, they are much smaller and more agile and alert than moose. An Indian once pointed out, on a deer I had shot, what appeared to be a recess or gland deep in the cleft of each hoof. He said, "See, Tommy? 'E got four ears on de ground beside two on 'ees 'ead!"

Usually we hunted on the move, by canoe and on foot. However, there was a large rock surrounded by young spruce trees near the stream from Long Lake to Eagle Lake that made a natural watching place for the more patient Indian method. From its top, usually in the difficult light of early dusk, when deer sometimes crept out of the woods and walked shoulder deep in the wild meadow grass, I shot a buck from time to time. My friends still call it Tom's Rock.

Ordinarily we hunted in pairs to share the work of carrying the meat, but to cover more country each man often hunted alone. Any of us at a pinch could shoulder a gutted carcass and stagger through the woods to a lake or stream where we could pick it up with a canoe.

Thus we lived two distinct lives. One was in the town and office, neatly attired in business suits or on summer evenings playing tennis in white shirts and flannels. The other was in shabby and much-worn bush clothes, hunting, fishing, or simply exploring, with one man throwing the canoe on his shoulders upside-down and toting it over the portages. For this active life of work and play we had a very good base at Liverpool, and we approved the ancient Indian name for it, *Ogomkegeok*, "the-place-where-we-go-out."

171

In the autumn of 1932 for a change and a look at one of my dream islands, I took my wife to Bermuda in a freighter of the Canadian National Steamships named *Colborne*, which had cabins for a few passengers. My wife scribbled a message to her mother as we left Halifax harbour, saying that we were on our way. When I took it to the radio cabin I was astonished and delighted to find that the brasspounder was my old shipmate Walter Hunter. After a chat to catch up on the past he told me to send the message myself, and I did. For lack of practice in the past ten years my hand was slower than in my Sable Island days, but the old code came back to mind as easily and fluently as if it hadn't been ten minutes.

In Bermuda motor vehicles were then taboo and my wife and I rambled about in a surrey with a fringe on the top, like the singer in *Oklahoma!* in later years. While we were there, *Mauretania* arrived on a cruise from New York, carrying what seemed to be thousands of American fugitives from Prohibition, all sucking up booze like camels at a waterhole. One day we drove clippety-clop to see the house where Irish poet Tom Moore spent a year during a lull in the Napoleonic Wars. We were disgusted to find it converted to a way-side pub called Calabash Inn. The Bermudians were catering in every way to the vast American thirst.

* * *

My scrapbook contains a licence dated September 12, 1932, and signed by the sheriff of Queens County, authorizing Thomas Raddall to carry "one gun or revolver" while taking money from the bank to the paper mill. This was occasioned by a series of robberies in our region, all done with stolen cars, something very strange in rural Nova Scotia in those days. The lone provincial policeman in the county was completely baffled. One night the robbers broke into a Brooklyn store, robbed the till, and fired a shot at the owner. This was just a few yards from the entrance to our paper mill.

As I have mentioned, one of my routine jobs was to pay the ships' crews twice a month in cash. I had no car, and Brenton Smith drove me to and from the bank in his. After the shooting in Brooklyn our boss decided that we should be armed, and we were equipped with small revolvers, concealed beneath our jackets with underarm holsters in the best Chicago fashion. The procedure was for me to enter the bank while Smith posted himself at the door. When I came out with a satchel full of money, Smith followed at a distance of about twenty feet in case somebody jumped me from behind. After a few months of this I said casually, "Brent, this gun business is dam' silly. Those fellows always operate at night. Why not leave the guns in the office? The boss will never know." He agreed heartily. Only kids played cops-and-robbers nowadays.

A few weeks later I got a satchel of money at the bank in the usual way, but my jacket happened to be unbuttoned. Smith exclaimed, "Hey! You've got your gun!" I grinned and said, "Brent, I figured that if anybody jumped me from behind I didn't want you there banging away at him." He was indignant for a moment and then saw the fun of it. I doubt very much if the mysterious rural gangsters would have tried armed robbery by daylight. Their game was nocturnal burglary. Finally one of them, shot while breaking into a village store, thought he was dying and blurted out the whole story. He and his pals were a gang of young loafers led by a village ne'er-do-well who had gone away to the States for a few years. There he joined a gang of thieves and became expert in everything from locks and keys to cars and guns. The American police must have wanted him badly when he fled back to Nova Scotia in 1931.

Here he lay low for a time and then began to teach some other idle louts the modern arts of car theft and wide-ranging robbery after dark. I daresay he was quite resigned at the last to a few years in Dorchester Penitentiary amid the Fundy marshes. In the States, police kept inconvenient records and fingerprints, and judges were harsh with old offenders toting guns.

* * *

In March 1933 Franklin Roosevelt was inaugurated President of the United States. The financial panic there was at its worst and every bank in the country was closed. It was amazing to see all of our Canadian banks open and doing their everyday business, with nobody perturbed, while on the other side of a pencil line across the map of North America the richest nation in the world was apparently flat broke. It was not, of course. Among other activities, the American papers continued to print the news, our mill continued to sell paper, and we continued to eat.

In that year I bought my first car, a second-hand Ford coupe with a canvas top that had run less than eighteen thousand miles. I got it for $240, which seems incredible now. What is more, it ran very well on our rough gravel roads for the next three years and carried my wife and me all over Nova Scotia. It was useful, too, in my own woods rambles, for I was no longer dependent on somebody else's car to reach a jumping-off point.

* * *

That summer a tennis team from Dalhousie University made a tour of the province playing clubs in the country towns, and one of the team was a tall handsome chap of twenty-six named Hugh MacLennan. He was rated the best player in Nova Scotia. Realizing that we had nobody who could even give him a good game, the tournament committee of our small Liverpool club asked Peter Aitken if he would mind playing a singles match with one of the visitors. Peter was a son of Lord Beaverbrook, sent over here to study the manufacture of newsprint paper. He had an athletic figure, and sometimes in the evening he strolled to our courts for a game. He was as careless about tennis as he was about dress or the manufacture of paper, but we noticed that he could play well when he was in the mood.

In his nonchalant way he agreed to play against MacLennan, about whom he knew nothing, and his only preparation on a very hot afternoon was to drink a lot of beer. He arrived on the courts wearing a soiled shirt, shabby grey flannel trousers held up by an old necktie run through the belt loops and knotted, and very dirty canvas shoes. Immaculate in white shirt and flannels, MacLennan won the first set easily and quickly, 6-0. Sweating and red in the face, Peter looked like a stumblebum in every way, but this exertion under an August sun appeared to burn the alcohol as well as the indifference out of him. The second set became a long-drawn-out affair that Peter eventually won, to everybody's surprise. The third was a complete reversal of the first, with Peter playing a brilliant and smashing game and winning 6-0.

I believe that Hugh's writing up to that time had been more or less confined to academic subjects, and on the physical side he cherished his game of tennis. To be defeated in a small country town by an apparent bum must have given him a shock. Soon afterwards Peter Aitken drifted back to England where he took up racing cars and then fast motorboats. Shortly before War Two we heard that he had perished by drowning in the North Sea. Had he lived, he would have made an indomitable air fighter like his older brother Max.

* * *

Early in 1934 my wife found herself pregnant and we were both alarmed, remembering that other horror. Abortion was unobtainable, so there was nothing to do but go through it and meanwhile try not to think about it. During that spring and summer we spent weekends and holidays rambling about in our little car. On one trip to Halifax I visited my former station at the harbour mouth. The small wireless shack and the old army signal station on Camperdown hill had been abandoned in 1924 and were falling into ruin.

On another jaunt we visited Oak Island in Mahone Bay, one of the many reputed burial places of "Captain Kidd's treasure." The island, like others in the bay, is composed of stones, gravel, and pockets of clay and loam, the typical debris of an ancient glacial movement, quite common in Nova Scotia. Such material is easily pervious to water, and any digging below sea level is bound to be flooded by saturation. Still, many people like to believe the Oak Island treasure fable, regardless of historical and geological facts. There are even maps showing a shaft with timbered sides and platforms, going down at least 150 feet to "the money pit," which has side tunnels deliberately made to flood it from the sea. Nobody has explained how Kidd did all this without powerful pumps to keep out the Atlantic Ocean while he was at it, or how he expected to recover the carefully drowned treasure at any time in the future, or indeed why he came there at all. History records that his piratical booty was buried on Gardiner's Island, near the upper tip of Long Island, New York. His crew revealed the spot, and the treasure was dug up and produced at his trial in London in 1701. By order of the court it was sold to pay the very large expense of the trial, in which witnesses had to be brought from Madagascar and India, and the sum left over went to endow the soon-to-be-built hospital for seamen at Greenwich.

In time I wrote a story for *Blackwood's* called "A Matter of History" in which I took a healthy crack at the Oak Island nonsense.

*   *   *

My wife expected the birth of the child in November. We dreaded the day, but in the hope that mother and child might survive I sought a larger dwelling than the tiny bungalow by the railway station. I had met the owner-skipper of a schooner chartered to carry wood along the coast to the paper mill. Expecting these freights to continue, he bought land on a quiet lane near the tennis

175

club and built an attractive wooden house in the Dutch colonial style with six rooms, a bathroom, and central heating.

In the fall of 1933 the paper company bought an old steamship to carry their wood cargoes, and the schooner captain was out of luck. The depression was at its worst, and he could not find another charter anywhere, so he sold his vessel at a loss and went into the seagoing branch of the RCMP. He leased the house to me and gave me an option to buy it at what it had cost him. We moved into the house in the summer of 1934 and it has been our home ever since.

Here on a frosty night of November my son Tom was born. There was no hospital in our town then, but my wife was attended by two hospital-trained nurses, cousins of hers, and by an excellent medical friend of mine, John Wickwire, who had started a practice in Liverpool when the paper mill was built. The birth was much easier than that frightful ordeal of six years ago, with a better anaesthetic and far better attendance. Nevertheless I was anxious, and it was an enormous relief when the doctor came downstairs smiling and said, "Your wife is all right and you have a fine healthy son."

He sat down while I rummaged about to find glasses and a sup of wine with which to pledge the newcomer. It had to be a Canadian wine, and I found some Niagara sherry. The doctor relaxed in an armchair and remarked that the first cry of my son reminded him somehow of a birth he had attended in the Canadian Arctic. After graduation from Dalhousie he had served as doctor to a Canadian government expedition to the North in 1927. They were mapping Hudson Strait by sea and air for about a year.

In the course of it he had ventured from Nottingham Island in an open motorboat to attend a trader's wife in childbirth on Baffin Island. The distance was more than a hundred miles over a sea littered with ice floes, but he and two Eskimos got there all right. On the way back the engine broke down. Then a gale closed up the ice and they were trapped, with no food but a seal they managed to kill. Only after days and nights of struggle and peril did they get back to the post on Nottingham. Some years afterwards I wrote that adventure for *Blackwood's*, calling it simply "North." It more than repaid my doctor's bill.

* * *

In talks with my Indian friends, and in my curious scratchings on ancient camp sites along the Mersey River, I had learned that *Sa-*

ak-a-wach-kik ("the-folk-of-the-olden-time") made seasonal wanderings up and down the rivers and along the coast. Despite its name, Indian Gardens had been mainly a winter gathering place. When spring brought wild fowl and sea fish back to the coast, most of the people went down the river in canoes. From the mouth of it ("the-place-where-we-go-out") they scattered along the coast in family groups, pitching a wigwam or two wherever there was a sheltered creek with a clam flat and a trickle of fresh water. Here the sea breezes drove off the woodland pests of blackflies and mosquitoes, and whenever hunting or fishing failed the squaws could dig up a meal from the flat. In the course of generations the sites of these summer camps became circular flat-topped heaps of shells mingled with bones of fish, fowl, and every sort of animal from squirrel to moose.

The only scientific research for such camp sites in Nova Scotia had been made in 1915 by a pair of archaeologists from Ottawa. I obtained a copy of their report, which had photographs of the middens and the artifacts found in them. Whenever we picnicked on the seashore I looked about for such middens but found nothing. In June 1935 a sporting parson told me a curious thing about a long sandy inlet called Port Joli. He had been hunting for partridges there one day last fall, and about three miles along the uninhabited west side he noticed a tree, killed by a bush fire years before and at last blown down. It was a good two hundred yards back from the shore and yet there were clam shells tangled in the roots.

How come?

At the first chance I went with him to the spot and soon recognized the roughly circular mound of an ancient midden, covered over with trees, bushes and ferns. The parson was sceptical until I dug in the mass of shells under the ferns and turned up a fragment of pottery with the typical Indian decorative marks.

During several summers after that, Parker, Smith and I, with our families and baskets of food, made Sunday expeditions to the place, getting a fisherman to put us across the inlet in his boat on the morning tide and to pick us up in the evening. The sea water was warm in this sandy nook, and the women and kids bathed happily while we dug in the middens, finding pottery fragments, stone tools and arrowheads, and one or two arrowheads made from sharks' teeth. The pottery bore the same simple decoration as fragments we had found inland at Indian Gardens and elsewhere along the Mersey River, proof that they had been made by the same

177

people. We found other camp sites at Port Joli and a few miles further along the coast at Port l'Hebert. These expeditions were a pleasant and interesting diversion for all of us.

One might have been a tragedy. I had gone to dig in a site at Port l'Hebert, taking along my wife and child and my wife's sister and young brother. Again the site was some distance back from the shore, where my companions were paddling in the shallows. None of them could swim. I warned them not to venture far because the outgoing tide in the main channel was a very powerful stream. The sister did venture, though, and she was swept off her feet. Fortunately she did not panic but remained passive on her back, breathing in and out quickly to keep air in her lungs and stay afloat. The others screamed for me. I reached her just before she drifted into the channel, which would have swept us both away to sea at a rate of knots. Even so it was an inch-by-inch struggle before I got her ashore.

*   *   *

In the summer of 1935 a businessmen's club at Halifax invited me to address one of their weekly luncheons. Someone on their program committee had seen a copy of *The Markland Sagas* and asked me to talk about the Norse voyages. I drove there in my little car, taking Tom Hayhurst's drawings and maps and a scale model of a Norse long-ship. It was my first attempt at public speaking and my first view of a businessmen's luncheon club.

The clubs engage in good works of various kinds, which are all reported and discussed before the guest speaker gets his turn. The chairman calls on Bob Somebody to report, and then on Harry Somebody Else, and they are followed by a succession of Jacks and Joes with things to announce or discuss. Before all this is done, busy men in the club steal away in twos and threes to their shops or offices. Unless he is famous or important in some other way, the guest speaker finds that at least half the audience has reached for its hat and gone before he gets up to speak. The rest hang on grimly unless he is telling jokes, and when he has said his last word there is a rush for the door. By the time the chairman shakes his hand in farewell they are alone in the dining room amid a scurry of waitresses gathering up the dishes.

On this occasion I recited my piece, carefully prepared to last no more than fifteen minutes, and I indicated the drawings and the model ship, suggesting that club members examine them closely afterwards. After the chairman had murmured a few words of thanks came the rush for the door. Two men remained, one of whom I recognized from newspaper photographs as Angus L. Macdonald, the Premier of Nova Scotia. He and his friend examined the drawings and the Norse ship, and Macdonald plied me with questions for half an hour.

As I drove home I reflected pleasantly on the premier's keen interest, for of all of the men in that room his time was surely the most precious. Later on, when I knew him better, I realized that he had stayed from natural courtesy as much as an interest in bygone Norsemen. An unknown young man from the South Shore had driven a hundred miles to say his piece and show his things, and the Scot from Cape Breton felt that he was entitled to at least one man's full attention and appreciation. It was typical of Angus Macdonald.

Several years later, when I knew him well, I met him strolling along Barrington Street in Halifax. Somebody had given me a gorgeous tartan necktie, which Angus spotted at once. "So you're a Scot too!" he said. "You never told me!"

I said, "Mister Premier, I have to confess that I'm sailing under false colours. My blood is all Sassenach. My father came from Cornwall and my mother came from Kent."

Angus considered that for a moment or two. "Wait a minute! If your father was a Cornishman, your blood is half Celtic. That makes you a half-brother to a Scot. Tom, you have my permission to wear any tartan you like." And after another brief pause, "*Even the Macdonald!*"

* * *

In the autumn of 1935 I took up the option to buy my house, paying about half from my savings and borrowing the rest from a bank. In this year I had sold three short stories to *Blackwood's* and received $452. Now I was labouring every possible hour to increase my production, but a severe critic slowed me down. Thinking ruefully of the slapdash stuff I had written for those New York "pulps," and now appreciating *Blackwood's* quality, I was never again satisfied with anything I wrote. The famous old monthly, with its worldwide circulation, enabled me to insert my small Canadian slides in a magic lantern that displayed them on a screen far wider and more sophisticated than any to be found in Canada itself. Consequently every story I sent to *Blackwood's* was written and re-written again and again, with a careful choice of word and phrase to get the right flair of the tale, and occasionally (as Kipling used to say) "putting it aside to drain."

I got a glint of encouragement in 1936 when an American publication, reprinting what its editors considered the world's best modern short stories, included one of mine from *Blackwood's*. I found myself in the company of Ernest Hemingway, William Faulkner and Morley Callaghan. With this fillip I slogged away harder than ever, but my output remained small for the hours of thought and work I put into it, and I wondered if I could ever produce enough to make a living.

* * *

In the spring of that year, when our child was teething and allowing us little sleep after my nightly writing stint, I wrote in my diary, "After a bad night, the day in the office is a long agony and I find myself making stupid mistakes, which is bad business. Sometimes I think I must give up writing, or give up working for the paper company, or go mad."

For some physical relief I took a week of my annual vacation to labour on the rough grounds about my house, working from morn to night with pick, shovel, crowbar and wheelbarrow. It meant grubbing up scrub trees and bushes, removing all the rocks I could lift, digging out pockets of loam between the boulders and using it to make a small lawn in front of the house. There were large boulders in the little wilderness behind the house. I hired a couple of men to drill and blast them, and to build the fragments into a low wall around my property. They were adventurous with dynamite and old-fashioned fuses, and my neighbours shared my daily trepidation. When all was done the stretch behind the house was like a rock-lined swimming pool without the water. I forget how many truckloads of earth I bought to fill it and make a back lawn. The rest of the cost was in sweat, all mine.

In August my wife gave birth to our daughter, Frances, in a small private nursing home lately opened in the town. Again there was no difficulty or danger. We could not afford more than two children on my slender income, however. From this time forth we had to make sure of it, like so many other middle-class couples of our time. During the long depression the most intimate and exquisite part of conjugal life had to be carefully insulated, like a dangerous electric current.

* * *

That summer I had a new experience which gave me a story. An American sportsman came to Nova Scotia hoping to catch a world-record tuna on rod and line. He was a friend of Hemingway's and fished with him at Bimini in the Bahamas, but the fish there were not big enough. He knew that another American sportsman had found huge tuna on the coast near Liverpool some years before. This was Zane Grey, who made an immense fortune out of saddle-and-shoot-'em-up novels of the Wild West but personally liked to ride a luxurious yacht and kill big fish with hook and line. After his encounter with what some of our fishermen called "horse mackerel" he went away to the Pacific, where fish were just as big and the weather much more comfortable.

The man I called Van Dopper and his wife Trudy turned up in our little town with much baggage and a lot of expensive sea-angling gear. Van liked to see his name in print, and when someone told him I wrote for a famous British magazine he invited me to accompany him in a hired fishing boat. We set out at three o'clock in the morning to be at the herring nets by dawn. There we got fresh bait and began the day's fishing. It proved an interesting one. Van hooked a big tuna in the harbour mouth, and after a battle over miles of open sea he brought it to the fisherman's gaff. On the fish dock in Liverpool it weighed about five hundred pounds, far below the world record but apparently bigger than the average Bimini fish. Van telegraphed to Hemingway in triumph and went on fishing eagerly for a week, in which he caught several more, but none bigger than the first. His wife had done some fishing in the Gulf Stream at Bimini, and one day Van harnessed her in the special swivel chair and put the rod in her hands.

She hooked a tuna almost at once. Then followed hours of painful struggle, in which the big fish with erratic lunges towed the boat over miles of sea. At last she managed to draw it within reach of the gaff. It was a whopper, well over seven hundred pounds, but still not a world record. Nevertheless, Van seemed satisfied for the moment. At the fish dock he had the tuna hoisted by the tail until it appeared to be standing on its nose, and he sent Trudy back to the hotel for a bath and a change into something eye-catching. She returned, slim and sexy in tight white pants, a frilly blouse and a big white hat, and posed beside the enormous fish with a rod in one hand and a cigarette carefully displayed in the other. Van sold the resulting photographs to a famous American cigarette company, which used them in advertisements showing the pretty lady, the big fish, and down in one corner a small but significant camel.

I called my story "Lady Lands Leviathan" and sold it to *Blackwood's*. Soon afterward the Nova Scotia government's bureau of information, eager to foster a new attraction for American tourists, asked me to write a booklet on the art of catching huge and energetic fish on rod and line.

*   *   *

In November 1936 I traded in my little Ford coupe and bought a new Chevrolet sedan. I planned to drive it for five years and then trade it in on another, in the economical manner of those times; but Hitler started his war within three years, our auto-makers devoted their plants to war machines for the duration, and after the war there was a long delay before they got into full civilian production again. The small towns got their new cars last. Altogether, my '36 Chev had to last thirteen years.

During 1936 I earned $773.77 with my pen, mostly from short stories in *Blackwood's*. I was then thirty-three. By careful economy and thrift I had saved nearly three thousand dollars, apart from my house and life insurance. I knew I would need more than that before I could cut away my office mooring and launch forth as a professional writer. I was determined to remain in Nova Scotia and to write about my own country and people. I was also determined to stand on my own feet.

To my mind Charles G.D. Roberts, the acknowledged dean of Canadian literature at this time, was an amusing poseur. His early verse was good, and so were some of his nature stories, but his other writing was mostly rubbish. He had lived abroad many years, supposedly on the largesse of moneyed women, and returned to Canada at the age of sixty-five when wealthy ladies were no longer interested in his verses or whatever else it was that pleased them in his younger years. Since his return to Canada he had sponged on his friends and acquaintances until finally they got him a monthly allowance from a newly raised fund for indigent Canadian writers.

I wasn't going to let that happen to me.

*   *   *

In August 1937 my employers introduced a group insurance scheme for which premiums would be deducted from our pay, and we were told to sign on the dotted line or give a good reason for refusal. I refused because I intended to leave the company's employ next spring. I noted in my diary, "It seemed silly to give such long notice but the insurance business brought the matter to a head. It is rather mad, I suppose, but I have money enough to support my family for three or four years, and by that time I shall know whether Joss meant me to be a writer or not."

In November a letter from George Blackwood told me that Lord Tweedsmuir (John Buchan) had asked him, "Who is the admirable man writing Nova Scotia stories for Maga?" Subsequently I had letters from Tweedsmuir himself from time to time, saying kind things about my work.

By this time bold speculator I.W. Killam had enlarged his paper manufacturing by acquiring control of a big Quebec mill, and he placed the Colonel in charge of that as well as the Mersey mill in Nova Scotia. As the Quebec mill was the larger of the two, the Colonel made his headquarters there, visiting our town briefly from time to time.

Soon after the New Year of 1938, the treasurer called me into his office and tried to talk me out of quitting a steady job for anything so precarious as writing Canadian stories for a living. The Colonel had told him to caution me about this rash step, saying the times were hard, that I had a wife and children to consider, and that no author living in Canada and writing full-time about Canada and Canadians had ever been able to make a living at it. He authorized the treasurer to raise my pay a bit, and if I ignored that, to offer me a year's leave of absence. If I didn't succeed in making a go of it in that time I could return to my job at the mill.

I told my boss to thank the Colonel for me and to say that I had found long ago (at Sable Island in fact) that I couldn't learn to swim with one hand on the side of a boat. Besides, it wouldn't be fair to the man who took my place. He'd be on tenterhooks for twelve months wondering if the job was his or not.

So the treasurer fetched a man from another office, and I spent some weeks explaining the various accounting chores that now comprised the cashier's job and standing beside him while he got into the routine and met the various men from the mill, the woods and the ships who had business with him. After a time he asked what I had been paid for all this and was dismayed when I told him twenty-one hundred dollars a year. He said, "Downstairs, we thought you must be getting about twice that." Within a year he left the job himself.

The last day of April 1938 ended my toils at the paper mill. Shortly before noon, people from various offices gathered in the treasury department, and my boss made a little speech and presented me with a leather travelling bag as a gift from them all. I stammered something about nine years of good fellowship, and everybody shook my hand and wished me luck. That night I wrote in my diary, "It would have been so easy to keep on in that round. Nine years had slipped by like months, and I knew it was now or never if I was to do something with a life which to date has been wasted. Ambition is an uncomfortable disease. Perhaps I shall regret my lightly resigned job before three years are out, but I know I shall never regret this attempt to establish myself as a writer."

*　*　*

During my last months at the paper mill I hired a pair of carpenters to build an annex to the rear of my house, to my own design. It gave me a large study lighted by five windows and with household and telephone chatter sealed off by soundproof walls and double doors with an air space between them. The view from the west windows was a pleasant one, facing over the back lawn and its low stone wall, and beyond that a field, a pond where frogs sang in spring, and a tall wood of spruce trees where many birds nested in summer. After ten years of study and writing by night on a dining-room table or a bedroom bookcase with a hinged flap for the typewriter, I had a good workshop at last.

*　*　*

The Colonel was in Quebec when I left the Mersey mill. Several weeks later he came to Liverpool on business and gave a farewell party for me at the company's luxurious fishing and hunting lodge up the river, where visiting VIP's were entertained. After a lot of drinks and a very good dinner with my former staff associates about me at the board, the Colonel arose and said pleasant things about my service with the company and predicted jovially that I was going to be another Dickens and (a few minutes later) another Thackeray. He then presented me with a silver tray etched with the signatures of the men with whom I had closest contact on the staff, including his own. In the centre was this inscription:

> Presented to Thomas Head Raddall in appreciation of his co-operation and good fellowship, and to signify that in severing his business connection to embark upon a literary career he carries with him the highest esteem and utmost good will of his associates in the Mersey Paper Company February 1929 – April 1938

* * *

In June 1938 I began to write a novel about the scene and circumstances at Milton when I came there, the old mills and their timberlands in the hands of a greedy speculator, the resultant poverty in the village, and so on. I had told Blackwood that I intended writing a novel, and he asked me to let him see it. I went ahead with it, pausing now and then to write a short story for Maga. During 1937 I had earned $811 with my pen, mostly from Blackwood. During 1938, when I was dividing my time between short stories and the novel, I received $690, again mostly from Maga.

In August 1938 I wrote in my diary:

> I get in about 1,000 to 1,500 words a day on my novel. I have about one third done on the first writing and it seems very dull and lifeless. Europe all excited over Hitler's mobilization of one million troops for "manoeuvres." In Spain the insurgent drive on Valencia and Barcelona has been forestalled by government attacks, the first in a long time, and there is now every prospect that the war there will continue into next year, in spite of continued reinforcements, German and Italian, going to Franco's armies. In China the Japanese are driving steadily towards Hankow, bombing all large cities cruelly.

* * *

In the heat of summer I found time for sea fishing and for happy joint-family expeditions to Port Joli and the Indian shell heaps. In the fall with two companions I made a canoe trip across Lake Rossignol, the largest on the Mersey watershed, and up a tributary stream to Coad's Lake, where we tried calling up bull moose for our cameras.

I spent a few days deer hunting with my friends at Eagle Lake. I still had no big-game rifle, depending on borrowed ones. Other than my old .22 rifle, which was good enough for rabbits, my only weapon was an ancient double-barrelled shotgun, which I had bought for a few dollars. I put ball cartridge in this relic if I saw a deer but it was useless at any range over fifty yards. I used it chiefly with pellet shot for wild fowl.

In November I went to Halifax for a chat with the head of the provincial bureau of information about the sea-angling booklet, which I revised every year. Suddenly I was offered a salaried post with the government. It involved writing or editing some government literature, writing speeches for unspecified persons, and now and then speaking myself, to represent the government at minor luncheons and dinners. I declined, saying I'd thrown up a steady job to establish myself as a free-lance writer, and I didn't care for public speaking and handshaking.

* * *

In January 1939 George Blackwood suggested a selection from my short stories written for Maga to be published in a case-bound book with a foreword by Lord Tweedsmuir. I was delighted.

I finished my novel on the thirteenth of February, an ominous day of the month. For many months I had been slogging away at it from early morning until long past midnight, taking some time out for a walk in the afternoon. I was very tired, and the book was not satisfactory, with characters either too stiff or on the other hand too garrulous. I sent it to Blackwood saying frankly that it was not a Blackwood sort of book.

He returned it at the end of March and agreed, saying that it was too vague in its characters, too sexy, too political, and too long. I knew he wouldn't like it, but I was not prepared for such a sweeping condemnation. On careful rereading I realized myself that much of what he said was right, but some of it was good, so I hadn't wasted all the time and drudgery I had put into it. I put the bundle of typescript aside, thinking I might salvage the good parts later on, but eventually I destroyed the whole thing. Years afterward I used the basic scene and theme in a very different novel called *The Wings of Night*, which was successful.

* * *

The war came in September, and Brenton Smith and I determined to enlist in the armed forces. Parker and Gordon suggested one more weekend at the Eagle Lake camp, Gordon saying "perhaps for the last time together," rather a grim way of putting it. While there we built a new footbridge where the trail crossed Eagle Brook, and Smith said confidently, "It'll be there when we come back." Neither of us had the slightest doubt that the navy or the army would accept us for war service.

1939
1945

O n September 6, 1939, I noted in my diary, "I hope to get a commission using my experience as a wireless officer, but until the Canadian government makes its position clear about aims and objects in this war there seems no sense in rushing off to enlist blindly on a something-or-anything basis. There are rumours that no troops will be sent overseas at all, merely a home guard raised."

About three weeks later I wrote, "These are restless days. I sit for hours every morning, part of the afternoon, and every evening, racking my head for stories, but the war keeps drifting across my mind. So far in September I have written one short story and made some notes from Perkins' diary, a poor show for a month's mental wrestling."

There was another factor in my worries. My main source of income was *Blackwood's Magazine*, which paid me with cheques in sterling drawn on Coutts' Bank in London. The dollar value of the pound was shrinking fast.

In October I became the voluntary secretary-treasurer of a newly formed branch of the Red Cross Society, very busy raising funds. Such diversions grew rapidly as the war became the most insistent and demanding fact of daily life. Groups and societies raising money for war activities asked me to speak at public meetings and write advertising for their benefit, and I never refused. Before long I was involved in half a dozen other things.

* * *

In November I had a surprising letter from a professional authors' agent in London. Without consulting me he had torn two of my stories out of *Blackwood's Magazine* and sent them to Napier Moore of *Maclean's*, representing himself as my agent and offering to sell the Canadian magazine reprint rights. Moore bought them at once and sent him a cheque. The agent then wrote to me and enclosed his own cheque for the amount, less his 10 per cent commission. He did not even know my address and sent his letter and cheque to Blackwood to be forwarded. In a covering letter, George Blackwood described the agent as "a very pushing gentleman" and added, "He has no authority from us to carry through a transaction without first obtaining the author's sanction."

I was furious. Long ago I had resolved never to send any more of my work to *Maclean's*, and now I wrote my displeasure to Napier Moore. There was an amusing side to it, though. One of the tales that Moore had bought so eagerly was "Tit for Tat," which he had rejected with explicit contempt eleven years before. He had forgotten all about it, of course, and was now impressed by its publication in a world-famous magazine. He wrote to me, pleading that he had bought the Canadian rights in good faith from the London agent and already had one tale (it was "Tit for Tat") set in type and illustrated by an expensive American artist. So I agreed.

In the months and years to come, *Maclean's* copied many of my stories after they had appeared in *Blackwood's*. One day in Toronto, in the presence of his editorial staff, Moore asked me why I hadn't shown these Nova Scotia tales to *Maclean's* in the first place. As he had stuck out his chin, I let him have the blunt and simple history of "Tit for Tat." Really, I should have thanked him for rejecting it in the first place, because this and subsequent stories in *Blackwood's* brought me correspondence with John Buchan, Theodore Roosevelt, Jr., Kenneth Roberts, Thomas Costain and others who led me to take up a career as a teller of Canadian tales to the world at large.

* * *

At Christmas I drove to Halifax to dine with my mother, and while there I inquired about a commission in the Canadian Navy, citing my experience afloat and ashore. I gave my age as thirty-six, which was the truth, but a supercilious young officer at the dockyard looked at the bald patch and the greying hair at my temples and told me in a bored voice that radio apparatus and practice had changed very much since "the last war," that I would have to be trained all over again, and that the navy would train young men only.

I came away feeling like Methuselah.

* * *

By this time Blackwood had published my first book of fiction under the title *The Pied Piper of Dipper Creek and Other Stories*, with Lord Tweedsmuir's foreword. Early in 1940 I found that a few copies had been placed on sale in Toronto and Ottawa but none elsewhere in Canada. The book was mainly on sale in Britain alone, where in the uproar of war it was barely noticed. It sold 333 copies in 1939, 315 in 1940, and 825 copies between 1940 and 1944, when Blackwood's reported it out of print. The total sales brought me $191.71 in royalties. Obviously this was no way to get rich.

During 1939 I sold eight stories to Maga, and with the second-hand sale to *Maclean's* my income for that year was $1,131.19. I had to dip into my savings to make ends meet, even with the utmost economy. I had foreseen this in the first two or three years of struggle to establish myself, for which I had saved so carefully, but I was not prepared for the war and its many distractions. I could only go on doggedly, writing as best I could and hoping for a break.

In the spring of 1940 a break came. I had a letter from another professional agent, this one in New York. He too had been reading my *Blackwood's* tales, but unlike the pushing gentleman in London he asked me to send him a new story to offer for sale in the United States. I sent him one I had just finished, "Blind MacNair," a tale of a singing contest between Nova Scotia chantymen in the days of the windjammers. He sold it promptly to the *Saturday Evening Post* for five hundred dollars. At that time the *Post* was the foremost American magazine, with a huge weekly circulation and a rich income from advertising. Each issue had articles on matters of American interest, especially politics and finance, but it was composed mostly of fiction, including half a dozen short stories and instalments of serials. The hope of most writers and would-be writers in the United States and Canada was to get into this magazine – in the phrase of the time "to crack the *Post*." So I had cracked the

Post. Lofty-minded critics and disappointed authors, a curious combination, always held the *Post* up to scorn as a packet of trash. A lot of it was, but during my own connection with the *Post*, which lasted two years or so, I remember tales by C.S. Forester, James Thurber, Kay Boyle, Stephen Vincent Benét and others with first-rate pens. My sales for 1940 included three stories in the *Post*, which brought my income to a little over twenty-five hundred dollars, a big improvement over last year.

*   *   *

In January 1941 I made a coast-to-coast radio broadcast on prime evening time, a tremendous thing in those days before television, when millions of people listened eagerly for every word. The CBC had asked me to give a talk about some feature of Canada's naval history, and naturally I chose the Nova Scotia privateers, the first ships designed, built, manned and commanded entirely by Canadians for warfare on the high seas. I made the broadcast from the Halifax studios of the CBC, of course. Among the listeners were a Commander Gow and his wife, who phoned to the studio an immediate invitation to a small cocktail party in their flat.

I went, and in the course of chat someone remarked that I had been a seagoing radio officer in time past. Mrs. Gow turned to me, saying, "Careful! Gow is always grabbing men who can do things."

I answered promptly, "Let him grab. I'd like nothing better."

She brought her husband over and he asked, "Do you mean it?" Of course I did. He said quickly, "I'd like to have you on my staff. You'll have to go through the proper channel and have your name registered on the Naval Volunteers List, which means volunteers for commissioned rank. It's kept by the Naval Secretary at Ottawa. I can do the rest from here." He revealed that he was in charge of naval radio installations on the Atlantic coast.

I obtained an application form and sent it to the Naval Secretary with all dispatch. The form warned applicants that there was a long waiting list, but I knew Gow could get around that. Months passed without further word from him or from Ottawa. I was perplexed by the silence. Then I heard indirectly that Gow and several of his staff had perished on a flight to Newfoundland – the naval censorship was always very tight. So my name on the Naval Secretary's list remained merely a name, far down.

It was strange to think that one had to have influence to get into a war.

*   *   *

Among other stories for *Blackwood's* back in 1937 I had begun a sporadic series about colonial days in my town, which I called Oldport. The fifth of the Oldport series, entitled "At the Tide's Turn," appeared in the magazine early in 1941. It described the dire position of the Nova Scotia settlers of Yankee origin, caught in the British and American crossfire during the Revolution. Persecution by their own brethren in New England eventually became the worse of the two, for it took the form of privateers, many of them no better than pirates, marauding along the Nova Scotia coast on the excuse that "them that ain't fer us is agin us." George Washington tried to stop it, seeing where it led, but in this direction he was powerless.

My studies of that time especially in the Perkins diary, gave me rich material, including a crucial episode in which the Yankee settlers of Liverpool, led by Perkins, at last met some of their predatory cousins with gunfire and so placed themselves firmly on the British side. A small affair at the time, almost lost in the general sound and fury of the war, it set an example for all of the hitherto neutral Yankees of Nova Scotia and proved to be the first faint crack of a widening breach between the Nova Scotians and the other thirteen colonies. At the final peace conference in Paris this breach secured for the British an abiding foothold on the Atlantic coast of Canada, because the province of Nova Scotia then included the Gaspé peninsula and the whole of what is now New Brunswick, and it had the only harbours free of ice. Without it the Canada of today would not exist. With a fourteenth American state commanding the Gulf of St. Lawrence, the United States would have swallowed Upper and Lower Canada in 1812 if not before. I used the affair at "Oldport," and what it dimly foreshadowed, as the theme of my story.

*   *   *

One of many American subscribers to *Blackwood's Magazine* was Theodore Roosevelt, a son of the former president, a veteran of the American Army in War One, and at this time chairman of the board of Doubleday Doran, one of the foremost book publishing firms in the United States. In 1940 or early 1941 he and some other men prominent in the American publishing industry were dinner guests of the Canadian Club in New York, and D. Leo Dolan, head of the Canadian government's Bureau of Information (or whatever it was called at that time), went down from Ottawa to address the meeting on the subject of Canada's image abroad. Dolan told me about it years later.

In conversation after the club dinner, Roosevelt remarked, "There's a man named Thomas Raddall writing Canadian stories for *Blackwood's Magazine*, the best dam' writer you've got up there, and you," pointing to Dolan, "are the first Canadian I've met who knows anything about him."

Already Roosevelt had drawn my *Blackwood's* stories to the attention of Thomas Costain, a Canadian on the editorial staff of Doubleday Doran. Another regular reader of my *Blackwood's* tales was Kenneth Roberts, the leading American historial novelist, who mentioned the fact in his autobiographical *I Wanted to Write* in 1949. In 1941 Roosevelt wrote to Blackwood asking for my address. In his cautious Scottish way, George Blackwood refused all such requests but agreed to pass a letter on to me if it was addressed in care of the magazine. The wartime convoy system delayed the mails but eventually I got the letter. Roosevelt praised my tales and asked particularly about "At the Tide's Turn." Was it based on historical fact? I replied that it was. He wrote directly to me then, saying that this was an aspect of the American Revolution utterly unknown to the people of the United States, and he suggested that I write a history of Nova Scotia during the Revolution, using "the Macaulay or Parkman approach." I replied that I was not a historian, that I wrote short stories for my living and must keep on with them. There the matter rested for a time.

* * *

I had read most of Kenneth Roberts's books, and he seemed to me a violently biased chauvinist. In his novels about the American Revolution and the War of 1812 his Americans were long suffering, brave, ingenious and chivalrous, whereas anybody on the British side was either a villain or an idiot. Early in 1941 I read his latest novel, *Oliver Wiswell*, with deep interest and astonishment. It was a complete reversal of his old attitude, setting forth the Loyalist side of the Revolution with all of his characteristic vehemence. I sent him congratulations and mentioned that I had hoped some day to tackle that theme in a book, as I had done briefly in my Oldport tales about "Colonel Larrabee," a Carolina Loyalist driven away to Nova Scotia.

Roberts replied that I should write a novel telling the full story of the Nova Scotians themselves during the Revolution, which I had merely touched in "At the Tide's Turn." He sent a copy of this letter to Costain, who consulted Roosevelt and wrote, urging me to write such a novel, and offering a contract with Doubleday Doran. On April 12 I noted in my diary, "I have resolved to do a book dealing with the Yankees of Nova Scotia and their painful position during the American Revolution, squeezed by both sides."

*　　*　　*

Meanwhile Hitler's war in Europe spread like a grass fire in a gale, and the news got worse and worse. Some worried men in my town decided that our little port must have a system of air raid precautions on the British model, and at their request I helped to draw up a plan suited to our conditions. When it was done they insisted that I become superintendent of operations. I felt that they were unduly alarmed, but I agreed.

The nearest hospital was thirty miles away, and in the long winter season a snowstorm could block the road for two or three days. Thus an important part of our plan was to gather equipment for a small hospital and practise setting it up quickly in the high school. For staff there were three local doctors, several women who before marriage had trained as nurses in hospitals elsewhere, and many untrained volunteers. We started vigorous practice of our precautions in April of 1941. As things turned out, the hospital was the only part of our plan that came into actual use, and then in an utterly unexpected way.

Added to my various other undertakings, this ARP business put a new strain on my finances along with my thought. The other top men involved in the plan had good salaries at their regular jobs. When I wasn't writing I wasn't earning a cent. In May I noted, "All these posts accepted in the name of Duty. I'm always told it's my duty anyway. All worthy causes, no single one particularly onerous, but together they bring phone calls, letters, meetings etc. Added to the terrific distraction of the war itself I find it almost impossible to do any decent writing. I have written nothing saleable since January. God only knows what is to become of my living if this keeps up."

As I read those lines again after nearly thirty-five years I recall my bewilderment about my own affairs. I was floundering along, taking on these various tasks as patriotic duties like Don Quixote taking on the windmills, and like him getting nowhere.

*　　*　　*

In June 1941 the *Saturday Evening Post* raised their price for my short stories to eight hundred dollars, adding in a note to my New York agent, "Hope this raise in payment will encourage Mr. Raddall to send us stories with somewhat greater frequency than he has done these past few months." This was encouraging. Unfortunately the U.S. Department of Internal Revenue took a dimmer view of money going to foreign authors. In 1940 they imposed a tax of 5 per cent on such payments. By June 1941 it was up to 15 per cent. In August of that year it rose to 16½ per cent and in October it jumped to 27 ½ per cent. Eventually it settled back to 15 per cent.

*　　*　　*

The Public Archives of Nova Scotia were housed in a grey stone building of Georgian design on the campus of Dalhousie University, and the chief archivist was a tall grey man who had been teaching Canadian history in schools and colleges most of his life. He meant well, but his mind had become pedantic in the extreme, and as an archivist his attitude to the public was unconsciously defensive, as if the documents in his charge must be shielded as much as possible from profane hands and eyes.

His own view of Nova Scotia's role in the American Revolution was the banal one handed down by a succession of schoolmasters in the past – that the other thirteen colonies had rebelled against His Majesty and the rest of the British people, but by a marvellous dispensation of Providence our fourteenth remained stoutly loyal, without a seditious thought or deed. This was precisely the fallacy I intended to attack.

Roughly two-thirds of the people in Nova Scotia at the outbreak of the Revolution were of Yankee birth or the sons and daughters of Yankee settlers, and their sympathies naturally were with their own people in New England. A few individuals in Nova Scotia were ardent rebels or loyalists from the start of the Revolution, but the majority, like Simcon Perkins at Liverpool, tried earnestly to keep out of the quarrel. Unlike the other colonies, they had no broad interior farmlands to which they could retreat and subsist if the king's forces dominated the coast. The Nova Scotia settlements were small, scattered, and almost all exposed to armed ships. In fact, the Yankees of Nova Scotia were pinned to the coast like a pelt to a barn door, and the result of their reluctance to commit themselves one way or the other was persecution by both sides. A time came when their American brethren harassed them beyond endurance, and they turned dourly to the king.

* * *

I introduced myself to the chief archivist and set out my intention, a novel based on what really happened in Nova Scotia told from the viewpoint of a son of Yankee settlers, with all his initial prejudice and ignorance, his harsh experiences at the hands of both British and Americans, and his eventual decision. The archivist said stiffly, "I'm not sure I want to see a book written from that viewpoint!" Almost immediately he realized how stuffy and arrogant that sounded and corrected himself, saying coldly that I could do what I liked and the archives were at my disposal.

As I say, he meant well, and when my novel was published I thanked him in the acknowledgements as I thanked his assistants, James Martell and Margaret Ells, who had given me the real help and encouragement. It was the beginning of a congenial and fruitful association with these two young archivists in the examination of Nova Scotia history from a fresh point of view, which I set forth in short stories and novels.

First they put me at ease in what hitherto had been a mere tomb of documents. The rules in the reading room were repressive and strict. You were not allowed to smoke. You could not use a typewriter or anything else that might make a noise. You were seated at a small table with your pen or pencil, and all talk was discouraged except your requests for this document or that, made in a low voice. All of this, of course, was before the invention of the tape recorder and the photo-copying machine.

Martell and Ells found me a small empty room on another floor where I could smoke as much as I liked and bang away at my typewriter for hours or days on end, making copies of documents or copious notes. In that room, too, we had animated discussions of Nova Scotia history in general as well as the particular matters in my mind. Often they brought documents that had nothing to do with the matter in mind, saying, "Here's something interesting. Read it and make notes if you like. You may find it useful in some other connection later on." For years I spent sessions in that room gathering material that proved very useful indeed. I was the first novelist to have the use of the archives and the aid of the staff in this facile and stimulating fashion. To give the chief archivist his due, all this was done with his knowledge and consent and later his active encouragement, for he changed his attitude entirely when my books from these sources were published, not only in Canada but also in Britain and the United States. From that time others had the best use of the archives, and not only academic thesis writers a‸ in former days.

* * *

In the summer of 1941 I spent several days at Fort Beauséjour (called Fort Cumberland at the time of the American Revolution) and tramped over every foot of the ground involved in the revolt of the Yankee settlers in Cumberland, the only open rebellion in Nova Scotia. In the fort museum I spent many hours copying documents and noting references. In later years the museum attendants used to tell visitors that I wrote most of *His Majesty's Yankees* right there!

In mid-November I drove 250 miles to Cumberland again to go over the landscape as it was at the time of the siege, with snow on the marshes and ice floes on the tide, and to get the look of the earth and sky and the general feel of the place at that time of year. The roads were icy, and on my long drive there and back I had a nightmare journey over the hills.

All these matters were good discoveries. My main discovery, of course, was that I could plunge myself into the eighteenth century and swim about freely under its surface, entirely at home with its inhabitants because I had learned to talk and think as they did and because I knew life in the forest and on the sea from experience, not just from reading about it. This was "the Parkman approach" that Roosevelt had suggested, but as a novelist I needed something more. When I was a boy I had seemed too much of a dreamer to my schoolmasters. Now I had to teach myself to dream deliberately. It was no great task, for I think I had some of my mother's imagination and intuitive human insight to begin with. The challenging thing was to make all this real to people in the world of today.

* * *

Up to this time my contributions to the *Saturday Evening Post* had been no more than three or four a year, but they drew a lot of fan mail, and the editors took note. In October 1941 I had a letter from the chief editor offering a substantial bonus over my price of eight hundred dollars for a short story if I contributed more than four a year. In other words he was inviting me to join what sneering critics called "the *Saturday Evening Post* stable of writers," whose work appeared frequently in the magazine. The implication was that all were mercenary hacks writing to the specifications of the editorial board.

In my case so far there had been no specifications or even suggestions from the *Post* editors. I continued to tell stories according to my own notions and in my own style, describing Canadian scenes and people utterly unlike the average American's picture of a country usually under snow and inhabited solely by red-coated Mounties, Eskimos, and a comic French character named Jan Bateese. The *Post* printed my stories as I wrote them, with no editorial hanky-panky. Later on, in 1942, when the editors began to ask for changes in theme or treatment that obviously would make the tales generally American and not just Canadian, I told my agent to sell the stories somewhere else, even if the price was less.

The *Post* published an annual book containing what the editors considered the best short stories of the previous year. These were well printed and bound, and they had a large sale. Stories of mine were chosen for the collections of 1940 and 1941. My connection with the *Post* ceased in 1942.

* * *

I had just got back from my November visit to Cumberland and several days of research in the archives at Halifax when my phone rang. A sudden visitation of bigwigs from Halifax, service and civilian, wanted to see a full-dress rehearsal of our air raid precautions. I took my post as superintendent of operations in an office of Town Hall, notified everybody concerned, and before long received reports of bomb damage, fire, and casualties by phone and runner. I phoned the various posts concerned, called for ambulances and fire apparatus, and checked on the first-aid stations. Within an hour the emergency hospital was set up in the high school, fully equipped even to X-ray apparatus, and staffed with doctors and nurses. After all this the chief bigwig made a little speech and said ours was the best emergency organization in the province. I daresay he told that to every group he visited, but we knew that ours was good, anyhow.

Privately I still considered German air raids a wildly remote possibility. As for submarine or surface raiders, Hitler was keeping his sea weapons well away from the North American coast so that the Americans could have no excuse for belligerence. In my view this was likely to continue indefinitely. We would never have actual use for our carefully planned and practised set-up. Like millions of other people (including Hitler himself), I was utterly wrong. In December Pearl Harbor changed the whole face of the war. As Japan's ally, Germany declared war on the United States a few days later, and the U-boats moved in. Their presence was a very painful fact along our coast by January 1942, with its bitter weather for torpedoed crews in open boats. The shift came so suddenly that the U.S. and Canadian navies had no escorts or even a plan for convoying shipping anywhere south and west of Halifax. The U-boat crews had the easy and cruel sport of shooting defenceless fish in a barrel of icy water.

*   *   *

During the fall and winter I had been working hard at my novel. I arose early each morning and stopped for a hasty snack at noon. Dinner was at five o'clock to give me a long evening shut up in my den. Usually I worked till midnight, but if the juice was flowing (as Hemingway used to say) I wrote into the early hours of the morning. Often I fell asleep at my desk, but I was alert again by seven o'clock for another day's work.

After a month or two of this I began to find that incessant work blunted my own sense of criticism. Sometimes after a session of many hours I thought I had written a masterpiece, or I was so disgusted that I hurled whole chapters into the wastebasket. I found that a long solitary walk was necessary to clear my mind so that I could see what was right and what was wrong. Thus I came to the routine of a full morning at my desk, a whole afternoon outdoors, fishing, hunting, or just plain walking, and then the long evening session that was always my best working time. On the whole this routine served me well throughout my writing life.

*   *   *

Expanding furiously in view of the U-boat attacks, the Canadian Navy had a tough problem in maintenance and repair. The shipbuilding and repair plants up the St. Lawrence were closed by ice in the four worst months of the year, when the navy's thin-skinned frigates and corvettes and minesweepers were battered by winter storms and seas. Because the facilities at Halifax were not enough, the navy financed the expansion of small ship-repair plants in the ice-free outports of Nova Scotia. The plant at Liverpool employed less than fifty men before the war. It grew quickly to a work force of seven or eight hundred. Similarly the big paper mill, with its excellent machineshop and wharves, engaged hundreds of shipfitters for the repair of naval craft.

These ships deposited their ammunition in the Halifax magazine before coming to Liverpool, and most of their crews went on hard-earned leave or to take courses of instruction, leaving a few officers and men as ship-keepers during the weeks of refitting.

One day in my den, discussing a coastal watch by the fishermen, the corporal of our small RCMP detachment made what seemed to me an amusing remark. He said an armed party from a German submarine or submarines, landing at night on any of the uninhabited beaches to the east and west of us, could easily reach the coastal highway, seize the first cars or trucks to come along, and swoop down on our quiet little port like a bolt from the blue. At our repair docks nowadays lay as many as a dozen valuable naval craft, with skeleton crews, no ammunition, and not even steam for escape. All could be sunk or badly damaged by well-placed explosives. A small platoon of the Reserve Army, recently formed in the town, had a few old rifles for drill but not a single cartridge. In fact, the only properly trained and armed people here were the Mountie corporal and one constable, and they had exactly two revolvers and two Lee Enfield rifles.

I chuckled at this picture in the late autumn of 1941. It was not so funny on a bitter cold day in February 1942, when our emergency organization got a message asking us to prepare immediate hospital facilities. I quote from my diary:

A plane on dawn patrol had sighted men in lifeboats rowing towards Liverpool. By 9 A.M. our school-hospital was set up and ready, and about that time the first lifeboat arrived, towed in by a fishing boat. A second boat landed at Western Head, and a third at Beach Meadows. The men were brought to our hospital, all wearing their dark blue kapok lifejackets for some protection against the cold. One chap had nothing else but his boots and an oilskin coat. Some were barefoot. We carried them in. The doctors and nurses were on hand, and the men were put into beds warmed with hot-water bottles. I arranged for food from the restaurants, and with my car I got dishes, cups, spoons, etc. from the stores.

Their ship was a new British steamer, *Empire Sun*, 10,000 tons, loaded with grain at Portland, Maine, and heading for Halifax to join a convoy to Britain. At midnight she was hit by two torpedoes amidships and sank in ten minutes. This was about 12 miles off our harbour and the sky reflection of the lighthouse was visible. After a vain search for other survivors, the boats rowed towards the light. They had only a few oars, and the set of tide out of Liverpool Bay made it a terrible struggle. They were eight or ten hours in the boats, suffering from exposure. One had a mangled hand. Many had severe bruises. Total crew 72, of whom 19 are missing including the captain and wireless officer.

*   *   *

That was the beginning. A few days later there was a curt hint by phone from Halifax. We sent out an old schooner with a volunteer crew to look for men in boats. We telephoned the new naval base at Shelburne, forty miles to the west of us, but they declared they knew nothing about a torpedoed ship in our area. Halifax, seventy sea miles to the east, had sent a couple of naval craft to look for survivors and remained officially mum to our people down the coast, whose fishermen in their motorboats were in the best position to help. Naval craft found the survivors after many hours of exposure in the cold, and in Halifax there was a terrible toll of amputations at the hospitals. Again the wireless officer had stayed at his post, trying to send forth the distress call and the ship's position, and so went down with the ship, all for nothing.

I went with several other men of the South Shore to confer with the naval officer in charge at Shelburne and get this muddle straightened out. After some brisk talk we got a promise of prompt information in the future, and the navy carried it out faithfully and well.

*   *   *

With time out for such alarms and excursions I went on writing my novel. There was a curious parallel in these raids on our coast and the raids of the American revolutionists, who had given my colonial predecessors at Liverpool so many alarms and excursions of their own. There was one main difference. Our war was still offshore. So far we had not been compelled to turn out with old fowling guns to defend the place against raiders afoot.

* * *

I finished *His Majesty's Yankees* towards the end of April and began to type clean copy for the printers. At the same time I was arguing by mail with editor Tom Costain over the title. He thought it very bad and asked me to suggest alternatives. I replied with a list of the most awful titles I could think of. One I remember was *Red Flows The Fundy Tide*. At last he admitted defeat. Much later when I met him in person he told me *His Majesty's Yankees* was such a striking paradox that it amounted to a stroke of genius. Its virtue to me was that it summed up my story in three words.

* * *

As soon as the book was out of my hands and into the printer's, I walked into the "armoury" of our local defence unit, the newly raised platoon of the West Nova Scotia Regiment. The armoury was an old church, and sunlight through its coloured windows gave a holy aura to the sergeant-major and other unsaintly persons, including me. When the U-boats brought the war to our doorstep, the authorities at Halifax had promoted the platoon commander to captain and ordered him to recruit a full infantry company of three platoons. He asked me and my friends Parker and Smith to take command of these platoons, and we agreed. Parker and Smith had served in the Canadian Army in War One, and I had been born and brought up in the army, so there was no basic difficulty. For our people in Nova Scotia, the Reserve Army was just a new name for the old militia, which had maintained armed companies all along the coast, and our task was precisely that of His Majesty's Yankees long ago, to keep watch and ward against marauders from the sea.

It was now confirmed that German submarines were landing parties of trained saboteurs at widely scattered places all the way from Gaspé to Florida; indeed, several had been picked up by local police in Gaspé and elsewhere. With their natural daring, the Germans were quite capable of trying something spectacular like the notion of our Mountie corporal.

* * *

A basic principle of the reserve force was that its company and platoon officers must find and enlist their own men, and that was my first task. In recruiting we were limited to men between eighteen and forty-five who were below the physical standard for service overseas, to youths between sixteen and eighteen, and men between forty-five and fifty. Most of the officers and sergeant-majors were veterans of War One.

On duty we wore Canadian Army battledress from boots to steel helmets. Our weapons came from arsenals in the United States. Officers were armed with Smith and Wesson revolvers, NCO's with Reising automatic carbines, other ranks with U.S. Army .30 calibre bolt-action rifles, made during War One and stored away in thick grease ever since. All were effective weapons. The only British firearm in our company was a Lewis machine-gun, a worn relic of War One.

Training was vigorous in the church-armoury twice a week, and on weekends we practised musters and patrols of likely landing places along the coast. In summer, troop trains gathered up the various companies and took them to Aldershot Camp in the Annapolis Valley for battalion training. Ottawa was urgent about all this but with the usual stupidities. With the help of our new American allies there was no stint of arms or equipment except in the personal equipment of officers. We officers were given a long list of things to obtain at our own expense, ranging from sleeping-bags to field glasses. Adding up the list roughly, we found that a platoon or company commander was expected to spend up to five hundred dollars of his own money. Of course I had such things as sleeping-bag and field glasses, as did many another sportsman in the Reserve Army, but few bought the entire list or anything like it.

We were paid only for the time spent at drill or on coastal patrols or at Aldershot Camp, where the money was hardly enough to pay our mess bills. With experience we found that a lot of similar demands, issued by staff dugouts from War One revelling now in new rank and full pay and allowances, made no sense whatever to the man on the spot, who had to earn his living somehow and be a soldier for a pittance on top of that.

My pay as a second-lieutenant at Aldershot Camp was twenty-one dollars a week. The first time I drew it from a pay officer there I noticed a mysterious deduction, which applied to us all. We asked what it was and were told that it was Defence Tax, levied on every civilian employed in Canada. We could only laugh, but it was a wry laugh.

I spend much of the summer of 1942 under canvas at Aldershot,

where our brigade (West Novas, North Novas, Pictou Highlanders, and the usual medical, signal and transport units) had assem-
bled. Training went on from dawn to dark, and for officers there
were lectures in a marquee after dark. At thirty-nine I was in good
condition, well able to dash over the camp's assault course, with its
walls to climb and pools to swing over, with no more than the
natural amount of puffing in such activities.

Most of our West Novas were from small towns and villages on
the coast, where the woods come down to the sea and almost every
boy has a gun in his hands by the age of ten. It was wildly absurd
for instructors at Aldershot to go through the old ritual for raw
recruits: "Now this is a rifle. It will be your best friend when you get
into battle, so take good care of it. This part is called the butt, this is
the breech, this is the barrel" – and all the rest of it. At first our men
and boys looked incredulous ("This guy has got to be kidding!"),
but as the drill sergeants went on with it, wooden-faced and gravel-
voiced, the troops just grinned and bore it.

All this was rendered absolutely idiotic when our men got their
chance to test these weapons on the Aldershot ranges. Every rifle
has individual characteristics in sighting and firing, and the only
way a man can get familiar with his weapon is by target practice.
From some stupid idea of economy our men were limited to fifteen
cartridges for their entire range practice with the unfamiliar American rifles.

Stupid, too, was the repetitious and monotonous foot drill
("square bashing"), the repeated re-aligning of rows of tents in the
camp, with all the tent pegs to be pulled up, moved a few inches,
and hammered down again, and especially the arrangement of kit,
which every man must pile outside his tent in a neat and exact
order every morning. The exact order of piling the kit varied with
the notions of the regular army instructors, who seldom had served
in the same regiment. ("This is the way we did it in the RCR," or
"the Princess Pats," and so on).

One morning a fat and pompous brass hat, finding fault loudly
with trifles right and left, noticed that the West Nova kits were
piled in a different order from those of the North Novas, and he
bellowed like an outraged elephant. I happened to be Orderly
Officer of the West Novas that day, accompanying him and his
brigade major on a tour of the camp, so I got the full blast. By that
time the fuse of my own temper had burned short, and I asked the
brigade major what the hell any of this had to do with the patrol

and defence of our coast, for which we had enrolled. I answered my own question by saying it was more important for our men to shoot straight than to pile kits any way at all.

Fatty turned scarlet. I daresay he would have liked to have me shot, but he couldn't even court martial a reserve officer who obviously would have a lot more to say, given a chance. He waddled off to report my insolence to my colonel and to order that the whole battalion be recalled from field training to re-pile the offending kits. At mess that evening the colonel said nothing of the matter, but the second-in-command brought up the subject, approving my remarks and adding his own opinion of "the bloody stupid waste of our men's time today." Both he and the colonel had good fighting records in War One. I don't know what the brass hat had ever done. The man might have made a fussily efficient corporal in charge of a latrine detail. He was obviously unfit to command even a rifle platoon in action. His present rank was one of the anomalies of the Reserve Army that were never resolved in action, which so quickly weeds out the incompetent.

*   *   *

Through the autumn of 1942 and into the winter we carried on our coastal defence practices. In addition to this routine there were sudden muster-and-patrol alarms from Army HQ in Halifax, usually in cold weather and sometimes in the middle of the night, and we officers bustled about, getting our men together and then away to various outlying parts of the coast.

In one of these alarms, with specks of snow drifting down from a gloomy November sky, I was ordered to take a fighting patrol to remote Cadden Bay, which had perfect landing beaches of sand facing towards the solitary hump of Little Hope Island, a notorious seamark and lurking place for German submarines on the surface at night. Several ships had been torpedoed in the vicinity. That part of the coast was uninhabited for many miles, so I with my ten riflemen took an army lorry as far as it could go and then tramped through scrub woods and barrens to the sea. Just before we reached the shore there was a sudden crashing in the bush, coming straight towards us. I said quietly, "Boys, here they are." Most of my patrol were hunters from boyhood. We lost no time in cocking our weapons and getting set for business.

Out popped about a dozen sheep led by two rams. We learned later that they belonged to people at Port Joli, who turned them

206

loose in the wild shore pastures in spring and rounded them up in December for feeding and shelter through the winter. With the early onset of cold weather I suppose the sheep were glad to hear us coming. We searched the sands of Cadden Bay but unlike Robinson Crusoe found not a single footprint. Indeed, in all our alarms and excursions we never found anybody to shoot, capture, or even challenge. Naturally we cursed the brass hats at Halifax who thought it witty to turn us out for nothing, at such times and places, and in such weather, but our comment was not altogether just. After the war I was told that some of these alarms were given on tips from the British Admiralty, decoding German naval radio messages. In the game played by both sides, most of the messages were bound to be false, to divert attention from real landings elsewhere. Other "flaps" of course were cooked up at Halifax, just to keep us on our toes. We had to take them all seriously, just in case.

*   *   *

While I was tramping about the coastal woods in the hunt for mythical Germans, my first novel arrived in the bookshops. *His Majesty's Yankees* did not set the world afire, but it had favourable reviews in respected quarters (the *New York Times Book Review* called it "the historical novel discovery of the year") and in the next two years it sold about ten thousand copies in the United States and Canada.

The man who first suggested it to me had since rejoined the U.S. Army and was commanding an infantry division in the expedition to Algeria. Before leaving New York he had given instructions for sending him a copy of *His Majesty's Yankees* as soon as it came from the bindery. I had a belated letter from him.

Somewhere in N. Africa,
Jan. 13th '43

Dear Mr. Raddall:

Among the stray and casual packages that reach us out here came a copy of your book. I have read it with the keenest enjoyment. It is excellent. All that I hoped it would be when I first wrote you. It gives the most vivid picture of those times. David is a finely drawn character. I hope to heaven we still have enough of the type left. I liked also the way you show the constant injustice, knavery and stupidity that cling to all sides in all struggles. I'm over here with my troops – have been since we attacked on the 8th of Nov. It's a long road that lies before us but at least we're moving in the right direction now. I'm looking forward to the next novel.

Theodore Roosevelt

*   *   *

Financially for me this original edition of *His Majesty's Yankees* was a failure. A case-bound novel sold for $3.75 at most in those days, and my royalty was 10 per cent. When Doubleday Doran let it go out of print in the United States two years later I had got less than four thousand dollars in royalties. In Canada, however, it brought me the prestige of those halcyon days when a native author achieved book publication, not merely in Canada but in the United States. Suddenly I was known, though far short of famous, in my own country.

In my home town there was the warmth of heart that goes to the local boy who makes good. The Town Council, the Board of Trade, the Kiwanis Club and others combined to honour me with a dinner, a toast, a hearty singing of "For He's a Jolly Good Fellow," and the gift of a barometer with a plate inscribed, "Presented to Thomas H. Raddall by his fellow townsmen in affection and esteem."

*   *   *

Adding up the little cashbook which I kept faithfully for income tax purposes, at the end of 1942 I found that I had received $3,922, most of it from magazines. This was enough to pay my bills and even to add a bit to my shrunken savings, for the first time since I quit my job, sink or swim, in the spring of '38.

*   *   *

In January 1943 I signed a contract with Doubleday Doran for a second historical novel. This time the publishers agreed to advance me $250 a month for the next twelve months. I knew I could add to this by writing an occasional short story or article for magazines. I sent no more stories to the *Saturday Evening Post*, but my agent was getting the same price (eight hundred dollars) from another prosperous American magazine, *Collier's*, whose editors worked on *Blackwood's* excellent principle: accept a story whole or reject it whole, but never try to tell the author what to write or how to write it. My agent sold the rejections to lesser magazines at smaller prices, but that was all right with me.

Thomas and Ellen Raddall with their children Nellie, Tom and Winifred in 1912.

Lieutenant Thomas Head Raddall of the Winnipeg Rifles early in World War I.

Tom in his first merchant marine officer's uniform, "splendid with gold braid on the cuffs."

(Top), Tom as wireless operator of SS. Watuka; (above), with fellow operators beside Sable Island's radio mast.

C.S. Mackay-Bennett, *which lifted and repaired damaged telegraph cables in the North Atlantic. Tom served on her for more than a year.*

Tom with Edith Freeman, his future wife, in August 1925.

The author dressed "suitably for a journey in the bush."

A successful deer hunt in the Mersey Woods, 1926.

The family home on Park Street, Liverpool, that Raddall bought in 1933. Later he added a study at the rear.

Historical research: the author with relics of Nova Scotia privateers.

T.H.R. at the wheel of Colonel Jones's yacht Awenishe *on a cruise in 1933. Jones is seated second from left.*

At the testimonial dinner on Raddall's retirement from Mersey Paper, 1938: talking with Hubert MacDonald.

The cabin at Eagle Lake and companions Jim Parker, Austin Parker, Roy Gordon (above), Hector Dunlop and Brenton Smith (below).

The forest could restore Raddall's serenity after a gruelling bout of writing.

(Left) Lieutenant Thomas Raddall of the West Nova Scotia Regiment, Aldershot Camp, 1942.

(Right) Beginning in 1941, Raddall spoke often over CBC radio on historical subjects.

(Below) Survivors of torpedoed S.S. Empire Sun *taking leave of the Liverpool emergency organization.*

In 1943 Raddall made research for Roger Sudden *at Louisbourg in the museum and among the ruined ramparts.*

His work included examination of old French coastal defences and the British invasion route.

The Simeon Perkins House in Liverpool. Raddall was instrumental in preserving the home of the colonial diarist.

Old King's College, the dream school young Tom was unable to attend.

An autographing session at a store in Halifax after publication of Roger Sudden.

Raddall with Nicholas Monsarrat during the Canadian Authors Association meetings, Toronto, 1953.

A family picnic, 1939: left to right, Tommy, Aunt Marie Freeman, Frances, T.H.R., and Edith.

T.H.R. and Edith on the White Point golf course near Liverpool.

In 1961 the author visited the shipyard of W.C. MacKay and Sons in Shelburne, where these photographs were taken. He is seen chatting with founder Winslow MacKay. The building of ships, particularly sailing ships, had been a favourite study since he first built a crude model brig on Sable Island.

T.H.R. with Governor General and Mrs. Michener at Rideau Hall, Ottawa, in November 1971.
He was made an Officer of the Order of Canada, one of Canada's highest honours.

In May 1972 the author was awarded an honorary degree by the University of King's College, which is now associated with Dalhousie University in Halifax. This was the fourth such honour given him.

In sessions at the archives I had talks with Martell and Miss Ells about a subject for the next novel. After you have worked long and intensely on a book there is a mental hangover in which you can think of nothing but that book and how it might have been improved. My mind remained full of *His Majesty's Yankees* for many weeks, shutting out all else.

My first new notion was a tale of the settlement of Halifax in 1749, beginning with the poor cockneys herded into ships in the Thames and going on to the harsh facts of life (and death) awaiting them across the sea. Then I mused on the rise and fall of the great French fortress at Louisbourg, a theme used in the past by two or three novelists without much delving into facts. One evening Jim Martell said, "Look here! Why not combine the two? Halifax was founded by the British government to offset the French naval and military base at Louisbourg. They were the little Rome and Carthage of their time in North America. One was bound to destroy the other."

Of course! Research began at once, in the archives and in a multitude of books and maps borrowed and studied far into the nights at home. Among other things I had to enlarge and improve my schoolboy smattering of the French language. To do all this I had to disentangle myself from the time-eating obligations and chores that had involved so much of my life since the war began. It was absurd for anyone struggling for a living to tussle with such a lot of windmills in the name of duty. I began with my commission in the Reserve Army, with had taken so much of my time and energy in the past year.

The western aspect of the great war had changed completely with the Allies' victories in North Africa. The Italo-German Axis was now revolving anxiously on the defensive, watching more and more powerful American forces coming on the European scene to join the British. It was only a matter of timing until these tremendous forces hit the Italians and Germans where they lived.

On our North American coast the furtive and scattered landings of saboteurs from submarines had accomplished nothing. There was now an efficient air-sea patrol and a convoy system. Many of the U-boats had shifted their operations to the more comfortable waters of the Caribbean Sea. Here in Nova Scotia the chances of an exploit such as our Mountie corporal had envisioned had gone with the winds of war. So what was the role of the Reserve Army on our coast? As far as I could see, its only useful purpose now was to give basic training to seventeen- and eighteen-year-olds who eventually would pass into fighting battalions overseas. This could be done by a couple of drill sergeants in each company depot, without the elaborate set-up for defensive musters and patrols which consumed so much time and effort.

In January 1943 I sent in an application to resign my commission, stating the plain truth that in making my living I could not afford so much time on military affairs here on the home coast. The fat brass hat's opinion of a mutinous orderly officer at Aldershot had not mattered to my commanding officer, who replied from Battalion HQ at Middleton, Nova Scotia:

> Dear Raddall:
>   We have your application to resign, which I regret very much to see. I can appreciate the reason for your complete attention to your work, but none the less I regret losing an officer of your high calibre. I wish to thank you very sincerely for a job well done, and I hope that in the future I may have the opportunity of working with you again.
>
>   Yours very truly,
>   C.A. Good. Lt. Col.

*   *   *

In Ottawa and Halifax the brass hats of the Reserve Army carried on blithely as if a German invasion might come at any moment, right up to the war's end. Like boys with boxes of tin soldiers they changed and rearranged the coastal units all that time. For example, the infantry company at Liverpool was plucked away from the West Nova Scotia Regiment and rearmed and trained as part of a machine-gun battalion based at Halifax. Later on it was retrained again as part of an engineer company.

In the early scurry of 1942 a friend of mine who lived at Lockeport, near the Shelburne naval base, was asked to raise a company of infantry there at once. So he did. Then, because he had fought in War One as a captain of artillery, he was ordered to change it into an artillery unit. He did that, too. By the end of 1943 he had a complete modern field battery – guns, trucks, searchlights, radios, range-finders – everything except a single round of ammunition. At that time there was no artillery practice range nearer

210

than Camp Petawawa in Ontario, well over a thousand miles away by rail. Like many other Reserve Army officers on the coast he resigned his commission when the role became not only useless but ridiculous.

* * *

My duties as superintendent of operations in our emergency organization at Liverpool had passed to someone else when I joined the West Nova Scotia Regiment, so now I was free of both. I continued to help in fund-raising drives for Victory Loans, the Red Cross, and so on, and I never slackened my efforts to aid needy war veterans, who soon began to include men of the new war, wounded and discharged. Now, however, the big wastes of time and thought were gone. I could devote the better part to my own work.

I had to wait a bit, though. In May 1943 I was smitten by the first serious illness of my life, a vicious kind of influenza that developed into pneumonia and laid me low for weeks. In the convalescent stage I began to mull over plot and material for the new novel, which I decided to call *Roger Sudden* after its star-doomed hero.

* * *

All this time on the Mersey River I had not owned a high-powered rifle. I hunted deer with borrowed ones and occasionally with ball cartridge in my shotgun. My preferred game was small – rabbits, partridge and wild duck.

Increasingly tight rationing of meat during the war made a special hardship for people on the coast, where few or no cattle were raised and even fish were scarce at times because so many fishermen were away in the armed forces. At last I adopted the practice of shrewd pot-hunters who shot a couple of deer in the season every fall, cut the venison into steaks, roasts, stew-meat and so on, wrapped each portion in waxed paper, and placed it in the local cold storage plant for use when other meat could not be had.

The manufacture of sporting rifles and ammunition in Canada had practically ceased for the duration of the war. Because lenders of rifles naturally clung to their own stock of cartridges, I searched about the town and countryside for someone willing to sell me a big-game rifle with a supply of ammunition. In these times it proved difficult, but in the summer of 1943 I was lucky enough to get an excellent Springfield 30-06 rifle, with the Krag-Jorgensen breech mechanism, and a stock of cartridges with high-velocity 220-grain bullets.

Long afterwards I was amused to find that Ernest Hemingway, the insatiate slayer of just about everything that walked, swam or flew, preferred out of his large private arsenal this same make and model of the Springfield, firing the same bullet, for his big-game hunting in Africa and America. It was the only thing I ever had in common with the trigger-happy life of Ernesto MacHemingway.

In that summer of '43 I went to Louisburg for research in the museum and on the ground. There was no hotel or boarding place in the little town, but three miles away the museum caretaker kindly gave me room and board in his residence, right in the heart of the old ruined fortress. During the 1930s the Canadian government had done some tentative work in clearing debris out of the foundations of the citadel but nothing more.

The seaward windows of the museum had no screens or blinds, so the coastal defence authorities forbade lights after dark. Ships loading coal and sometimes steel from Sydney passed down the harbour channel in clear view of the museum, like my old *Hochelaga* in 1920. Each day I pored over documents, maps and books as long as I could read print and make notes. Then I took an evening stroll around the ancient ramparts, which had been damaged by the siege guns of 1758, blasted afterwards by British demolition engineers, and further crumbled by more than eighteen decades of frost and thaw.

Deer were plentiful in the surrounding woods, and at this time of evening they crept forth to nibble some dainty that grew in the moat and on the glacis. In my semi-circular walks I came on them singly and in small groups. They were quite bold in the dusk. When I drew near they merely walked away a few steps and returned to their grazing when I passed on.

One day I heard the caretaker's wife grumbling about the meat ration, a familiar complaint. She had her coupons, but by the time she got to the butcher's shop in Louisburg there were only scrag ends left, and today there was nothing at all. Her husband said, "I'll fix that tonight." He had fought in War One and was now a sergeant in a reserve company of the Cape Breton Highlanders at Louisburg. Under the latest coast defence arrangements these home-guard soldiers kept a rifle and ammunition along with their uniforms in their homes, ready to turn out at any moment.

That evening towards dusk, as I was about to leave the documents for my usual stroll, the caretaker put his head in the museum doorway. Visitors were unlikely at that time of day, but he asked me to stay a bit longer in case any did come because he had a little job to do. About ten minutes later I heard a loud crack of a gunshot. It was intriguing for a moment to fancy that Wolfe's redcoats were back again but I knew what it meant. I ran out and found the caretaker with his army rifle and a slain deer. I helped him to clean out the carcass and carry it to the house, where we skinned it and carved up the meat. For the rest of my stay in the old fortress built by King Louis and his clever mistress and adviser, La Pompadour, we feasted royally on steaks and roasts of venison.

* * *

The mayor of Louisburg, a Mr. Huntingdon, had a small old-fashioned grocery store on the main street. His lifelong hobby had been a search for relics and traces of the siege of 1758, and whenever I came to him for information he delightedly locked up the store and went off to show me. The first time this happened I said, "But what about your customers?" He made a gesture. "Never mind *them*. Who's more important than General Wolfe?"

Although an elderly man he was as nimble as a goat, and he knew the site of every battery and outpost of the British army as well as the French. One day I asked the museum caretaker to drive us in my car to distant Kennington Cove, where Wolfe had made his first dramatic landing in the face of dug-in French troops. Huntingdon and I got out of the car there and scrambled over Wolfe's route through the woods along the shore to Louisbourg, outflanking one after another the French forces guarding nearer and better landing places. It was a rough landscape of rock, scrub forest and bushes, little if at all changed since 1758. Another day we scrambled through the woods on the east side of Louisburg harbour from Big Landing to Lighthouse Point, following the route of the British eastern attack and finding traces of French earthworks and of the British camp with its defensive redoubts. The redcoats had been methodical in protecting their camps and road with walls of piled stones. (It was difficult to dig a trench in most places about Louisbourg without striking water or bedrock.) We waded through swamps bright with blossoming iris, trampling the blue fleur-de-lis underfoot as Wolfe had trampled the white, and my mind's eye saw hundreds of soldiers and seamen dragging can-

213

non up from the beaches on the huge-wheeled carriages of Admiral Boscawen's design. Their wooden ("corduroy") tracks over the swamps had rotted and vanished ages ago, but their other works in that stony landscape will be there for ever.

* * *

Whether engaged thus with on-the-ground research or just clearing my mind after long desk work, I always enjoyed walking. At home one of my favourite hikes was along an inland road to Western Head at the entrance to Liverpool Bay, returning by a road along the shore, a round journey of ten miles. One fine afternoon in 1943 I had just left the little fishing village at the Head on my way back to town when I was overtaken by a funeral procession. I knew the undertaker well, a friendly and very practical man of Liverpool who made a hand signal to the little motor cortege and stopped the hearse. "Get in, Tom," he said. "Take you as far as the Baptist cemetery in town." I said Thanks, but I was just enjoying a walk, and on they went. It did not occur to me until they were out of sight around a bend that I had passed up a chance that comes to few people in this world, to ride in a hearse and smell the flowers.

I had a more memorable encounter with this amiable man just before Christmas, when I was returning with a friend by car from the country village of Caledonia. In a long stretch of woods we came around a bend and found the road blocked by the Liverpool hearse, on its way home from a funeral at Caledonia, and a horse and wagon facing the other way and laden with firewood. Three small firs cut for Christmas trees lay on top of the load. The undertaker and his assistant, solemnly attired in black trousers, claw-hammer coats and bowler hats, were standing in the road in earnest talk with the woodsman. I got out and hurried up to them, thinking something serious must have happened. The teamster was saying, "Well, I cut them trees fer m'self and two neighbours, but I can git more. You want a couple, okay. Cost you a quarter apiece." At this point the undertaker noticed me. "Tom, you want the other one? We can stow all three of 'em in the hearse." So I got a Christmas tree and had it delivered at my house in town, all for twenty-five cents. My motoring friend had an errand in the village of Greenfield, several miles off the main road, with the result that we got back to the town long after the hearse. My wife and neighbours were startled when it stopped at my house and the two sombre-garbed servants of death got out, went to the back of the hearse, and opened the doors. But there was a roar of laughter when they drew forth, not a defunct Tom Raddall, but a fresh green Christmas tree.

*   *   *

In September 1943 *Maclean's Magazine* asked me by wire to cover a special story for them at Halifax. The naval authorities at Ottawa had decided to reveal that a German submarine or submarines had laid mines across the mouth of Halifax harbour one night last May. It was the Germans' first and only attempt to mine the entrance, and the mines they laid were soon swept up. One small ship strayed out of the channel made by Canadian minesweepers and blew up.

Everybody on the coast had known about this for the past four months, and during that time a swarm of ships out of Halifax had carried the news to most parts of the world, but Ottawa sat cautiously mum as if this were a tremendous secret. Late that summer Churchill made a trip to Canada, and the British authorities were about to announce his safe return. The brass hats landlocked in the woods at Ottawa decided that this was a good time to take the cover off the great Halifax mine story, which of course had nothing to do with Churchill. Various Canadian newspapers, magazines, and news-camera people were invited to send representatives to go out with the minesweepers on a routine patrol to get the background for it.

I drove to Halifax and stayed overnight at my mother's flat. At five o'clock the next morning a navy car picked me up there and took me to their public relations office in a shabby old wooden house on North Street near the dockyard. The other people were there, and we were briefed by a junior PRO, a short and dour lieutenant. He said we would board H.M.C.S. *Comox*, the flotilla leader, on a routine sweep of the war channel, which extended from the harbour mouth a distance of thirty miles over the coastal shelf. This would take all day. We would see how everything was done and on our return the PMO (Port Minesweeping Officer) would tell us anything we wanted to know.

There is a detailed account of this jaunt among my papers. The main feature was not the day's wallowing in the war channel, which made some of the passengers very sick, but the denouement after our return to the dockyard, which sickened us all. Navy had told *Maclean's* that they wanted particularly to see a good magazine article on the minesweepers, which had such a monotonous but sometimes dangerous job.

From my notes at the time:

> We were now taken to the Port Minesweeping Officer's office. There we found the PMO with the Director of Naval Information, the great Howard himself, who had come down from Ottawa to see the press properly nursed for the big Halifax minefield story. There was also an Intelligence officer, resplendent in gold braid. In an unhappy voice the PMO invited questions and we questioned him with gusto. At once it was clear that the PMO was mortally afraid to give any information at all. When he did make one or two quibbling replies the Intelligence Officer cut in and said we mustn't use this and we mustn't mention that.
>
> Again and again we were referred to the brief press release furnished by Howard, a few bare bones, and obviously the Halifax PMO was forbidden to add any flesh to them. All the world knew that the Germans had magnetic and acoustic mines as well as the ordinary contact mines, yet we were forbidden to make any mention of such things. We were forbidden to describe what we had seen this day, the simple method of fishing for contact mines, well known to every sailor since War One and still essentially the same. We were even forbidden to mention the name of *Comox*, although she had been mentioned by name several times in Canadian newspapers as the leader of a minesweeping flotilla at Halifax.

By this time the cameramen were openly bored and scornful. So were the CBC man and nearly all of the press men. And so was I. The conference broke up when the CBC man and I walked out, followed by the others. As we left someone said to me, "Are you doing this story for *Maclean's*?" I answered, "No, certainly not."

The CBC man said, "Why don't you do an article on naval censorship?" It was a temptation, but I knew it would never get printed.

When I got home I wrote to *Maclean's* saying I had no story and why. I added that as long as this stupid policy continued to hide the tasks and doings of the Canadian Navy, the rest of the world would go on thinking as it did now, that the war in the Atlantic was being fought mainly by the U.S. Navy and partly by the British Navy, with some fringe assistance by Canadian, Brazilian, and other little tinpot outfits that didn't really matter much. Even our own newspapers found little real news in official releases from Ottawa. The editor of our Liverpool weekly once showed me a wastebasket half full of what he called "naval publicity stuff" from Ottawa, every bit of it worthless.

A good occasion for a story on the minesweepers never came again because the Germans never mined Halifax again. They had much more urgent employment for their minelayers on short runs in Europe. *Comox* and her flotilla, like a mama duck with a train of ducklings, continued to paddle along the Halifax war channel every day until the war's end. Literally and figuratively they, and other more sophisticated types of minesweeper at Halifax (which we were not permitted to see, let along mention), were sitting ducks for an occasional U-boat on the prowl, and two were torpedoed and sunk with many of their seamen right outside the harbour mouth. But they never found another mine.

I had heard that under wartime security measures the post office in every Atlantic coast port, no matter how small, sent a random selection of every day's outgoing mail to the censors' office in Halifax. And they sent every letter addressed to a newspaper or magazine. After just the right time for my letter to reach the Halifax censor and then get to the chief naval PRO's desk, my phone rang. It was the chief PRO, an amiable man. He mentioned the article for *Maclean's Magazine* and asked if everything had been satisfactory. I guessed that he had my letter in front of him. In case he hadn't, I repeated my remarks and said I'd heard the words and music of "Hush-hush-hush, Here Comes the Bogeyman" when I was a child, and I didn't like it any more now than I did then. He asked if I would come to Halifax again if he guaranteed a story with lots of facts. I said Yes, but not right away. I was busy with a novel.

*   *   *

After my researches in and around the ruins of Louisbourg I plunged into the story. Before winter I was in trouble with it, or rather with a New York editor, who persuaded me to change the story line. This is the way of editors, of course. They have their own ideas and feel they are not earning their own considerable salaries unless they impose those ideas on the author. Sometimes they are right and many an author owes a lot to a brainy editor. The classic case is that of Thomas Wolfe and Maxwell Perkins.

Getting a little closer to my own acquaintance, Kenneth Roberts freely acknowledged a lot of help from his editor Tom Costain and from his neighbours and fellow authors Booth Tarkington and Ben Ames Williams. When this kind of co-operation works well it may produce a good novel for which the author gets all the credit, not to mention the cash, but really it all depends on the nature of the author's mind and how it works. I was always glad to have suggestions that made good sense to me, but any approach that made the editor practically a co-author was absolutely not for me. By every instinct and habit I was a loner. In the case of *Roger Sudden* I wrote several chapters under the editorial influence, like a planchette under the fingers of a medium, and then I rebelled. I scrapped all of the imposed stuff and went back to my own hunches and punches.

In essence my story was a tragedy, every chapter a step towards the death of Roger Sudden before a French firing squad just as Louisbourg fell. Beneath all this, if any reader cared to look deeper, my story was an allegory showing why the French failed in their attempt at empire in America and why the Anglo-Saxons won.

When I shot my hero on the last page of the book my New York editor was appalled. After all, the French were about to surrender the fortress, why not have him rescued at the last moment? I was wicked enough to ask by whom – the United States Marines? That would be quite in the Hollywood tradition, no matter what history said. So Doubleday Doran let me have my own stubborn way. I could see their shrugs away up here in the wilds of Canada.

*   *   *

In December 1943 I had a salutary break in my concentrated efforts on *Roger Sudden*. Again it came from *Maclean's Magazine*, but this time the result was happier and a good story came out of it. *Maclean's* asked me to fly to Montreal and get an account of some airmen in hospital there after a remarkable adventure in Greenland. Except for a brief flip over Liverpool in a rickety Gypsy Moth in 1931, this was my first travel by air. The plane was a DC-3, seating twelve passengers. The cabin was not pressurized. I had a bad head cold and congested nasal passages. At full altitude some mucus was forced violently into the inner channels of my ears, and I landed in Montreal almost deaf and in excruciating pain. I spend a miserable night in the Mount Royal Hotel.

By morning the pain had settled into a severe ache in my right ear, but I could hear well enough with my left for conversation.

Some time afterwards I went to a specialist and found that my right ear had suffered permanent damage. For the rest of my life I had poor hearing on that side. An experienced RCAF doctor told me I was lucky. He had known cases of airmen rendered utterly and permanently deaf under the same circumstances.

My airmen were under treatment for frostbitten feet and fingers in the Royal Victoria Hospital, two Canadians and their lean drawling captain, a man from Louisiana. They were employed by Ferry Command and were bringing an old Hampden bomber from Britain to Canada when both engines failed. They were off the east coast of Greenland just as winter was setting in. They scrambled into a small rubber raft a few seconds before the aircraft sank. After many hours of paddling among ice floes, they landed at the base of a high rock that stood up like a tusk from the sea. The "coast" behind it, vaguely seen in the dawn light of a far northern latitude, turned out to be the face of an enormous glacier. They found a ledge on the rock wide enough for all three of them to lie down, and of necessity they had to deflate the rubber raft to cover them against the wind and snow. They had no food but a few sugar tablets in an emergency kit and a couple of chocolate bars from a canteen in Reykjavik. After ten days, slowly perishing of cold and starvation, they were rescued by an absolute miracle, a chance sighting of their little helio mirror flashing in the sun by a small ship alone on that coast and hastening south before winter shut it tight. Her engines chanced to break down, and she paused for repairs in the icefield a few miles off their rock. While the engineers strove to get her going again, a man on deck, a U.S. Army officer, noticed the far twinkle of light and insisted on putting off a boat to see what it was.

I found the airmen silent and hostile. A newspaperman had badgered them for the story and then written it in a paltry way that angered them. They were not disposed to tell it again to anyone. The American skipper's wife was there, and I contrived to meet her casually in a hallway. I said, "I'm not a professional reporter. A Canadian magazine has asked me to write the story for that very reason. I think this is one of the great human stories of our time and the public should know the whole of it. Please help me. If your husband will talk to me, so will the others."

With her help, and a bag of pecans, I got the whole of it. She had brought the pecans from trees on their home property in Louisiana. The skipper showed me how to crack them in one hand. You take two nuts in your palm and squeeze hard. One breaks and the other stays whole. So you have a whole nut in your hand all the time, and you go on to crack another and another.

It reminded me of sessions in an old forge on the Mersey River, where retired loggers and sawyers sat on benches and with jack-knives whittled away at pieces of pine from the sawmill. It was useless to ask them for a story. You just took out your knife and whittled too. After a time someone would start a yarn about the river or the woods, not looking at you or anybody else, just keeping a careful eye on his whittling.

So the skipper told me his story in the hospital, punctuated by the soft crunch of pecan shells. After that, carefully spacing the sessions because these were men in recoil from a cruel experience, I got the stories of the others. In three days and a morning I had the details.

During all the years since then, the skipper and I have exchanged cards at Christmas and sometimes the mail brings a small carton of pecans. *Maclean's* had stipulated that the story should appear under the American captain's name so that the *Reader's Digest* would pick it up and pay part of my fee and expenses. Except for my paper-mill boss's speeches and articles, this was the only ghost writing I ever did. Years later, using other names for the men, I rewrote this affair as a short story entitled "Resurrection" and included it in my book *A Muster of Arms*. Several anthologies of Canadian writing have chosen it since. I consider it one of my best.

* * *

In March 1944 McClelland and Stewart informed me that their publication of my book of *Blackwood's* stories, *The Pied Piper of Dipper Creek*, had won the Governor General's medal. A day or two later I had a letter from the national secretary of the Canadian Authors Association. He informed me that (*a*) although these awards had been established in Lord Tweedsmuir's time and named in his honour, he had never contributed a penny for them, (*b*) in fact, the cost of the medals was borne entirely by the CAA, and (*c*) he enclosed a membership form for my signature and requested my cheque for the annual membership fee. In short, I should help to pay for the medal I was getting.

I had heard of the CAA, but the only thing I knew about such groups was what Thomas Macaulay had said long ago: "I detest all such associations. I hate the notion of gregarious authors. The less we have to do with each other, the better." Nevertheless I filled out the form, sent my cheque, and became a member. Things have changed a lot since then. Nowadays the Governor General's medal is provided by a Canadian government grant, and a cheque for $5,000 goes to the author for good measure.

*   *   *

In February 1944 my wife had a sudden notion to create an extra chamber on our second floor, so that each of our children could have a separate bedroom. I protested that this was not the time for such a project, in winter and in a time of war. Materials were scarce, labour scarcer still. The only men available were the dregs of the work force, lazy, slipshod, demanding big pay for little effort, and failing to turn up for days and weeks at a time.

I should have saved my breath, of course. There is nothing in this world more determined or ruthless than a doting mama. She sent for a building contractor right away, and the work began, a noisy business of tearing out interior walls, building new ones, shifting the plumbing to a new bathroom, and so on. It came just when I was in the final throes of *Roger Sudden* and as usual after such long effort I was plagued with taut nerves and insomnia. All this racket added to the strain. Only a grim effort of will enabled me to finish the novel exactly as I had intended it, right down to Roger's defiant shout of the old Kentish motto, "Invicta!" as the French firing squad pulled their triggers.

On March 16, 1944, I wrote in my diary, "Finished Roger Sudden after 12 months and 10 days of the most earnest labour. Sent a carbon copy to Jim Martell and Margaret Ells for perusal. Our house still in a semi-wrecked condition. Plumbers and plasterers waiting for supplies. Blood clinic tonight in the high school, my fourth donation since last autumn."

*   *   *

Our Canadian Legion branch had elected me president this year, and now I turned to a backlog of Legion work. The first men disabled by the fighting in Italy had lately returned to our town. They reported slipshod arrangements for their reception at Halifax and for transportation to their homes. I wrote sharp letters to shake up authorities in Halifax about this new but obvious feature of the war. Eventually the proper things were done, but as usual there was a lot of inertia to be overcome. I also set up among our businessmen a committee to look into such matters as employment, housing, vocational training, and so on.

Then I collapsed under another violent attack of influenza. On April 12 I scrawled in my diary:

> Got up after hours of hell, sneezing, coughing and weeping. No better now but can't stand lying in bed any more. This is the sixth week we have lived with a torn-up second floor and no bath. The idiocy of doing anything like this in wartime.

> *April 13, '44.* Plumbers in, shifting toilet etc. They went off coolly at 5 P.M. leaving waste pipes from kitchen and bathroom emptying on the cellar floor. I am up, though still very sick. A bad session last night. Thought a great deal of IT, but considered the mess and gave it up.

* * *

I had sold my old revolver long ago, but there was another in the house, and some cartridges for it. In the middle of the night I went into my den and loaded it. I must have sat an hour in agonized mental wrestling before I put it away, having "considered the mess." I had been driving myself so hard for so long that the maddening wreck of the house and the utter misery of flu had pushed me to the edge. Looking back after all the time since, I know there was something else in my long contemplation of the gun that night. It was my father's Webley, taken off his body before his soldiers buried him, and sent home with his kit. Something in the back of my wretched mind that night refused to put it to such a use.

* * *

When May came I had recovered enough to drive to Halifax for another meeting with Jim Martell and Margaret Ells, talking over a theme and material for my next novel. One evening Martell took me to a meeting of The Haliburton, the literary society of King's University, and in the usual informal chitchat he brought somebody over to me, saying cheerfully, "Here's a man who wants to meet the best Nova Scotian writer since Haliburton." I turned and recognized Andrew Merkel. He was still head of the Canadian Press at Halifax, but after all the years gone by he failed to recognize in me the slim dark-haired youth who once asked him for a job. He had utterly forgotten that brief meeting in 1923, and I never reminded him of it. We became very good friends.

222

For the past twenty-five years Merkel and his talented wife, "Tully," had made their home the favourite rendezvous of Nova Scotia writers and especially poets, for Merkel wrote verse himself as a change from his press work. In the mid-1920s some of the poets formed a sort of flying squad, calling themselves whimsically the Song Fishermen, including Charles G.D. Roberts, Bliss Carman, Robert Norwood, Evelyn Tufts, Stewart MacAulay, Kenneth Leslie, Ethel Butler and other lively spirits. The first three lived elsewhere but came to Nova Scotia in summer. From time to time this group made sallies by car into the countryside or by sail along the coast, always on the spur of a moment, and staying a day or a week wherever they chose to alight.

Sometimes this worked in reverse; indeed, the Merkel house at 50 South Park Street was a sort of wayside inn for itinerant poets at any time of year. On an autumn occasion right after his return from many years abroad, Roberts came to give an evening's recital of his poetry in a public hall in Halifax, and the Merkels invited him to stay with them over the weekend. He stayed the weekend, the next week, the next month, in fact nearly the whole winter, and would have remained indefinitely if the Merkels had not told him, gently but firmly, that he must move on.

* * *

My gross income for 1943 was $5,414, mainly from the United States, on which the U.S. government levied a tax of 15 per cent. *Maclean's* was running my *Blackwood's* stories and paying $175 for Canadian rights.

* * *

I returned from my discussions and studies at Halifax in May 1944 still unsettled in mind about another book. I spent a refreshing week in the Mersey headwaters, travelling by foot and canoe and staying at logging camps and the shacks of forest rangers.

A letter came from Doubleday Doran, whose books were sold in Canada by McClelland and Stewart. Both firms wanted me to start another novel at once, for publication in 1945. I was unwilling to start another so soon. *Roger Sudden* had nearly killed me in more than one way. I replied that I wanted several months to write short stories before tackling another novel.

In July 1944 I was sorry to read in the dispatches from Normandy that Theodore Roosevelt had died in the midst of the great battle, from a heart stroke as swift and deadly as a bullet, while commanding the infantry division he had led through Algiers, Sicily and Italy. I thought of his letter to me from Algiers in '43 – "It's a long road that lies before us but at least we're moving in the right direction." His brother Kermit also died this year on active service with the U.S. Army.

All those brothers were valiant.

* * *

I now had a summons from the Canadian Authors Association to attend the annual dinner and presentation of the Governor General's Awards, to be held in Toronto this year. It stated that the people at the head table, including those to receive awards, were to wear formal evening dress. My Toronto publishers urged me to go and offered to pay half my expenses, but I balked at the fancy dress. Merely to receive a complimentary medal, why should a struggling writer be required to wear a costume utterly ridiculous to anyone of plain habits? I refused, and made it a principle for the rest of my life. None of the working writers of my acquaintance would have cared to be found dead in white tie and tails. McClelland and Stewart sent somebody to receive the medal on my behalf.

William Deacon, long-time literary critic of the Toronto *Globe and Mail,* and a leading figure in the Canadian Authors Association, afterwards chided me for inverse snobbery about this. I retorted that a lot of people regarded the CAA as a gaggle of poseurs and dilettantes rather than a company of working writers, and they could point to this annual masquerade as an example.

I think Bill Deacon must have heard this before and known the truth of it. After that, the formal dress demand was dropped from invitations of this sort, to me at any rate, and when I received a second G-G Award in person in the summer of 1948 I wore a plain blue jacket and white flannel trousers, my customary garb at summer evening parties at home. At the time of my third award I was in Europe, so the matter did not arise. No doubt I missed some interesting people here and there by refusing to wear any but my usual clothes, but in the course of my life it got me out of a lot of boring stuffed-shirtery, too.

* * *

Another old friend died in 1944, much closer to home than Normandy. As a young man he had been expelled from Acadia College for a prank, and he had spent most of his life wandering about northern Canada, British Columbia, Australia and the Philippines. At the age of sixty or so he returned at last to the vacant family home in Milton. There he lived holed up like a tramp in the kitchen, keeping his firewood stacked in the living room and parlour because the barn leaked, and for something to do studying local history in old documents at the Recording Office in Liverpool. He had in the house a small library, and one of his prized possessions was the logbook of a Spanish brig called *El Ercules*, captured by a Liverpool privateer in the Caribbean during the 1790s and handed down by the family. I spent many hours in that soiled and smoke-grimed kitchen listening to him, and years later when I wrote a novel called *The Wings of Night* I described him as "Jim Pelerine."

When he died, a nephew came from British Columbia to settle up his estate and sell the house. The family furniture had been sold to itinerant second-hand dealers long before, and what remained, including the much-thumbed books, he intended to burn. He told me to take any of "those old books" I wanted, and I wanted several, including that logbook, but I couldn't find it. The old fellow had been a careless housekeeper to say the least, and in one corner of his kitchen abode, just where he had flung them, lay a pile of old newspapers. After much fruitless searching I was about to leave in disgust when I had a wild hunch and went through that heap of newspapers, one by one. I found the logbook tucked out of sight near the bottom – the old man's notion of safekeeping, I suppose.

The book was of the durable old-fashioned rag paper, well bound between thick parchment covers. By holding a page to the light you could see the watermark of the papermaker and the date 1792. The log entries had been made by a good penman and a first-rate navigator for his day. His precise record of each day's sailing and the calculation of his noon position were neatly set forth, ending always in a pious little phrase of thanks to God for the continued safety of the ship. With what my old friend remembered of his Spanish in the Philippines, plus careful study of a Spanish-English dictionary, plus his own experience as a sailor crossing the Pacific in a square-rigger, he would translate the entries aloud for me. The very sails had names like music. The main topsail was *la gabia maior*, the fore-royal was *el juanete de proba*, and so on.

With this in my hands something began to stir in my mind, a projected and enlarged image of my first little book about a Nova

Scotia privateer fighting Spaniards in the Caribbean Sea. I was still busy hunting material for short stories and still reluctant to let myself in for the long stress and struggle of another novel, but somewhere behind all that my subconscious *daemon* must have been sketching a novel about Nova Scotians adventuring in those waters long ago. That is what came out of it, anyway.

* * *

On my forty-first birthday copies of *Roger Sudden* were appearing in the bookstores, and McClelland and Stewart sent George Foster to handle publicity in Halifax, as he had for *His Majesty's Yankees*. Personable and energetic, George arranged a radio broadcast, a splurge of bookshop advertisements in the newspapers, and autographing in the leading shops. In those days a real live author, writing his name in his book right under your nose, was considered well worth the price whether you read the book or not. Halifax was swarming with army, navy, air, and merchant marine personnel, as well as the swollen and prosperous civilian population of a bustling war base, and like every other shop the bookstores were doing a roaring business.

* * *

One evening the Merkels invited me to attend a session of a poetry society in their house. I found there about two dozen people, mostly ladies of a certain age, with papers at the ready. They did not resemble in any way the vivacious feminine half of the bygone Song Fishermen, scattered long since by time and circumstance. My fellow guest was the Chief Justice of Nova Scotia, Sir Joseph Chisholm, a small man with a noble face and long white hair, and I sat beside him while a succession of earnest ladies read their rhymes aloud, to solemn applause by the others. Then came a long lecture on Keats, read from a book. Comic relief was supplied by a little old man whose specialty was writing hymns. He simply went to sleep and snored.

When the society went home to bed at eleven o'clock Merkel brought forth a bottle of West Indian sunshine and showed me his collection of Nova Scotiana, especially the complete works of James D. Gillis, author of *The Cape Breton Giant*, *The Great Election*, and other remarkable flights of the pen. Merkel described a merry sortie of the Song Fishermen in 1932, when with Gillis as their special guest they sailed an old schooner named *Drama* from Halifax to Shad Bay and had a picnic on the shore.

The next morning Merkel took me to Shad Bay by car, along with Jim Martell and a genial professor of history at Dalhousie named George Wilson. We dined with a hospitable old fisherman and his wife, who gave us a feast of roast venison and vegetables and a pie made with maraschino cherries plucked from a shipwreck at Sambro.

This man's shore pasture had been the scene of the 1932 frolic, which Merkel had recorded at the time with a little movie camera. For the pleasure of the fisher-folk we set up a screen and projector and ran the old film. It had no sound track, of course, which was a pity because a lot of fun had lain in the recitation of verses composed on the spot by the poets (not a bit like those of last night) and in the final coronation of Stewart MacAulay as King of the Song Fishermen with a crown of seaweed. From Shad Bay we went on to Peggy's Cove and visited a lady known to the Song Fishermen as Windblown Nelly, a lightkeeper's widow, still hearty and merry, who insisted that we stay to tea. Merkel's light-hearted group had known everybody on that shore.

*   *   *

In November 1944 I signed a contract with McClelland and Stewart for publication of another book of short stories previously written for magazines. The title was *Tambour and Other Stories*. The winter and the war dragged on, and so did I, for I was still in the grip of a mental block, that occupational hazard of the writer's trade which may last weeks, months, or sometimes years. Merkel's busy mind was still hitting on all its cylinders, however, and our chat about James D. Gillis had given him an inspiration. It was to send Gillis money for travel and invite him to come down from his mountain in Cape Breton and visit us at Halifax.

I motored up to the city in mid-March 1945, bringing with me a few budding plants of the mayflower, which in spite of its name blooms much earlier on the South Shore. I intended planting them on the grave of Nova Scotia's great patriot, Joseph Howe, who had written verses in praise of this sweet-scented harbinger of spring.

Andrew Merkel, a whimsical lawyer named Roy Lawrence, Jim Martell and I formed a reception committee for the author of *The Cape Breton Giant*. He got off the train with little baggage other than his fiddle and bagpipes, wearing a shabby suit of hand-me-downs, a greasy cap, and an ancient coat made from the pelt of a buffalo obviously afflicted with mange.

As it was impossible to get a hotel room for him in wartime Halifax, Merkel cleared out a small room on the second floor of the Canadian Press offices and installed a cot and bedding, with washing and sanitary facilities close by. Our first job was to provide the visitor with a better outfit of clothes – shirts, underwear, socks and so on. For footwear he chose a pair of seamen's boots, calf-high, which would be "useful on the hills back home."

On the first opportunity we gathered at Merkel's house with a few friends, and Gillis played his fiddle and bagpipes and talked about his contributions to Canadian literature, a series of small paperbacks put out at intervals of years by a stationery firm in Halifax. He had never married. After teaching a country school for many years he had retired to live alone in a shack on the hillside overlooking Lake Ainslie in Cape Breton.

He was eccentric but not the self-important half-wit that some mistaken people thought he was. His indifference to soap and water was apparent, but his bald head was noble, the brow full, the eyebrows thick and black, his eyes a dark brown that glowed whenever he warmed to his subject, the eyes of a poet and philosopher. A grey moustache covered his upper lip and drooped at the mouth corners. He must have stood six feet in youth but hunched his shoulders now, and he walked with the long loose stride of a man of the hills. In Cape Breton, where he and many other people still spoke Gaelic, he was known as Sheamus Dhu (Black James) to distinguish him from other Jameses in the numerous Gillis family.

In chat with Jim Martell I mentioned my little mission with the mayflowers and suggested that he come with me tomorrow to Camp Hill cemetery. Merkel overheard. At once he protested, "You can't just go and stick some flowers on Joe Howe's grave without saying something. At the very least you ought to recite Joe's ode to the mayflower. And hey! What about Gillis playing a lament on his bagpipes?"

We drove into the cemetery on a quiet Sunday morning when there would be nobody about. The snow had gone and the ground was free of frost. Martell helped me to plant the flowers on Howe's grave. I recited Joe's ode – "Lovely flow'ret sweetly blooming" – and then Sheamus Dhu tramped up and down in his old buffalo coat, with his pipes wailing the ancient tune of "Niel Gow's Lament." When we drove in there, Camp Hill seemed void of life, but after a few skirls of the pipes we had a small crowd about us (Merkel vowed they must have jumped out of the graves), and after a decent interval we withdrew.

By this time, of course, all Halifax knew that the famous James D. was in town. Halifax millionaire F.B. McCurdy was a native of Cape Breton, and he invited Gillis to dine at Emscote, the McCurdy mansion down by the Northwest Arm. Sheamus Dhu (who ate with his fingers mostly) was not used to elaborate dinners of several courses. He complained to us afterwards, "I wass full before supper wass half over." After "supper," to bring luck to the house in the old Highland fashion, Sheamus marched from cellar to garret playing his pipes, followed in procession by the McCurdy family and all their servants. For a good job of luck the pipes had to be played in every chamber and closet. Sheamus told us later, "That house is ass big ass a university!" He was so much occupied at Emscote that he forgot a later engagement at Pine Hill College. The students sent a delegation to claim him and carry him off, pipes and all.

The Halifax radio stations asked me to interview Sheamus for them and I did. The talk was about the Highland settlers in Cape Breton, their traditions and their songs. They should have been recorded permanently, for Gillis had a thorough knowledge of his people. To illustrate it, he sang various Gaelic songs and then explained in English what they meant. One was very old and much used at "fulling" parties, when Highland folk gathered to prepare new homespun cloth for wear. The process was to soak and beat and scrub each bolt on a long table of rough boards, in order to shrink it and to "bring out the nap." This tune had just the right rhythm for the work, which was the same rhythm as rowing a boat, and the words were addressed to a curly-haired damsel named Morag, begging her to return to the Highlands and help her folks to "drub the red cloth." It was an old Jacobite allegory, begging curly-haired Bonnie Prince Charlie to come back over the water and help his people to wallop the redcoats.

When Merkel took Sheamus off to the train for Cape Breton with a shoebox full of Tully's sandwiches, the old man went happily, vowing it was the best time he'd ever had in his life. Back home at Lake Ainslie ("near the international border between Inverness and Victoria counties," as he said on the radio) he wrote to Merkel a full and glowing account of his visit to Halifax. There is a copy in my papers.

* * *

During all these busy times I did not neglect my family. I taught my boy and girl to swim in nearby lakes and in winter took them bob-sledding on a hill behind the town. I gave young Tom a .22 rifle and taught him how to shoot, clean and take care of it. As far as the gasoline ration permitted I took my family on picnics in the woods and by the sea. It was always a relief from the strain of work for me, and we had a lot of pleasure together.

* * *

All through the spring of 1945 the news had been full of victory in Europe. On May Day, just as we were sitting down to the evening meal with our radio tuned to London, the BBC announced the fall of Berlin to the Russians and the death of Hitler. It ended with an apt quip from Shakespeare's *Richard III*: "The day is ours. The bloody dog is dead." Less than two weeks later the German land, sea and air forces remaining in western Europe surrendered to the Western allies.

Andrew Merkel came to my house with a naval officer named Bill Sclater in his car, telling me mysteriously to grab my pyjamas and shaving gear and hop in. Sclater had served in the destroyer *Haida* in the cut-and-dash fighting in the Channel and Bay of Biscay after France fell to the Germans. Now he was on the admiral's staff at Halifax. Among other duties he acted as an unofficial liaison man with the Canadian Press.

On the way to Shelburne they revealed their errand. It was to witness the surrender of a U-boat, one of Hitler's latest, and they told me I would come along as "special correspondent of the London *Times*." This proved so impressive that nobody at the Shelburne base demanded to see my credentials. We found the lone hotel in Shelburne full to the rafters, but Sclater arranged food and berths for us aboard the frigate *Toronto*, which was refitting there.

Complying with the surrender orders, the U-boat had surfaced, hoisted a black flag (the British signal for a submarine on the surface), and reported her position by radio to Canadian naval forces. Remembering the scuttling affair at Scapa Flow after the surrender in 1918, the Canadian authorities prudently decided not to admit any surrendered craft into Halifax harbour and directed this one to

230

Shelburne under the escort of the Canadian frigates *Buckingham* and *Inchallan*.

I quote from my diary:

> *May 13, '45.* A dull cold misty day. Lunch on *Toronto* and then went down to the jetty and boarded a Fairmile launch. Three other Fairmiles in our little procession out of the harbour. One held the boarding party, 8 or 10 ratings armed with Sten guns and 2 officers with revolvers. Also an explosives expert. He is to board the sub at the moment of surrender and explore it for time-bombs or any other attempt to sink her.
>
> We ran outside and lay rolling (and how those Fairmiles can roll!) about twelve miles off MacNutt's Island, until the submarine was sighted coming slowly with the shadowy forms of *Buckingham* and *Inchallan* in the mist astern. About two miles off Shelburne lighthouse the U-boat stopped at a signal from the leading Fairmile and our little flotilla closed in. There were two or three officers in the conning tower in white-topped caps with large Nazi badges and glazed black peaks. On deck stood half a dozen seamen in trousers, grey coats reaching the knees, heavy rubber sea boots, and wedge caps of dark blue. It looked more like an army than a navy dress.
>
> She was U-889, 750 tons, with twin anti-aircraft guns on a platform abaft the conning tower, and two more on the conning tower itself. The explosives expert jumped aboard and vanished below. The boarding party prepared to board also. Captain "Gus" Miles, RCN, called out formally, "Do you surrender this ship?" and the German captain said "Yes," in English. There was no saluting. A Canadian seaman cut the black flag out of the halliards, a bit of bunting about two feet square, dyed apparently with a mixture of oil and exhaust soot. Up went the British white ensign in its place.
>
> About half of the German crew were ordered to board one of the Fairmiles and stand on the deck, which they did promptly. Canadian seamen with Sten guns watched them closely. The other half, under guard, operated the sub on the final surface hitch into Shelburne Harbour. The German captain was at the controls, a handsome blond man of 26. He and the other officers looked very gloomy but their spirits picked up after the sub was moored safely off the naval base. The seamen were mostly kids of 18 or 19, short, well fed, but with

faces pale and hair shaggy from the long confinement of the voyage. The boatswain wore a dark blue jacket like our own Navy battledress, with a white-topped cap. He had an old-style German Imperial Navy beard, the only whiskers in the ship as far as I could see.

* * *

Questioned by newsmen through an interpreter, the young German captain now relaxed and talked freely, laughing at some of the questions. After trials in the Baltic, U-889 had departed from Norway on April 4, making her way towards the North American coast. She did not surface until May 8, having been more than four weeks under water using the Schnorkel air intake and engine exhaust device, which could be thrust above the surface like a periscope.

Asked what he intended to do after the war, the captain said his home city of Hamburg was in ruins and he would like to live in Canada – "after all, your government is very much like ours." (A newsman chortled, "Another voter for Mackenzie King!")

QUESTION: "When did you feel that Germany had lost the war?"

ANSWER: "I knew we could not win it after Stalingrad."

QUESTION: "When did you feel the U-boat war was lost?"

ANSWER: "Never! You gave us some bad times, but now we have the Schnorkel. You cannot find us but we can still find you. When the surrender order came we had many U-boats at sea or preparing for sea, with plans for a hard-hitting attack on your shipping."

* * *

On June 8, 1945, I wrote glumly in my diary, "No urge to write for months. Need a complete change. Some travel would be marvellous but no hope of it with present gas rations, and I loathe trains and buses." The climactic months of the war in Europe had made creative thought impossible, and the war with Japan was still booming towards its macabre finish. My mind was weary with more than five years of concentrated effort. Yet a few days after I wrote that disconsolate entry the mental block began to dissolve. I saw the outline of another novel. As I have said, it must have been forming in the back of my head from the time I found that old Spanish logbook, and of course there was the research I had done long ago for my first little book, *Saga of the Rover*.

With these for a start, other ideas and material suggested themselves as the creative juice began to flow. A Milton family had shown me a book of sailing directions used by their privateer ancestor on his Caribbean voyages. Its flyleaves were covered with noon notations of latitude and longitude, lists of washing sent ashore in Saint Kitts and other West Indian ports of call, and a priceless pencil scrawl:

> Francis Kempton is my nam
> Seaman is my stashon
> Nova Scotia is my dwelen plas
> And Ingland is my nashon.

This book contained exact and often delightful descriptions of a sailor's approach to ports and islands in the Caribbean and along the Spanish Main. Then there was the diary of Simeon Perkins in Liverpool. That busy little man had built privateers, owned shares in them, recorded their cruises, their prizes and cargoes, and the final ruling on prize money by the Vice-Admiralty Court at Halifax. I knew, too, that Enos Collins, the great merchant-banker of Halifax, who lived to see Confederation and died probably the richest man in Canada, had begun his long career as lieutenant of a privateer out of my town of Liverpool. He'd had many adventures on the Spanish Main. He also knew well the coast of Haiti (Hispaniola to our seamen in those days) where in later years of peace he made a deal with black King Henri Christophe and got a monopoly of the Haitian coffee trade. Ruthless, cold, grasping, and capable in every way, he made a notable character for a novel. I called him Amos Pride and my book's title became *Pride's Fancy*.

I chose a brig for my privateer because I knew how to sail one from my studies of that rig, beginning long ago with my little model at Sable Island. I got charts of the West Indies, ancient and modern, and pinned them about the walls of my study for total immersion. I gathered books about the Caribbean islands in the 1790s, and particularly I studied accounts of the revolt of the Haitian slaves led by Toussaint L'Ouverture and the subsequent massacre of the whites by Dessalines, all of which were important to my tale.

* * *

On July 16, 1945, I drove to Halifax to combine a session at the archives with a family reunion. My mother and sister Hilda had taken a new apartment on Chebucto Road, and my older sister

Nellie, after many years in Alabama, had come to join them with her youngsters for a summer holiday now that travel was possible again.

Early in the evening of July 18, in stifling heat, I left my mother's flat to have tea with Margaret Ells and her brother Donald at her new apartment in the south end of the city. I had driven only a few yards along Chebucto Road when I heard a loud bang. For a moment I thought one of my old tires had blown out, a thing I had experienced several times during the war and constantly expected again. Being a free lance, I had none of the privileges of a regular journalist, and consequently I had been unable to buy new tires since 1940. Like others in my case I had to rummage the town and countryside for old tires, discarded in the easy days of peace, that still had a usable amount of tread.

Then I saw a shop window falling in fragments and guessed that an explosion had happened with much more force than a blown tire. I was actually in sight of our old home on Chebucto Road, with all its memories of 1917. Jumping out, I saw a small grey cloud of smoke rising swiftly in the northern sky like a puff from a cigarette. It was nothing like the huge and hideous mushroom of 1917, so I knew the cause was much less. I drove on south to Margaret's place. We were chatting at her tea table when Donald's wife phoned, saying that the big magazine at Bedford Basin had caught fire and the situation was dangerous.

I left at once, dropped Donald at his home, and went on north-ward to Mother's flat. She had fainted at the explosion, and my sisters were trying to revive her. By this time there was a steady *woomp-woomp-woomp* of explosives – depth charges by the sound of them – with intervals of small-calibre ammunition rattling like kettle-drums and sometimes a blast of noise and rushing air as if several depth charges had exploded together.

After the German surrender the Canadian Navy had drawn its ships back to Halifax and prepared to refit some for service against Japan. As a routine precaution all of the ships put their ammunition ashore at the Bedford Basin magazine, which consisted of many small brick storehouses, each surrounded by a thick earth-and-concrete rampart as high as the roof and all spaced well apart. In theory no single storehouse would hold a dangerous quantity, and if it did explode the rampart would confine the blast and throw it upward where it could do no harm.

Since May, however, the storehouses had been stuffed to the

234

roofs, and a huge amount of munitions had to be stacked over the slope down to the jetty on the Basin shore. By July 18 that slope (whose original name, before the erection of the magazine, was Burnside) held enough shells, mines, torpedoes, depth charges, rockets and other powerful stuff to blast Halifax and Dartmouth flat and burn them off the face of the earth.

The first bang was the explosion of an ammo barge at the jetty. It blew the barge, the jetty and a watchman to bits and a puff of smoke, but otherwise it was not much. The trouble began when the flash of this blast set a dump afire just above the jetty, and from then on the dumps on the slope caught fire one after another, and set off a continual rumbling and concussion that went on for something like thirty-six hours.

As a spectacle it was magnificent. The sun went down with a fine red blaze of its own across the western sky, and as the huge cloud of burning explosives and dust arose and diffused over Bedford Basin it produced a tint in that sky which Turner alone could have painted. When darkness fell, the burning dumps made a golden glow in the northern sky, with crimson underlights, sudden blue-white flashes as if a gigantic searchlight had been switched on and off, and fountains of rockets, star shells and flares. All this with accompanying sound and air-blast effects.

At 9 P.M., Naval Headquarters broadcast a radio warning to all people living between Bedford Basin and North Street, advising them to leave their homes and go southward at once. Later the warning was extended to everyone living north of Quinpool Road, more than half the population of the city. This included us.

Some people fled to the extreme south end of the city, but the greatest number headed out of the peninsula altogether. In those days the isthmus of the Halifax peninsula was a perfect bottleneck. Only two roads led out of it, and the main one ran along the Bedford Basin shore, fully exposed to blasts from the magazine across the water. The whole evacuation had to be made by the single road through Armdale toward Saint Margaret's Bay, which soon became a solid mass of vehicles ten miles long, crawling slowly westward.

In 1917 I had seen a torrent of terrified people pouring afoot down Chebucto Road towards Armdale. With the addition of modern motor traffic I foresaw a hopeless jam at the crossroads there. Mother had revived, and I discussed this with my sisters and her. If matters came to the worst I proposed to take them in my car southward to Point Pleasant Park, about six air miles from the magazine. There we could shelter under the trees in the warmth of a summer night. For the time being we decided to stay where we were, opening all the doors and windows wide to save them from air blast. My sisters primly pulled down all the window blinds to shut out the gaze of the refugees hurrying afoot towards Armdale.

About midnight the sounds and the glare died down, and thinking the worst was over I went to my bedroom, changed into pyjamas, and began to write the day's events in my diary. A few minutes later there was a very loud explosion and a crash of crockery and glassware falling from the kitchen shelves. Oddly, the most startling noise came just afterward, when the air blast arrived and pushed the window blinds inward. It tripped the roller springs and they all flew up together with the racket of so many shotguns.

I dressed hastily and moved Mother and her armchair down to the street porch. On a little jib of turf in the angle of North Street and Chebucto Road I could see men, women and children lying on the grass. Army jeeps, trucks and an ambulance or two rushed past. Smaller explosions continued as we watched the fantastic fireworks in the sky. About 3.30 A.M. these died down, and again I told Mother and my sisters to go to bed, setting the example myself. But sleep was not to be had. A few minutes before 4 A.M. a huge yellow flame shot up to the zenith and made the street as bright as day, and a terrific blast rocked the house on its foundations with a series of shuddering bumps.

Mother collapsed again, and while my sisters worked over her I kept watch at a north window. In a few minutes another huge yellow blaze was followed by another terrific bang. Again the house rocked and shuddered, and this time the electric lights went out. Rain was falling now, a wet and chilly prospect for an elderly lady in a state of shock, so we continued to take the risk indoors. About 5.30 I fell asleep. When I awoke two hours later, the explosions were still thumping on a lesser scale, but daylight had killed the glare in the sky and there was nothing to see but a mass of smoke writhing and dancing as the blasts went on.

At noon on this second day of the magazine fire, the mayor of Halifax made a radio broadcast warning all citizens that the Navy expected a tremendous explosion from a store of depth charges containing the new explosive called RDX. He advised everybody to get away. Calmly we sat down to lunch, and then I packed the family into my car with blankets, cushions and food, and took them to Point Pleasant. After that I called for Jim Martell and his family, who had no car, and took them to the bus terminal behind Citadel Hill. By this time the traffic jam at Armdale had resolved itself and they were able to board a bus to Saint Margaret's Bay, where Jim had planned to spend his summer holidays and had engaged rooms.

He told me most of the archives staff were on duty because the Dalhousie campus was far enough south to be safe, and I went there and spent the rest of the afternoon doggedly trying to read the material for my novel. It was no good. After that wild and sleepless night my head nodded dopily over the documents. Towards the end of the afternoon I managed to get a phone call through to the Canadian Press, and Merkel told me the worst danger was over. He had this assurance from Bill Sclater, just back from Bedford Basin in *Moby Dick*, the admiral's barge, after a close look at the naval parties battling the fires.

I drove to Point Pleasant, picked up my people, and returned to the flat on Chebucto Road. The doors and windows were intact. There were a few cracks in the plaster and some broken crockery, but that was all. Through that night there were occasional pops and bangs, but I heard them only fitfully in a sleep of exhaustion.

* * *

Before coming up to Halifax I had agreed with the CBC to tell three true stories of Nova Scotia on the national radio network. After the magazine noises ceased I went to their studios on Sackville Street and recorded them. Also, I made a direct talk to Britain at the request of the BBC, describing the fires and explosions and their effect on the city and its people.

* * *

There was a much bigger bang in the making on the other side of the world. On August 6 the first atomic bomb fell on Hiroshima. Three days later another destroyed Nagasaki, where my father had cruised with the Far Eastern Squadron nearly fifty years ago. Far from these tremendous affairs, we had one of our joint family picnics on the sands of Port Joli, including a feast of clams baked in seaweed in the ancient Indian fashion. Thunder had been grumbling in the west all afternoon, and about sunset a bank of cloud there caused a fan of red sunrays. Somebody said, "Look! There's the Japanese flag, and it's going down!"

237

So it was. Two days later the long war ended. A week after that I began to write my novel about a Nova Scotia privateer in the Caribbean during the Napoleonic wars. The temporary working title was *Lia*, the name of my French creole heroine; it was published as *Pride's Fancy*.

* * *

One or two reviewers of my work as a whole have remarked airily that my first three novels, all historical, were written as "escape literature" during the Second World War. This was news to me. With as much truth they might have said that Rudyard Kipling wrote *Kim* as escape literature during the Boer War, or that Charles Kingsley wrote *Westward Ho!* as escape literature during the Crimean War.

The simple fact was that the historical novel had been widely read in North America ever since its renascence in 1933 with Hervey Allen's delightful *Anthony Adverse*. As I was interested in history, and writing novels for my living, I chose this very good genre for my first three books. *Pride's Fancy*, incidentally, was written *after* the war.

* * *

At this point I should say something more. It was never my wish or intent to be a historical novelist or, for that matter, a sea novelist, a forest novelist, or any other stereotypist. From early days when I was writing for *Blackwood's* I went back and forth between present and past, between sea and forest, between humour and drama, seeking always to portray men and women in the scenes I knew and in the context of their times and circumstances.

Conrad used to protest angrily against the "sea novelist" tag that critics and reviewers tied on him for life. He wrote just as well (and much more) about people ashore, but the sea tag clanged at his heels wherever he went like the tin can on the dog's tail. Some reviewers and academic thesis writers have a lazy weakness for cramming an author's work into a convenient slot like that, which saves them so much further study and analysis.

Pride's Fancy was my third historical novel in a row. Then I determined to write three novels of my own time in a row. After that I moved between present and past to keep my mind fresh and my readers entertained. No groove, no type, no tag. Just people.

1945
1960

In the autumn of 1945 George Foster came from Toronto to spend a weekend with me, and I showed him the chapters of *Pride's Fancy* I had written so far and gave him a rough outline of the rest. He mentioned that the advance sale of my new volume of short stories, *Tambour*, was going well and suggested a big autographing party in Halifax when the book appeared in the shops. I thought that kind of thing looked cheap with repetition, and we decided to skip it this year. We discussed a further volume of short stories for publication in '47 and a one-volume history of Halifax, tentatively set for '48.

The book on Halifax was first proposed to me by Doubleday Doran during the late war. They had published a series on the chief American ports and fostered a Canadian series through McClelland and Stewart. Stephen Leacock had started the series with his book on Montreal, and the second was done by Mazo de la Roche about Quebec. Leacock's book was good as far as it went, but he ignored the seamy side of Montreal life as if it did not exist. Perhaps behind the ivied walls of McGill he didn't know much about it. Mazo de la Roche had no flair for historical research; she made a lot of errors, and her book was sharply criticized. I agreed to write the third volume about Halifax, but I specified a year or two after

239

the war, when I could tell the whole story of the port's recent war-time activities and tribulations, free from the clamp of censorship.

* * *

In addition to *Tambour*, McClelland and Stewart brought out a new edition of *His Majesty's Yankees* in 1945. Their Toronto print-ers being busy with *Tambour* and with another printing of *Roger Sudden*, they arranged for the printing of *His Majesty's Yankees* by a firm in Vancouver.

In November I went to Halifax to fulfil some engagements, in-cluding an address to the Commercial Club, which my father had addressed a little over thirty years before. Also, I made my first appearance at a meeting of the Halifax branch of the Canadian Authors Association. At their invitation I talked a little about my work and methods, but only a little. I said there was too much talk about writing in Canada and not enough writing. Pleasantly I quoted some doggerel that I had noted years ago and adopted:

> A wise old owl sat on an oak,
> The more he saw the less he spoke;
> The less he spoke the more he heard;
> Why aren't we like that wise old bird?

* * *

McClelland and Stewart had been the publishers of Dr. Archibald MacMechan, whose works were all out of print. Now George Foster asked me to make my own choice of selections from MacMechan's work, and write a foreword, to be printed in a single volume. Archie, as his students called him (not to his face, for he had a Victorian dignity), had been head of the Department of English at Dalhousie University more than forty years when he died in 1933. A versatile man, he had written poetry, essays, stories from Nova Scotia history, and much more. I had read most of it. Naturally I liked best his true stories of the sea, most of them taken down carefully from the seamen themselves, for MacMechan had lived when the days of sail were passing and he knew it. I chose a selection of these and called it simply *Tales of the Sea*.

Walking along Barrington Street and discussing this book, George Foster and I chanced to meet Donald Mackay, a Nova Scotia artist who knew ships and the sea. He agreed gladly to do the illustrations, a work after his own heart. All in all it proved to be a good production, and I'm sure Archie's spirit must have been pleased with it.

* * *

One November evening in Halifax I had a special invitation to The Haliburton. The members met in their clubroom in King's College, a large chamber with a portrait of the author of *Sam Slick* over the fireplace. It was filled with undergraduates and alumni. As soon as they were called to order, Jim Martell arose, talked a bit about my work, and moved that I be honoured with a fellowship. This was seconded by a fluent young student and followed by a vote of approval with much applause. I spoke my appreciation and talked about Haliburton's work and what it had meant to me.

The current president of this old but lively literary society was a professor with a fund of broad stories quite in the spirit of Tom Haliburton, but unlike him the professor had a fanatical hatred of alcohol. In deference, the toasts were sipped in ginger ale, a spectacle that must have shaken the convivial man over the mantelpiece. When the meeting ended Martell drew the dean of King's College and Foster and myself to his house not far away, where we talked into the small hours over a bottle of what Sam Slick would have approved as "high proof Jamaiky."

* * *

Our little historical society in Liverpool had been in abeyance during the late war, when most of us were absorbed in the history being made under our noses. Now we could look back again to colonial days. Shortly before the war we had ventured to borrow money and buy the charming little wooden house built by Simeon Perkins, the diarist, in 1766. At the end of the year 1945 the society regathered to resume operations and elected me president. My first concern was to pay off the debt we still owed on the house. My aim was to restore and furnish it as it was in colonial days and open it to the public.

Our society was small; we had no well-to-do members and no large interest on the part of the townsfolk in a monetary way. Soon I realized that our goal could be reached only with government funds. First I tried to convince the National Historic Sites and Monuments Board that the home of the leading spokesman of the Nova Scotia Yankees during the American Revolution should be preserved and shown as a Canadian national monument. I got a flat

No. At that time the board's sole activity was in putting up cairns with plaques, carefully allotted province by province according to the voting population. Our Nova Scotia voters' list being small, so were the allotments and monuments. I believe the limit was three cairns a year.

I turned with more bravado than hope to the provincial government. Premier Angus Macdonald was a man of culture with a deep interest in history, but most of his government members had neither one or the other. In fact, Nova Scotia was in a cultural ice age and the pace was glacial. For years I battled the inertia and often the open hostility of politicos who cared for nothing older than the last election. They ran true to form with capital city politicos everywhere – ignoring the country constituencies until three months before election day, then suddenly appearing with glad tidings of road contracts and other goodies, orating loud and long about our priceless heritage, and promptly forgetting all about that when the votes were in the box.

I pestered buck-passing officials with letters and personal raids on their Halifax lairs. Success came only by degrees – very long degrees. To start, our society presented the historic house and grounds to the government, free of all debt. After a long interval, with an election looming, we got them to repair the house exterior. It remained empty and closed. Just before another election we got them to restore the interior. Gradually they furnished it, one or two rooms at a time. And finally they opened it to the public.

It had taken eleven years!

Since then the Nova Scotia government has saved and restored other historic buildings for posterity, and people swarm to see them and to learn something important from them. In the frantic world of today, with everything in a ceaseless uproar like a forest in a hurricane, it's a good thing to see that your roots go a long way down.

* * *

I have mentioned the worst ailment of a writer, the mysterious mental block which comes from nowhere, without warning, and stops his production for weeks, months, in some cases years. There are minor blocks, too, but for these there is a remedy. It is simply to turn your thought to something else and write it down, even if it is only a description of the scene from your window or the pictures on the wall or the funny thing that happened on your way to the post office. Usually this is enough to start a current trickling, which you can then turn to your work.

One day in January 1946, as I laboured on *Pride's Fancy*, I had one of these temporary blocks, which I melted by a long diary entry:

> This is the pattern of my life these winter days. I wake at 5 A.M. or more rarely 6, and lie abed till 7 thinking of my novel and other matters. Then I get up, shake the coal furnace, light the oil stove in my den, and make my breakfast. I am at my desk by the time Edith and the kids get up.
>
> I read over yesterday's work, look up various bits of information, write a sentence or two, ponder a great deal, write a little more, ponder again, walk up and down, look at the snow outside for half an hour at a stretch (seeing a small brig in the West Indies). Towards 10 A.M. I emerge from my den, still in pyjamas and dressing gown, tend the furnace, wash and dress. At 11 A.M. I return to my desk and find that my mind now had gathered itself for a spurt. From then until noon I write perhaps 500 words, seldom more.
>
> At noon the kids come home from school and Edith knocks sharply on my study door. I join them at dinner. Afterwards I listen to the news broadcast diffidently – none of the anxious wartime manner – and go upstairs and shave. If the day and the road are fit I put on my walking shoes, my old fur-collared blue pea-jacket, my old brown hat (a cap on windy days), gloves or mittens, and sally forth.
>
> In winter I hike up the east side of the river to Milton, cross the bridge, and return down the west side, 1½ hours smart walking, plus time for conversation with acquaintances along the way, so the journey usually takes at least 2 hours and sometimes as much as 4, especially if I stop at the Milton forge.
>
> On wet or snowy days I walk uptown, cross the river on the railway bridge, follow the long curve of the line to Bristol Avenue, and thence to the post office where I collect my mail. Then down to the waterfront for a yarn with the fishermen, or to the undertaker's parlours (in an old shipyard) where a game of forty-five absorbs a little group every afternoon when there are no funerals in the offing. They used to play on the white-enameled corpse table, surrounded by bottles of embalming fluid, but a year ago they fitted up a little room apart,

with a card table, and a heavy curtain to shut off the gaze of passers-by.

I do my simple shopping, cigarettes usually – I smoke 30 to 50 a day – and reach home sometimes between 4 and 5. I read the newspaper and my mail, glance through magazines (Blackwood's, Maclean's, Reader's Digest, Saturday Evening Post, The Legionary, Time, Life, The New Yorker) which arrive at convenient intervals. I write my letters nearly always on the typewriter. Towards 6 Edith raps on my door and I emerge for supper.

After supper I tend the furnace, dump ashes etc. About 7.30 I am back at my desk. The process of the morning is repeated. A few words, a long wait, more words, more waiting, studying, smoking, fiddling with things about my desk, taking down my rifle from the rack and sighting it on something, walking up and down the shabby carpet. Then the gathered mind and the spurt, usually between 10.30 and 11.30 or midnight.

I emerge, stoke the furnace for the night, sometimes eat a few crackers and a glass of milk, sometimes mix a nightcap if I have some rum or gin. Then to my bedroom, where I lie reading for an hour or so before turning off the light and opening the window.

I am now in my 43rd year and weigh 195, which Doc. Murray says is 25 lbs too much. [So it was, and subsequently I reduced it to 175, my natural weight.] When I look in the glass I see a bald long-headed man with clipped grey hair at the sides and back, bushy black eyebrows in which one or two white hairs have appeared lately, a pair of quizzical brown eyes, a fleshy nose, a long mouth intended by nature to be lax and indulgent but firmly held for the past 15 years and now a little grim. The face is lined and sallow, losing the summer's brown but reddened a little by the winter air.

When I look at my somewhat worn exterior I marvel that I feel so ridiculously young. At heart I am still the romantic fellow I was at twenty, despite a lot of cynical wisdom picked up along the way, and with the same vague wistful longings and restlessness.

* * *

Later that month I had shocking news. My young friend James Martell had fallen ill suddenly and was dead. I went to Halifax for the funeral. Andrew Merkel and I were among the honorary pall-bearers at the service in All Saints Cathedral and on the slow march along the snowy streets to Camp Hill cemetery. I thought of our meeting there less than a year ago, when Jim helped me to plant mayflowers on Joe Howe's grave, and Sheamus Dhu played the lament on his bagpipes. It seemed to me, by second sight now, that the lament that day was for Jim, too.

It was bitter cold weather. Tully brought the Merkel car to the cemetery gate and took us down to 50 South Park Street, where she mixed hot buttered rums to stay the rattle of our teeth. Reverently and affectionately we turned down an empty glass for Jim.

The next day I called on his widow and his mother. We talked about Jim's enthusiasm in everything he undertook and especially the application of his keen young mind to the archives, urging people like me to take a fresh look at old matters. I remarked sadly and truly, "We all warmed our hearts at his fire."

* * *

That evening Bill Sclater sent a Navy car and chauffeur for me and we dined together at Admiralty House for the last time. He was leaving the service to take a job in Toronto. It was visitors' night in the familiar mess, and a number of discharged naval officers were there in civilian clothes, with a noticeable wistfulness about them. As we left Bill remarked, "This place is full of ghosts."

So it was. Indeed, change was afoot everywhere in Halifax, erasing everything but memories. Andrew Merkel was about to retire from the Canadian Press, and he and Tully were preparing to sell their house and make their home on the other side of the province, where they had bought an old farm overlooking Annapolis Basin. So the long-time rendezvous for Nova Scotian writers at 50 South Park Street would soon be haunted too.

* * *

Halifax was never the same to me after 1946. In one way or another nearly all of my friends there departed, taking with them the lively and stimulating atmosphere I had enjoyed so much. From my private lair on the South Shore, at long and longer intervals, I made fleeting visits. As the years went by I saw most of the familiar city demolished to make way for tall gleaming monstrosities of ferro-concrete. They reminded me of the gleaming fungus growths that spring up and flourish on a fallen tree in the forest.

245

*   *   *

Book publishers pay their authors twice a year. In March 1946 I
received cheques for the six months ending December 31, 1945,
and noted in my diary:

> Latest royalty returns show that the total sales of my immortal
> works, beginning with the Pied Piper volume in 1939, amount
> to:
>
> The Pied Piper of Dipper Creek .... 4,255 copies
> His Majesty's Yankees .... 15,262 "
> Roger Sudden .... 53,456 "
> Tambour and other stories .... 4,245 "
> <u>77,218</u>

*   *   *

Books of short stories do not sell well compared with novels, as
these figures show. When my first novel was published I thought I
could die happy if the sales of my books ever reached one hundred
thousand. With these figures before me, and with another novel
nearly finished, I began to dream of two hundred thousand.

*   *   *

I wrote the last word of *Pride's Fancy* in April 1946. As no printer
would bother to read with care my original working script with its
mixture of type and scrawled pencil insertions and deletions, I
began to type clean copy as fast as I could. On April 23 I noted in
my diary, "Hard driving at the typewriter, usually from 7 A.M. to 1
A.M. I am such an insomniac when deep in a book that it is no
trouble to keep awake. I quitted yesterday's work at one o'clock
this morning, slept till 3.30 A.M., woke up completely, lay an hour
tossing and thinking, came downstairs and got to work again."

I typed the last sheet on April 29 and packed the whole thing off
to New York. After all that I needed a long breath of the forest, and
I spent a week in the backwoods, fishing on the Tobeatic stream. In
mid-May I was in Halifax again to make final preparation for the
MacMechan book, including long discussions with artist Don
Mackay, with MacMechan's widow (who lent me his diary), and
with his colleague and successor at Dalhousie, C.L. "Ben" Bennet.

The headmaster of King's Collegiate School at Windsor invited
me there for a weekend, so from Halifax I drove on to Windsor. The
school occupied the spacious and beautiful grounds of the original
King's College, which was destroyed by fire in 1920. It was the first

246

time I had stood on this spot since I visited old King's as a boy. That evening in Convocation Hall I addressed an audience combining the staff and boys of KCS, the staff and students of Edgehill School for young ladies, the graduating class of Windsor Academy, and a number of town folk.

On Sunday morning the Head asked me to attend morning services in the chapel and read the scripture lesson. As he said, it was a good seafaring bit well suited to me (Acts 21: 1 – 17). He informed me also, "On your departure the cadet corps wish to have the honour of marching with you through the town, something they reserve for special people." In the afternoon we set off with the drum-and-bugle band in the lead, then my car with the Head driving and I sitting beside him trying to keep an attitude of modest dignity, then the colour bearers and colour guard, and finally in column-of-threes the corps itself, marching smartly in green tartan kilts and scarlet tunics, with glengarries, sporrans, white spatterdashes and gloves.

Leaving the school by the winding road through College Woods, we passed the natural pit of limestone that is called the Devil's Punch Bowl and then went right along Windsor's main street, stopping finally at the junction with the Chester road on the outskirts of the town, which was my road home. The corps lined up at the roadside for a formal inspection. I walked slowly up and down the ranks with their commanding officer and then thanked them for their compliment and gave them well-earned praise for their bearing and their good march discipline. They responded with three cheers and a tiger as I got into my car and drove away. All of this was in Tom Haliburton's home town, of course. In 1946 it was still something special to be a Nova Scotia writer visiting the place where he created Sam Slick, Squire Poker, the Old Judge, and the rest of that immortal company.

*   *   *

One midnight my phone rang, and I was told that the oldest and best guide for salmon anglers on the Medway River was very ill, with internal bleeding, and the Bridgewater hospital was seeking suitable blood donors. Early the next morning I set off in my car for the hospital, thirty miles away, with three others whose blood was the right type. At the hospital a doctor told us, "Old So-and-so is just alive and that's all." A nervous female lab technician took samples of our blood and examined them under a microscope for

247

"cross-matching," whatever that is. I had given blood many times during the late war to a travelling Red Cross unit at Liverpool but never before as a direct transfusion. With a grave smile the doctor told us that if the old fellow recovered he ought to be quite versatile, having in his veins the blood of a car salesman, a garage hand, an author and a papermaker. Alas, the poor old chap didn't get a chance to be versatile, or even to catch another salmon. In two days he was dead.

*　　*　　*

At the urging of the Canadian Authors Association, and of my Toronto publishers, I attended the 1946 convention of the CAA in Toronto. I went by train in the last week of June. George Foster met me at the railway station and took me to 215 Victoria Street, where I met my Canadian publishers for the first time.

John McClelland was a slim man, sixtyish, hardheaded, precise, the obvious business mind of the partnership. George Stewart was the jolly good fellow, always laughing, with a large face and frame, gleaming dark eyes, and white hair. He had been a travelling salesman of books in earlier days. They made a good team.

They told me they were giving "a little luncheon" in my honour at the Granite Club. It turned out to be eighteen people, among them poet Earle Birney, Napier Moore and his wife, a popular Toronto radio broadcaster named Rex Frost, and young Jack McClelland, who had served in the navy during the late war and was now getting acquainted with the publishing business.

That evening I made my way on foot to Hart House for a meeting of the executive committee of the CAA, to which I had been appointed. After much wandering in dim passages and opening wrong doors, I found the committee halfway through their business. The retiring president, Roderick Kennedy, was an editor of the Montreal *Family Herald and Weekly Star*. His successor, William Deacon, literary critic of Toronto's *Globe and Mail*, was a tall man with greying black hair, large black eyes behind glasses, and a brisk voice and manner.

The next morning I walked the short way from my suite at the Park Plaza to Hart House again, joined a general session of the CAA, and shook hands with Gwethalyn Graham, Kathleen Strange, Will Bird, Dorothy Dumbrille, Maida Parlow French, Grace Campbell and others prominent in the CAA of those long-ago days. A tall handsome woman, thirtyish, humorous, direct,

Gwethalyn Graham was the most striking personality and the most successful writer there.

At dinner that evening in the Great Hall of Hart House I sat with Birney and afterwards removed to a lecture room, where the gathering consisted of about one hundred and fifty people, of whom four out of five were women. John Murray Gibbon had arranged an hour of Canadian ballads written or collected by himself, set to old tunes, sung by a baritone and accompanied by a harpist. Mazo de la Roche gave a brief and light talk on Toronto and Torontonians. She was a slight person about sixty, with a bush of hair dyed baby-blonde and a nervous tic that made her head quiver as she spoke.

At the close of this session Bill Deacon brought over and introduced a woman journalist, a rangy blonde in her late twenties with a strong Baltic accent and the studied mannerisms of film actress Greta Garbo. I shall call her Miss Helsinki. She said she wanted to write "personality sketches" of me and of George Hardy, a professor at the University of Alberta who wrote sexy novels about ancient Rome and Palestine.

Kathleen Strange had invited us to a cocktail party in her room at Whitney Hall, but Miss Helsinki declared that would be too much of a crowd for her purpose. She said, "Ay vant to valk oonder som trees," and led the way adroitly through the little park to the Plaza and the suite, mentioned by Toronto papers, that my publishers had engaged for me on the top floor. Up there we went.

It seemed to me that Miss Helsinki had dallied a bit too long at a cocktail party somewhere, but she was quite an actress and I'm not sure to this day. Now and then she seemed to pull herself together and questioned us briefly, scribbling on a large pad of blue paper with a yellow crayon pencil. For hours she sprawled full length on my settee, demanding that Hardy recite poetry, and he obliged with everything from ancient Greek to Masefield. Whenever he paused, she renewed her demand. At the same time, she looked utterly bored and sometimes half asleep.

Once, for fair exchange I suppose, she jumped up and announced that she would sing for us "the marching song of THE FINNISH SOLDIERS when they are only TWO HUNDRED and the Russians are TWO HUNDRED THOUSAND and they are all going to DIE and they don't give a GOOD GOD DAMN." (I can't reproduce all that in her accent, but it was as thick as Scandinavian fish soup.) She marched up and down the floor yelling the song. It was a hot night, with every window open, and my fellow dwellers on the Plaza's top floor must have been in the Russian mood when she finished. Then she slumped on the settee again. I wondered what to do with her if she passed out. Hardy solved that problem for me at some time towards two o'clock in the morning, when he took her downstairs and poured her into a cab.

The next day two of my Toronto publishers' staff were coming to lunch with me, and I had invited also one of my father's war comrades, Colonel Charles Corrigan of Toronto, who had been wounded with him at Vimy Ridge in 1917. At ten o'clock in the morning Miss Helsinki phoned to say she had left her notes in my room and was coming for them. She did not turn up until 12.30 and then sat making conversation, obviously expecting an invitation to lunch. I told her I was expecting three men for lunch but she didn't seem to believe this until they arrived. Then she departed with her notes, which as far as I could see were just some yellow doodles on the fancy blue paper.

After lunch Colonel Corrigan took me away to Toronto Island, a beautiful place with tree-shaded creeks, and we spent some time in the yacht club, of which he was a member, in a refreshing breeze off the lake. We returned to a city sweltering at 89° in the shade. Corrigan led me into the Royal Military Institute, the ancient club for former army officers, where he thought I might find the library useful in future historical studies.

In that temperature I was perspiring in a sport shirt, open at the throat, and carrying my jacket on my arm. Suddenly a sergeant-majorly type sprang before me like a jack-in-the-box, announcing in a loud barrack-square voice that I was improperly dressed, that I must button up my shirt and put on my jacket or leave the premises at once. My own strong impulse was to say something rude and walk out.

Colonel Corrigan, a former president of the institute and one of its most respected members, had stepped toward the bar to fetch me a cold beer. He came back hastily, very disturbed, and for his sake I smiled, buttoned my shirt, and put on my jacket. Corrigan then called over and introduced the current president of the institute, who apologized for the fuss and explained that the rule had been imposed "because young officers lately out of the service are inclined to be careless about dress, and we can't have that sort of thing."

250

I wondered, and I wonder still, if this could have happened any-where else in Canada. It was too much like what we are told of the stuffy Guards' Club in England to be quite credible on our side of the sea. When Corrigan delivered me back to the Plaza I met Roderick Kennedy, and we walked together to Hart House, where Hugh MacLennan was giving a lecture on the writing of a novel. He was as tall, dark and handsome as when I saw him first in that memorable tennis match with Peter Aitken, and the overwhelm-ingly feminine audience went into rapturous murmurs at every pause.

Back at the Plaza, I turned on the radio and heard Rex Frost describing me as "a strongly built man with keen brown eyes and an air of quiet resolution." The next day I read Miss Helsinki's personality sketch in a Toronto newspaper. Among other things she said I had "the good square face of a sailor" and that I carried the salt air of my Nova Scotia about with me.

In that weather I wished to God I did.

*   *   *

Learning from newspapers and radio that I was staying at the Plaza, several of my father's old soldiers phoned or came to chat with me, and in their discourse I heard much more about him than I had known as a boy. Veterans of the Winnipeg Rifles now living in Toronto had formed a branch of the regimental association, and they were full of yarns about "Uncle Tom," vowing he was one of the finest soldiers in the old Canadian Corps "and just as salty as any of those characters you write about." They told me how he took command of the regiment after it had been shot to a remnant at Passchendaele, and how he rebuilt and trained it until it was acknowledged in First Division as one of the best to wear the fa-mous "old red patch." With grins they mentioned encounters with his discipline and assured me he was just as tough with brass hats whenever the welfare of his men was concerned.

*   *   *

Bill Deacon gave a luncheon at the Royal York for the newly ap-pointed executives of the CAA, of which I was a vice-president representing the Maritimes. By good chance I sat with Kathleen Strange, a handsome and vivacious woman with greying hair. She was an English girl who married a Canadian soldier during War One and afterwards worked devotedly with him on his prairie farm.

251

She wrote about this later in a book called *With the West in Her Eyes*, which was widely read and acclaimed in Canada, and she was invited to join the CAA. She told me that for the past twenty-one years her annual holiday had been attendance at the CAA conventions held in various cities across the country.

She gave me an amusing anecdote about Charles G.D. Roberts after his return from his long sojourn in Europe. The CAA was holding its convention in a western city, and Roberts was at the convention hotel looking over the female talent, as he always did. He selected young Kathleen for his attentions, and she was flattered by the famous author's interest in her book and herself. After a time he invited her to his room upstairs "just for a minute" to see some interesting photographs of his travels abroad. Unsuspecting, she went.

The photographs were all of himself at the time of his encounter with Isadora Duncan in Paris, wearing sandals and flimsy tunics of the pseudo-ancient-Greek style that she and her little coterie affected. Each successive photo showed less of the tunic and more of Charles. Finally he thrust under her startled gaze one of himself in no costume at all, with full frontal exposure, as they say nowadays. Then, she said, "he pounced," and there was a short struggle that ended abruptly when she slapped his face with the full swing of a healthy and indignant right arm. She fled, leaving him on his knees declaring that he wanted her embrace to inspire him to new poetry – a line he must have used many times in his long career with ladies other than the muse.

During several conventions after that, Roberts ignored her. Then he came up to her in a hotel foyer somewhere, announced in a dignified voice, "My deah, I forgive you," and passed on.

* * *

Napier Moore took me to dine at his elegant new home in the suburbs. A small dapper man with a protruding lower lip and jaw, he liked to talk and was full of little jokes and anecdotes. He had turned over the chief editor's chair at *Maclean's* to W.A. Irwin and was now boss of the entire Maclean-Hunter complex.

After dinner we drove around to York Mills to spend the evening with Walter Allward, designer and sculptor of the great Canadian war memorial on Vimy Ridge, on which he had spent fourteen years. He was a tall broad-shouldered man, quiet and unsmiling, seventyish, with a long lined face, dark eyes, white hair, and the nose of a Mohawk warrior. He addressed his wife affectionately as "Girl."

When he went off to get drinks, Girl took us quickly into a room hung with many of his drawings inspired by the war, male and female nudes in attitudes of grief, fear, resolution, hope. One struck me especially. Three huge cannon formed the background. Before them stood a slim male figure, face to the sky in an attitude of defiance, with a violin and bow in his hands. Allward was touchy about strangers seeing his private work, and he came along with a tray exclaiming "Here! Here! What's this?" Diplomatically, Mrs. Moore declared we had asked to see the drawings and Girl had been too polite to refuse.

We drifted out to the cool shade of a flagged court, looking on lawns and fruit trees full of greedy robins and grackles. Moore ran off with the conversation in his cheerful way. Allward and I sat together, listening. He knew that I was a writer from Nova Scotia and that was all. Out of a silence – even Moore had stopped talking for a minute – Allward turned to me with a sudden glow in his eyes and said, "It seems to me that you are a man like Robert Louis Stevenson, with a mind full of eighteenth-century sea characters." I was so surprised that I gaped for a moment. Allward turned to Moore and picked up a thread of the former conversation. I turned to Girl and said, "How did he know that?" My book was not out, and only one or two McClelland and Stewart people knew what I had been writing during the past year or so.

She replied quietly, "Walt is psychic sometimes," and went on to give instances. One was about the Vimy memorial. After that long work was finished in 1936, Allward ordered several more large and heavy slabs of the expensive stone to be brought from the distant quarry in Dalmatia and had them buried deep in the side of the famous ridge, as if he foresaw another war and another battle that would damage the monument. He was terse about his motive and perhaps did not realize what instinct made him do it, just three years before Hitler began the second world war.

I was so astounded by his remark that I brought it up again, asking how he knew what was in my mind. He said simply, "I just knew. It came to me very clearly. Do you know, I have often seen in mind a rocky inlet on a sea coast, with small white houses, and pole stagings built down the face of the rock to the water. I have described it to people who told me it was an exact picture of my

253

father's birthplace in Newfoundland, although he never described it to me and I have never been there."

Later he told me that the Vimy monument had not been damaged in War Two except by a few vandal rifle shots that had smashed a hand on one of the figures, and the like, and he would go to France soon to repair it. He said his original intention in designing the war memorial (and he still thought it was right) was that it should stand on a cliff top facing the Saint Lawrence estuary, where it would be seen as a landmark by every ship coming in or out of the river. He showed me a drawing of it, a magnificent conception, with a massive strengthening apron or buttress down the face of the cliff.

* * *

Back home, I worked on maps for the inside covers of *Pride's Fancy*. Doubleday (the firm had dropped the name of Doran) sent copies of two ancient maps they had found in the New York Public Library, one French, the other God-knows-what, with all the names in Latin. Both were very inaccurate. I made a tracing of the French one, substituting eighteenth-century English names. I made another from the modern admiralty chart, marking all the points mentioned in my book and the track of the Nova Scotia privateer from her first appearance in the Florida Strait to the place of her destruction off the coast of Haiti. With these guides the publishers got it right.

* * *

Later in the summer of 1946 I drove to Cape Breton to attend another session of the Gaelic Mod at Saint Ann's and to enjoy again the Highland pipers, singers and dancers. There I chanced to meet J.A.D. McCurdy, the man who flew Alexander Graham Bell's experimental airplane off the ice of Bras d'Or Lake in February 1909 – the first man to fly in the British Empire. Among other interesting things he told me some anecdotes of Marconi in Nova Scotia during his early experiments with transatlantic wireless telegraphy, including his love affair with a Cape Breton girl.

I found the little hotel at Baddeck full of people attending the Mod, so I just got my meals there and slept in a private home outside the town. When I first lunched at the hotel, the young man at the desk recognized me from newspaper photographs and asked me to sign my name in the register "to bring honour to the house."

He said he had read *The Pied Piper of Dipper Creek* and *His Majesty's Yankees* while a prisoner of war in Germany and that both books, sent by the Red Cross, were very popular in the camp.

* * *

After dining one evening at the hotel I sat for a time on the verandah. The house was bustling with people from the Mod, including several little girls in costume who had been competing in the Highland dancing, half a dozen soldiers of the Cape Breton Highlanders, and a pink-cheeked man in a bus conductor's uniform. Darkness had fallen, rain was coming down in a torrent, lightning flashed and thunder boomed.

A red-coated piper left his instrument in a chair on the verandah and went inside to get his supper. Immediately the bus conductor picked up the pipes and began to play a tune. One of the little girls stepped out and began to dance a fling, then a reel, then a strathspey, as the piper changed the airs. When she tired she made a bow and another small girl took her place. The piper in the red coat returned to the verandah, wiping his mouth. He showed no surprise at finding another man playing his pipes. After the busman had got enough tunes off his chest he passed the pipes to their owner, who struck up another tune at once. He played and played, and the little girls danced. Then one of the young soldiers asked for a "lend o' the pipes" and went on to play tune after tune.

All this time the rain poured and the thunder and lightning went on. Once all the lights went out and we thought the house was struck, but the piper didn't falter a note. He went on playing in the dark, and eventually the lights came on again. A bus loomed through the rain and halted outside the hotel, and away scurried most of the girls and their papas and mamas, the soldiers, and the pipe-playing busman.

All of which could have happened only in Cape Breton.

* * *

In August 1946 I was working on another book of short stories, but at the request of *Maclean's Magazine* I took time out to do an article on Tancook Island, off the south coast of Nova Scotia. I had sailed past it a number of times as helmsman of the Colonel's yacht, but I had never set foot on it. At Chester, where a little motor ferry ran once a day to the island, I paused to chat with a doctor who knew the islanders well. He warned me not to reveal myself as a writer. In the mid-1920s a literary professor named Frank Parker Day had spent two or three summers on Tancook's small neighbour, Ironbound Island, whose people are all close blood relations of the Tancookers. In 1928 he published a pseudo-novel called *Rockbound*, portraying the Ironbounders as a backward folk, the result of generations of intermarriage, speaking English with a thick Old German accent, and lusty in their quarrels and amours. According to the doctor, Day never returned to Ironbound. The Tancookers and Ironbounders would have hanged him if he did.

I took passage in the ferryboat and after chugging five or six miles landed at a decrepit wharf. I wore a khaki trench coat (a relic of my Reserve Army days) and carried in one hand a club bag and in the other a briefcase containing paper and pencils. I encountered an immediate hostility in everyone I met. Nobody would rent me a bed, or sell me a bite of food, or even tell me anything. As the ferry had gone back to Chester it looked as if I must spend the night hungry in a fish shed and come away next day with absolutely nothing on that paper in the briefcase.

Finally the wife of one fisherman agreed reluctantly to let me sit at the family table and to make a bed for me on the parlour couch. Wherever I had gone about the Nova Scotia coast I always found the people warmly hospitable, and I was puzzled by this exception. In the course of an awkward evening's talk with the family I rejected the doctor's advice and mentioned casually what I did for a living and my purpose in coming there. The effect was magical. All the suspicion and hostility vanished. Then they told me what was in their minds when I appeared. In the long years between the two great wars the price of fish was very low, and the fisherfolk of Tancook had a very hard time; but they endured it and never asked a cent of relief.

Since the outbreak of the second war, the price of fish had soared beyond all peacetime belief, and now that peace had come it was actually climbing higher still. The people of the island were saving a lot of money for the first time in their lives. They had heard about income tax and would not risk putting their money in the bank at Chester. They were stashing it away in mattresses and other hiding places, and every day they kept their eyes peeled for "a spy from the Income Tax" who would come to ferret out their hard-earned cash. When I stepped off the boat with my trench coat and the briefcase, I was obviously the spy.

From the moment I revealed my true mission everyone smiled on me, and my stay on the island was a happy one. After my habit I made research far beyond the needs of a magazine article, out of sheer interest in people. One item was the Tancook speech. I had expected the typical German accent of rural Lunenburg County in those days, and it was there all right; but with it I found traces of Irish accent and idiom and some old Yankee expressions right out of the eighteenth century. The reason was simple. They were derived from an Irish settlement long ago at Blandford, just across the bay, and from the colonial New Englanders who settled at Chester. I did not include any of this in my article but as *Maclean's* wanted more, I sent my notes and told them to take as much as they liked. Among other things they added my modest little note on linguistics.

Much later I was told that Tancookers resented the *Maclean's* article because I said they "talked funny." I said nothing of the sort. When I paid my hostess on departure after two or three days, I remarked on the attitude I had met when I came to Tancook and asked out of curiosity why she took me into her home. She chuckled and said, "Well, the Bible says everyone's got a guardian angel walking about with him. Who was I to turn an angel away from my door?"

* * *

McClelland and Stewart urged me to make a public appearance tour in central Canada at the time of the publication of *Pride's Fancy* in November. It would involve some speeches here and there, various interviews by the press and radio, and a special coast-to-coast radio broadcast on the CBC. I wrote in my diary, "I don't like this monkey-show business and have refused on previous occasions, but I realize its importance to the publisher and feel I should agree this time."

Meanwhile I gave myself a break. October is usually a pleasant month in Nova Scotia, and I spent some of it sailing, deer hunting with my friends at Eagle Lake, and pheasant shooting with Andrew Merkel in his place of retirement above the Annapolis Basin marshes. On November 13, 1946, my forty-third birthday, I left home to make the first and last public appearance tour of my life. I stopped in Halifax to confer with a group of ex-officers of the West Nova Scotia Regiment, veterans of the war in Europe, who had asked me to write a history of the regiment from its colonial beginnings down to the present day. I agreed to do it, and when they asked my fee I said, "Nothing." The publication cost would be up to them, and I stipulated that if any profit came from the book I wished it to go in some way to needy veterans of the regiment.

* * *

At the Toronto railway station I was met by some of the M & S staff, including a proficient young man named Hugh Kane, who had made all the arrangements for the tour. The next morning I went to the Carlton Club for a quiz by the Toronto press. In the afternoon there was an official reception by Mayor Saunders at City Hall, in the presence of reporters and photographers. The mayor welcomed me to Toronto, introduced me to his staff, and presented me with tickets for two box seats at the Winter Fair, to which all Toronto was flocking that week. Then I was rushed away for another broadcast with Rex Frost.

That evening I had a private engagement for dinner with the Walter Allwards. I was to call first at Napier Moore's house, and I arrived late to find Moore peering up and down the street for me. In the Moores' car we drove away to Walter Allward's lovely house. The Allwards' son "Chips" was there with his handsome and witty wife, and so was Mazo de la Roche.

Moore had spoken of Mazo with affectionate irreverence as "something like a desiccated turkey." I found her charming, and we had a long and pleasant conversation. She had moved into Toronto from the countryside but still lived in an ivory tower, scarcely knew what was going on in the world and didn't want to know. Her latest book was selling very well, despite critics who generally condemned it as "another sausage in the Jalna string" and other words to the same effect. She told me she was charmed with my tales of Nova Scotia, especially those in *Tambour*, and asked me to find a secluded cottage on the seashore near Liverpool for her next summer. Allward asked me how I liked the notion of this personal appearance tour, and added seriously, "Don't let them spoil you, Raddall, and don't ever be tempted to live here. Stay down there on the coast where you are and *as* you are."

Learning that I was to take part in a radio show called "The Readers Take Over," Miss de la Roche threw up her hands. "Do you know what they do? They pick your book to pieces right before your eyes and in the hearing of all the world. I heard one, and they were saying horrible things, and the poor author sounded so confused. I wouldn't submit to that for the world!" Moore spoke up, saying he had been chosen as one of the "readers," and while he had some criticisms to offer he admired *Pride's Fancy* and intended to make that clear. I said he was at liberty to say anything at all if the author was given a chance to defend himself. Miss de la Roche retired about ten o'clock, asking me to be sure to get in touch with her again, especially if I could free myself from the tour arrangements long enough to have dinner with her.

* * *

I must say something more about this conversation with Mazo de la Roche. I cannot recall my exact words, but I remarked that the American market had seemed closed to novelists living in Canada and writing about Canadians until she and Martha Ostenso broke through in the 1920s. Recalling my remark ten years later in her strangely allusive and more than a little illusive memoirs (*Ringing the Changes*, published in 1957), she forgot Martha Ostenso and quoted me as saying, "You cannot imagine what your winning of the *Atlantic Monthly* prize meant to us other Canadian writers. It was as though you opened a door that had been inexorably shut against us." She was perfectly sincere, I'm sure, but her memory or her interpretation was at fault. *Jalna* was first published in the United States in 1927, the year of my marriage, when I began experimenting with the short story. Far from any hope of the American market my sole hope was to sell some in Toronto.

* * *

When Mazo asked me to find a cottage for her on the Nova Scotia coast, I assumed that she merely wanted a holiday by the sea with her cousin and lifelong companion, Caroline Clement. She was very specific. It was important that the cottage be near (but not in) a small fishing village where she could talk to the people and see how they lived and worked. It must be comfortably furnished, with two bedrooms, a living room, a well-equipped bathroom and kitchen, and, of course, electrical connections. Also, there must be no other summer cottages or visitors nearby.

With those terms, it was a tall order. I wrote to her that I knew of only one such cottage. It was near the fishing village of Port Mouton and owned by an American couple, friends of mine, who made visits from time to time but did not stay continuously all summer. They did not lease it to other people in their absence and I would have to write to them with a special plea.

Mazo reminded me of this in the following winter, when my Christmas card showed a Nova Scotia fishing cove under a summer sky.

307 Russell Hill Road
Toronto
7th January, 1947

Dear Mr. Raddall,

It was so nice of you to send me that gorgeous card at Christmas. It stands alone on the chest of drawers in my study warming my heart in this wintry weather, to think such scenes can be.

I so enjoyed meeting you at the Allwards'. I am afraid that when your week was over you must have been tired out. At such times one is like a piece of bread on a duck pond, torn to bits by the greedy. And for what? If you can write you can write, and no speeches are needed to prove it.

Do you remember telling me of a house belonging to an American, near a fishing village? It is possible that we shall want to go to Nova Scotia next summer and I should like to have some place in mind. With all my good wishes for the coming year.

Very sincerely,
Mazo de la Roche

*   *   *

I wrote to my American friends but got no reply. They were a manufacturer and his beautiful and rather eccentric wife. He had branch plants in Britain and elsewhere, and they did a lot of travelling. I was still hopeful in June 1947 when I wrote to Mazo with an exact description of the cottage and its setting, but shortly afterwards I had a note from the owners saying politely No. They liked to have the cottage available whenever they had a notion to motor up to Nova Scotia and could not consider letting it to anybody. I wrote to Mazo accordingly.

That summer the Napier Moores made a visit to Nova Scotia and renewed our acquaintance. They mentioned that Mazo had found a place on the Bay of Fundy where she and Caroline could stay several weeks studying the fishing people. It was the

New Brunswick island called Grand Manan, where the American novelist Willa Cather formerly spent summers working on her books. In the fall I had a letter giving some detail of that visit.

307 Russell Hill Road
Toronto
10th September, 1947

Dear Mr. Raddall,

The Napier Moores came in the other night and told me how much they enjoyed meeting you again and making the acquaintance of your wife. They told me that you spoke of your disappointment in not being able to get that lovely cottage for Caroline and me this summer. Your description filled me with longing, for it was just the sort of place we wanted.

We went to Grand Manan which in many ways suited us very well. But there was a great deal of fog and the food was far from good, which is a pity for a convalescent and indeed for anyone who is making a stay of nearly six weeks. Perhaps another summer we may have better luck. Next year we hope to go to England but in these days one really cannot make plans ahead. I hope that by now you are well on the way to a new book. I so much enjoyed your last one. I had hoped to do some work this summer but there were far too many people about. Thanking you for all the trouble you have taken over the cottage.

Very sincerely,
Mazo de la Roche

*   *   *

I realize now that when I had my first conversation with Mazo in the autumn of 1946 she had a notion of stepping out of the Jalna rut to write a novel about Canadian fisherfolk. Long ago she had visited Nova Scotia and was charmed with the coast and its people. But when she made an attempt to recover that old enchantment at the age of sixty or so there was too much fog, too many people about, and the food too bad.

In fact, alas, the Jalna rut was too deep and the gap too wide.

We exchanged Christmas cards with a scribbled note each year, but I can find no further correspondence except a pathetic note from Caroline just a year before Mazo's death. She was a little confused about the Doubleday Award.

3 Ava Crescent
Forest Hill Village
Toronto 27-6-60

Dear Mr. Raddall,

My cousin Mazo de la Roche has asked me to send you a few lines to say how happy she is that you have won the Doubleday Award. And may I add my own congratulations. It is especially pleasant when one's own country shows its appreciation of one's talent.

I regret to say that my cousin has been ill for many months now – gravely so. We have had three nurses in the house since the first of this year. Since the warmer weather has come she is picking up a bit of strength but this extreme nervous exhaustion from which she is suffering is very difficult and slow. Indeed it has been a sad winter for us.

We have just finished reading your stories of early days in Nova Scotia and greatly enjoyed it, though we shuddered at some of the hardships endured by those fine brave people.

Vy. sincerely,
Caroline Clement

*　　*　　*

I return to my adventures in the urban wilds of Ontario in November 1946.

Diary, Nov. 19, '46. Spent most of the morning at the McClelland & Stewart office, autographing copies of *Pride's Fancy.* John McClelland asked me into his sanctum and said he had something of great importance to tell me. The long association of M & S with the New York firm of Doubleday was coming to an end next spring, because Doubleday were about to establish their own branch in Toronto. M & S therefore are transferring their American connection to the Boston firm of Little, Brown & Company. He urged me to do the same. He said frankly that handling my books in Canada had become a valuable part of M & S business and they did not want to lose it. Doubleday were a huge corporation, a grasping lot, absolutely without a soul, and so on.

With some of this I could agree, for I have never felt that Doubleday made much effort to advance the sale of my books in the U.S. At the same time I felt little assurance about the proposed transfer to Little Brown. I have always thought authors damned silly who keep shifting from one publisher to another.

*　*　*

One of my engagements in Toronto was a very cheerful affair. It was lunch with the Shellbacks' Club, an informal group of Toronto sailors and former sailors who gathered weekly at a hotel for a meal and songs. An amusing thing occurred beforehand. M & S had spread information about me including the fact that I practised the unusual art of calling moose. This intrigued many people in Toronto, and the Shellbacks asked if I would demonstrate the art at their luncheon. I agreed, and Hugh Kane phoned the Royal Ontario Museum to ask if they had in their Indian section a moose horn and if he could borrow it. They said they had and he could. Like a good promotion man, Hugh scented some useful publicity – after all, how many sea novelists can call moose? – and he arranged for reporters and photographers to witness me receiving the moose horn at the museum. Alas, at the last minute the museum phoned Kane asking what size of antlers he wished to borrow. Antlers! The fact was, they hadn't a birchbark calling-horn at all. So the stunt had to be called off.

The Shellbacks gathered in a small dining room seating about thirty. We had a good lunch. A man with a foghorn voice led them in singing several chanties including my favourite, "Shenandoah," in which I joined heartily.

He then led them in a long doleful ballad about the sinking of the *Titanic*, which they performed with great feeling, especially the chorus:

> Oh it was sad, mighty sad,
> It was sad when that great ship went down.
> All the husbands and their wives,
> Little children lost their lives,
> It was sad when that great ship went down.

In a verse that mentioned the ship's band playing "Nearer, My God, to Thee," they all stood and rendered with great solemnity a stave of that lugubrious hymn.

Ian Armour introduced me as "a former sailor with some yarns to spin," and I spun some which they received merrily. The chairman then asked me to do a couple of moose calls with a piece of rolled-up cardboard. I said, "All right, but I won't be responsible for whatever may come in the door." (There was said to be a small but plush brothel on the next floor.) After all this the chairman informed me that the Shellbacks were unique in that every member was a commodore. Therefore they had decided to confer on me the title of Honorary Vice-Admiral of the Royal Cibola Yacht Club. The club was mythical, of course. Cibola was the name of a creek in Toronto Island where some of the Shellbacks kept their sailing craft. Two new sloops in the creek actually had been named *Pride's Fancy One* and *Pride's Fancy Two*.

I still rate this one of the best of my honours.

* * *

The editorial staff of *Maclean's Magazine* gave me a luncheon at the University Club, with Napier Moore presiding, although Arthur Irwin was now the chief editor of the magazine. The others were Arthur Mayse, Ralph Allen, R.G. Anglin, N.O. Bonisteel, John Clare, A.S. Marshall, Hal Masson and Scott Young. There was talk about my work, quoting from this story and that, and Irwin remarked that *Maclean's* so far had run nineteen of my short stories, more than any other writer's works. Scott Young wickedly asked how much *Maclean's* had paid me for the first one, and when I said sixty dollars, Moore denied it indignantly. I insisted, while the others roared, and finally Moore said he would look it up. (He never did.)

We then removed to the Maclean Building, where I was shown the printing and binding plant and the offices. Prominent on a wall in the editorial office was a large oil painting. It was the picture of Scabby Lou at the sawmill, which Moore had commissioned from artist John Clymer when he bought "Tit for Tat" at second hand in 1939. I pointed and said it belonged to me for a special reason, which of course the editors knew. They protested, chuckling, that they liked to have it on that wall, but Moore agreed that I should have it, and he had it newly framed and sent to me in Liverpool. There it hangs in my study to this day.

Irwin drew me aside after this and said he would like to have a serious discussion with me on my next visit to Toronto, when he would make me an important proposition. I said politely that I'd be interested to hear it, and let it go at that. As things turned out I did not visit Toronto again for a long time, and I never knew what Irwin had in mind. Soon after this mysterious hint he left *Maclean's* to take charge of the National Film Board, and from there he went to Australia as a Canadian trade commissioner.

*   *   *

The Toronto branch of the Canadian Authors Association invited me to an evening reception, and I found the chamber full of people. Don LeBourdais, who presided, said it was the largest gathering of Toronto writers since Charles Roberts came there on his return from Europe. I thought of Kathleen Strange's anecdote and wondered if I should feel flattered. Bill Deacon introduced me in a nice little speech and asked me to address the gathering. I asked what I should talk about, and various voices called out, "Yourself! How you came to write. How you work." And so on.

So for the first time I risked the wrath of the gods with what Kipling called "the evil I." A barrage of questions followed. Then refreshments and random conversation. I noted in my diary, "Many compliments about my work and – what seemed strange – about myself. Deacon explained that I had remained aloof from the CAA so long that many had the impression that I was stiff-necked and swollen-headed by my own success. Now they found me 'easy and modest' and were agreeably surprised."

*   *   *

Kane had drawn up a busy schedule for me. I was rarely in my hotel room except in the early part of the morning and late at night, and even then the phone rang frequently. Whenever I returned to the room I found chits clipped to the door – people who had phoned when I was out and left numbers to call. Many were former naval men whom I had met in Halifax and Liverpool during the late war.

At one luncheon, M & S had invited 104 people ("Toronto's top crust," according to Kane) and the food was served buffet style in the "library" of the Royal York, a chamber furnished like an immense drawing room. (I didn't see a book in it.) John McClelland, George Stewart and I formed a little receiving line at the door, and I was introduced to a procession of pleasant well-dressed people, most of whose names I cannot remember. B.K. Sandwell remains in mind, a man despised in Halifax for his sneers at its people in *Saturday Night* at the time of the V-day riot in '45. What I'd read of his other opinions had given me the impression of an intellectual snob. Now his face and tone confirmed it, although he was polite enough.

John McClelland asked me *sotto voce* to address the gathering. I pleaded weariness with so much talking in the past few days, but when "Sandy" Sanderson of the Toronto Public Library urged me to say something, I got up and uttered my pleasure at meeting so many charming people, threw in what I hope were some clever remarks, and sat down in a patter of polite applause.

A luncheon address to the Canadian Club was an ordeal. It was to be broadcast, which I had not anticipated, and I had not written and timed my talk as one must for radio. I had determined to speak extempore, so within a few minutes I had to arrange it all in my head, with a beginning, a middle and an end, to fit the time slot. I wondered how many of the club would have a genuine interest in what I had come to talk about, the little privateer warships of Nova Scotia and their part in Canada's story. As the moment approached a small black microphone was pinned to the lapel of my coat. A radio technician sat manipulating instruments on a little balcony, and when his red light glowed I began to talk. It was a simple recital of what was to me a memorable chapter in Canadian nautical history. No oratory. No funny stories. I managed to finish on the second of the allotted time and sat down feeling that I had bored them all. Although many came to shake my hand afterwards and say polite things, I retained a bleak impression that most of the club felt let down by the distinguished author as advertised by M & S. They were used to much better speakers on much more important subjects.

One evening I submitted myself to the radio show "The Readers Take Over," which Mazo de la Roche had so deplored. Napier Moore, Frank Willis, James Scott and I sat about a table with microphones. Scott was interlocutor. Moore and Willis had the criticisms. Moore opened by saying that Dolainde's dying speech in *Pride's Fancy* was too long and too lucid for belief. "Reminds me of the dying father in a Victorian melodrama." I retorted that I wouldn't have my book reduced to his Victorian memories. Any lawyer or notary could give instances of dying men making long and lucid testaments.

In general, however, they had good things to say about the book, Willis reciting a long extract about the building of the ship, and Moore waxing lyrical about my descriptions of the Nova Scotia countryside in summer and winter. At the close of the show we

266

adjourned to my suite at the Royal York for drinks and talk. Mrs. Moore came along with Napier because she refused to stay alone in their fine new house. There was a female maniac next door who turned in fire alarms and insisted that the Moores were murdering a pair of "English refugees" in their basement. Moore chuckled about this and other adventures with their uncomfortable neighbour. He appeared to be enjoying the whole thing.

* * *

In London, Ontario, I was interested to learn that the scene of Proctor's defeat and Tecumseh's death in the War of 1812 lay about forty miles down the Thames. A knowledgeable newsman told me that the Indians dragged Tecumseh's body out of the fight and buried it in a secret place before their flight. It was never found. I reminded him that Henry Clay used to boast possession of a miniature razor strop made from Tecumseh's skin. He laughed and said the Yanks were always adept at skinning strangers and lying about it afterwards.

We drove outside the city for an unscheduled visit to the University of Western Ontario. Soon I found that I was to address a class in English literature for three-quarters of an hour and submit to questions afterwards – one of the little surprises that Kane was continually popping at me. The room proved too small for the students who gathered, and we had to adjourn to a larger one. There were many ex-servicemen in the class and nearly everybody seemed to have a question. I had to break away at last for a brief chat with the head of the university, Dr. Fox, and then a dash back to the city by taxi.

With no time to wash, I addressed another club luncheon and then was whisked off to a splendid modern public library and art gallery. The biggest bookshop in London had arranged a public reception in the art gallery and issued one thousand invitations. By this point in the tour I was beginning to tire of all this talking and dashing about. Insomnia, my old enemy, was haunting me night after night, and the strain of being literally on exhibit day after day, from morn to night, was wearing to body and soul. In the London art gallery I had to stand for three interminable hours, sipping tea now and then and making conversation with a procession that seemed to consist largely of ladies in middle age, all beautifully dressed but without much to say. I suppose they had come out of natural feminine curiosity to see if the novelist from Nova Scotia was exactly as advertised. I had to rack my tired wits for new things to say, or rather to find new ways to say old polite clichés. After an hour and a half, the primitive savage inside me wanted to yell like a bored wolf and take to the woods.

When finally we got back to the hotel I was angry with Hugh Kane and George Stewart, feeling that they should have rescued me somehow long before. I started to tell them in blunt sea language, but poor old Stewart begged, "Don't say it! Don't say it!" After a drink or two I simmered down, but I resolved that once this tour was over I would never go through all this again.

* * *

George Foster accompanied me to Ottawa, where I was to address the CAA branch and their guests. First I met their executive committee at a luncheon. They included Robert Stead, who said the great need of the day was a book he intended to write entitled "How to Refrain from Writing a Novel." I asked them what I should speak about tonight, and again the reply was, "Your experiences as a man and as a writer. Everybody is curious about you."

Foster and I were staying at the Chateau Laurier. Before we left for the evening's affair he insisted on my taking two or three whiskies poured with Cape Horn measure "because it's a cold night." We walked the short distance to the Senate on Parliament Hill, where the big Railway Committee Room was filled with people. I was soon introduced and invited to speak. I don't know how long I spoke or exactly what I said, but Foster declared afterwards that it was brilliant and why didn't I always talk like that? A good question, as they say. The truth was that the whisky had put me at ease, as I never was before in the presence of an audience. I reminded him that, brilliant or not, I'd got along very well for fifteen years without any of this jawing in public.

After my talk came the usual question-and-answer session, which everyone seemed to enjoy. It is much better than a speech because people can ask what they really want to know. A friendly affair. I heard again what I'd been told at the CAA meeting in Toronto, that my apparently aloof attitude towards other Canadian writers for so many years had given an impression of snobbishness, whereas in person I was "unpretentious and outgoing." I could only say that I regarded my writing with humility, and my "aloofness" was simply a matter of circumstance and geography.

268

(After all, how many Ontario writers would have travelled a thousand miles to see me in Nova Scotia ten years ago, or even five?)

When the meeting closed, Evelyn Tufts was waiting by the door for a private word. The *femme fatale* of the merry group of Song Fishermen in Nova Scotia in the 1920s, "Eve" went on to become a famous journalist based at Ottawa and travelling all over America and Europe. *Saturday Night* in those days described her as "a ball of fire, a kaleidoscope of words, blonde, green-eyed and terrific."

Alas, time had overtaken Eve at last. She was now fifty-five, plump, fashionably dressed, heavily rouged and powdered, and with hair dyed baby-blonde in the same tint as Mazo de la Roche's. Her political reports from Ottawa were still tart and merciless to public personalities, however, and I was surprised to hear her saying, "My dear boy, how tired you must be . . . and what a bore all this . . . but you must face your public . . . bear your burden . . . everyone's simply entranced with you tonight . . . you're so vital and sensible."

That whisky of Foster's must have been great stuff. I should have made a note of the brand. Finally Eve said, "Now do go to bed and get a good rest." I thanked her and did exactly that.

*   *   *

The last stop on my tour was Montreal, where I made two addresses and attended a luncheon at the Ritz-Carlton, given by the Montreal branch of the CAA. Later there was an autographing session in the book department at Morgan's, which Hugh Kane had advertised well beforehand. In the long line of people with books was the man who had given me my first job, W.J. Gray of the Marconi Company, and we stopped the autograph production line to have a happy chat.

Not long after that I was on my way home, almost gasping for good salt air and peace and solitude.

*   *   *

I relate these patches of my first and last public tour because in patchy ways it was an education. I saw what advertising and ballyhoo can do to puff sales, especially when the author is willing to play the performing monkey to the organ-grinding of the publisher. I had met a lot of friendly people and lost the instinctive Bluenose suspicion of "Upper Canadians."

Until I made those two visits to the heart of Canada in 1946 I had never been more than fifty miles from the sea in my life. It was a venture in the spirit of Marco Polo to travel a thousand miles or so inland and meet "those freshwater fellows" on their own ground, and to find so many of them interested in a writer from a remote corner of the Atlantic coast. The important fact about me, naturally, was that my books were being published in London and New York as well as in Toronto. At that time very few Canadians living in Canada and writing entirely about their country and its people had done this literary hat-trick. Thus I was a curiosity, and they wanted to have a look at me and ask me how I did it.

I didn't like the monkey's role, though. As a boy I had felt sorry for the poor beastie, capering, chattering, doffing his little red cap to the tinkle of cash and the blast of the hurdy-gurdy. From the time I started to write I had a conviction that if I chose interesting characters in my own familiar scenes, and wrote well enough about them, a sufficient part of the world's people would pay to read my tales. I would never need to stand on my head and gibber in the marketplace or to bellow into every microphone that I could reach.

Back in the early 1930s when I was merely turning out a few short stories, I chanced to meet Morris Longstreth, an American author who told me a few things about the writer's life as he had seen it. I made note of one bit, probably because it flattered me with an assumption that I was bound to succeed:

> Sooner or later you'll have to make an important decision. As your writing becomes known and you achieve a certain amount of notoriety, you'll be assailed on every hand by people wanting you to get up on your feet and talk. Never forget that your proper attitude is on the seat of your pants and pushing a pen. The art of writing and the art of public speaking are very different things, and the time and thought you give to one must always be at the cost of the other.

* * *

Looking back over forty-seven years since the publication of my first short story, I say Amen to that. When I quote it, some people contradict me with the dual brilliance of (for example) Winston Churchill. Well, Churchill was a genius and I am not. But they are wrong anyhow. From his twenties Churchill wrote with care and increasing skill to become one of the best English authors of his time. Painfully practised elocution enabled him to recite with sonorous eloquence anything he had written. He could make a biting phrase in a House of Commons debate, but whenever he spoke at length extempore he was a lame and halting disappointment.

By the same token the silver-tongued orators of the world, the men who can arise at any moment and hold an audience spellbound by the sheer flow of a mellifluous voice – these are dead ducks the moment they sit down to write. Their words then fall as flat as the paper they are written on.

*   *   *

Diary, Dec. 18, 1946. At 10 P.M. Jack Brayley of the Canadian Press phoned, "We have a report that your novel Pride's Fancy has been sold to Paramount Pictures for $200,000. Will you confirm this, please?"

*   *   *

I was stunned for a moment, but my native caution revived me. I told Jack to check with Doubleday at New York before releasing anything.

Wonderful news, if true. Even with the terrific income tax deducted, such a sum would remove the shadow of penury in old age which has haunted me ever since I took up writing as a whole-time job. But I could not permit myself such a dream castle on so flimsy a bit of evidence. No sleep all night. Lay restless till 4 A.M. Then got up, lit the stove in my den, sat smoking cigarettes and trying to read, suffering all the pangs of a desert wanderer in the presence of a mirage.

*   *   *

The next evening Brayley phoned again. "We've been in touch with Ethel Hulse of Doubleday about that movie sale. She says it's all news to her."

I asked my American agent to look into this. Just what was going on? I knew that as preliminary ballyhoo for a picture the movie companies commonly "leaked" news of the outright purchase of a novel for a tremendous sum, when actually they had merely taken an option, and for a much smaller sum. Just the same, Hollywood was then at the height of its fabulous prosperity and anything was possible.

Kenneth Roberts was Doubleday's top historical novelist, and the firm always gave his books lavish promotion. I was on a very much lower shelf, a fellow up in Canada with some capability but a strange insistence on writing about Canadians. Consequently an elderly woman sub-editor was assigned to handle my work, and the firm spent little on promotion. Mostly my books had to sell themselves.

My agent discovered that Kenneth Roberts had been writing a novel called *Lydia Bailey* at the very time when I was writing *Pride's Fancy*. By a fantastic chance, both novels dealt in part with the black revolt against the whites in Haiti in the 1790s, and both had among their characters the actual persons of Toussaint L'Ouverture and Dessalines. Nobody in the Doubleday editorial offices discovered this unfortunate coincidence until my novel was published first and the matter of motion picture rights came up. Doubleday always insisted on handling those rights and deducting 10 per cent for their commission.

Exactly what happened after the editors did make their discovery I never knew. Inquiring in Hollywood, my agent picked up a hint that Paramount had been ready to take an option on *Pride's Fancy*, as the Canadian Press had learned. Doubleday then denied any option or sale. After a silence of several months Doubleday announced with éclat that *Lydia Bailey* had been sold for a large sum to the movies.

If the Hollywood rumour was true, the movies' interest in my novel had been switched to the novel of Doubleday's top man. Hollywood rumours are seldom worth a damn, but true or not, this contretemps convinced me that I should have another publisher in the United States. My original sponsor at Doubleday, Theodore Roosevelt, had died in Normandy. The most friendly man on the Doubleday staff, Tom Costain, a Canadian himself with an abiding interest in Canada and Canadian writers, was about to leave his editorial desk to write best sellers of his own.

There was something else. Publishers strive to keep their authors in convenient pigeonholes, and to Doubleday I was just a writer of "costume stuff." I knew they would balk at a modern novel from my pen, whether staged in Canada or anywhere else, and I was now determined to write some novels of contemporary life in Canada as I had seen it.

*   *   *

Just before Christmas, 1946, among the jolly greetings of the season I found a cold note from the income tax department, stating that I must pay a surtax of 4 per cent on my book royalties. Under this income tax ruling an author's royalty on his book was the same as a speculator's royalty on an oil well and therefore subject to extra tax as "unearned income." God knew it was hard earned, every cent of it, but God was a poor witness in the view of the income tax department. If my plumber earned $5,000 in a year, and I received $5,000 from the sale of my books in the same year, I had to pay 4 per cent more tax than the plumber because he worked for his living and I didn't.

This was only one of several penalties for anyone daring to earn a living as a writer of books in Canada. Another was the lack of a Canadian tax agreement with other countries about their authors' earnings. An English author whose book was published in London and New York paid income tax only to Britain on his royalties in both countries. By the same agreement an American author whose book was also published in Britain had to deal only with the tax machine in Washington.

The Canadian government ignored Canadians writers except to mulct them by excessive taxes when by some incomprehensible chance their books were successful abroad. In those days no author could live on his or her earnings in Canada alone. This was mainly why successful Canadian writers in the 1920s, like Martha Ostenso, Norman Reilly Raine and Thomas Costain, moved across the border where the market was much more lucrative and the tax machine much more lenient. Not until 1949 did Ottawa admit that a Canadian author actually worked for his living. The surtax of 4 per cent on his book royalties as "unearned income" was finally revoked in that year.

Years more went by before Ottawa got around to an arrangement about Canadian authors' royalties in Britain. During all that time my British publishers deducted 50 per cent (ten shillings in the pound) of my royalties in their country for income tax. My London agent collected his 10 per cent fee on the gross earnings too, so that during all those benighted years I received only 40 per cent of my British earnings.

* * *

A letter from Doubleday now declared that they had contacted no less than thirteen moving picture companies about the film rights in

Pride's Fancy. "All admitted heartily that the story was excellent motion picture material but felt that the costumes and settings involved made it too expensive to produce." The letter writer forgot to mention that Doubleday were then arranging to sell the movie rights in *Lydia Bailey* for a very fat sum, despite exactly the same Haitian settings and costumes.

In January 1947 I notified Doubleday that our connection was at an end.

*   *   *

An author who has had some success, but not enough yet to make him too important to trifle with, gets sophistry from more than publishers. One day Frank Willis, then one of the most prominent figures in the CBC, telephoned from Toronto and introduced a man I shall call Soper. Soper came on the line and said he was head of a new Canadian film enterprise, affiliated with one of the chief British film companies. His company was building a large studio at Toronto and was committed to three first-class pictures this year and six each year to follow. His company had an arrangement with the biggest chain of theatres in Britain for full-circuit playing, quite apart from the U.S. and Canadian markets.

He said he would like to film *Roger Sudden* next year. In the meantime he wanted me to write a story around the famous Nova Scotia sailing ship *Bluenose*, "involving a romantic element," to be filmed in the coming summer. He wished me also to act as an adviser in the filming of the story. As all of this would involve a lot of time and work, I asked how much his company proposed to pay me. He coughed and paused. Then, "We hadn't given much thought to that side of it." I told him to write me a letter setting forth his whole proposition, including that side of it, and rang off.

Promptly I got an airmail letter with an elaborate and imposing letterhead, showing the huge new studio building as if it really existed. Soper apologized for stalling when I asked about payment and said he didn't like to mention a figure on the phone. Now he offered me five thousand dollars for the *Bluenose* story. He would come to Liverpool on a certain date, bringing his script writer and Frank Willis, who was to be a technical adviser on the film, and he asked me to make hotel reservations in my town.

On the date set I drove to the railway station to meet the daily train but found no Soper, no Willis, no script writer. When I did the same thing the next day with the same result, I cancelled the hotel reservations and went on with my work. I was busy revising and typing my Oldport tales from *Blackwood's Magazine*, which McClelland and Stewart were to publish that fall in a book called *The Wedding Gift and Other Stories.*

I never heard of Soper again, and in after years when Frank Willis came to see me on his summer trips to Nova Scotia he avoided any mention of the matter. We had both been conned by a glib parasite of the movie business, propelling himself with his own wind like a jet plane. It was my first encounter with the tribe of fluent liars who make pictures in Cuckooland. I was to hear a lot more from them as the years went by.

* * *

With my deep interest in the story of Halifax I had long studied the city's records. In the spring of 1947 I began particular research for my book on Halifax. Most of my work was in the archives, but I rambled over Halifax and Dartmouth to refresh my mind with the sites of things past.

Now came something else. After signing documents making myself responsible for safekeeping, secrecy, and what not, I received from Army Records, Ottawa, two large bundles containing the official war diary of the West Nova Scotia Regiment from 1939 to 1945. The sheets were bound in monthly sections together with those holy testaments of the army that are called Part Two Orders.

I put aside my work on the Halifax book to study all this, to write to former commanding officers and others who now lived outside of Nova Scotia, asking for additional information, and to arrange interviews with officers and men living in the province. Preparation and writing of the book entailed three months of hard work, but I found it highly interesting. Many of the West Novas who fought in the Second World War were descendants of "His Majesty's Yankees" and of exiled American loyalist soldiers like my "Colonel Larrabee" of Tarleton's Legion.

* * *

My American agent was anxious for a personal conference about a new publisher in the United States. To me it was of no immediate concern because I would be busy for the next year or two on the Halifax book and the West Nova history, both of which would be Canadian productions. Nevertheless he insisted on flying up to Nova Scotia, and I agreed to meet him at the Yarmouth airport.

275

We stayed at a Yarmouth hotel and held a long discussion. He was very keen for me to sign a contract with the John C. Winston Company of Philadelphia, an old established firm with a big non-fiction business that was thinking of a wide extension into fiction. To begin with, they proposed to republish *His Majesty's Yankees* as an adventure story for teen-agers, with some revision on that account and therefore under another title. They hinted at a first printing of thirty thousand. Also, according to the agent, they wanted my next adult novel and were prepared to advance me five thousand dollars on it sight unseen.

When I put my agent on the plane next day I told him there was no hurry about a new contract in the United States because of my present Canadian commitments. I might come to Philadelphia this summer to talk things over with Winston's chief editor before making a decision. On that we parted.

The Winston Company printed the version of *His Majesty's Yankees* edited for teen-agers under the title *Son of the Hawk*. I was much occupied with my West Nova book that summer and did not get to Philadelphia. Before long, Winston's changed their minds about putting forth a large fiction wing. I had no desire to be part of the remaining stub, so that was that.

*   *   *

My boon companions, Parker and Smith, had taken up golf several years ago and urged me to do so too. I pooh-poohed "that sissy game" after our years of adventure together in the woods. I was now in my forty-fourth year, however, and I realized that a time was coming when I could no longer throw a canoe on my shoulders or tramp all day in the bush, and I might as well start getting used to some less strenuous outdoor sport.

In June 1947 I joined the small Liverpool golf club, which had a nine-hole course, converted from old farm pastures, on a grassy point in the sea a few miles outside the town. As it happened the club's pro was seriously ill, and my friends tried to teach me. Also, I got a book on the game and studied the golfing form plates in my *Britannica*. None of this did me any good. I was too old a dog for such new tricks. At last I settled for the best I could do in my own way. In the woods I had seen good axemen at work, and I had swung an axe a lot myself. The stance was utterly different from the orthodox golfer's, but in the downswing the important wrist action was pretty much the same, and on impact the stroke was accurate to a small fraction of an inch.

I tried it with a golf club and after some practice found that I could hit the ball straight in this way, instead of slicing off to the right as I did invariably with the orthodox stance and swing. My style became the favourite joke of the club, of course. On his summer visits to Nova Scotia, Napier Moore always spent an afternoon at golf with me, and once he wrote a merry description of "Raddall's lumberjack swing" in *Maclean's*. Still, after two or three years I confounded the jokers by playing eighteen holes in the low eighties. As exercise it was much better than walking, and for a bonus there was the view over the sea, especially after storms when a big surf broke on well-named White Point. Year after year I have played there from the time the snow goes off the ground until it comes again. In winters when the snow came late, in spite of icy temperatures I played often in December and January when there wasn't another player (or nut) on the course.

None of this altered my work schedule. For many years I had spent the afternoons outdoors whenever the weather was fit. In my late sixties arthritis in my right hip ended my cherished travels in the forest, but today I can still limp quite nimbly about the course by the sea, where there are no boulders or fallen trees to leap over.

* * *

All the summer of 1947 I worked on the West Nova history, starting at daylight and going on far into the night, with the afternoon break for golf when the weather was fine. In addition to the war diary of the regiment I had obtained the brigade diary, various intelligence reports, large-scale maps, and air photographs of the battlefields. Also, I consulted field notebooks, personal diaries, letters and other documents. As I wrote in my foreword to the book, "The happiest part of these labours came through the various quiet but keen young men who visited my house and took me through this or that action yard by yard, with maps spread on the floor of my study and the Regiment's war diary at our elbows."

By August these long daily and nightly labours were having the familiar effect. I was getting along well with the history, but my nerves had gone to fiddle-strings and killed the boon of sleep. There was no ease to be had from drugs in those days, or from alcohol. I had found long ago that good writing and grog were utter enemies, and there was no compromise. The time for grog was when the long travail came to its end. Hence a somewhat exalted entry in my diary towards the end of August:

> Finished my history of the West Nova Scotia Regiment after long and hard labour. Tonight, feeling the need, I left home in my car and wandered through the streets and finally to Greenfield and the Medway River, where it was very wonderful and rather eerie in the moonlight with the mist rising in tall wisps from the water. Parked a long time by the river, somewhere near Glode's Falls, I think. I had no hat or coat and the night was cold, but a drink of Trade Wind from time to time kept the blood warm and left the mind free for enjoyment. All was very still and I could hear a deer moving in the woods across the river and all the little sounds of the night, and these and the mist and the moonlight very lovely and exciting as when I first spent a night in the woods 24 years ago, and very soothing to the mind and to the heart bowed down by weight of Whoa! About 2 A.M. came away feeling absurdly young and driving fast and wishing to God I really was young again, and knowing what I wanted this time and not just drifting into things.

* * *

About two weeks later I resumed work on the Halifax book. Also I resumed golf . . . very badly, my left hand and wrist half crippled with writer's cramp, arthritis or whatever it is.

I had cut my left hand deeply when I was a child. The Halifax explosion cut it again in 1917. One day in the 1930s, splitting kindling wood with a sharp hatchet, I cut the back of the hand near the wrist. Each time the hand healed well, but in later years when I typed clean copy of a book script for the printers, which meant continuous labour at the typewriter keys for two or three weeks, the tendons controlling my left fingers became painful and eventually useless. Towards the last of the job I could use my right hand only, which made the work tedious and rasping to nerves already taut.

* * *

In Toronto the year before my friends McClelland and Stewart had assured me that the Little, Brown company would be delighted to publish my future work in the United States, and as it chanced, the chief editor of Little, Brown, Angus Cameron, had come to Ontario that fall on a hunting trip. M & S arranged for us to meet briefly at one of the luncheons or dinners on my public appearance tour in

278

November. I cannot remember now what Cameron even looked like; his face was just another in the swiftly passing crowd of those days. But I remember very clearly that I disliked the man in the space of a few polite remarks, and the feeling obviously was mutual. We weren't on the same wavelength in any way at all.

Consequently I was not surprised or perturbed in October 1947 when my American agent informed me that Little, Brown would not contract for my next novel if it had a modern theme. I was deep in the Halifax book and there were other matters to be tackled before I could turn my thoughts free for a new novel, but one thing was sure. The next novel was going to be as modern as wireless telegraphy – as my own life, in fact.

*   *   *

Publication of *The Wedding Gift and Other Stories* was delayed by the illustrator, C.W. Jefferys, whom I had chosen because he was the best-informed artist in Canada on historical matters and costumes. Unfortunately he was old and ailing now. The page proofs arrived just as I got back from a deer hunt at Eagle Lake, and Hugh Kane phoned from Toronto asking me to wire the corrections to save time. I sat up long after midnight and arose again at daylight to finish the job.

A few days later I was in Halifax for more research on the book that I had decided to call *Halifax, Warden of the North*, after a line from Kipling. While there I conferred again with the group of ex-officers of the West Novas, this time to select photographs and maps for my history of their campaigns in Europe. Typescript of the history was already going the rounds of other officers now scattered across Canada, to be checked for errors and omissions.

Now arose the matter of money for printing and binding. My own publishers had warned me that regimental histories never sold enough in the ordinary book market to earn their cost and consequently had to be financed privately. When the West Nova officers got home from the war and formed their history committee, they had easy verbal assurances about the money from two well-to-do men. Neither of them was a native of Nova Scotia, but they had been connected briefly with the West Novas and were proud of their association with such a famous fighting unit.

The chairman of the history committee, back at college studies like so many of the wartime officers, had lately approached these gentlemen in person, saying the history was almost ready for printing and what about the money to pay the printers? Both side-stepped their promises adroitly and turned the talk to something else. They did the same thing when I wrote, giving them an exact statement of the cost. I knew the other officers had no money for anything but their struggle to establish themselves in the postwar world.

Rather than see my work wasted and the regiment's record buried in a file at Ottawa, I finally put up the money myself. The former officers, not knowing anything about business, had committed themselves to a contract with a printing firm in Montreal, which now urged me to pay for an edition of five thousand copies. I decided to limit it to one thousand, each numbered, and autographed by myself. The cost was about $2,750, a big outlay for me in those days. I set a retail price of four dollars a copy, of which the booksellers would get eighty cents, and I told the officers' committee that the profit should go to a charitable fund for needy veterans of the regiment.

The hypothetical profit was based on a notion that out of several thousand men who passed through the regiment from 1939 to 1945 at least one thousand would be eager to read its history. I was only half right. I should have considered that most men who have suffered the hardships, pains and terrors of war don't want to be reminded of it afterwards. They prefer to talk about the funny things that happened in the line and the jolly good times at the rear. There was something else. In the shifts of war many men serve briefly in the regiment and then are transferred to another. In 1944, after the great wastage of battle and sickness in Italy, all Canadian army reinforcements were pooled in depots, and men were drafted to the West Novas from every part of Canada. Few of these had any interest in the history of the regiment.

Nova Scotian bookshops quickly sold about five hundred copies and the provincial department of education bought two hundred for school libraries in western Nova Scotia. The rest gathered dust in my attic until in later years book collectors suddenly sensed a value in them.

I never regretted the work or the money I spent on the book. If I had shirked it, the deeds of many brave men would have been lost in an Ottawa limbo. That happened to my father's regiment after War One because nobody was willing to assume the work or the expense of a book with maps and photographs telling the whole story of the Winnipeg Rifles on the Western Front. I determined that it would not happen to my own West Novas, a regiment with no large and prosperous city in its home recruiting area, simply a gathering of lads from small coastal towns and farming villages who fought their way through Sicily, Italy and Holland and emerged with one of the finest fighting records in the Canadian army.

In March 1948 the wandering typescript of *West Novas* came home like a boomerang, loaded with corrections and additions suggested by the various officers who had examined it since the previous August. I made the changes. Then, in the formal procedure, I sent it to the postwar colonel of the regiment, who endorsed it and sent it to the Historical Section, General Staff, Ottawa, for inspection and approval. All of which was mandatory before the book could be printed.

*   *   *

Since the spring of 1947 (with time out for *West Novas*) I had been working on *Halifax, Warden of the North.* I found it a refreshing change from a novel, in which you have to wring your mind for every line. The plot and the timing were clearly set by history itself, and the old records of Halifax furnished a cast of characters beyond the invention of any novelist. As Macaulay observed of another matter long ago, "So much is history stranger than fiction, and so true is it that nature has caprices which art dares not imitate."

I was mystified when the committee selecting the Governor General's Award for 1948 gave my book a medal for "Creative nonfiction." From this apparent contradiction in terms I concluded, perhaps wrongly, that in their view history by itself wasn't supposed to be all that interesting.

> *Diary, April 6, '48.* Wrote the last word of my Halifax book at 1 A.M. Very tired. It has been a long job with much research and tedious checking. This evening I started to type clean copy for the printers, putting in corrections and new matter discovered since first writing. Probably a month's work.

> *Diary, April 25, '48.* Working very hard the past two weeks, without taking time to exercise, answer mail, or even to enter this diary. Terribly hampered by my lame left fingers. On the verge of a breakdown sometimes but always succeed in pulling myself together. This morning I awoke at 5 feeling awful. Got

up, moving quietly not to disturb my family and had break-fast. Phoned Brent Smith and suggested a trip to Eagle Lake. After dinner at the camp we worked down the east side of the lake, chopping the winter's windfalls out of the hunting trail. Got back to camp exhausted and hot. Had a drink and got supper. Reached Big Falls at dusk. Very tired physically but much better in mind.

* * *

In May I sent the finished typescript to McClelland and Stewart. The next day I began final changes in the *West Novas* typescript suggested by the Historical Section, General Staff. Mostly minor things like the spelling of some Italian place-names. I refused to agree with one pointed suggestion, that I omit any reference to "scrounging" (looting) by Canadian troops. To my mind, a half-truth is a lie like any other, and when I write a history I want the whole as far as I can discover it. I had met veterans from all parts of Canada who told merry yarns of scrounging by their own and other Allied troops in Italy, although it was nothing like the systematic pillage of the Germans. William Napier's famous history of Wellington's Peninsular campaigns never failed to mention looting by British troops as well as their heroism in battle, so I let my small but authentic references stand as they were.

With that off my hands I went to Halifax and spent a couple of days with artist Donald Mackay, looking over old prints and paint-ings to illustrate the Halifax book and discussing the scenes for his own drawings to accompany them.

* * *

Now came time for a brief holiday at last. An old friend named Jerry Nickerson had started his working life as a boy fishing for lobsters at Seal Island, which lies far off Cape Sable, the westerly tip of Nova Scotia. Surrounded by reefs in the powerful ebb and flow of the Fundy tides, often hidden by fog or snow, Seal Island had a reputation for shipwrecks almost as bad as Sable Island's, far away in the ocean to the east.

Getting old and ailing, Jerry longed to see the scene of his boy-hood once more while he was still able to travel. One day in May I phoned him to pack some clothes, picked him up in my car, and drove eighty miles to Cape Sable. There we found a younger kins-man of his, Dewey Nickerson, still active in the lobster fishery, and

Dewey took us to Seal Island in his fishing boat. He and his crew of lobstermen lived in an ancient wooden dwelling there, and we bunked and ate with them.

We called on the owner of the island, Mrs. Winifred Hamilton, the abiding descendant of a family that settled there in 1823 mainly to rescue and care for shipwrecked sailors. She was the daughter of a lightkeeper and widow of another, and like her father she kept a flock of sheep. She made a daily walk of seven miles around the island in all seasons and all weathers to rescue any of the sheep that might have fallen over the steep sea banks. One of the most remarkable women I ever met, at sixty she had the figure and complexion of a young woman, a gentle face and manner, and hands calloused like a lumberjack's from carrying driftwood up from the shore and sawing and splitting it to supply her stove and fireplace through the long winters.

She took us on a tour of the island, pointing out many slight mounds where drowned sailors had been buried long ago. In one place, where the tides and winter storms had eroded the sea bank, she picked up a human thighbone and used it as a pointer on the rest of our journey. (Dewey took it for a moment and measured it against my leg. "Man about your size, Tom.") Most of the graves were unmarked. Her forbears had made, and she herself had renewed from time to time, three wooden headboards for a pathetic little group at the south tip of the island. On each she had painted neatly:

WOMAN NAME UNKNOWN
WASHED UP FROM BRIG TRIUMPH 1861
SUNSET AND EVENING STAR
AND ONE CLEAR CALL FOR ME

I took a camera shot of her sitting by these graves amid the daffodils she had planted about them. On my return home I typed a description of all this and in my custom added a brief history of the island and drew a detailed map showing Blonde Rock, Mother Owen's Rock, The Devil's Limb, The Limb's Limb, Hospital Shoal, Loch Sloy Shoal, and the other hazards that had killed so many ships and men. I thought of sending some of it to *Maclean's* as an item of Canadian interest, but just then a letter came from my American agent. On a recent call at the offices of the *Saturday Evening Post*, the chief editor had asked him about that man Raddall who used to send them short stories. I mailed the typescript to my agent, who promptly sold it to the *Post* for a thousand dollars, a generous fee in 1948. The *Post* sent a photographer, and I took him to the island. It was a cameraman's paradise, what with the graves, the curiously stunted and twisted trees, the litter of old ship wreckage, the ancient wooden lighthouse braced inside with stout ship-knees to stand hurricane winds, the lobstermen's shacks built mostly of washed-up wreckage (one actually had a mahogany floor), and so on.

I mentioned in my article that Mrs. Hamilton was getting old and hoped to sell the island to someone who would live there and care for the sheep, the graves, and the nesting rookeries of the sea birds, as she and her people had done for 125 years. The *Post* printed the article with several excellent colour photographs under the title "ISLAND FOR SALE." It drew an enormous response from readers all over North America. Many wanted to visit Seal Island and some to buy it, but none were willing to live there on Mrs. Hamilton's terms.

The lady of Seal Island refused to sell.

* * *

In June 1948 a convention of Canadian Clubs met at Saint John, New Brunswick. Well beforehand they had asked me to address them. Ordinarily I would have sent a polite refusal, but there was something I wanted to say, so I went. I told them how instead of encouraging its authors, Canada treated them scurvily. In addition to the drawbacks I have set forth already in these memoirs, I said that alone among civilized countries Canada did nothing whatever to help talented writers in need of money.

The Canadian Authors Association once tried to raise an endowment fund for the aid of young writers, but the income tax department effectively squashed it, ruling that donations to such a fund were taxable because the CAA was "a trade organization." I reminded my audience that the only honour available to a writer in Canada was a medal called the Governor General's Award, which was provided by the "trade organization," not the Governor General. And so on. I urged them to talk about these things to other people when they got home.

* * *

The Saint John newspapers reported my speech fully and favourably, but in my home province the Halifax *Chronicle* in a tart editorial declared that authors should stand on their own feet like everybody else and hinted broadly that I was advocating a public subsidy for people like myself. I didn't bother to reply. I had made clear in my address that I had been on my own feet from the start of my writing career and was in no need of a crutch now.

I did express regret for the gap of ten years between 1928, when my first short story appeared in *Maclean's*, and 1938, when painfully earned and saved money enabled me at last to quit a steady job for the perilous chances of a free-lance author in Canada. I was thinking of Britain's civil list, the Guggenheim Foundation in the United States, and suchlike subsidies in other countries for native writers of promise. For example Australia, less wealthy than Canada, spent fifty thousand dollars a year to foster a native literature. With grants from some such fund I could have been writing full time, with a free mind, long before I reached the age of thirty-five.

Years were to pass before Ottawa set up the Canada Council with plentiful funds to foster native culture in all ways from literature to the ballet. When that came I was dismayed to see the result where writers were concerned. The ease of getting a Canada Council grant drew a swarm of greedy free-loaders, including professionals well able to finance themselves, a flock of shallow cadgers eager to enjoy a year or two in London or Paris or wherever else their fancy went, most of them without talent or energy enough to write an interesting postcard, let alone a readable book. I suppose one should forget about those and think only of the talented writers who do need help and get it; but when I look back at some of the names on the Canada Council grant lists, I can't avoid the sensation in my stomach which, on my first voyage, made me run to the lee rail.

*   *   *

All through the summer and fall of 1948 I was unable to settle down to a new novel because I had to deal with a succession of printers' proofs and write letters about them. The *West Novas* history alone brought a stream of proofs and letters through July and most of August. Then came the galley proofs for my Halifax book, and after the galleys the page proofs, for of course I had to prepare an index.

One day in October I sent off the index and the last batch of page proofs for *Halifax, Warden of the North* with the eager feeling of a lover free to turn at last to his darling waiting in the shadows. In the very next mail I got a wilting surprise – another mass of proofs, this time for a volume of selections from the colonial diary of Simeon Perkins, to be printed by the Champlain Society in Toronto. Originally the society had asked me to compile this volume with explanatory footnotes, but I was too busy with other work. They gave the job and the fee to a Toronto university professor, who asked me to send the diary there for his examination. The diary was in the custody of the Liverpool town council, who refused to send the precious bundle of manuscript so far away as "Upper Canada." I persuaded them to place it temporarily in the care of the Public Archives at Halifax, where the professor could come and study it in a secure place with proper facilities and then return it promptly. Then came a long delay. The professor actually took three years to get around to it, and I had to stall the town fathers again and again. And now that it was selected and edited he had sent me the printers' proofs with a bland request that I check them before publication.

For those who do not know what it means, the checking of proofs is a slow and painstaking chore for any honest examiner. The setup of every sentence in the book must be checked, re-checked, and checked again, because with long knowledge of the material your own mind is actually too familiar with it, and wherever the printer has missed or mangled a word or a phrase your own brain is apt to supply what is missing or wrong and glide right on. Not only the words but every bit of punctuation must be checked. I remember a publisher's copy-reader in New York who had a mad passion for commas. Sometimes I suspected that he or she must have loaded a blunderbuss with commas and shot them at the type. In several instances, however, the insertion of a comma in a certain place, as if by diabolical intent, changed utterly the meaning of what I wrote.

*   *   *

Diary, Oct. 16, '48. After long and vexatious delays I am able at last to turn my whole mind to the novel I had hoped to begin last summer. The difficulty as always is the start, the plunge from the diving board. It will deal with wireless opera-

tors and a woman on a lonely island 25 or 30 years ago. In a
sense it is a story I've been waiting all this time to write.

* * *

Each morning I wrote, or went through the agony of striving and
getting nothing at all. On afternoons when the weather was fit I
played golf alone at White Point, continuing through November
when the course was otherwise deserted for the winter. Each
evening I shut myself in my den with my problem. At that early
stage the characters always appear dimly and talk in a flat sort of
way. You know vaguely what you want but you can't get them
alive on the paper. Every third or fourth day you scrap what you've
written so far and start again, fumbling for the note you want and
must have to go on with. This is what some writers call "living with
your characters," I suppose. To me it seems more like a passionate
effort to make their acquaintance. Even on the golf course the novel
was never out of my mind. White Point and Sable Island happen to
be on exactly the same line of latitude in the North Atlantic. Whenever I gazed true east over the sea I knew my island was there,
hidden by distance and the wet curve of the globe, but close and
vivid in my memory.

* * *

After nearly a month of struggle with the story I took a week off
with my friends at Eagle Lake. On my forty-fifth birthday, hunting
alone on the wooded ridge west of the lake, I fired at a buck deer
running and circling as they often do and felled it with a single
bullet through the spine at the base of the neck. It is a preferred
shot if you can make it, because it kills instantly and does not damage the meat. If that sounds a bit like Hemingway let me add that I
made no attempt to shoot another deer that year. I contented myself with paddling a canoe about the lake, walking in the woods,
and doing firewood and other chores about the camp.

Over a glass with my friends I said something like, "This is what
I've enjoyed most in the past twenty-five years. Just being in the
woods, hunting, fishing, or simply wandering along the old trails.
Outdoors all day, every day. When a man can't enjoy that any
more he can't enjoy life any more. He should be content to die at
fifty, really. After that he's had the best of it, and the rest is all
down hill."

Probably the dram after a long day's exertion had much to do with this profound observation. I promptly forgot it, anyhow. Unknown to me, Austin Parker made a note of it in the camp log. When I did reach my fiftieth birthday we were all together at Eagle Lake again, and after a round of drinks Parker turned the log pages back and read the note aloud. "Now," he said to me solemnly, "how will you have it? Do you choose to pick up a rock and jump in the lake? Or shall we take you out behind the camp and shoot you?" I could only grin and utter a complaint about the cold-blooded friends I had. Years went by before arthritis put an end to my travels in the forest, but then nobody offered to shoot me as a favour.

*   *   *

In January 1949 I noted in my diary, "The novel is going well, after many fits and starts." In February I had a surprising phone call from John McClelland, saying that Stanley Salmen of Little, Brown and Company would be in Halifax next Monday on his way to England, and he would like me to tell him about my new novel. This was a puzzle. When my agent approached Little, Brown about my proposed modern novel in 1947, Angus Cameron had refused to have anything to do with it.

I learned that Salmen had come from the *Atlantic Monthly* to be executive vice-president of Little, Brown, that he had been working long and hard since he took the post and now for a rest he was taking a slow boat across the sea to talk with English writers. The chosen boat was a small steamship of the Furness Withy line, which carried freight and passengers back and forth between England, Newfoundland, and Nova Scotia.

I made a date to meet Salmen and his wife in Halifax, and because the roads were icy I went by train, taking with me in a battered old attaché case the novel as far as I had written it. Like all my first drafts, for economy's sake it was typed on cheap letter-copy yellow paper, with numerous scrawled pencil additions and deletions. I doubted if Salmen would have time or patience to read much of it, but at least he could see that I had a book well under way.

I found the Salmens waiting for me at the agreed rendezvous outside the dining room of the railway hotel, and after dinner we removed to their cabin aboard the ship at Pier Two. Salmen was about my own age, with thin silver-blond hair and shrewd blue eyes. Mary Salmen was slender and somewhat younger, with brown hair and grey eyes, and she had a casual friendliness that concealed an acute mind and a warm heart. We discussed the theme of my novel. Salmen was doubtful about it, especially because it involved a deep and passionate love affair between a middle-aged man and a spinster of nearly thirty. He shook his head and said, "That will be a very difficult thing to bring off!" He must have guessed that my case contained manuscript but he did not ask to see it, and I made no attempt to show it.

His frank disbelief and my own stubborn faith in what I was doing brought about a glum silence, which Mary Salmen broke by asking me to tell her about life on Sable Island. I thought she was just making conversation, and my reply was brief and stiff; but she pursued the subject with questions intuitively good and perceptive, and suddenly I found myself responding. I did not address myself to Salmen. I had written him off by that time as I had written off Angus Cameron before him. I simply opened my heart and mind to a woman who showed sincere interest in what I was trying to do.

When I finished, Salmen remained silent but she exclaimed, "You *can* do it! I can see that island, and I can see your people and their very human situation. You go ahead and finish it no matter was Stan says!" I thanked her and said it was exactly what I intended to do, and I arose with my unopened leather case and bade them bon voyage. Salmen's only manifestation of interest was in parting, when like any publisher he said, "When you finish your novel I'd like to see it before you show it to anyone else."

As I left the ship I felt that my journey had been wasted.

*   *   *

In March 1949 I received my first honorary degree from a university. It was Dalhousie, where long ago my father had wished to see me graduate. President Kerr invited me to address a special convocation, and I chose for my subject "The Importance of Things Past." Three of my former school teachers in Halifax were in the audience, and I had the pleasure of a chat with them afterwards. The citation was given by my friend C.L. Bennet, head of the English department. The final and finest accolade came from my gentle dark-eyed mother. In private after the ceremony she said quietly, "Tom, your father would have been so proud."

It was strange to hear people calling me Doctor. I had to restrain an impulse to look around for a man with a little black bag. When I got on the train the next morning the conductor called me Doctor, and when I said, "Where did you get that?" he smiled and pointed to a Halifax morning newspaper, which had an account of the ceremony and a photograph. Several other acquaintances on the train also had seen it, so I got the Doctor all the way to Liverpool. When my wife and I alighted, a taxi driver came up and said, "Wanna cab, Tom?"

I was home again.

* * *

Diary, May 19, 1949. The novel goes slowly but it marches well, or so I think. One thing is certain. It will be the best or the worst thing I have written.

* * *

I took time out from the novel to make inspections and suggestions for the restoration work being done on the historic Perkins house, to do a few CBC broadcasts, and to attend the convention of the CAA, which was held at Halifax that summer. I traded my faithful old Chevrolet after thirteen years' service and bought a new Ford for a change. I made another trip to Seal Island, and while stormbound at Cape Sable I visited a woman renowned for many years among Canadian coastal brasspounders. Much later I described her and her role in a short story called "The Mistress of C K U."

In August 1949 I had a visit from Arthur Mayse, who was one of the editorial staff of *Maclean's Magazine* when I met him in Toronto in 1946. I took him to some of my favourite places on the seashore and then up the river to Eagle Lake, where we paddled a canoe to look at beaver houses and other interesting things. As we sat in front of Kitpoo Lodge looking down the lake he said, "When the editors lunched with you that day at the University Club, and you were answering our questions about your life and work, I said to myself, 'There's a happy man.' Now I see why."

Some time after that meeting in Toronto he had quitted his job with *Maclean's* and struck out as a free lancer himself, moving to live in British Columbia at a place like Liverpool, where a river and the forest came down to the sea. His first book had just been published after appearing as a serial in the *Saturday Evening Post*, and he was sharply wounded by a review in a Vancouver newspaper, written by a former colleague, who gibed that he had turned away from good work to write cheap adventure tales for money.

I told him a lot of good writers had been accused of that, including R.L. Stevenson, whose work holds a well-acknowledged place in English literature. Literary snobs are always poised to fling this dart from envy of success, or from sheer ignorance of true art in the story form, which consists of a tale unique and good in itself however told, and for full measure told with style and craftsmanship. Most fiction that remains imperishable in the world's literature is just that, and written usually by men and women earning their living with the pen.

* * *

That fall I was guest of honour at a dinner given by the current officers of the West Nova Scotia Regiment in their mess at Aldershot. After toasts to the King, Fallen Comrades, and the Regiment, the Colonel arose and made a pleasant little speech, thanking me for my history. As a token of the regiment's esteem he presented me with an inscribed salver, which has an honoured place in my den.

* * *

Diary, Jan. 1, 1950. We ushered in the New Year with éclat, playing hosts to a large and convivial gathering. The party went on merrily all night, with dancing and singing, including the chanteying of "Shenandoah" and "Blow The Man Down" by four old sea dogs including myself. The last guests, including some utter strangers who drifted in on the New Year tide, departed at 5 A.M. We then cleaned the house, washed an enormous pile of soiled dishes and glasses, and finally got to bed at 6.30. All good fun, and a lovely frosty moonlit night.

Diary, Feb. 5, 1950. Dewey blew in from Cape Sable and presented us with half a dozen fine lobsters. Wearing a fur-lined parka over his Sunday clothes, drinking whiskey neat, and blowing out cigaret smoke in furious gusts, he entertained us with the latest gossip from the Cape and from Seal Island.

* * *

In April 1950, with a snowstorm sweeping in from the sea and scratching at the panes, I wrote the last word of the novel I had begun in October 1948. The typing of clean copy remained to be done. I wrote in my diary, "Now that the novel is finished the plot seems simple, even trite, and the characters in no way distinguished; yet it is the product of the longest and most arduous labour I have yet performed – deliberately refusing to dash off so much as a paragraph, and spending an hour sometimes over a single phrase. It is a romance, but I think I have sketched truly the life in an isolated wireless station as I knew it nearly 30 years ago, and a glimpse of Halifax and the Annapolis Valley in the hectic postwar days of '20 and '21."

*　　*　　*

I gave my island the fictitious name of "Marina" because I wanted to make clear that my story was a romance with an assemblage of characters drawn from various directions. "Matthew Carney" actually was a former chief operator in the coastal service whom I never met, although I heard a lot about him. I added something to and subtracted something from the actual man to shape him for my tale. Long afterwards an old Canadian brasspounder told me he had met the original of "Carney" living in retirement somewhere about the Great Lakes. "Carney" had a copy of my book and treasured it, saying I'd given the true feel of life on Sable Island, as well as many other things about life anywhere. He did not say that he had recognized himself, and there was no reason why he should, because the girl who came into his life was not at all like "Isabel," and he did not go blind or suffer any other disability that might excite her love and pity.

The picture of a man going blind in that desolate and lonely place came to me in a graveyard watch there, one of many spent poring over radio textbooks and intricate wiring diagrams in the meagre light of a kerosene lamp. Suddenly my vision was blurred with a peculiar greenish haze. I could see things in the watch room all right but as if I were looking at them through a fathom of sea water. I put my books and diagrams aside, and after some anxious days and nights my vision cleared. After that I avoided long study in bad light. The mere notion of losing my sight was frightful, with my nightmare memories of people blinded in the Halifax explosion of 1917. They haunted me all my life.

"Skane" was a real man too, a sea officer, handsome in a lean sardonic way, disillusioned about the sea, and women, and life itself for that matter. Women were attracted to him as women often are to a man of his qualities, and in various ports he had occasional affairs with remarkably good-looking ones, who obviously were not whores but ladies made adventurous by some quiet study of him in a restaurant or a seat in a park or anywhere at all.

What I wrote of "Skane" was true of him in every word: "Skane was no Lothario, Lotharios are gay, they flash and whir like hummingbirds entering every flower along the way, whereas Skane was a mixture of self-pride and self-contempt, he wanted to be whole master of himself and hated the need that could make him slave to a woman, even for an hour; and there was a kind of fury in the passion he expended in her flesh when at last he admitted her victory."

The original "Skane" made no secret of these feelings to his shipmates, but I think he revealed himself more to me than any other, perhaps because I was still young and vulnerable, an image of himself before the sea and a woman who mattered very much had both mistreated him. When I left the ship he did not shake hands with me, merely saying curtly, "So long, Sparks. We may meet again." We never did. I still wonder if by some chance a woman did get inside that cynical armour of his at last and give him peace.

"Isabel" was drawn mainly from a woman I was able to study at close hand, but not on Sable Island. By no means beautiful, she had that mysterious quality called sex appeal without being in the least aware of it, keeping her emotions locked up like a vestal waiting unconsciously for release. She was ripe for such a release as I gave "Isabel" on that haunted island in the living arms of Carney and Skane.

*   *   *

Again I was exhausted after so much sustained effort at my desk. For months I had worked at least nine and sometimes as many as eighteen hours a day and night. After three more weeks of straight typing I had clean copies ready for submission to prospective publishers. For a title, after considering *Castaways* and several others, I decided on *The Nymph and the Lamp*. It was suggested by two bits of dialogue in the story. The first was from Captain O'Dell, telling Isabel about Carney's naïve belief in Ran, the legendary Norse goddess of the sea. "She had caves at the bottom of the sea, a sort of Fiddler's Green, where drowned sailors were entertained with food and drink, and each found a nymph waiting for him shaped in the image of the woman he'd most desired on earth." The second part came from Skane's brusque "Look here, you don't mean you'd chuck everything that's good in life to go back to that barren heap and be a lamp for Carney?" And Isabel's reply. "Yes, that's it. A lamp for Carney."

* * *

After two impatient weeks there was no word from Little, Brown, so I mailed a copy to my New York agent, telling him to sell serial rights to a magazine. Then I had a telegram from Salmen. He had just got back from California and read the novel. "I am pleased, impressed, and moved. It is a magnificent story of real people in a challenging situation. Letter and contract soon."

The words reminded me of Mary Salmen in the ship's cabin at Halifax.

* * *

Now and then I heard something good about other work of mine, and from unexpected quarters. On invitation of the admiral I attended a ceremony in the naval dockyard at Halifax. A block of old wooden quarters for sailors called Stadacona had got into a decrepit state, and contractors had begun to build a large and well-designed brick barrack to replace it. The ceremony was the laying of a new cornerstone with full naval ritual. A lead box containing various documents and a bright new Canadian silver dollar had been inserted into the stone, and Commodore Adrian ("Boomer") Hope told me the presence of the dollar was due to my novel *Pride's Fancy*, in which each mast of a new privateer was "stepped" on a silver coin for luck.

Evidently the book had been well read in the Canadian Navy, for the admiral discussed it with me at length. He assumed that I had sailed all round the island of Haiti, and when I said No, he was surprised. "We were down there last winter on exercises, and we found that your descriptions of the coast, your sailing directions among the reefs, and so on, were all very accurate."

I told him why.

* * *

A letter from the CBC gave me a pleasant surprise. The year before I had given a half-hour talk on the national radio network about Canadian sailing ships ("Canada's Heritage of Sail"). The CBC informed me now that it had won first prize in the Radio Awards for 1949. I did not know that such awards existed. With the prize money I bought an oil painting by Donald Mackay showing the old shipyard at Lunenburg with a half-built schooner of the *Bluenose* type on the stocks, and the bigger windjammer *City of New York* hauled out for repairs after her adventures in the Antarctic with Admiral Byrd.

* * *

Stanley Salmen phoned from Boston to talk over points in a contract for *The Nymph and the Lamp*. He wanted an option on my next book and (contrary to Angus Cameron) suggested that I go on with modern themes now that I had "broken away" from costume novels. Later he sent advance copies and wrote, "We are all agreed that this is a book of the first order." Other publication arrangements were coming up. McClelland and Stewart would bring it out in Canada. Lovat Dickson was anxious to have the British publication rights for Macmillan, but my London publishers, Hutchinson and Company, were quick to use their option. Doubleday's Dollar Book Club made it their choice for the next February and predicted a sale of not less than 100,000 copies. At first glance this looked like a lot of money for the author, but at that price, and with the big club's bargaining power, the author's royalty was only a few cents per copy, and under their contract with me Little, Brown took half of it.

More profitable to both of us under this hard-fisted arrangement was adoption by the huge *Reader's Digest* Book Club, a quarterly publication in hard covers containing a condensed edition. It was printed first in English and later in almost every European language west of the Iron Curtain, reaching a total of more than 750,000 case-bound copies. Quite apart from these *Reader's Digest* editions, *The Nymph and the Lamp* has sold to date more than 700,000 copies, case-bound and paperback (about half and half), in many languages. It has been performed also as a play on radio and television networks in the United States and Canada. These figures seem picayune nowadays, when a popular novel runs to millions of copies and major production in the movies. I mention mine because *The Nymph and the Lamp* is a story of real people in real Canadian scenes, and it has been sold entirely without personal ballyhoo by the author and (with one exception) with very little by the publishers.

The exception was the Dollar Book Club, which placed full-page advertisements in the New York *Sunday Mirror* and similar U.S. weeklies, with a sensational illustration in colour and a misleading blurb, both aimed at the mass of readers who want sex first, last and always. The actual sexual episodes and references in my book added up to about three pages, if all were put together.

Ignoring sales figures, which have no relation to merit, I consider *The Nymph and the Lamp* the best of my novels, not only for style and workmanship but also because so much of the story came out of my own observation and personal touch with life. The book did not make me rich. It did make me famous for some time in the world at large, and in all humility I believe it will continue to be read as a Canadian classic.

* * *

Diary, March 6, '51. My mind keeps turning over material for another novel without coming to any sort of conclusion. I should have been at work on a new book all this winter, and the failure haunts me and takes all the zest out of life. Food seems tasteless, liquor just gives me a headache, cigarettes taste bad. All this effort to get my mind working is like running a bucket up and down an empty well from morn to night.

* * *

In the spring of 1951 I bought a piece of wooded shore at Moose Harbour, a small inlet on the west side of Liverpool Bay about two miles outside the town, and that summer I hired carpenters to build a cabin of peeled logs on the spot. It formed a single spacious room, furnished simply with a stove, two or three chairs, a small table for my typewriter, and a couch-bed. Usually I thought and worked in it during the day, returning to town at night, but quite often I slept there. The whole front was plate glass. I could lie abed and watch the sun rise out of the sea, and in the right lunar phase I could see the moon arise in golden splendour from the waves, like Aphrodite herself.

In the afternoons I could keep an eye for Moose Harbour fishermen returning from their lobster traps, and it was only a few steps to the wharf to buy a feast. I cooked them in a pot of sea water over my stone fireplace outdoors, the simplest and best of all ways to prepare lobsters.

The seclusion of the cabin, hidden by a wood of spruce trees, without a phone, and unknown to the autograph hunters who called at my house on their way through town, gave me the boon of utter privacy and quiet. Sometimes my family joined me for a picnic meal, but our teen-agers found the place dull and preferred the more distant sands and crowds of Summerville.

* * *

I had a letter from Wallace MacAskill of Halifax, a devotee of marine photography. Years before, he had published a selection of his photographs of ships and the sea called *Out of Halifax*. The edition was limited and was soon snapped up. Now he had put together another collection and asked me to write a foreword. I called on the old man in his cluttered little shop on Barrington Street, and he showed me the pictures, every one unique and beautiful. In the opinion of connoisseurs he was the best photographer of sea, coast, ships and seamen then living in North America. I described him in my diary in April 1951: "He is a short stocky Cape Bretoner, speaks in a mild voice with a faintly Gaelic intonation, has a pale face, blue eyes, white hair, a jutting nose. Simple and pleasant in his ways and speech, a poet with the camera, fascinated all his life with the sea."

Later he sent me the printer's dummy of his book, asking me to do something about the captions under the photographs. I could see what was bothering him. Most of the captions had been written apparently by one of those ecstatic lady poets who used to come out of the Halifax woodwork at the slightest whiff of tea and buns. I replaced nearly all of them and wrote the foreword. MacAskill had the book printed in a single edition (some bound in sailcloth) under the title *Lure of the Sea*. Like his first, it was soon snapped up. Several years later he began assembling pictures for a third volume and again asked me to write the captions and foreword, but he died suddenly and so did the book.

* * *

Through the summer of 1951 I mulled over the plot for my next novel. It would be different from *The Nymph and the Lamp* in every way, with the leading character drawn from a seafaring scoundrel I had known. I knew I would have to cut out some of his exploits and tone down others, merely to make him credible. The man himself did not belong to this century at all. He would have fitted quite happily into the time of Captain Kidd and bold bad Henry Morgan, for he had all of the daring energy, the arrogance and the utter treachery of the out-and-out pirate.

I made a start, worked hard for days and weeks, came to a stop, and threw away all I had written. This went on through the autumn, hence a gloomy entry in my diary on November 13, 1951: "My 48th birthday. My family forgot it and I should be glad to forget it, too. The best part of my life has slipped past and I have accomplished none of the bright and wonderful and beautiful things I used to dream about when I was young. Now that most of my friends are beginning to talk comfortably of retirement in a few more years, I think on Stevenson's remark, 'The writer has the double misfortune to be ill paid while he can work, and to be incapable of working when he is old. It is thus a way of life which conducts directly to a false position.'"

Just after New Year of 1952 I made another start on the novel. After a week's hard work I again destroyed what I had written and began again.

> *Diary, Jan. 22, '52.* I now have about 24,000 words of my new novel written. It is a sort of Rogue's Progress suggested by the career of So-and-so who used to live here. Had a long chat with old Captain Manning today, going over points of navigation in the West Indies and descriptions of Nassau and Belize as they were in 1926.

> *Diary, May 19, '52.* Tonight about midnight I finished the last page. Don't know what the title will be. *The Cheat* perhaps. I sat through the night reading it from start to finish. It was 5.30 A.M. when I finished. Daylight had appeared and the robins had begun the day's chirping when I turned out my light and went to bed.

*   *   *

Stanley Salmen was disturbed about this book as soon as he read the script, and in June he motored all the way from Boston to say so in the seclusion of my cabin at Moose Harbour. He said the first half contained too much narrative and not enough incident. Also, I had been too lavish with material. "Your manuscript contains the bones of two other novels in addition to the main one." His chief worry was that after the success of *The Nymph and the Lamp* the critics and the public would expect a well-knit story of the same type and workmanship. As I saw it, however, the two books could not be compared, notably because *The Nymph and the Lamp* dealt mainly with vital and open-hearted people, whereas *The Cheat* (a title that neither of us liked) dealt with an unscrupulous rogue and two weaklings, male and female, who came into his power.

I said hotly that I refused to write pretty-pretty stuff and I had chosen this theme and cast of characters to keep myself out of any sort of rut. Salmen quickly agreed, saying that if I felt strongly about it he would publish the book as it stood, and then I could go on to something else. I could see that he would prefer a revision, though. It would mean rewriting the novel, which would delay publication until the autumn of 1953.

Mary Salmen joined us at my house in town. With her usual intuition she saw the anger and frustration in my mind and talked lightly of other matters. On their way to Nova Scotia they had stopped to chat with novelist John Marquand and almost persuaded him to come with them, Mary telling him jauntily that it was "time for the top American author to meet the top Canadian author." For perusal along the way they had brought the manuscript of a novel lately written by Lionel Barrymore, the famous American stage and movie actor. Salmen showed it to me, and we agreed that it was a horrible piece of tripe. It is strange how some actors, after reciting other people's lines for years with notable success, get the notion that they can write better stuff themselves. Mary convulsed us by reading parts of it aloud with the celebrated Barrymore voice and mannerisms.

We dined together at White Point, and as we sat gazing over the sea a new title for my novel came to me. I said, "What about *Tidefall?*" The Salmens were enthusiastic. I added dourly that apparently I must improve it a lot or it would be Tomfall, and Mary said, "Nonsense!" and Stanley said, "Oh no, not at all." When they left for Boston I gave Mary a book of MacAskill's photographs.

* * *

Diary, June 30, '52. Began work today re-writing the first half of *Tidefall.* Still very depressed about it and tempted to tear up the whole thing.

* * *

By the end of that summer I needed my old medicine, a long plunge into the forest. I went with a timber cruiser to Saint Margaret's Bay, where we followed a logging road inland and then carried our stuff over an old Indian portage to the head of the St. Croix River, which flows across the province to the Bay of Fundy. The September weather was perfect, warm in the days and cool in the nights. When I got home I felt better, and with my new work and insight *Tidefall* began to shape better.

* * *

Diary, Dec. 19, '52. I wrote the last word of *Tidefall* this morning, a complete re-write with a sounder plot. Many chapters retained almost entirely, others entirely scrapped, but all changed in some respect. The book satisfies me now as it didn't before. I took one copy of the typescript to the Royal Bank vault for fireproof keeping, and will send the other two to the Canadian and American publishers after the New Year.

* * *

A telegram came from Arthur Phelps, head of the Department of English at McGill: "Art willing I submit you selection committee Royal Society?" I guessed that he meant the Royal Society of Canada, which is devoted to science and the humanities like its model, the ancient and famous Royal Society in Britain. Feeling ridiculously like Dickens's Barkis, I wired back that I was willing.

* * *

In February 1953, dealing directly with my Toronto publishers, the CBC bought the right to make a television play from *Roger Sudden*. Television was new in Canada, and the publishers had no idea of the value of such a right. The CBC got it for five hundred dollars, a sharp bargain, for they used *Roger Sudden* as their first serial play and lavished money on the production. The man who played Roger was British actor Patrick McNee, who liked the part and the story so much that he asked my permission to approach Hollywood people for a full-scale moving picture of it with himself in the leading role. I agreed, but McNee was unable to swing it and he returned to England. I did not hear of him again until he forsook drama to take the lead in an absurd but immensely popular and long-lived BBC series called "The Avengers."

* * *

I now received a letter from Thomas Costain, asking me to take part in writing a history of Canada in several volumes, to be published by Doubleday in New York and Toronto. Originally Costain intended to write the whole set, and he had made an announcement to that effect at a literary luncheon in Toronto a year or two

300

before. He was now finishing the first volume, entitled *The White and the Gold*, which dealt with the early part of the French regime. Meanwhile he had changed his mind about writing the whole thing and decided that the rest should be written by other Canadian authors. He asked me to undertake volume two, dealing with the French regime from 1700 to the British conquest.

As I had told Roosevelt long before, I was not a historian; I was a writer who studied and used the work of historians, an important difference. I had studied the history of Canada for many years, but having only a superficial knowledge of French I could do little with French documents. I thought I might be interested in writing a history of Canada from the end of the French regime to the achievement of home rule by the individual Canadian provinces about the middle of the nineteenth century, but I was doubtful of my qualifications even there. I mentioned this to George Wilson, who had taught history for so many years at Dalhousie University. He said, "My dear fellow, there are two good ways to learn a subject thoroughly. Undertake to lecture on it or to write a book about it."

Following Costain's letter I had one from Ken McCormick, head of the Doubleday Company, offering a substantial cash advance if I would undertake volume two. My reply to both was a polite No, saying that I was not interested nor was I competent to write any part of a history of the French regime in Canada. McCormick persisted, increasing the proffered cash advance by half, but still I said No.

When *The White and the Gold* was published early in 1954, Costain's foreword began: "There have been many histories of Canada and some of them have been truly fine, but it seemed to a group of writers, all of whom were Canadians or of Canadian stock, who met a few years ago, that the time had come for something different . . . a version which would consider the lives of the people, the little people as well as the spectacular characters who made history."

This drew a slashing attack in the *Canadian Historical Review* by C.P. Stacey, who wanted to know, among other things, who comprised this "group of Canadian writers." Costain did not reply. I believe he did confer with some other Canadians before he made his first announcement in Toronto, but I was not one of them and I never knew who they were.

* * *

In March I had a letter from Stanley Salmen, just back from another visit to Europe. He said *Tidefall* was improved, but obviously he remained unenthusiastic about it. His attitude still was what he had told me at Moose Harbour: he would publish it to get it off my mind, so that I could go on to something better.

* * *

The Royal Society of Canada informed me that I had been elected a Fellow, by ballot, and that the society expected my attendance at their next meeting, to be held in London, Ontario, where my election would be confirmed. So in June 1953 I attended the meeting, which was at the University of Western Ontario. In Convocation Hall the newly elected Fellows were received into the society one by one. I was presented by historian A.R.M. Lower, a tall grey man in spectacles and rumpled clothes, with mobile lips and very emphatic speech. He spoke of my novels but stressed *Halifax, Warden of the North*, calling it "an audacious, revealing and interesting book."

In the following sessions I drifted instinctively towards a tall portly man of about sixty with shrewd and humorous grey eyes who turned out to be a fellow Maritimer. He was Fulton Anderson, head of the Department of Philosophy at the University of Toronto. The sessions consisted of lectures on various academic subjects, each followed by a discussion. To a novelist the inability of these learned men to put their thoughts in an interesting way was distressing. They were at their best in the free discussion after each lecture, but the papers they read were as stiff and dry as a bundle of old cedar shingles.

Fulton Anderson was one of the exceptions, an erudite lecturer who was also a lively personality, on and off the floor. I made diary notes of some of his remarks to me, including this:

> Don't be the least impressed by the academic mind. This Society is full of academic minds, and it's a good thing to see some fresh minds like yours coming in. You've attained success in your field because you never went to college. College would have ruined you in all probability. Observe these men. They're clever, learned, and quite good fellows in their way; but they're all neurotic, all of them, and their heads have been in the clouds for years. Stay on the ground where you belong and

keep in close touch with life, of which the academic mind knows nothing. I've read some of your books. You have a good style and you know what you're talking about.

One of the lectures was given by a professor from Queen's University, and his subject was "The Battle of the Books: Some Remarks on Censorship." A short dark bald man with beady eyes and a large sharp nose, he reminded me of a busy little woodpecker. He spoke of the present flood of fiction devoted to violence and sex and various measures now proposed to curb it. He mentioned the cover illustrations of pocketbooks on sale in every drugstore and said he had seen a paperback copy of Hawthorne's *The Scarlet Letter* showing a semi-nude woman wearing her letter in "a very strategic place." Then, without a smile, "One of our new Fellows has a book on the stands called *The Nymph and the Lamp*, the cover of which shows a good deal of the Nymph but not very much of the Lamp."

In the discussion that followed I got up and said, "Mr. Chairman, as the Fellow whose book, *The Nymph and the Lamp*, was mentioned a few minutes ago, I feel I should add a footnote to the professor's paper. In the present publishing system the author makes a contract for a cloth-bound edition of his book. Under this contract the publisher reserves the right to make further arrangements with pocketbook and other people without consulting the author at all, and so he does. By the time I saw the cover picture on the paperback edition of my book about 150,000 copies of it had been sold. I could only comfort myself with the thought that 150,000 unsuspecting people were going to find themselves reading a good book under false pretences."

This brought a roar of laughter, an unusual sound at lectures of the RSC. Later on I met the professor, who said he hoped I did not mind his reference to my book. He had read it and enjoyed it.

* * *

A few weeks after this my wife and I attended the annual convention of the Canadian Authors Association in Toronto. The woman who was head of the Toronto program committee had written to Nicholas (*The Cruel Sea*) Monsarrat and me, asking us to make a joint debate on "Writing a Sea Novel." We had refused. At our separate arrivals in Toronto she confronted each of us with a formal printed program in which she had set our names down for the debate anyway, saying archly, "Oh, please don't let me down!"

303

We were both annoyed by this bit of cool effrontery, but it worked. We were too polite to let a lady down.

I met Monsarrat and his wife at a cocktail party the next evening. He was tall and clean shaven, with greying dark hair, a pasty complexion, and a jerky manner and speech. She was his second wife, a handsome and shapely brunette, exquisitely dressed and groomed, a native of Johannesburg where she met him. I was told that she formerly conducted a smart society gossip column in a Jo'burg newspaper and was remembered there as "The Cruel She." She was very pleasant that evening in Toronto and they made a striking pair, so obviously pleased with each other that I was surprised when they were divorced a few years later.

At the party Monsarrat and I had no chance to discuss our debate because people were continually edging in for introductions. We met next in a hallway of Hart House shortly before going into the lecture room, and he said, "Look here, old boy, we ought to have a battle plan. I suggest you talk for two minutes, then I'll talk for two minutes, and after that we'll just be funneh." I told him that since the audience was sure to include a number of earnest persons with notebooks, we ought to do a cross-talk about writing in general and then throw the meeting open to questions and answers.

We went in, and I opened lightly by saying that in my opinion the way to write a sea story is the way to write any story. You plunk yourself down in a chair before a typewriter, put in a sheet of paper, and don't get up until you've got something on the paper. You do that day after day and month after month until you've got a book. Monsarrat agreed heartily and went on to elaborate with his own practice. First he planned the whole story exactly, chapter by chapter, and then he followed the plan exactly from beginning to end. As the story progressed he did not allow any of his characters to grow or diminish or change in any way from his original concept. He wrote a set stint of five hundred words a day and got a physical pleasure from hitting the keys as he followed his plot.

Then he tossed the ball to me, and I described my own way of feeling intuitively for the story to begin with and then working it out by intuition as I went along. I believed with Somerset Maugham that every story has a certain natural curve from start to finish, and the writer's task is to find that curve and follow it. Monsarrat observed rightly that it must make very hard work. We went on like this for a time with our utterly different methods and then threw the session open. At once we were assailed with questions. Monsarrat's wits were quicker than mine, and whenever somebody popped up with an absolutely silly question he turned with a swift gesture, saying gallantly, "I'm sure Mr. Raddall will be delighted to answer that one!" Finally out of the side of his mouth he said, "Now get us off the hook!" so I closed the show abruptly, saying it was time for lunch.

That evening Monsarrat and I appeared together in a CBC television interview. It was my first experience of TV and I think his too, although he was entirely at ease, as if he had been acting before a camera all his life. I thought of that some months later when a distinguished Canadian naval officer told me of his meeting with Monsarrat during the late war. "He wore a fantastic beard, a single earring, and a pair of enormous leather sea-boots that came to the top of his thighs. I had a strong impression that he thought he was Sir Francis Drake. Nowadays I can't resist a feeling that he was acting a part that some day he intended to write."

* * *

After the close of the convention Hugh Kane took my wife and me on a motor tour of the Niagara region, where I wanted to see the chief battlefields of the War of 1812. For a view of Queenston Heights I climbed the narrow spiral stairway inside the tall Brock Monument, and Kane followed, gasping, "Phew! I didn't even know this dam' thing was hollow!" I cheered him with, "Well, now you know how a bullet feels inside a rifle barrel." Altogether it was an interesting tour, and what I saw was useful three years later, when I made a documentary study of those battles for a book called *The Path of Destiny*.

The rest of that summer I worked on another collection of short stories to be published by McClelland and Stewart. A few had appeared in magazines during the late war. The rest I wrote now from notes made at that time. I called the book *A Muster of Arms*, saying in the foreword, "War is a fierce business and the flash and bang of it are apt to fill one's mind to the exclusion of all else. During two wars, chiefly the second, I was curious enough to look away from the blaze at intervals and see what sort of shadows it cast, and where. Of these I made note, for they interested me, and the stories in this volume have to do with some random flickers that fell across my notice in the Canadian scene. Some were plain, some tragic, some funny or grotesque, but all seemed worth recording for their origin in that twice-experienced phenomenon of my time, the spectacle of men and women under the strain of war and the effect of it on their lives."

* * *

Stanley Salmen came to see me again in September, and we went sea-fishing together. He was keen for me to start another novel. I had been busy with short stories, and my mind was vague about the next novel, except that it would be a contemporary story about life in a Nova Scotia village after the late war. Nothing specific came of the talks, but it was good for me to have the impact of Salmen's keen mind in my country retreat.

* * *

In the summer of 1953 the National Historic Sites and Monuments Board erected a brass plaque in memory of Canadian author Marshall Saunders in the place where she was born, the village of Milton on our Mersey River. As one of her kin ("second cousin once removed," whatever that is), my wife was asked to unveil the plaque. Watson Kirkconnell came over from Acadia University to make a public address on the occasion, pointing out among other things that Miss Saunders was the first Canadian to write books that sold over a million copies. After the ceremony the representative of the board quipped heavily to me, "I don't know who will arrange for the plaque to you, for of course I shall be dead."

I could only shrug and say, "So shall I."

* * *

My son Tom had spent the summer working as a seaman on a freighter, and now I took him in my car to university. I wrote in my diary, "One of the happiest days of my life . . . he can enjoy a privilege and an experience that I never had."

Tidefall went on sale in October 1953, and Jack McClelland wrote: "I thought I would drop you a line and tell you again how very proud we are to be your Canadian publishers, and to have the opportunity of bringing another of your books to the Canadian market. There are three reasons for our enthusiasm. First and foremost you're a wonderful guy to do business with. Secondly, you are Canada's most outstanding author today. And thirdly we think you are Canada's best-selling author. What more could a publisher ask?"

306

Diary, Nov. 1, '53. All the newspaper reviews of Tidefall I have seen to date have been favourable. Some like Morgan-Powell's in the Montreal Star, and Bill Deacon's in the Globe and Mail ("the most powerful novel ever written by a Canadian") were too fulsome. The book is not that good by any means.

Tonight on a CBC radio program called "Critically Speaking" a professor from Bishop's College, speaking in a lofty Oxbridge accent, gave Tidefall a blast. First by way of compliment (like Powell, Deacon and others) he likened me to Conrad, which is absurd. Then he said I was all right when I wrote about the sea, but when I wrote about domestic contretemps my dialogue was trite and humdrum and in places almost ridiculous. He also reviewed Monsarrat's new novel *Esther Costello* in much the same vein and advised us both to stick to the sea.

I would have been willing to compare my own or Monsarrat's experience of domestic contretemps with the professor's any day of the week, so I found this comment hilarious. I had a letter from Monsarrat not long afterwards saying, "*Esther Costello* excited howls of dislike and derision all the way round the world. However I am glad to tell you that this is not stopping the sales, and I have just sold the film rights and am negotiating for the stage rights."

I could not boast anything like that about *Tidefall.* Salmen wrote from Boston, "The general impression here is that it is an excellent book about the wrong hero." With that opinion his firm made little effort to promote the book in the retail bookshop trade where the author gets his full royalty. They made an easy profit by selling it to book clubs and paperback firms and then taking half of the royalties. As it turned out, the book club and paperback editions sold very well in the United States, Canada, and Britain.

The book publishing business is not run for the benefit of authors, except in one class. Prolific writers of huge best-sellers are able to dictate not only their royalty rate but also the elaborate promotion of each book, and consequently their sales and profits are self-escalating, year after year. For most authors the business is contrived so that they get the least possible reward for their pains.

* * *

After many months of pondering I began to write my third contemporary novel in April 1954. It had to do with a place like Milton when I came there after my sea service and found those decrepit pulp mills and the village itself in the clutch of a greedy speculator. I took my title from some lines of Longfellow's, "The day is done, and the darkness/Falls from the wings of Night." As always, *The Wings of Night* grew slowly and painfully.

In my early struggles at writing I consoled myself with a notion that the work would become facile with experience. It never did. Always I had to go through a brain-racking struggle in which the creative ecstasies were separated by long tortures of doubt and despair like a Morse code of travail. When I had come to the end and had the whole plot and characters set forth clearly at last, I always wondered why I couldn't have seen it all like that from the start, planning everything and everyone exactly as Monsarrat and others did. I had heard several boasting that they could have written any chapter in any order, as a film director works from a neatly comparted shooting script.

I came to realize that I simply lacked this gift, which made everything so much easier. Looking back over my life, nothing desirable ever came to me easily. I had to work long and hard for it. Perhaps there was something after all in what that silly woman told my mother on the day I entered this world – "How unfortunate for the poor child to be born on a Friday the thirteenth!"

* * *

Diary, May 31, '54. In the Saturday Night issue of May 29 is an article by Scott Young on "What's wrong with the Canadian novel?" Just about everything, thinks Young. He has never attempted a novel himself and is frank to admit it. Pays me a compliment. "Only a few novelists in the world have been able to persuade the novel to provide their daily bread. Thomas Raddall is the only Canadian within my knowledge who makes a living from novels. The others are housewives, professors, editors, publicists, radio or television performers, who combine one or more of those fields with novel writing."

* * *

I determined that the illustrations for *A Muster of Arms* should be done by a young Nova Scotian named Jack Gray, whose marine painting I liked. I wanted small pen-and-ink drawings to appear at the head and tail of each story and an oil painting for the jacket. On a day in June 1954 I drove to Chester with carbon copies of the short stories and found Jack, his wife, and their charming baby Johnnie living aboard a rickety old twenty-foot motorboat at the end of a wharf. A large electric refrigerator stood in the cockpit aft for lack of room inside. The baby's crib was placed in the sunshine on the wharf top, and they kept a small life jacket tied about him in case he found his way overboard. Jack used the loft of an old boat-house for his studio. Living thus in the summers they saved rent and taxes, and in their happy-go-lucky way they enjoyed themselves.

Although half a gale was blowing, Jack insisted on a short cruise in Mahone Bay, so we took the baby aboard, unplugged the shore electric cord, cast off the lines, and went forth. The going proved rough and wet. The boat shipped several waves as soon as we got outside Quaker Island, and after a time the engine failed just when we were on the windward side of an uninhabited island with a lot of nasty-looking rocks. Jack's wife checked the baby's life jacket and clutched him in her arms. Jack dived below and managed to coax the engine back to life as we were about to hit the rocks. Finally he brought the boat back into Chester Cove with all the nonchalance in the world. On a personal choice I wouldn't have left the wharf aboard that thing, in a flat calm, with Neptune himself at the helm.

* * *

R.J. Rankin, managing editor of the Halifax *Chronicle-Herald* and a board member of the Canadian Press, urged me now to edit the papers of Nova Scotia's late Premier Angus Macdonald and write a biography for publication. He mentioned casually that the papers amounted to truckloads. I pondered and then replied that in other circumstances I would consider the task an honour, but with my financial bind it was impossible. It meant a very long commitment because I would have to get much information from other people. My friendship with Angus was conducted for the most part at a distance of one hundred miles. Over a period of many years we rarely got together. I had no interest in politics, and so I knew little of the political history in which so much of Macdonald's life had been concerned, not only at Halifax but in Ottawa. A proper study of his papers and searching interviews with his social and political intimates would take a year's hard work at the very least. Writing the book itself would take as much more, to do it well. I simply couldn't afford so long a hiatus in my own work. With young Tom at college, and with the utmost economy at home, I needed at least five thousand dollars a year merely to pay my bills. Rankin suggested that the biography would sell well on publication, but I had before me the plain fact that my careful book on Halifax, which took years of part-time study and then a whole year to write, had brought only $2,800 in royalties so far. However interesting to me, history and biography were luxuries I could not afford. My daily bread was fiction.

* * *

In August I sent McClelland and Stewart the corrected galley proofs of *A Muster of Arms* and again went to Chester to see how Gray was getting on with the illustrations. In his carefree way he grinned and confessed he hadn't done much. Pen-and-ink was an unfamiliar medium, and what little he had done was experimental. He hadn't even started the oil painting for the jacket. I said the publishers' deadline was close and he must get to work.

When I checked again he had finished the head and tail pieces, which were just passable, and he had done the oil, although the paint was not quite dry when he put it on a plane for Toronto that evening. It was excellent, showing a wartime convoy coming out of Halifax harbour. Sandwich Battery's big guns watched over it from a steep crag to the left, and there was snow on the ground at Sleepy Cove below.

Some time later I asked McClelland and Stewart to let me have the painting, now that the jacket had been printed, but I was told it had "disappeared." I guessed that old Navy hand Jack McClelland had waved the magic wand, but long afterwards Jack denied it indignantly, saying he'd wanted the painting all right but like me didn't claim it soon enough. Some unknown so-and-so had made off with it. Whoever he was, the magician with the vanishing painting got one of the best things Gray ever did. I knew that view of the harbour mouth very well. It was practically the view from my old station at Camperdown.

In several summers after that I joined Gray for a bit of exploring, sketching and lobster-spearing on the coast east of Lunenburg, from the reefs called Hell's Rackets to Heckman's Island, and then around to Blue Rocks. In a small dory with an outboard motor we cruised along Tanner's Pass, a strange little salt waterway that looks like a man-made canal, and explored other creeks and bays between the pass and Blue Rocks. It was a region of low slim islands and reefs, some bare, some covered with bushes and cat-spruce. All lay roughly east-and-west like stony fingers in the sea, created by an ancient upheaval that folded the bedrock like corrugated iron. The tides flowed in the troughs, and the dry folds were broken conveniently here and there so that a dory could pass from one through to another, finding charming clusters of fishermen's dwellings in odd corners.

Jack kept a sketchbook on his knees and went along slowly, making framing gestures with his lean hands at the sight of a ramshackle fish-shed, an old boat hauled out to perish of rot, a cottage with nets hung to dry on a pole wharf before it, and so on. Each sketch was done with rapid skill in charcoal, and in small loops Jack noted in detail the exact tints to be used in every part of the land, sea, and sky. He spent his winters in New York making oil paintings from these sketches. Strangely for a good artist, he worked best at night, hence the careful notations of colours observed by daylight. His painting for the jacket of *A Muster of Arms* was the sustained effort of one whole night in the loft of the old boathouse in Chester Cove.

*   *   *

Diary, Dec. 28, '54. Telegram from George Nelson, head of Doubleday's branch in Canada, asking for an interview here. Wonder what he wants.

*   *   *

Nelson arrived by rail on a cold January weekend, a tall, dark and genial man with short curls of grey hair. At a recent conference in New York with Tom Costain and Ken McCormick he had been told to call on me in person with another proposal about the Canadian history series. The second volume (which I had declined to do) was being written by Canadian author Joseph Rutledge for publication in the autumn of 1955. They wanted me now to undertake volume three, covering the period from the British conquest to 1850. This was right in my own line of study, as Costain knew, but as I knew very well I couldn't afford to write it.

Apparently Nelson foresaw some such reply, for he said carefully, "We feel that you turned down our first offer because you thought Doubleday wouldn't give your volume the promotion they gave to *The White and the Gold*, and that the cash advance would be your entire income from the book. I'm here to tell you that we would give your book exactly the same promotion as Costain's, and that we can almost guarantee that your income from it, including book club and other avenues, would be close to $20,000."

I remained silent. Nelson went on, "Costain is very anxious that you do this book. He's a great admirer of your work. If you wish to stick to Little, Brown in the U.S. and McClelland and Stewart in Canada, it's your affair. In that case we suggest that you get a one-book release from them to do this history for us. I don't mind saying that we hope to show you, with the sales of this book, that you would be far better off as a Doubleday author than with anybody else. It's not a case of getting you away from other publishers, it's a case of welcoming you back where you were in the first place, with us. However, don't give me an answer now. Think it over carefully and let me know your decision later."

*   *   *

I put this proposition away in the attic of my mind and plunged back into my novel. After another month of its throes and toils I had a note from Nelson asking for my decision. His proposal emerged from its niche in my mind as if from a quiet debate there, of which I had been quite unconscious, and it had come to a decision. I should write the book. With my daughter joining young Tom at college next year I would need the money.

It was not so cold blooded as that. Indeed I saw a challenge in the book, remembering George Wilson's aphorism about the best way to learn a subject thoroughly. I had long studied the period when Canada's destiny as a free nation was blindly worked out and fought out in spite of internal quarrels and two determined American efforts to take and hold the country by force of arms.

Towards the end of February I got two letters in the same mail. One was from Doubleday enclosing the new contract for my signature. The other was a surprising little hand-written note from Stanley Salmen saying he had left Little, Brown. He made no explanation and did not say where he was going. I never heard from him again. Much later I heard indirectly that he had disagreed sharply with the board of Little, Brown over a matter of publishing policy and had taken a post in New York with Columbia University. Thus my only personal and friendly contact with Little, Brown vanished as the Doubleday contract came into my hands. I could not forget the cold unconcern of Little, Brown when I was writing *The Nymph and the Lamp*, or their penny-pinching promotion of *Tidefall* after the fat profits they had got from *The Nymph*.

Following the standard publishing form, the Doubleday contract had a clause giving them a world-wide option on my next book. If I signed it as it stood it meant breaking away from my present publishers in the United States, Canada, Britain, and various others in Europe. Nelson had attached a note about this clause, saying it was not vital to the agreement for the history. I could strike it out if I wished. For the time being I held the contract unsigned.

In March, Costain asked me to come to Toronto for a brief conference about the history with George Nelson, Joseph Rutledge and himself. I took the unsigned contract with me. We lunched at the Granite Club and moved to a small side room where we discussed Rutledge's volume, my volume, and the general tenor of the whole series. Costain had determined to have this history of Canada written by non-academic authors for the sake of a fresh approach, and they must be Canadians whose knowledge and ability had been proven to the public.

Tom Costain was then a handsome man in the late sixties, tall, broad-shouldered, with white hair in vivid contrast to the bright blue eyes of a boy. He'd had a remarkable career. Born in Ontario, he became chief editor of *Maclean's Magazine* in his twenties. Then, as he said, he decided to go where the money was, and headed for California, where he spent some lucrative years writing movie scripts. Then differences of opinion with Hollywood moguls and dissatisfaction with Hollywood life caused another move, this time to a post on the editorial staff of the prosperous *Saturday Evening Post* in Philadelphia. Then he had gone to an editorial desk on Madison Avenue with Doubleday, and it was there that I came into his view. Although he spent most of his life in the United States and made a large fortune there he was always proud to call himself a Canadian.

We dined that evening at the Royal York, the party now including Ethel Hulse, the little grey woman editor assigned by Doubleday to handle my work, and Toronto critic Bill Deacon. Afterwards Costain and Miss Hulse left to catch a plane for New York, and I went off to stay a few days with a friend living in retirement on a beautiful farm estate outside Toronto.

One evening I dined with George and Lily Nelson in their home on Royal York Road. I had the Doubleday contract in my pocket. At my request Nelson struck out the next-book-option clause, making it simply a one-book agreement. I noted later in my diary, "Doubleday would like me to come back with them completely, but I said I would not break off with my present publishers in so abrupt a manner."

My Toronto host took me to a cocktail party given by a woman lawyer, a large amiable person who looked like the singer Kate Smith. There I chatted with Arthur Meighen, still erect and keen witted at eighty, his son Max, Max's vivacious wife, and other interesting people. In side glances I noticed my friend tossing off whiskies, and I thought of the long drive into the heart of the city that was to follow. Leonard Brockington had invited us and poet Edwin Pratt to dine with him at the York Club.

The drive there exceeded my worst expectations. My friend Jehu tore along with violent swerves across two traffic lanes despite angry hornblowers and my own futile commands to pull over to starboard and slow down. At the club he shot through the narrow entrance of the parking lot like a swallow diving into its nest hole in a cliff, stopped inside successfully, and gave me a comical look as if to ask what all the fuss was about.

I had never met Brockington although we'd had some correspondence, and I had heard him broadcasting on CBC radio from time to time. He was an eloquent speaker with a well-informed mind, and somehow I pictured a king-sized man to match that mind, the rich tones and the beautifully articulated speech. I was astonished to see a hunchback of medium height, with wild white hair and eyebrows, a small beak nose and a determined mouth.

We had a very good dinner and Brockington did practically all of the talking, a lively and often brilliant monologue that ranged all the way from the origin of the Newfoundland word "brewis" to a dissertation on *Hudibras*. Throughout the meal he leaned back in a special chair, talking nearly all the time, conveying food a long way to his mouth and frequently spilling some of it en route. He remarked cheerfully that he always ordered three eggs for breakfast, two for himself and one for his necktie.

A lawyer by training, he was Canadian representative of the Rank Organization, the biggest British movie company with all its various industrial complexities, and above his Toronto offices was a private theatre seating twenty-five or thirty persons where on Sunday evenings he invited friends to see the latest Rank films. We went there from the York Club. After the show, to my relief, my friend's son drove the car back to the suburbs.

* * *

In April 1955 I resumed work on *The Wings of Night*, after long delay caused by the Toronto trip and its distraction of thought and then another prostration by influenza and the subsequent lassitude and depression that invariably came with it. I had lost more working time by illness during the past winter than in any other I could recall. My weight was down to 164, almost thirty pounds less than the bulk I had reached four or five years before. With the coming of warm sunshine and long walks my condition improved rapidly, and by mid-May I had brought *The Wings of Night* nearly to its close. I worked on the story in my Moose Harbour cabin and left the typescript there when I slept at my house in town. On the evening of May 21 I took it back to town with me for no reason that I can recall.

* * *

Diary, May 22, '55. Very hot. About noon a bush fire sprang up near Town Lake and another near McAlpine's Brook. At the same time a gale sprang up from the west and blew in very strong gusts until night.

My wife had prepared picnic baskets for ourselves and two guests and was all set to go to Moose Harbour, but I said we'd better wait and see how the fire went, otherwise we might be trapped in the cabin between the woods and the sea. Late in the afternoon I drove alone towards Moose Harbour but found police turning back all traffic. Dense smoke hid everything. I was told that several houses and barns were afire along the road and that two families that lived at Moose Harbour had been obliged to flee by boat. Later I learned that all the fishermen's shacks and stagings there had been destroyed, together with thirteen fishing boats, two summer cottages, and my cabin. It was just about four years since I bought the land and cleared the site for it.

Diary, May 23, '55. Drove to Moose Harbour and found everything razed and black. Had we been there on our picnic we'd have had to jump into the sea.

Diary, May 24, '55. Fires are still burning in the bush about the town, we breathe smoke night and day, and through the windows open in the heat my desk and papers are covered with fine grey ash. In these circumstances I finished my novel tonight. The last few chapters will need re-writing, having been ground out doggedly amid so much distraction.

Diary, June 3, '55. A week of intense labour at my novel. Continuous typing as usual has produced the cramp in my left hand. The tense attitude required to force that hand to work in any way at all produces agony between my shoulder blades, so that from time to time I have to throw myself down on my cot to ease the pain. I work ten or twelve hours a day typing clean copy for the printers, and between nine P.M. and midnight I have to sip rum to keep myself going. I don't drink any other time. I have no appetite for food or drink, no interest in life other than to get this book done. All this effort is complicated by people writing or phoning, demanding that I address everything from a school closing to a mass meeting at the Apple Blossom Festival at Grand Pré. With illness and everything else, the older I get the more difficult it is to do my work.

Diary, June 22, '55. Finished typing clean copy of the novel this afternoon, with much new work on the last six chapters, especially the final two which I had written amid the forest fires.

Diary, June 24, '55. Packed up and placed in the Royal Bank vault for safekeeping one copy of the novel, thus ridding myself of the nightmare that always haunts me from the time I've worked six months on a book to the day it is acknowledged in the hands of the printers – a fire that might destroy the whole thing, as it so nearly did at Moose Harbour.

* * *

Like Sindbad the Sailor when he got the Old Man of the Sea off his back at last, I felt an enormous relief. With carefree hours outdoors in the fine summer weather, my spirits made a tremendous rebound from the gloomy deeps of last spring. Hence this cheerful entry:

Diary, July 1, '55. This is a good life, although I have to fight off various people who want to waste my time. My health was never better than right now, after the miseries of the winter and spring.

*　*　*

I wrote to Little, Brown asking them to cancel the option on my next novel, and a polite reply said, "While we grant this with sincere regret, because we all have an enormous respect and liking for your work, we certainly do not want to stand in the way of your establishing a relation with another publishing house."

It was clear to me that I must take the proffered hand of Tom Costain in New York. Back in 1941, at Roosevelt's suggestion, he had made the contract for my first novel. Later he took indefinite leave from the editorial desk at Doubleday to write novels of his own. He was fertile and ingenious, and long editorial experience had given him a formula for best sellers. With the full thrust of Doubleday's powerful promotion machine his novels sold in millions, and lucrative movie sales followed as a matter of course. In ten years he was the most popular and the richest author on the Doubleday list.

Most of his books were staged in ancient times in Europe, the Levant, and Asia, but he remained keenly interested in Canada and Canadian writing, as he had shown in persuading Doubleday to publish the Canadian history series at small profit to themselves. When he first wrote asking me to join in writing this series I jotted in my diary a strong doubt about "playing the tail to Costain's kite," but he dispelled that on our first meeting in Toronto, when he assured me that my volume would stand on its own feet. So it did. Tom Costain respected my values and remained a friend to me until his death.

In my rugged passage through this world I was always moved strongly by intuitive likes and dislikes in my encounters with other people, an inheritance from my Cornish ancestors. Usually I found the feeling mutual. I had an early and well-sustained rapport with Jack McClelland, and that made my decision to return to Doubleday a painful one. McClelland and Stewart were now firmly linked with Little, Brown in the States. Doubleday now had their own branch firmly established in Toronto. There was no way out of this impasse except a complete change of publishers, and the ever-increasing financial needs of my family gave me no choice.

I had other troubles. For example:

Diary, Nov. 28, '55. My old friend and woods companion Brent Smith died today of cancer.

Diary, Nov. 29, '55. No work yesterday or today. I feel too sharp a loss in my old comrade's death to settle my mind on history.

Diary, Nov. 30, '55. Snow squalls all morning but the weather cleared for Brent's funeral this afternoon. A Canadian Legion party carried the casket. Parker, Dunlop and I were honorary pallbearers. As we drove away Dunlop said, "When we were sitting in the church with the coffin before us, somehow I kept seeing us all tramping up the trail to Eagle Lake with our packs on our backs."

* * *

Towards the end of 1955 I had a letter from Watson Kirkconnell saying,

The Halifax branch of the Canadian Authors Association has been urging me to let my name stand for the national presidency of the Association. I have demurred on two grounds, one that you are the logical and ideal nominee; and two, that I have already put in a two year term (1942-1944) in that office. They retort that you have refused to let your name stand. Might I, in all fraternal good will, urge you to reconsider the matter? The CAA would benefit greatly by having a bona fide, full time, distinguished professional writer like yourself as its national president. There have been too many academic folk giving it leadership in the past and I am not keen on perpetuating that tradition.

This was flattering, but my answer again was No. Two years ago a clash of personalities in the Toronto branch, the largest in Canada, had been spread by its factions into a national brawl that disgusted me with the whole lot. I did not mention this in my polite letter of refusal, but I noted in my diary that Kirkconnell was best qualified for the job because, in addition to his other abilities, "a lifetime of experience with college students will enable him to cope with the childish problems which from time to time absorb the CAA."

* * *

My left hand was getting worse, and any prolonged typing brought the painful and crippling cramp. This did not happen in the process of creative writing because then the spells of typing were spaced by much walking up and down the floor, or staring out of the windows, or hunting up and checking references. What I dreaded was the ultimate continuous labour of typing clean copy for the printers from my slowly composed and intricately amended first draft. In our small country town there was no typist to engage as a temporary amanuensis. I could not send my first draft to a professional typist in Halifax because she would not be able to understand my pencil scrawls with their looped additions and changes, any more than printers could.

In 1956 I asked my wife if she would learn to decipher my daily drafts and practise typing so that she could turn out clean copy when the book was finished. She was pleased with the idea, got a book of instructions on touch typing, and began to practise daily on my portable machine, set up on the desk-flap in my bedroom where for so many years I had done all my writing.

* * *

Diary, Feb. 26, '56. All day and evening indoors, I working away in the den at my history, E. tapping away upstairs with her typing practice, and both of us stopping now and then for a game of Scrabble.

Diary, March 1, '56. I have got my history as far as the departure of Dorchester and Simcoe from Canada in 1796.

* * *

In June 1956 I attended the annual meeting of the Royal Society of Canada, held this year at the University of Montreal, where I was bidden to receive the Lorne Pierce Medal "for distinguished service to Canadian literature."

We heard an opening address on existentialism by Doctor James S. Thompson of McGill. Having no education in the fine points of philosophy I found it hard going, although in private conversation, with his good Scotch burr, Thompson was a witty and interesting man.

The next session was a symposium on Canadian literature by three professors of English whom I shall call Cumulus, Nimbus and Stratus. Cumulus was then teaching in British Columbia, Nimbus in Ontario, and Stratus in the Maritime Provinces, and I suppose this choice had been made to give their views some semblance of a national scope.

Cumulus chose to make some light comparisons between contemporary and past Canadian novels in their religious aspects. His paper was typical of pundits who have been lost in the literary forest so long that they can only pause to finger an odd bit of moss here and there.

Nimbus talked about Canadian poetry in an amusing fashion.

Stratus was the most pretentious, covering the whole field of Canadian literature, past and present. His general view was one of lofty disdain, with an austere ray of approval now and then. All through his discourse he belaboured his obvious theme, that the quality of academic criticism in Canada was very much better than the stuff it had to criticize. He was patronizing to three or four contemporary writers including Hugh MacLennan and me, dismissing us as "competent." MacLennan was sitting by me taking a wrathful hearing of all this. After a while he got up and walked out.

* * *

Dr. Thompson was to cite me for the literary medal, and he drew me aside and mentioned that it was customary for recipients of the society's medals to wear white tie and tails at the presentation. In my absent-minded way I had not thought of this possibility or I would have sent a polite note regretting that I couldn't accept the medal at all. As it was, I could only say that I never wore formal clothes under any circumstances. After a little hesitation Thompson glanced at my cool summer suit and said dress didn't really matter.

That evening the society and their guests filled the big auditorium of the university and the new medallists sat on the platform with their respective sponsors. The first French-Canadian medallist was a little old gentleman in correct white tie and tails. The second was a plump hearty cleric in a black cassock and a wide purple sash. The two English-speaking medallists, Lyman Duff and I, wore light tan trousers and jackets that were almost identical. I wondered if Dr. Thompson had suggested this to Duff lest I feel embarrassed on the platform, or if Duff himself felt as I did about clothes, especially on a very hot night.

Thompson's citation of my work was generous, and at the end of the meeting several members of the society came to me with congratulations, among them historians C.P. Stacey and George Stanley. They knew I was writing the third volume in the Doubleday history series, and Stacey discussed my period with me. Later he generously sent me some very useful material that he had written for the *Canadian Historical Review*. At his suggestion, too, I became a member of the Canadian Historical Association.

The next day I lunched in the university cafeteria with Hugh MacLennan, and in the course of our random chat I asked by the way how he liked being patronized by Professor Stratus yesterday. He was still annoyed and said Royal Society papers were always boring. In easier talk he said he was working on a novel but didn't get much time for it. He had found that he couldn't make a living from his novels and had turned to a variety of interesting occupations, teaching English literature at McGill, appearing on TV discussion shows, writing articles for *Saturday Night*, for a travel magazine, and so on.

* * *

To close the convention there was a dinner in the university's Hall d'Honneur, where long buffet tables held a succulent array of food and drink, adorned by small statuary carved in ice. The city was in a heat wave, and even up on the mountain the evening air was hellish. The statuary dripped and so did we.

Professor Stratus came up to me, introduced himself and his wife, and mentioned with obvious satisfaction that they had seven children. We filled our plates and I carried off a flagon of excellent burgundy to a table well out of the hubbub. At once Stratus began to ply me with questions about my working methods, my sources of material, editorial preferences, markets, authors' agents, and so on. These queries followed a familiar pattern and soon rang a familiar bell. Unsuccessful writers put them to any author who is getting published and paid. Finally Stratus confessed that he had been writing short stories, hoping to sell them to big magazines for good prices, but so far the magazines had rejected every one of them and he couldn't understand why. When I recalled his pontifications on published Canadian writing, I was first amazed and then amused, but I was not without pity. I knew only too well what it was to support a wife and children on an inadequate salary while trying to earn extra money with my pen. However, there was no time to go into all that. I was desperate to get out of that Montreal sweatbox and catch a plane back to good salt air.

* * *

A week or two later I left home again briefly to address the annual convention of the Canadian Authors Association, which was meeting in Halifax that year. The subject given me by the program committee was the historical novel versus the imaginative novel, a silly proposition because any good historical novel is imaginative, and nearly all novels are historical in that they deal with the past, if only the past of yesterday afternoon. I did the best I could with it.

For entertainment on the next day there was a mass sightseeing jaunt to Peggy's Cove on the coast west of Halifax. I skipped it and drove my car to the harbour mouth, where I spent a happy afternoon recalling scenes of my youth. The village of Portuguese Cove was much changed and enlarged, and the ruins of my old station had been bulldozed away during the late war, when the navy built a new radio and visual signal station on Camperdown hill.

I found the house where I used to get my meals, and where a girl of the family taught me to dance. She was a small and lively creature of eighteen, and it was sad to learn that she had contracted tuberculosis and perished at the age of twenty-five. Her old uncle told me this in the lee of a fish-shed where I had spent many an off-watch hour in time long past, gazing from the little cove to the sea. The rusty bow and forecastle of shipwrecked *Letitia* had vanished long ago.

York Redoubt and Sandwich Battery were at gunnery practice today, and we watched a small steamer towing the target far astern and tall fountains leaping and glistening in the sunshine as the shot plunged into the sea. Then came the sharp crack of the guns and the delayed *boom-oom-oom* of echoes dying away in the harbour hills. These sights and sounds, long familiar to dwellers at the harbour mouth, were about to end for ever. That autumn the Canadian Army disarmed the forts and left future defence of the port entirely to sea and air forces. In the new era of atomic explosives and long-range rockets to carry them, the battery of guns fixed on the face of the earth had gone the way of the log blockhouse and the musket.

* * *

George Nelson had come down from Toronto to attend the convention with Montreal-born Lionel Shapiro, a Doubleday author who was to receive a Governor General's Award at the annual dinner. Nelson also wanted to talk to me. At lunch tête-à-tête he reminded me of Costain's influence with Doubleday in New York and my opportunity to become their top historical novelist "in the northeastern area." They were publishing my modern *Wings of Night*, but they were sure my proper field was the costume novel, and they were hoping to have one from me after I finished my volume of Canadian history.

Nelson urged me to go to New York as soon as possible for a personal conference with McCormick and his chief editor, Lee Barker, who could make a fortune for me as they had for Costain and Shapiro. I promised to think about this but my nature boggled over that bit about "the northeastern area," which obviously meant New England. I had no desire whatever to write historical novels in the field of the late Kenneth Roberts, and the hint that I might make this profitable switch reminded me of my experience with the *Saturday Evening Post*, whose editors printed my Canadian stories without a quibble for two years and then wanted me to write things more American. I could see that Lionel Shapiro was an ideal Canadian author in the eyes of Madison Avenue, for I don't think he ever wrote a book entirely about Canada and Canadians. From his native Montreal he had gone to Europe in 1940 as a war correspondent, and except for flying visits to consult Lee Barker in New York he remained there, writing books about the war, the Nazi death camps, the Nuremberg trials, and so on. With Barker's expert tutelage and Doubleday's promotion, these books sold in enormous numbers. Now a rich expatriate had come to Canada to pick up a medal for what he openly considered tardy recognition.

I knew of course that Doubleday were not in business to sustain a Canadian or any other foreign ego. Like the rest of Madison Avenue, their business was to make money and I did not blame them for it. They had published three novels of Costain's that were set in the Canadian scene, but this was an amiable indulgence to their very best selling author, whose most profitable themes and scenes lay much farther away. My own belief was what it had been from my early work for *Blackwood's Magazine*, that if a Canadian story was good enough it would find sufficient readers anywhere. My trust was that Madison Avenue could see that, too.

* * *

Diary, Oct. 25, '56. Spent the morning and evening writing letters, especially a long screed to Ralph Allen, managing editor of *Maclean's Magazine.* Tom Costain asked him to write Volume Four (1914-1945) of the Canadian history series, and Allen wrote me asking some advice on how to go about it.

*   *   *

Doubleday now set the limit of my own volume at "about 230,000 words." Rapt in my subject I had written 200,000 already, which did not leave me room enough for the rest of the period. To gain room now I had to go back over what I had written, cutting out what was not absolutely essential. Much of the scrapped material was highly interesting, and I had worked long and hard to dig it up and write it down. I realized now what a massive task I had undertaken with this period, containing as it did the American Revolution, the War of 1812, and the Canadian rebellions of 1837-38. It should have been given two volumes.

My fundamental problem was the wars, knowing the scorn of captious academics for what they call "drum-and-trumpet history," yet I could not write my way around the wars, dismissing them in a few pages as a wretched waste of blood and treasure. No doubt it seemed clever to say (as one pundit had) that the price of beaver pelts at Hudson Bay was more important than a fight at Lundy's Lane, but that was academic nonsense.

In the period of my book (which I called *The Path of Destiny*), most Canadians lived on or near the border, in easy reach of marauding American forces. The wars affected them cruelly and profoundly and fixed the Canadian attitude towards the United States for generations to come. The bold attempt to seize Canada during the turmoil of the American Revolution was really the first act in the doctrine of Manifest Destiny, which was to obsess the Americans for another hundred years. That first attempt failed, and the inevitable sequel was another try, which was adroitly timed in 1812 when Britain was locked in a life-or-death struggle with the empire of Napoleon. It failed because the invaders were little better than armed mobs expecting an easy conquest and led by men more adept at party politics than war. Again and again they blundered and were beaten back by the few but experienced British soldiers in the country, supported valiantly by Canadian regulars and militia. In dispatches to Washington the American generalissimo complained of "the universal hostility of the inhabitants of the country," and Canadian farms and villages were ruthlessly pillaged and destroyed along much of the border country.

Actually the War of 1812 was Canada's war of independence. Release from the rigid rule of London was bound to come with time and Canadian development, and the Canadians could await it with patient certainty. The urgent thing in 1812 was absolute freedom from rule by Washington, and it had to be fought out then and there. I wrote in my book:

> The expansionist demands of the Jeffersonian party in the United States spelled domination to the Canadian as clearly as the supercilious and dictatorial manner of the British officials sent overseas to rule him. The difference was in the distance. John Bull was at least three thousand miles away. Brother Jonathan was peering right over the fence. When it came to a choice of imperialisms, the broad Atlantic distance lent enchantment. . . . If the War [of 1812] showed clearly their [the Canadians'] military dependence on Britain and set back the vague dreams of home rule for more than thirty years, it also set hard their determination to live apart from the United States.

*　　*　　*

Regardless of beaver pelts at Hudson Bay I described every aspect of the war as it affected the Canadian population, including every American thrust into their country, which invariably drew Canadian farmers and hunters hotfoot to the scene along with the regular British and Canadian redcoats. Such small but desperate affairs as Chateauguay, Lundy's Lane and Queenston Heights were our Bunker Hill, Saratoga and Yorktown, something to sing about, as the Americans sang about theirs.

No doubt this raised the hackles of Lee Barker in New York, but my book got favourable reviews in the United States as well as Canada. Indeed, the prosaic *Wall Street Journal* mentioned it in an editorial on Canadian-American relations, which were then in one of their periodic touchy spells, and advised its readers to study *The Path of Destiny* for a clear understanding of the Canadian attitude and its origins.

*　　*　　*

Diary, Jan. 12, '57. The snowplough in the street wakened me at 3.30 A.M., and as I couldn't sleep any more I got up and

325

worked straight through till 10 P.M., stopping only for meals and a walk to the post office. Today I sent 51 chapters of my history to Doubleday by registered mail. This is about 90% of the book and should keep them and Costain happy until I can forward the rest.

*　*　*

While I was composing the last chapters of *The Path of Destiny* my wife was typing clean copy of the rest, consulting me from time to time on the more cryptic pencil changes in my working typescript. I wrote the last word on January 22, 1957. I had signed the contract in Toronto in March 1955, when I was still working on *The Wings of Night*. Progress on the history was delayed by two bad spells of illness and the perilous edge of a nervous breakdown. The writing had taken nineteen months.

Soon afterwards I saw a television interview of Tom Costain in New York. In the course of it he waved a hand at a pile of typescript on his desk and said it was Canadian history as it should be written, "a beautiful piece of work by Thomas Raddall, up in Nova Scotia."

Meanwhile Doubleday published my contemporary novel *The Wings of Night* in New York and Toronto and arranged for editions in Britain and in various translations on the European continent.

My efforts went on without slackening. Already I was working on a one-book contract for Macmillan in Toronto, a revised and much enlarged version of my first little book about the *Rover* privateer. Also, I had determined on a new historical novel. In preparing my book on Halifax years ago I was intrigued by the character of Frances, wife of Nova Scotia's Lieutenant-Governor Sir John Wentworth. Beautiful, vain, ambitious, witty but shallow, unhampered by scruples or morals, she had parlayed herself from a flirtatious little housewife in colonial New Hampshire to the *femme fatale* of young British officers in the garrison at Halifax and then to the paramour of wild young Prince William (afterwards King William) when he commanded a frigate on the North American station and she was old enough to be his mother. Finally she had the triumph of becoming Lady Wentworth as wife of Nova Scotia's newly ennobled governor, with all the pomp and majesty of a viceroy's consort and with a list of all her personal enemies in Halifax to be snubbed and deprived of all patronage.

Who could ask a more piquant subject than a Becky Sharp and a Ninon de Lenclos rolled up in one artful bundle of petticoats?

* * *

In June 1957 I made a flying visit to New York and met my publishers for the first time. Tom Costain was there, of course, and George Nelson came down from Toronto for the occasion. I stayed at the New Weston on the corner of Madison Avenue and Fiftieth Street, less than a block from Costain's apartment and about the same distance from the Canadian Club in the Waldorf, where Nelson and I dined with him. Costain was now seventy-one, and although his mind was as lively as ever he confessed that his writing had slowed down to three hundred words a day instead of the two or three thousand he used to turn out.

He had reserved seats at Radio City Music Hall, and after dinner we enjoyed the show. The hour was getting on for midnight when we emerged, and the audience vanished as if by magic. It was a lovely night with a high moon shining down into the New York canyons, so we strolled along for several blocks enjoying it. The streets were deserted, a strange sight after the bustle of daytime, and if any muggers were lurking there they must have decided that three was a crowd.

Next day in the Doubleday offices on Madison Avenue I met the head of the company, Ken McCormick, with top editor Lee Barker. McCormick appeared to be on the sunny side of forty, with keen good looks and an amiable manner. Barker appeared to be forty-fivish, balding, with a deceptively bland face and air, and what seemed to me a distinct trace of the Harvard accent. If so, it must have been the Harvard Business School for behind the accent I soon recognized the cold clicking of a calculating machine.

Costain joined us, and we lunched together at the Regency Club, a quiet place with good food, favoured by writers and publishers. With the dessert McCormick opened the subject of my next book, and Costain immediately put forth two suggestions, both Canadian in concept. One was a biographical novel based on the life of Sir Guy Carleton and the other was a biography of Joseph Howe.

He then withdrew.

First I set forth my intended novel about Frances Wentworth, and the others agreed that it was good. McCormick asked, "What have you in mind after that?" I replied that I did one thing at a time, and for the present I must give my whole thought to the Wentworth book, which would require research in New Hampshire and in England, as well as Nova Scotia. So they turned to Costain's suggestions. Who was Sir Guy Carleton? They were very diffident when I told them he was the soldier who defended Canada successfully during the American Revolution and afterwards conducted the removal of a host of displaced Loyalists from New York. And who was Joseph Howe? When I told them, their faces were blank until I mentioned Howe's friendship with Samuel Cunard and Howe's voyage to England, in which he saw a steamship for the first time and conceived the idea of a regular steamship line to carry passengers and mails between England, Nova Scotia, and the United States. It was that idea which Sam Cunard made a fact.

Lee Barker seized on it and declared that I must write a history of the Cunard Line. Cunard was still a big name in New York, of course, whereas Joe Howe meant less than Joe Doaks, but I said quietly that any good advertising firm could turn out a history of a steamship line complete with pictures and details of the ships as they improved. I was interested in Sam Cunard himself, the busy little shipping merchant who began with a few small windjammers and trotted about the Halifax streets paying his bills with cash tied up in an old stocking. Accordingly I said I'd look into Cunard's story when I got a chance. Right now I must get on with the Wentworth book. On that we shook hands and parted.

That evening Nelson and I dined in Costain's huge apartment on Park Avenue, a whole floor of big rooms with ceilings twelve feet high and furnished with elegant antiques and bric-a-brac. Tom was probably a millionaire by that time and he lived like one. I told him the gist of the afternoon's talk. He made no comment except that he still wished I would write a book about Joseph Howe.

Some wizard on the Doubleday staff had procured two seats for that night's performance of *My Fair Lady*, which had been running only a year or so and was booked up apparently for ever. Nelson and I taxied over to the Mark Hellinger theatre well in time for the curtain opening. The seats were first-rate ones near the stage on the orchestra floor, and I enjoyed every minute of the play. It was like a dream to be only a few hours by air from my remote home in Nova Scotia and here at close view watching Rex Harrison and Julie Andrews make a better job of *Pygmalion* than Shaw himself.

I flew home the next day. I couldn't see what the conference had

328

accomplished except that I was no longer a stranger to my publishers, but I had enjoyed every minute in New York. I had not set foot there since I was a youngster aboard the *Mackay-Bennett* thirty-seven years before.

On the plane I opened the New York *Tribune* to find the outcome of yesterday's general election in Canada. After some search I found it in six inches of single-column type tucked away in the great bulk of the paper. Was this a good measure of American interest in Canadian affairs? I thought of Sir Guy Carleton and Joseph Howe. And Lee Barker and the Cunard Line.

* * *

When I finished the new enlarged text of *The Rover* in July, my wife typed clean copy and I packed it off to Macmillan. During the rest of the summer I read the papers of Sir John Wentworth in the archives at Halifax and sought in various directions for other Wentworth material. John had been governor of his native New Hampshire when he and Frances were driven out with the other Loyalists. They spent several years of exile in England before he got a minor post in Nova Scotia as official surveyor of Crown lands. Eventually with the aid of Fannie's wiles and charms he rose to be lieutenant-governor with a title in the British peerage. For many years before this they had cultivated the friendship of two great Whig families in England, the Rockinghams and Fitzwilliamses. I was fortunate in finding many of Frances's letters to them, written over a long period from New Hampshire and Nova Scotia.

I had learned that the best authority on New Hampshire history was Dorothy Vaughan, head of the public library in Portsmouth and a descendant of one of the old colonial families. I wrote to this lady but got no reply. I should have guessed that she received a flood of inquiries and could not undertake to dig out information for them all.

In September 1957 I went to Portsmouth and got a room in the old Kearsarge Hotel on Congress Street, three minutes' walk from the public library. I found Miss Vaughan, a pleasant middle-aged woman, very busy in her office. She was delighted to meet a writer who made a point of doing his own research, and she provided me with a small office equipped with desk and typewriter and brought me books, documents and maps to my heart's content. More than that, she accompanied me on walks and drives about Portsmouth, pointing out the surviving colonial mansions and relating the local traditions of John and Frances, their clandestine love affair while her first husband was slowly dying of consumption, and their hasty marriage ten days after the funeral. Miss Vaughan had compiled a map of Portsmouth in the latter half of the eighteenth century showing where the more important people lived, and she gave me a copy of it. She also permitted me to study her private collection of photographic copies of portraits painted by Copley, Blackburn and other artists of that time. This was especially valuable, because I could actually see the faces and figures of most of the people I wanted to write about.

With the Portsmouth research completed I went inland to see the site of Governor Johnnie's famous country residence near Lake Winnipesaukee. Again I was fortunate. I went by bus to Wolfeborough, intending to hire a car there and drive to the site, but there were no cars for hire, and anyhow the road to Lake Wentworth was too rough for anything but a jeep or an old truck. I lunched in a small restaurant by the shore of Lake Winnipesaukee and told an intelligent proprietress what I was doing there in the off-season when the summer visitors had gone.

She was interested at once, and after much phoning around she put me in touch with another authority, a woman who wrote a column in the Wolfeborough newspaper about the history of that region. This good lady came along in a battered truck driven by her husband, and they took me into the woods around Lake Wentworth, some miles east of Winnipesaukee, where we followed traces of the original "Governor's Road" from Portsmouth, and of his other road, cut through the forest to Dartmouth College. Then we jolted along to the site of John's country house, in the woods overlooking Lake Wentworth and still marked by the hewn stones of a huge cellar. It was all beautiful country with the sumacs in autumn scarlet on the lake shores and slopes like an army of redcoats deployed for battle. I had several happy and fruitful days like this, going over the Wentworth ground in town and country. As always, the ground work evoked that mystical touch with people in documents that I had found before in other places.

*   *   *

I spent the rest of that fall and winter at home in study of the Wentworth material and then in the usual struggle to get a novel started. It was no trouble to find a title. *The Governor's Lady* was obvious, although the book would have to deal with Johnnie as much as Fannie. There were some gaps in the material that gave me a problem because I was torn between a novel and a straight biography. This resulted in more than the usual writing and destroying, which I reported by letter to Tom Costain.

* * *

I determined to go to Europe in the spring of 1958, for several reasons. My wife and I needed a long holiday. For many years I had wanted to go over the battlefield of Amiens and find my father's grave. I wanted to see some of the European continent. Last but not least, I wanted to follow the tracks of the Wentworths in London and elsewhere after they were driven out of New Hampshire and before they came to Nova Scotia.

My financial burdens at home were increasing all the time, and I had to budget carefully for this trip abroad, crossing the sea in one of the small Furness Withy liners out of Halifax and using motorcoach tours on the continent as much as possible. We left home in April. It was a pleasure to be at sea again, and when the ship called at St. John's, Newfoundland, I was able to retrace some of my youthful tracks there. In England we went straight to Hythe and put up at the little White Hart Inn, where the poet Shelley once lived and where Joseph Conrad used to lunch on his trips into town when I was a child. One afternoon we visited the old Pent farmhouse. Walter Crane's couplet was still over the door and lately repainted. The interior had suffered much wear and tear when soldiers were quartered all over this countryside after Dunkirk in 1940. The room where Conrad wrote, and where he burned tobacco and candles far into the night with Galsworthy and Wells and the others, was now repaired and made into a small modern sitting room with a TV set; but nothing could change Conrad's old view across the fields, where sheep still grazed, or the bluff of The Pent looming behind.

I visited the School of Musketry and found it almost deserted. After Dunkirk the British Army had shifted its small-arms training inland and kept it there, far from the Straits of Dover. The ancient married quarters where I was born had been pulled down long ago. The rest of the buildings were on a maintenance basis and no more. In the town I walked to Saint Leonard's School and found it much the same as in my boyhood, and I attended a Sunday morning service in the old parish church on the hill where I had been bap-

331

tized. It was as cold as a tomb, and I shivered through a long dull sermon on the life of Saint Anselm.

Leaving my wife at the White Hart I made a lone pilgrimage across the Channel to the Picardy battlefield of August 1918, because I wanted to follow the route of the Winnipeg Rifles as the Canadian Corps fought their way over the rolling farmlands east of Amiens. I found my father's grave on the spot where he fell, with many of his officers and men, in the storming of Hatchet Wood. Among my papers at Dalhousie University Library there is an unpublished account of this as well as my other travels in Europe. I quote from it here:

Now I stood there myself, almost forty years after the battle. The maple saplings planted soon after 1918 had grown to fine trees. There was a soft green turf underfoot, and on each grave a few sprigs of a modest little creeping plant with pink flowers called London Pride, nothing else. When I came to Dad's grave I fell on my knees and closed my eyes, not praying but simply thinking deeply of the stern soldier, warm at heart, whom I had seen last when I was twelve years old.

At my mother's request the opening words of an Anglican hymn, "God be with you till we meet again" had been engraved on the stone long ago. (Dad used to write 494, its number in the hymnbook, at the end of all his letters to her from France.)

At last, remembering my mission, I had the chauffeur bring the little plastic bag, and I put in it two or three handfuls of earth from the grave, together with a cutting of the plant growing on it. While I was thus engaged I passed my camera to the chauffeur and he took two snapshots. I then walked out into the wheatfields, faced about, and took two pictures of the pitiful clump of graves, with Hatchet Wood on the rise just beyond. The spot where I stood must have been about the place where Dad and the others leaped to their feet and began their rush to attack the Germans in the wood.

I returned to the graves and motioned the chauffeur to leave me for a few moments. My father was forty-one when he died, and the gravestones showed that most of his soldiers were between eighteen and twenty-five. I looked slowly over the whole scene, so quiet and peaceful now. Caix and Le Quesnel were invisible, indeed there was not a single dwelling to be seen, so far off the main motor road. The fields, rolling like a pale green sea, capped here and there with dark green clumps of trees and undergrowth like Hatchet Wood, extended as far as the eye could reach. The German infantry perched in the wood had a clear field of fire in all directions, so they could not be by-passed. For the sake of other Canadian troops advancing on exposed slopes to the right and left of Hatchet Wood, this German force had to be attacked and destroyed at once, in the broad light of a summer noon, without waiting for tank or artillery support. When the brigadier's order came by runner Dad and his Rifles obeyed it without hesitation.

It was time to leave, and I knew I was leaving for ever. At the entrance to the little cemetery I turned about and faced the graves, drawing myself up instinctively and saluting army-fashion – saluting them all, with my eyes full of tears, thinking how young and brave these men had been, and how lonely they are now, forgotten, thousands of miles from home, in a world that considers 1918 as remote as the Crusades.

It was the first time I had wept since I was a child.

* * *

I rejoined my wife in Hythe, and we went on to London and boarded the first of the motor-coaches on our European tour. In planning it I avoided Paris and Rome, those haunts of would-be Joyces, Hemingways and Fitzgeralds, all rubbing elbows with each other and thinking they are touching Life and Art. There were other places I wanted much more to see.

Our party included four Australians, a New Zealander, a pair of Tasmanians, a South African army brigadier with his wife and daughter, and a mixed bag of English people ranging from a retired lawyer and his charming wife to three stout and merry old girls travelling together who appeared to be a trio of retired barmaids. Altogether our companions were as interesting as anyone or anything we saw along the way, and we made a lively company through Flanders and northern France, Switzerland, the Tyrol and northern Italy.

After a few days in Venice my wife and I visited the World's Fair at Brussels and then joined another party touring western Germany, Holland and Denmark. Back in England we visited some of my Gifford relatives in Kent and some Raddall kinfolk in the country outside London. As the rest of our schedule was drawn rather tight, there was no time for hunting up other Raddalls in Cornwall.

We returned home by the same little liner, *Nova Scotia*, having been away about two months. For exercise and auld lang syne, reliving old days at sea, I paced the ship's deck most of each morning and afternoon, sometimes accompanied by the chief officer. At table as we approached Halifax, the captain chuckled and said Furness Withy should refund my passage money, because I'd jolly well walked across the sea.

* * *

During my absence there was an announcement of my third Governor General's Award, for *The Path of Destiny. Maclean's Magazine* had put my picture on the editorial page and said among other things that I was "a towering figure in Canadian literature." *Time* magazine had tried hard to reach me, phoning and cabling all the way from Nova Scotia to Venice and badgering my family and friends at home for intimate details of my life, habits, income, present financial worth, and what not. Apparently they were panting to do a rags-to-riches story of a poor boy who ran away to sea and worked his way to fame and wealth as an author. If they had reached me they would have heard bluntly that the story was wrong at both ends.

* * *

Diary, Sept. 18, '58. My novel grows slowly, but it grows.

Diary, Oct. 18, '58. I haven't hunted deer for several years, and on this trip [to Eagle Lake] I brought only young Tom's single-barrelled shotgun and some bird shot. Difficult to follow any of our old hunting trails now owing to new growth and old windfalls.

Diary, Nov. 9, '58. Letter from Doubleday suggesting that I come to New York for a conference about my book. I suppose they're getting worried about my long silence, and no doubt Tom Costain has told them of my letters last summer, in which I expressed my own uncertainties about the style and content of the book. My course is chosen now, and I'm damned if I want those Madison Avenue hawks picking at the thing half born.

Diary, Nov. 13, '58. I'm fifty-five today. Letter from Jack McClelland. M & S want to issue a paperback volume containing some of my short stories. Also they would like to publish a cloth-bound volume of new stories if I have any and if Doubleday isn't interested. This, Jack says, "for old times' sake or any one of a number of good reasons."

* * *

In February 1959 a busy tapping of typewriters filled the house, as I wrote the final chapters of *The Governor's Lady* while my wife typed clean copy of the rest. For me this required more thinking than writing, so I had none of my old trouble with my left fingers, but I seemed fated to pain in that arm. Now it was an acute attack of bursitis in the shoulder joint. The pain became excruciating and the arm almost useless. I refused to consult my doctor, who would order me down to his offices for electro-heat treatment every day. I couldn't afford the time.

It was easier to write with a pencil than to type with one hand, so I went back to my early *Blackwood's* days, writing everything in longhand. Towards the end of March I mailed copies of my wife's neat typescript to Doubleday in New York and Toronto.

Tom Costain wrote urging another get-together with Doubleday's top men to discuss future writing plans. This insistence on future plans was a fetish with the Doubleday staff, who considered that a writer's mind, like their own huge printing plant on Long Island, must be scheduled well ahead for efficient and unfaltering production. I had no firm idea of what I wanted to do next, except that it would *not* be a history of the Cunard Line. As for a human-interest story of Sam Cunard himself, I found that his descendants, lofty with money and title in England, apparently had destroyed long ago everything that even mentioned his early days in Nova Scotia as a busy little nobody "in trade."

* * *

One day in June 1959 George Nelson phoned and asked cautiously if I was open to a few suggestions about *The Governor's Lady*. Tom Costain as well as the Doubleday editors had read the typescript, and they liked it but felt it was too long. Costain had suggested cuts. Also, he thought the novel would have more appeal to the book clubs if John Wentworth remained a high idealist, blind to his lady's infidelities, instead of condoning them and becoming a *mari complaisant*. My Doubleday editor would send me these suggestions if I had no objection. I was noncommittal except to say I would consider the suggestions. I knew that extra work on the novel now would mean a delay in publication until next year.

* * *

My daughter had married another student at university, and by this time they had a little toddler and another baby on the way. My son also had married this year. Mama determined that all of them would spend the summer with us. This was fine, but it gave me a problem as the general provider. I had a lot of money to earn and consequently a lot of work to do, and I couldn't do it in a house crammed with lively young people and their friends and visitors, with the phone ringing day and night.

My former retreat at Moose Harbour remained a black desert. I had to find a quiet place somewhere, so I put some clothes, a typewriter, and a carbon copy of *The Governor's Lady* in my car and cast myself on the hospitality of my widowed sister at Halifax. She had a small bungalow in the pretty little suburb of Jollimore, across the Northwest Arm, and spent every day in the city at a secretarial job.

Costain's suggested cuts were not so painful as I had supposed from Nelson's cautious approach. It was a matter of writing careful bridges for the gaps and rewriting one chapter to make it effective after the cuts. I retained a firm view of John Wentworth as a *mari complaisant* borne out by known facts, and I refused to alter that a bit. With this done and sent off to New York, I wrote some articles for magazines and then plunged into work for the CBC.

Learning that I was staying the summer at Halifax, they asked me to research and write script for a proposed film on the Halifax naval establishment, an extensive job that first required careful inspection of everything from the Burnside magazine to the boom defence yard at Point Pleasant. After all that was done, I researched and wrote background script for a film on the ancient French colony at Annapolis Royal, again a long job. The CBC also asked me to do a personal TV talk-show in Admiralty House next fall, so while I was there I dug into the history of "Ad House" and wrote the script for that.

For occasional exercise during these labours I walked along the shore of the Northwest Arm to Melville Island in one direction and to York Redoubt in the other. Joined by a short causeway to the shore of the Arm, Melville Island was the site of a prison for French seamen during the Napoleonic Wars, and nearby Dead Man's Island held the unmarked bones of those who perished in it. In the other direction, from the high crag of York Redoubt I gazed across the harbour entrance to McNab's Island and the grim hangman's beach that had so intrigued me as a boy. Although I had passed it many times in my seafaring days I hadn't set foot on the island since I camped there in the summers of '14 and '15.

Early one morning I went by boat to McNab's and spent a day scrambling over its three-mile length. Much of it was military property, disused but still taboo to eager Halifax real estate speculators. The extensive camp grounds, the long shooting ranges, the forts and batteries already were shaggy with a creeping overgrowth of trees and bushes, as the whole island had been when Peter McNab bought it more than two centuries before.

Preoccupied with the summer's work, I had no notion that I was viewing the scenes of another novel, but my faithful *daemon* was well aware, and in due time it spoke.

* * *

Back in 1956 the Toronto branch of Doubleday had announced a prize of ten thousand dollars for the best novel submitted by a Canadian author, but so far it had not been awarded. In August 1959 George Nelson notified me that the award would go to *The Governor's Lady* when it was published in the autumn of 1960.

I had drawn $5,000 from Doubleday to tide me over 1959, and I would need another $5,000 in 1960, so the net result for me would be nothing until the book's royalties exceeded $10,000.

* * *

My long absorption in *The Governor's Lady* had left the usual mental hangover that barred new creation for months, but as the winter of 1959-60 crawled past I sensed a new malaise. I was in my fifty-seventh year, an introspective time of life, with old age not at a hazy distance any more but staring me right in the face.

> *Diary, April 12, '60.* A sea gale all day, wet and raw. Spent this day and evening reading over my old letter files from 1935 to 1950. Highly interesting because so many matters and people have slipped from my mind since. But melancholy, too.

* * *

Despite a war, the years from 1935 to 1950 were the happiest of my life. In that period I achieved my dream of becoming a widely read and approved Canadian author, beginning with short stories, going on to novels, and reaching something like world notice with *The Nymph and the Lamp*. In those days our own people regarded almost with adulation a Canadian writer who had won success at home and abroad with tales of his own country, and apart from a flood of fan mail I had many interesting correspondents. In Halifax there were stimulating friends like Jim Martell, Margaret Ells, Andrew and Tully Merkel, all gone from the city now.

Then, too, I was charged with energy and getting a huge enjoyment whether at work or play. I had temperamental dumps but no real troubles. Since 1950, especially during the past five years, a succession of tragic deaths among friends and relatives, and of domestic and other problems, had fallen upon me one after another. Now, too, I had lost my zest for fishing, hunting, and rambling about the woods and lakes. I went sometimes, but the old good medicine was not there any more. Arthritis in my right hip had developed to a point where I couldn't step into or out of a canoe, or over boulders and fallen trees, without great awkwardness and pain.

*   *   *

There was something else on my mind, and it had the final importance. As a young man I had noticed once-admired authors scribbling away long after they should have stopped. Their product had sunk from good to mediocre and then to rubbish, and I heard a new generation discussing the rubbish with merciless voices, wondering what their fathers and mothers had ever seen in such a hack. I promised myself then, in my thirties, that when I had written the themes that interested and excited me I would throw the pen away and dig ditches or do anything rather than grind out books in which I had no heart or interest.

As it happened there was no need of digging ditches. Nowadays there was interesting and lucrative work to be had in writing television scripts. My friends in that industry had been urging me to "get into TV with both feet before books go out of style altogether." They said it gaily and confidently, and I retorted in the same spirit that books would never yield their place to talking pictures; it was only authors who went out of style.

As if to compound my troubled thoughts, Doubleday were harping again on future writing plans, and at Tom Costain's urging I made another flying trip to New York in May 1960. I lunched at the Regency Club with Costain, Barker, Nelson and George Shively, the editor who was now looking after the office business of my publications. We went on to Costain's magnificent new abode, the whole top floor and roof terrace of a tall building on Riverside Drive. I had regarded his former place on Park Avenue as the height of luxury, but that was a hovel in comparison. Among the costly antiques Tom showed me with pride his latest purchases in England, a writing desk that had belonged to Horatio Nelson and a huge and ugly baroque silver pen-and-ink stand once used by Charles Dickens.

From his beautiful garden on the roof we had a wide view of the Hudson River and could see the first steep bluffs of the Palisades on the farther side. With the publishers at my elbows I had a sudden impish thought of the Tempter on the mountain with the plain man from the boondocks south of Jerusalem.

When we got down to business in Tom's large book-lined study I was aware of an uneasiness in the company lest I propose another modern Canadian novel. When I refused the year before to write a history of the Cunard Line, saying that any good advertising firm could turn out a book of that kind, they seemed hurt by the phrase as if I had said something obscene.

As they saw it the publishing business was designed solely for the alchemy of turning paper into gold, and any worthwhile author must be eager to point his pen towards any positive lode. It was reasonable. I could see their viewpoint. The trouble was my own viewpoint, which they could not see at all. I wanted money all right, but I wanted it to come from good stories about my own country and its people.

Things had changed greatly in the outlook of Doubleday since Theodore Roosevelt went off to the wars in 1942. In the eyes of the firm nowadays Canada, like Mexico on the other side, had an actual drawback in being right next door. As they saw it, Americans went to those countries for summer or winter holidays, but they weren't interested in reading about them. Their first interest would remain naturally in books about their own land and its people. When their reading fancy did venture abroad they wanted books about Europe, the Near East, the Far East and Africa, where everyone and everything had the glamour of the far away. For years now in utterly different ways Ernest Hemingway, Pearl Buck, Tom Costain and others had catered to this American penchant for the exotic and made fortunes for themselves and for their publishers.

Costain himself, however, knew Canada as an interesting subject in the United States, and he remained my guide, philosopher and friend. On this occasion in New York he opened the talk by suggesting a novel drawn about Frontenac or Champlain, Canadian figures famous enough to be well known in the United States. Chief editor Barker pursed his lips and murmured agreeably. I demurred, saying that Frontenac and Champlain had been written to death, and there was nothing new to say about them. Costain grinned as if he'd known I would say that and asked, "What's your own idea?"

I had no idea. I needed more time to settle my mind after the disturbing doubts of last winter and spring. Yet I heard myself saying diffidently, "Well, there's the story of the La Tours." This meant nothing to the Doubleday men, but Costain himself had noted the La Tours briefly in his history of the old French regime in Canada, and he caught at this notion and urged me to elaborate it for the others. I had never made deep research into the La Tour story, but I knew the gist of it and I had been over the ground. So I described the Nova Scotia scene in the seventeenth century, the tactics of Claude La Tour and his son Charles, and particularly the bitter rivalry between Charles La Tour and his enemy d'Aulnay for the fur trade, the siege of Fort La Tour in the owner's absence by d'Aulnay's hired ruffians, the gallant defence inspired by Marie La Tour, the betrayal, the capture, the brutal hanging of her little garrison one by one, which she was forced to watch, and her heartbroken death soon after. There was nothing new about it. The story had been told and retold in Canada for generations, but so far the writing had been shallow and inept.

Lee Barker murmured that it *might* make a good novel. Then, looking me straight in the eye, he said, "You understand of course that we can't give much promotion to a historical novel staged in North America unless at least one-third of it takes place in what are now the United States." I knew what was in his mind. Nearly half of *The Governor's Lady* had taken place in New Hampshire before the Revolution. That made it as much American as it was Canadian, although it was the accident of history, not contrivance on my part. Any story of the Loyalists had to begin and develop substantially in what are now the United States.

However, I couldn't do anything like that again without blatant repetition in one guise or another. There was only one Fannie Wentworth in the history of the United States and Canada. Barker must have known that, too. I could only suppose he was hinting at the same notion that George Nelson had passed on to me from New York in the summer of 1956, that a rich opportunity was open to an adaptable historical novelist in the area of New England.

Hearing thunder in my silence, Tom Costain loyally switched the talk back to wholly Canadian concepts, and with genuine enthusiasm urged me to write the story of the pioneer La Tours and then follow it up with sequel after sequel branching from the family tree, like the Jalna tales of Mazo de la Roche. Tom glanced carefully at Barker when he said this, as if to remind him that Canadian author Mazo de la Roche had made and was still making fat profits for her publishers in the States and everywhere else.

I remained silent for a time. Then I said, "Tom, critics nowadays call Mazo's books 'the perpetual Jalna soap opera' and so on. As I see it, you may start with an interesting and valid book, but you can only dilute its value to nothing with a train of sequels." Costain looked at me sadly. In the presence of these hardnosed publishers he was trying to do his best for a Canadian whose work he liked, but I couldn't or wouldn't play Madison Avenue ball and my whole manner showed it.

At this point the chief editor arose abruptly, said he must get back to his office, and vanished. I stayed talking with Costain and Nelson about Canadian books and authors. Then I returned to the hotel, packed, and taxied to the airport. My subsequent diary entry of this encounter was equivocal, reflecting my uneasy mind. But later on I realized that I had left New York like the Loyalists long before me, with a mingled feeling of regret and of escape.

* * *

I never went back.

1960
1975

T o satisfy my curiosity and for something to occupy my mind for the rest of that summer and fall I made a search for the facts about the La Tours, turning aside now and then to do some necessary television work. The records of the ancient regime in Nova Scotia were sparse and often contradictory, but I found enough of the truth to convince my *daemon* that the story of the La Tours was not for me.

At a time when Catholics and Huguenots were at bitter strife in France, when the possession of Nova Scotia shuttled back and forth between English and French, and when rival French traders in the country itself were at each other's throats, the La Tours (like the Vicar of Bray in the song) casually changed their allegiance, their religion and even their personal affections whenever it suited the chance of the moment. To cap all, following the tragic death of his wife Marie and the accidental drowning of the ruthless d'Aulnay soon after, Charles La Tour actually wooed and wedded d'Aulnay's widow. This last and most sordid of his chameleon antics was designed to win back the property he had lost to d'Aulnay and give him all of d'Aulnay's own possessions to boot, a triumph won comfortably in d'Aulnay's bed, a much safer jousting place than the log ramparts of Fort La Tour.

Even Mazo de la Roche couldn't have done much with the

La Tour family tree. It was more like a family forest. As a young man roaming the Acadian wilderness Charles had offspring by Indian women, some of whom bore his name. Then he had offspring by his white wife, Marie Jacquelin. Now he begot several children with the new Madame La Tour – who already had eight young d'Aulnays. How could anyone make this mish-mash interesting or even credible?

* * *

By this time *The Governor's Lady* was in the bookshops of Canada, the United States, and Britain. Shively sent me a batch of reviews. As always, many were the brief paragraphs of a hack in a hurry, using the summary of the story on the jacket and letting it go at that. Papers like the *New York Times* and the New York *Tribune* gave good and pertinent critiques, pointing out among other things that my book gave a dispassionate view of the American Revolution and its aftermath for the Loyalists.

* * *

Time magazine had this to say:

Arts and Letters

Novel Honor

The fattest literary prize in Canada is Doubleday Canada's newly established $10,000 Novel Award. The first winner, announced last week, is Nova Scotia's novelist-historian Thomas Head Raddall, 56. The winning book, his 16th, is *The Governor's Lady*, a novel about the career of New Hampshire's Governor John Wentworth, who left America at the time of the American Revolution. *Lady* will be published this fall.

Tall, white-haired and soldierly-looking, Tom Raddall is a prolific novelist who has won Canada's coveted Governor-General's Literary Prize three times. Born in England in 1903, he was taken to Halifax by his parents when he was nine. In World War One, though a mere 15, he enlisted in the Canadian Merchant Marine, served as a wireless operator aboard ships and on lonely coastal stations such as Sable Island "the Graveyard of the Atlantic." After the war he settled down in Liverpool, N.S., married a local girl, took a course in accounting, got a job as bookkeeper, and began writing short stories. In 1934 Raddall's stories caught the eye of Scottish novelist John Buchan, who encouraged Raddall to publish a set of them, *The Pied Piper of Dipper Creek*. By the time the book came out in 1939, Buchan was Lord Tweedsmuir, Governor-General of Canada, and he (advised by a board of judges selected by the Canadian Authors Association) gave Raddall a Governor-General's prize for it. Since then Raddall has had no trouble living from his writing – no easy feat in Canada.

*   *   *

The most notable error was that I'd had no trouble living by my pen since 1939. One of *Time*'s Canadian stringers, Jack Golding, wrote me a note of apology, saying their rewrite desk had cut much out of his article and garbled the rest.

However, *Time* was no worse than my own publishers. Doubleday's blurb on the jacket of *The Governor's Lady* declared that I lived in Halifax, that one of my books was entitled *Nova Scotia, Warden of the North*, and that Nova Scotia was an island.

I got hilarious letters.

*   *   *

In the spring of 1961 my son was graduated from Dalhousie University and so was my daughter's husband. After eight or nine years of study they now entered lucrative professions.

A week or so later I sold my lumbering old Monarch car and bought a snappy little green Corvair for some new rambling in search of old tales, a happy return to the carefree days in the early 1930s, when I wandered about the province in a little canvas-topped jalopy. To begin, I chose the story of the mystery ship *Mary Celeste*, which was launched in Nova Scotia under the name of *Amazon*. A lot of wildly contrived nonsense had been written about her strange abandonment in mid-ocean in 1872, and the utter disappearance of her crew. As far as I knew, nobody had ever gone back to her origin and followed her story through.

I steered the new car towards the ship's birthplace, a village called Spencer's Island but actually on the mainland opposite the island. I made my headquarters in a little old wooden hotel on the shore of Minas Basin near Parrsborough. It was originally the summer home of Sir Charles Tupper, at whose wintry funeral I had shivered long ago. From there I ranged to Spencer's Island and a village called Economy, where *Amazon*'s first captain went to his untimely grave, and in the other direction to the village of Advocate, where I found the grandson of the man who built her, a knowledgeable old gentleman living alone in a house full of ship models and paintings, photographs, newspaper clippings, and documents.

Each evening at the hotel I typed the day's notes. It was the kind of on-the-ground research I have always enjoyed, and it included time spent in old graveyards, pulling up sunken tombstones in the search for an epitaph of the hoodoo ship's first victim, her own captain. From there I rambled about western Nova Scotia renewing my acquaintance with favourite spots and people. The new car had run over a thousand miles when I got back to Liverpool.

I had no intention of making an entire book out of the *Mary Celeste* affair. I had in mind a collection of stories, all true, all having some mystery about them in one way or another, and all touching on the Nova Scotia scene. In the course of research and observation over the years I had found interesting fragments which I noted and set aside, awaiting some time when I had leisure to trace the rest. Now at last I could take time to track them down.

* * *

In the summer of 1961 the Canadian Authors Association held their convention in Toronto, and as one feature of the show they asked my Toronto publishers to make a formal presentation of the Doubleday Prize Novel Award to author Thomas Raddall. They had a vision of George Nelson handing me a cheque for ten thousand dollars. George had to explain that – um – I had received the award already. However, he asked me to make an appearance at the convention with my wife, and then we could run up to Muskoka for a chat "about the new novel."

At the convention I was shanghaied into a typical futile CAA panel discussion. The given subject was, What is wrong with the novel? There were three male panelists (George Hardy, Ralph Allen and myself) and an amiable but garrulous old lady whose magnum opus had been published thirty or forty years before. She had been overshadowed a long time by later authors and like the legendary wolf from Bitter Creek she figured it was her night to howl. The chairman, a bewildered young professor from Victoria College, lost any hope of control within a few minutes, and the show became a rapid-fire female monologue, with the males getting a chance only when the lady paused for breath.

* * *

Doubleday Canada gave a large party in the Great Hall of Hart House, always an impressive place, where portraits of bygone college dignitaries look down on you and a long quotation from *Areopagitica* runs around the walls. George Nelson called me to midfloor, presented me with a copy of *The Governor's Lady* beautifully bound in morocco, and asked me to make a speech. I did the best I could. There was much chatter afterwards with CAA people, including an importunate woman who insisted that I collaborate with her in a book about the wives of all the governors general of Canada.

I had a good talk with Ralph Allen. He had finished volume five of the Doubleday History of Canada, dealing with Canada's part in the two world wars and with the years between. Blair Fraser, who had moved into Allen's vacated post as chief editor of *Maclean's Magazine*, was about to write the sixth and last volume, *The Search for Identity*.

Next morning the Nelsons took my wife and me by car to Muskoka. It was pleasant in the shade of old trees with a breeze from Lake Joseph rustling the leaves, and we remained there over night. Nelson was disturbed to find that I was not writing the La Tour novel. I told him why, but he urged me to do it anyhow. *The Governor's Lady* was proving to be such a success that the public would be eager for my next one, whatever it was about. He repeated Costain's suggestion that I plan a series of novels about the La Tours and their various descendants on the Jalna model.

I could only shake my head. I was occupied with *Mary Celeste* and other true tales that ought to be in print, and I was determined to see them in print. I forbore saying that I had worked long and hard to win repute as an author who wrote well about Canadian people and their times, and I refused to grind out romantic rubbish just for money.

We returned to Toronto for the final dinner of the convention, where I enjoyed talks with Wilder Penfield, with cheerful old Ned Pratt, and with Jack McClelland. Jack told me that he and Farley Mowat were thinking of buying a small sloop in Newfoundland. They hoped to cruise in it to Nova Scotia and would call on me in Liverpool. As it turned out, they didn't get this dream into fact for several years, and then they sailed to Montreal and Expo '67. Out of their misadventures came Mowat's hilarious *The Boat Who Wouldn't Float.*

* * *

From time to time, radio or television crews came to my house for interviews. One was a half-hour talk in a five-part TV series on

Canadian authors from coast to coast. The others were Earle Birney, Eric Nichol, Morley Callaghan and Robertson Davies. I noted Callaghan's statement that he often spent months without writing a line, and there was a period of eight years (1938-46) when he wrote nothing at all. I wondered what Doubleday would have thought about that.

For myself, I was busy enough but not with the sort of things that Madison Avenue would stand up and cheer about. I had written the *Mary Celeste* story, and I was digging into the mysterious murders aboard the barkentine *Herbert Fuller* back in 1896, which startled the people of Halifax and Boston and seamen all around the world. After that I would tackle the story of Archie Belaney, the English vagrant who made himself famous as "Grey Owl," the most cunning and successful impostor of the 1930s. All accounts of him so far said he came from England to Northern Ontario, that he enlisted in the Canadian army in Montreal and became a twice-wounded hero in Flanders, and that after the war, posing as a half-breed Indian, he devoted himself to saving the beaver from extinction in Canada.

Not even his sponsor, publisher and persistent apologist Lovat Dickson seemed to know that Belaney first appeared in Canada among the Micmac Indians of Nova Scotia, that he returned to them in 1914 and the next year went overseas in a Nova Scotia regiment. Nor did Dickson seem to know that Belaney's first wound in Flanders was marked "accidental" in his army medical record, that his second wound was a most suspicious one in the edge of his foot, sustained in a rest camp far behind the lines, and that in fact he had malingered his way out of the war with a "deformed foot" and "eyesight damaged by previous attacks of snow-blindness," both of which recovered miraculously as soon as he got his discharge from the army.

Later on, when he stepped into the limelight in buckskins and feathers as "Grey Owl," he set himself up as a kind of latter-day Hiawatha, the embodiment of the Good Spirit, not only to the Indian people but also to the entire animal kingdom. In this role he never missed a chance to decry the white man's treatment of the Indians. Yet as long as he lived he went on committing the oldest and most common of the white man's sins, cohabiting with Indian or half-breed women and leaving them, and any offspring of the

348

liaison, as nonchalantly as he cast away his empty whisky bottles.

Whimsically at first and then with set purpose he fashioned an image of himself as the inspired saviour of the beaver in Canada. The actual records show that he kept a few beavers as pets for his own amusement and later as live models for his nature stories, which with Dickson's promotion were sold in enormous quantities to the reading public. The truth was that the restoration of the beaver was begun by farseeing and capable men of the Department of Northern Affairs long before Archie the trapper stopped killing them, and their efforts continued successfully during his Grey Owl masquerade and long after he was dead.

Men who had known Belaney in the backwoods before his tongue-in-cheek metamorphosis chuckled over his escapades and described him as a clever rogue with no morals or scruples, a creature nothing like the folk hero that fanciful writers and talkers had made of him. At late as 1973 dear old John Diefenbaker, shaking all his wattles for emphasis, told a Canadian television audience that Grey Owl should be remembered as a "ger-RATE ca-NAY-jun."

It was time for somebody to expose plain truth about this artful dodger, and I might as well do it. There were other true stories of Canada, and particularly Nova Scotia, that invited research and publication. Apart from all that, I had in mind something else.

In research I always felt grateful to bygone men and women who had taken the trouble to write down what they knew for the information of posterity. Now I owed a debt to posterity myself, and it was time I began payments on account. With this in view, I began to sort out and type clean copy of my notes on the Micmac Indians and their remote predecessors who made the shell heaps on the coast. I researched and wrote a history of the militia in my part of the country and their part in the various wars and alarms during the period 1775-1875. And so on. These minor but interesting occupations carried me through the winter and the spring of 1962.

*   *   *

I have mentioned that the CBC chose *Roger Sudden* for their first television serial play in 1953. They lavished money on the production. Later the cost appalled them, and they did not serialize another novel for nine years. In 1962 they began again, and again they chose one of mine, *The Wings of Night*, a modern tale that would not require eighteenth-century costumes and settings.

In May 1962 director Ronald Weyman and producer Ted Leversuch visited me with a cameraman and a designer, and I showed them over the scenes of my story. In the old courthouse in Liverpool the designer made careful drawings and the cameraman took photographs that enabled the CBC to reproduce the court-room inside their Toronto studios with marvellous fidelity. I was told that the CBC would employ something like fifty technicians, actors and actresses in Toronto and on the actual scenes here, and their wages alone would amount to more than $100,000.

One difficulty was the river scenes, which called for canoes in rapid water. The Mersey nowadays was a tamed stream of hydro-electric dams and ponds all the way from Indian Gardens to the sea, so I took them to look at the Medway River, which had no dams to check the runs. After a wet spring it was a torrent with picturesque rapids and falls, and a motor road through the woods along one bank made filming easy. Weyman and his men were delighted. We stopped for lunch in a little hotel at Greenfield, look-ing out on the river, and I heard Leversuch making arrangements for hotel accommodations to begin on August 15. I said hastily, "Wait a minute! In the middle of August this river won't have enough water. It's got no storage dams and only a small lake sys-tem." They didn't understand. A river was a river all the time, wasn't it?

I explained, "Once the hot weather comes, this river dwindles fast. Last August, and the August before that, I could have crossed it right out there, simply by hopping from rock to rock." So we went back to the Mersey, which did have big lakes and storage dams, and picked a place in the woods where the canoe sequences could be shot, although lacking rapids or falls. As they left for Toronto, Weyman said to me wistfully, "Are you sure there won't be enough water on those Medway rapids in the middle of August? You see, all of our people and equipment are on rigid schedules, so it's all got to be done at that time." I said, "High water in the Medway then would take a miracle. The weather would have to start raining now, and keep on raining more or less continuously until August. That just can't happen." They went away murmuring regretfully about those fine shots on the Medway.

While they were gone, the impossible happened. The summer of

'62 was one of the wettest in Nova Scotia history, and when Weyman and his people arrived in August the Medway remained a foaming torrent. Weyman chaffed me about my prediction. He never knew how lucky he was. The last two weeks of August were the only consecutive days of fine weather in that whole summer. If all those expensive people had been obliged to sit indoors waiting for the rain to stop or the fog to clear, Leversuch's budget would have gone to the moon.

I watched the filming of the outdoor scenes with interest. At one point, the local railway station, Weyman invited me to "do a Hitchcock." I would be seen as an unimportant character greeting one or two loafers in the background while the hero walked up into the camera. Alas, the Canadian public never had the chance of seeing me as a makeshift Hitchcock. I fell to oblivion on the cutting-room floor along with a lot of much better film footage. The CBC had decided to run the serial in eight parts instead of ten, and the scissors were ruthless.

Weyman and Leversuch were enthusiastic about the story, and both urged me to put books aside and write TV plays instead. On the other hand, a letter from George Nelson congratulated me on the television sale and inquired pointedly about my next novel. I wrote in my diary, "I haven't replied yet because there is nothing to say, except that I've been working damned hard for many years, and I'm taking a sabbatical leave from all that. In fact I'm taking a long look back on my life and works, my dreams of old and the shortcoming of results, and wondering if I should write another word for public sale."

* * *

This does not mean that I sat gnawing my fist in a dark corner. On the contrary, I moved about, keeping the close touch with life that was always as needful to me as eating and breathing. For a random instance, in September 1962 I spent an afternoon with my wife on a rustic golf course at Clyde River. As we waited on one tee a bull moose swam across the river and trotted across the fairway in front of us. He had a fine set of horns, and his wet coat shone with a black gloss in the sun, a rare sight in those days when the moose had all but vanished from western Nova Scotia.

Returning towards Liverpool we stopped to dine at the Ragged Islands Inn, whose proprietress, Dorothea Arnold, greeted us and then introduced four or five old ladies who remained as guests now that the tourist season was past. We had a good dinner of roast turkey, pumpkin pie and coffee, and then a merry chat with the old ladies in the parlour, where I told them about the golf-buff moose and went on to spin yarns about Scabby Lou and other backwoods characters of my acquaintance in time past. When I paid my bill Miss Arnold said, "I shouldn't charge you anything. You've entertained us all."

Less than three months later, she was dead at sixty-eight. She was a slim erect woman, good humoured and efficient, who had gone to the States at eighteen and worked there for years with a dream in her mind. She would return some day to the old house of her colonial ancestors, facing the sea and the well-named Ragged Islands, and set up an old-fashioned country inn. She found another woman to share the dream and together they created it, serving good country meals at honest prices and furnishing a few small bedchambers. My wife and I stopped there for a meal and a chat whenever we passed that way. In those days the law forbade drinking anything stronger than tea in "a public place." If strangers were present I was always bidden to the kitchen by a crooked finger in a partly opened doorway, and there I joined the two cheerful old girls in a dram of rum.

They provided the travelling public on the coastal road with a wayside inn straight out of Haliburton's travels with Sam Slick. Once each winter, choosing a night with a snowstorm booming in the chimneys and hissing about the house, I open my copy of *The Old Judge* and turn to Haliburton's lively account of travellers snowbound at a Nova Scotian inn. Whenever the proprietress, "Miss Lucy," comes into the parlour, I see the smiling wraith of Dolly Arnold.

* * *

When I applied for naval service in War Two I wrote a short memoir of myself and my family background. The trend of the war was ominous then, and remembering the fate of my own father I wanted my children to know something about me when they grew up. The memoir remained in an old loose-leaf notebook. In January 1963 I found it there and resolved to write a more detailed account of my life, checking my memory closely with the diaries and correspondence; but a new turn in my publishing affairs postponed it.

Early in 1963 George Nelson asked me to meet him in Halifax.

352

There he informed me that the parent firm of Doubleday in New York had a large profit surplus and were now determined to use some of it in expansion abroad. In England they were about to purchase an old London publishing house and were planning to enlarge this footing. In Canada they intended to expand the business and plant of Doubleday Canada Limited, which hitherto had published a few established Canadian authors like myself but acted mainly as a Canadian distributing centre for the great Doubleday publishing and book club complex in New York.

Among other activities Doubleday Canada was to get many more Canadian authors on its list, and Nelson had been told to tour the country signing up new writers from coast to coast. The authors already on the list were to be persuaded to sign contracts for books far into the future. So what had I got in mind?

I told him about my occupations since publication of *The Governor's Lady*. I added an intention to write another historical novel, set in Halifax and Dartmouth during the Napoleonic Wars, when Peter McNab's family and retainers lived like a little Highland clan in the seclusion of their island, and when at least one of every ten people living about Halifax harbour was a French prisoner of war. Obviously it would not fit the Barker formula for a successful Doubleday costume novel because all of it would take place "up in Canada."

Nelson seemed unworried about that. He drew up the following list:

1. For immediate action, a special new edition of *The Wings of Night*, printed by offset process, to be in the Canadian bookshops by the time the CBC began to run its television serial of the story.
2. A new Canadian edition of *Son of the Hawk*, originally published by Winston in Philadelphia.
3. A fresh edition of *Halifax, Warden of the North* with the text brought up to date.
4. A novel about the McNabs and French prisoners at Halifax.
5. A volume of true short stories including *Mary Celeste* and "Grey Owl."
6. A history of Sable Island, "Graveyard of the Atlantic."

* * *

When I made a rough guess at the time it would take to fulfil all this with my laborious methods, I said, "George, I'm getting on for sixty, and that list looks like a tie-up until I'm carried off in a box. I don't mind telling you I've begun to jot down some of my memoirs just in case the men come soon with that box." He cracked right back, "Will you sign a contract for the memoirs?"

I laughed and shook my head. There were quite enough unhatched chickens on that list.

* * *

Diary, May 23, '63. Drove to Bear River this morning and called on James McKinnon, a man with a good memory and a sensible manner. He enlisted at Digby in March 1915 and remembered Archie Belaney joining the recruits there. Belaney wore his hair long enough to touch his shoulders and said he came from the West. He used to do Wild West stunts with a revolver, tossing sticks and cans into the air and hitting them.

* * *

By August I had completed the new material for *Halifax, Warden of the North* and had written a foreword for the new edition of *Son of the Hawk*. I had obtained microfilm of Archie Belaney's army documents, including all of the medical reports, and other documents relating to him during the years he was employed by the Department of Northern Affairs. Also, through the magazine of the Canadian Legion I had found three more men who served in the army with him, one of them the officer who commanded Belaney's platoon in Flanders in 1915. The real picture of Grey Owl the war hero was coming to light at last.

* * *

Tom Costain was keenly interested when he learned that the CBC were resuming the production of serials and beginning with *The Wings of Night* in the summer of '62. He promptly invited a CBC man to come to New York, all expenses paid, and sold him the television rights in his own Canadian novel, *Son of a Hundred Kings*. For some occult reason the CBC showed Costain's story first, beginning in September 1963 and running through ten weekly instalments. So the showing of *The Wings of Night* was postponed until December 1963, although it represented a CBC investment of well over $150,000 already tied up for a year or more.

*   *   *

Diary, Oct. 22, '63. Lovat Dickson has sent me a copy of an address on Grey Owl which he wrote for broadcasting years ago. The BBC had refused it, pointing out that he should say more about Grey Owl as an impostor.

Diary, Nov. 19, '63. Today a carpenter completed repairs to my old typewriter desk. Over the years the veneer on each side of the typewriter had been splintered by blows of my fists, thumping the wood in vexation whenever my thoughts ran ahead of my fingers and the fingers pied the type.

Diary, Feb. 10, '64. A note from Weyman: "I am pleased to tell you that Wings of Night had a greater audience than any drama on Canadian TV to date. I have hundreds of letters expressing their delight both with the play itself and with the book."

Diary, March 7, '64. Working at the novel. The vision of Ellen Dewar is in the back of my mind but elusive when it comes to words on paper. Yet I must find her. My original concept of her was trite and false, and my instinct told me so from the beginning. Her personality has got to be utterly individual and outstanding, otherwise McNab and Cascamond (whom I see clearly) will themselves seem false to life.

Diary, Sept. 9, '64. The truckman came and carried off my old bedroom furniture, bought by Trim. When the shabby bookcase-desk went out of my sight I had a pang of regret, remembering the nights I slaved at it, year after year, and the hopes and disappointments and subsequent glories that came from it.

Diary, Dec. 28, '64. I have at last mastered the new electric typewriter and find it a boon, very fast and precise, although my thought is still far ahead of my fingers. Fortunately I can blot out errors by holding down the X key, which runs on automatically as long as my finger is there, a marvellous device.

* * *

In January 1965 an attack of influenza again developed into pneumonia and knocked me flat for weeks. It delayed work on *Hangman's Beach* and made it too late for publication that fall, just as a similar attack had delayed *The Wings of Night*. This susceptibility to flu was a strange chink in the health of a man of strong body who exercised that body a lot outdoors. I never could understand it. I drove myself mercilessly whenever I wrote a book, but if debility from overwork had laid me open I should have suffered other ills. I never did. The flu bug alone seemed to have a passkey to my fortress.

* * *

Diary, March 20, '65. Received a bushel of Chesapeake oysters with the compliments of sea captain Charles Williams. This evening I shucked them with the Micmac crooked-knife that old Mike Mo-ko-ne made for me years ago.

Diary, Aug. 27, '65. This morning I wrote the last words of *Hangman's Beach*. E. has typed clean copy of most of the book, week by week, from my working script. No doubt I'll find some changes to make in the rest before it goes to the printers. After long research I began to write this novel in a tentative way on Jan. 10 '64, tentative because I was not sure whether to begin with the McNabs on their island or with Cascamond aboard *La Furieuse*.

* * *

Late in September I had a letter from my New York editor, George Shively. He had just read *Hangman's Beach*. "I congratulate you heartly. It seems to be a splendid novel, in fact just about the best you've done." He added cautiously, "Nobody else around here has yet had a chance to read it." I knew exactly what that meant. Shively was a low man on the editorial totem pole. A much loftier head would decide how much or how little the firm would do to promote a costume novel staged entirely "up in Canada."

Suddenly I had bad news in a double thunderbolt. Tom Costain had died in New York, and George Nelson was stricken by a heart attack and lay gravely ill in Toronto. Much later I realized that *Hangman's Beach* had come under the cold scrutiny of the machine on Madison Avenue without the presence of my two warmest advocates.

Back in '63 I had written to Vincent Massey about the portrait of Grey Owl painted by Sir John Lavery, which Massey had bought long ago in London. He replied, "We must have eliminated it from our collection before it went to the National Gallery in Ottawa. I am afraid I cannot tell you its whereabouts." This seemed odd. Later on I inquired through a friend of mine, an art connoisseur, and now at last I had the answer. The portrait was right there in the National Gallery, but carefully segregated from the Massey collection. Massey had been sensitive about the Grey Owl hoax and didn't want anyone to know he had been taken in.

How stuffy and silly!

* * *

I spent that winter working on *Footsteps on Old Floors*, which would include the Grey Owl story.

* * *

Early in 1966, Ken McCormick wrote that he was taking over the files of George Shively, who was ailing and had retired, and henceforth he would be my personal editor. This was meant to be complimentary, but I knew that McCormick was fully occupied with the management of Doubleday's huge business, and the decisive and overriding editorial voice at Doubleday remained that of Lee Barker, a man I disliked from the first time I met him.

I received one of the first copies of *Hangman's Beach* with McCormick's card tucked inside, but the spring and summer went by without any further word. In the fall I wrote to him, inquiring in the usual way about other editions, English and foreign. After a long time I had an answer from McCormick's secretary, who seemed to know nothing at all. She said McCormick was in Europe. Then I knew the score.

Barker had decided to print a single edition of *Hangman's Beach* in the U.S. and Canada, just to fulfil the contract and maintain an option on my next book. His promotion in the States consisted of one small advertisement in a New York paper and another in Boston. The reason was all too obvious. Having got this out of his head, that odd man up in Canada now could turn his mind to something better suited to the U.S. market.

The odd man up in Canada wrote his own opinion to McCormick and added, "I am seriously concerned, not only about this book, but about my whole connection with Doubleday." This time McCormick wrote a bland letter in reply. It was a quibble, and I was not appeased. I went on writing *Footsteps on Old Floors* to fulfil the next-to-last item in our existing contract and finished it in March 1967. I sent it to New York with illustrations, including a photo-copy of the Grey Owl portrait by Lavery. McCormick wrote at once, saying he'd just heard that my typescript had arrived and was delighted. "This is an exciting prospect which we'll publish with pride, both here and in Canada." I have no doubt that he meant what he said at the time, but I was under no illusion about the outcome.

Chief editor Barker put the publication of *Footsteps* over until 1968 and then disposed of the book by printing ten thousand copies and melting the plates, without consulting me or the Toronto branch of Doubleday, which sold its consignment and then had orders that it could not fill. This despite good reviews, including an enthusiastic one in the *New York Times*. In the same arbitrary way Barker had printed fifteen thousand copies of the new Doubleday edition of *Halifax, Warden of the North* back in '65 and then melted the plates without a word to me or Toronto. I had apologetic letters from Toronto, none from New York.

* * *

It was time to keep the promise I had made to myself long ago, to quit while my work was still in good repute and simply say, "That's all." I had been working hard in various ways for half a century and now I was sixty-five. As if to point out this milestone on the road to Journey's End, several institutions were seeking to acquire my manuscripts, correspondence, diaries, and other papers. They included Boston University, Dalhousie University, the Public Archives of Canada, the National Library at Ottawa, and the Public Archives of Nova Scotia.

* * *

Only one item remained in my multiple contract with Doubleday, the history of Sable Island, which was certain to get the same treatment as *Hangman's Beach* and *Footsteps on Old Floors* – a single printing to keep the Doubleday option open, just in case that man up in Canada came out with another *Governor's Lady* (which by this time has sold over 460,000 copies in the United States, Canada, and Great Britain) or maybe another *Nymph*.

*　　*　　*

For years I had kept a growing file on Sable Island, but there remained a lot of research to be done in the annual reports of the lifesaving establishment, going all the way back to 1801, and in other documents to be hunted out and examined. With my eyesight fading, I did not look forward with pleasure to all this visual strain, but I reckoned it part of my debt to posterity and I had put it in the Doubleday contract with that in mind.

Now came an unforeseen relief. In the summer of 1967 I was visited by a highly intelligent young officer of the Australian Navy named V.L.W. Vickridge, who had literary ambitions. On a Commonwealth liaison exchange he had been posted at Halifax for the past two years with the Canadian naval air service, and in flights over Sable Island he had become intensely interested in "the Graveyard of the Atlantic." During his off-duty hours in Halifax he had been studying everything he could find about it and planning to write a book. Someone had told him to see me, and now here he was on my doorstep, asking what I knew and eager to do the documentary research that for me would be a difficult chore.

Delighted, I showed him everything I had and my list of other source materials, telling him to copy whatever he wanted. Next I had a hurried note from him saying he'd been posted to the U.S. Navy at San Diego, California, on another assignment for two years. He would go on with his studies of the Sable Island material and then return to Australia to write the book. He did not know his future address, but when the time came he would get in touch with me. So I put the Sable Island book out of my mind. At the end of two years I had no word from Vickridge. As time went on I guessed that something had happened, an air accident perhaps, or merely a change of mind. By that time I had decided to write nothing more for publication.

*　　*　　*

In February 1968 I had a telegram from New York: "Dear Tom, we are proud to be publishing Footsteps on Old Floors. Happy publishing date. Best wishes – Ken McCormick."

*　　*　　*

The mail brought a letter from Lovat Dickson, to whom I had sent an advance copy of *Footsteps*. "I think you have done the piece on Grey Owl very well indeed. The Army bit, which I didn't know about, is extremely interesting and clinches your reading of his character. This should remain the final word on this very odd bird."

A few years later Dickson changed his mind on that and brought out a new elaborate book on Grey Owl under the title *Wilderness Man*. He refrained from sending me a copy. His previous biography called *Half-Breed*, published in 1939, was an unabashed defence of Archie Belaney, as Dickson admitted himself in the new book. This one was not quite so lopsided, admitting that Archie was a bit of a rogue, using my account of him in *Footsteps on Old Floors* in one or two places, but ignoring the rest of it and still portraying Belaney as a noble defender of all creatures of the wild, human and animal.

Dickson put aside my facts about "the Army bit." Now he preferred to say that Belaney "showed the reckless courage that was typical of him" and suffered two wounds before being sent back to Canada with an injured foot, and lungs damaged by "mustard gas." There is no mention of mustard gas in Belaney's army medical record for the simple reason that he got himself out of the war in April, 1916, and the Germans did not introduce mustard gas until July, 1917. In fact, the Canadian army records made no mention of his lungs or of any kind of gas at all. They did reveal exactly what X-rays showed about that "injured foot."

* * *

On a frosty night in February 1968 my phone rang, and the caller said, "Tom, I have been asked to find out if you would accept the post of Lieutenant-Governor of Nova Scotia. Our people have agreed that you would be an eminently suitable person in all respects, and asked me to persuade you if I could."

The retiring lieutenant-governor, Henry MacKeen, was an admirable man whom I knew well. He had served gallantly in War One and after the war became one of the most successful and at the same time the most respected lawyer in Nova Scotia. To round out a distinguished career he had served two terms in Government House, although, as he confessed to Lovat Dickson and me one evening at the Saraguay Club, he detested the endless round of ceremonial duties. He and his wife were beloved throughout the province. Their hospitality at Government House was wide and generous, and at their board my wife and I had met all sorts of interesting people, from a famous British soldier to a cheerful and witty little Acadian priest from Île Madame.

We could not begin to fill those shoes at Government House even if we had wished to try – and we didn't. When I said so, my caller mentioned carefully that the salary and expense account could be increased if I was deterred by money matters, but I said the post was not for me in any respect. I was honoured by the invitation but my answer must be No.

I told my wife, "You might have been a governor's lady, just like Fannie Wentworth." Her reply was a droll, "Well, hardly!"

* * *

There were other things in mind, among them Journey's End, and I began to put my papers in order, a herculean chore, rummaging about the attic and in my files, sorting the correspondence of a lifetime. Also, I went on paying my debt to research. Now and again, too, I took time out to address a group of students, a histori-cal society, or a university convocation in which I was given a hon-orary degree.

George Nelson had recovered from his illness and retired in 1968. In the summer of '69 I had a letter from the new manager in Toronto. "I am sure that you are aware how pleased and proud we are here that you are a Doubleday author. Our association has been a happy one in the past and I hope it will be just as happy in the future. I wonder if you would drop me a line to tell me how your writing is going." I replied that I had abandoned the book on Sable Island because someone else was doing it. Consequently the mul-tiple contract of 1963 was now at an end, and so was my connection with Doubleday. This brought a letter from McCormick in New York, asking pointedly about the Sable Island book "which is in our contract." I knew he had a copy of my letter to Toronto before him, but in any case I repeated that my connection with Doubleday was at an end.

That, as they say on television, wrapped it up.

* * *

Late in October 1969 I joined my long-time companions in a week-end at Eagle Lake, for old times' sake, leaving my rifle on the rack in my study, where it had reposed, clean but unused, for years. We went up the river from Big Falls to the outlet of Eagle Lake by motorboat, and stalwart sons of Parker and Dunlop carried our supplies and duffle up the steep mile of trail to the camp.

The next day I rowed a little skiff down the lake a mile or so to the stream from Long Lake and walked under gnarled red maples in the wild meadows where we'd had so many hunting adventures in time past. There was some snow in the shady places, and tracks and patches of flattened wild grass showed where deer had been. I climbed to the peak of the big boulder, formerly screened by young spruce trees, where I had spent many a vigil watching for deer to creep out of the woods. I had shot several bucks there. It was never easy, for the bucks were much more wary than their does; they never fully revealed themselves, and the target was always a moving one in fading light. I used to stick my spent cartridge cases on twigs of the concealing spruces. Since those faraway days the porcupines had killed these trees by gnawing the bark, and in the course of time the trees had fallen and rotted away, leaving my old aerie naked to view. I looked for some of my old brass cartridge cases, but they were buried under many seasons of fallen leaves from the swamp maples. It was like trying to recover the time when I fired those shots, at a physical prime far back on the other side of the hill. I returned to the boat and rowed slowly back to camp.

That evening, on a whim, I took one of the birchbark horns that still hung on the camp wall, stepped outside, and made several moose calls. In the stillness the sounds went along the lake shores and echoed from the ridges, but there was no reply. No moose had been seen in these familiar woods for at least twenty years. I still knew how to call a live moose, but I couldn't call one back from the dead.

The next morning I departed for home with my old knapsack on my back. Parker wanted to take me down the river in the motorboat but for auld lang syne I limped out by the old trail through the woods to Big Falls. Just where it turned towards the hydro-electric dam and the motor road I met a trigger-happy youth hunting deer. He threw up his rifle to shoot, and I saved my hide if not my life by yelling a quick "Hey!"

I was over the hill, but I wasn't ready to drop just yet. There were still some things to do.

*　*　*

In 1970 I began to write memoirs, not for publication but to accompany my papers for the information of future students. I had noted, too often, what a mess a biographer can make of a man's life when he does not know what he was like or how he lived and thought and worked. I determined to write my own life story. Anyone in the future could read what I had to say about myself, and if sufficiently interested could check it with my diaries and correspondence.

* * *

I put it aside in the autumn to revise and update *Halifax, Warden of the North* for a new edition to be published by McClelland and Stewart. Then the CBC asked me to come to Halifax and record a two-part television interview about my life and times. On my lone motor drive to the city I ran into a terrific storm of wind and rain from the sea, and my life and times nearly came to an abrupt end on a long downward slope in the hills behind Saint Margaret's Bay. The flood of rain made the asphalt as slippery as ice. I was driving too fast for such conditions and a gust of the gale sent my light car skidding into the left-hand lane. By a miracle there was a gap in the fast oncoming left-hand traffic, and I managed to regain control and get back to my proper lane before I was smashed to pulp.

I was still a bit shaken when I reached the CBC studios, but I pulled myself together very well. I wound up the interview by saying that in *Footsteps on Old Floors* I had written my last book. There would be no more. When the interview was shown on Canadian TV I got letters deploring this decision, but naturally I did not change my mind and I had no regret whatever.

* * *

In October 1971 I was summoned to Ottawa to receive the Order of Canada at the hands of Governor General Michener in Rideau Hall. Thirty-four others were included in the solemn and glittering ceremony. The selection of the semi-annual list was apparently modelled on the Queen's Honours in Britain, marking people from all walks of life, from scientists and clerics to the inevitable jockey. In the audience room I sat beside Guido Molinari, who observed in a musing voice, "As you see, of all these worthy people you and I, a writer and a painter, are the only representatives of the arts. Doesn't that say something about the place of the arts in Canada?" I said, "You're forgetting old Dan George over there. He represents Drama, doesn't he?"

Later on I had a long and interesting chat with Dan George, who was in full "Indian" costume, including a pair of much-decorated moccasins with shanks up to the knee, made by a sporting goods firm in California and a popular item in their catalogue. For much of his life Dan George had worked as a stevedore on the Vancouver waterfront. When he retired to a little Indian community outside Vancouver he let his hair grow long enough to twist into a pair of pigtails. A television producer discovered him there, with his wise old eyes, his deeply lined face and slow half-whispering voice, and coached him to play the part of "Old Antoine" in a play about a backwoods ranch in British Columbia. It made him famous, and he had appeared since in Hollywood movies as well as television plays in Canada. He was a consummate actor by nature, and now he played the ancient and venerable red man on and off the stage, wearing a costume designed mainly in Hollywood, nothing like the plain and skimpy garb of his Salish ancestors.

* * *

I completed the first draft of my memoirs in 1973. It ran to more than 400,000 words, much of it of value only to a student. McClelland and Stewart, and the firm of Macmillan Canada, heard that I was writing an autobiography and wanted to publish it, but I demurred for various good reasons. Jack McClelland persisted and flew down to see me. After lunch and an afternoon's talk he persuaded me to let him take it away and read it. I had qualms because I had made no carbon copy, and Jack was literally a bird of passage, flying all over North America in the course of his busy life. That bundle of typescript was the sole product of several years' patient work, consulting the correspondence and diaries of more than fifty years, together with notebooks, photo and snapshot albums and scrapbooks.

When I heard from Jack next he was in Bermuda, where he had gone for a rest and a chance to read the memoirs at leisure. He insisted on the phone that it should be published. He would return the typescript to me in person within a few weeks and hoped for a favourable answer.

When he came I vetoed publication of the whole, pointing out that it would take two or three volumes as it stood, and I was no Winston Churchill. Finally I agreed to reduce it to a single volume, which you now have in your hands. My life has not been dull and I trust that this account of it has not been, either.

In the earlier years I gave details of my sales to show something of my long struggle for financial independence as well as literary worth. If it is of any interest now, my books have sold to date about 2,500,000 copies in various languages, roughly half of them casebound and the rest in paperback. Many were sold through book clubs, which have a low royalty rate and divide that half-and-half between the author and the original publisher. So I never got rich, but I was able to educate my children, to travel a bit, and to enjoy my life as much as any man can. In the long course of it I achieved financial security, and after that money ceased to matter.

On the aesthetic side, I have received more honours than I deserve. I cherish best of all a few words spoken to me by Bob Chandler, proprietor of a small fishery business at Moose Harbour, where I used to write in my log cabin before it was laid in ashes. One day in 1966 I went to buy some lobsters at Moose Harbour, and just as I was leaving Bob said, "Tom, I'm not much of a hand for talking and I don't rightly know how to say this, but I am proud of you and proud to know you, because you write about our own people and our own country, and you live here and you're one of us."

I would like an epitome of that carved on my tombstone.

And now there is nothing more to say except the familiar phrase of my old Micmac friends when talking of things past: *Kes-pe-ah-dook-sit* – "Here the story ends."